Ōoku

☉ THE INNER CHAMBERS

by **Fumi Yoshinaga**

VOL. 9

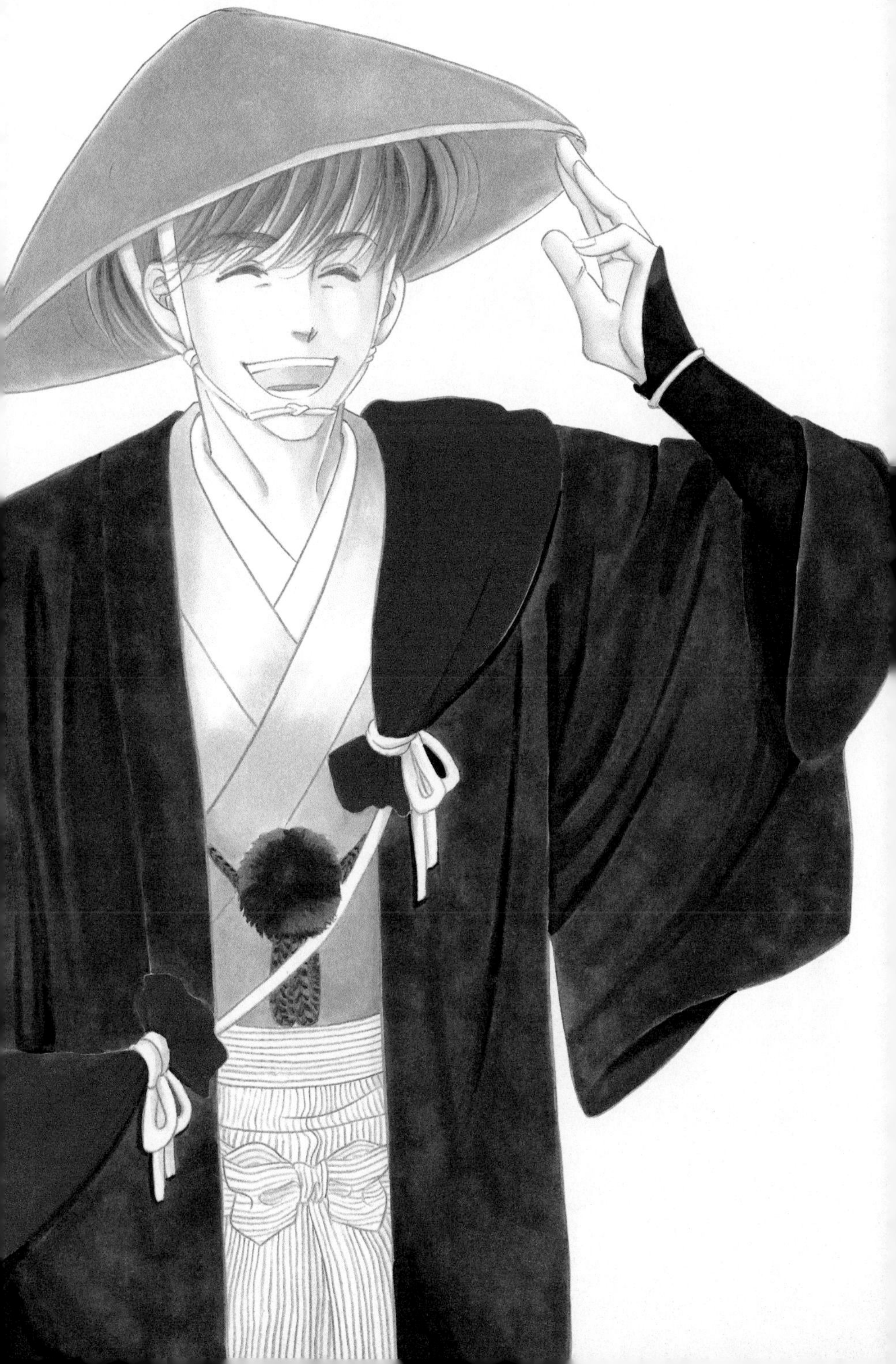

TABLE *of* CONTENTS

Ik ga naar

Japan

Ōoku

THE INNER CHAMBERS

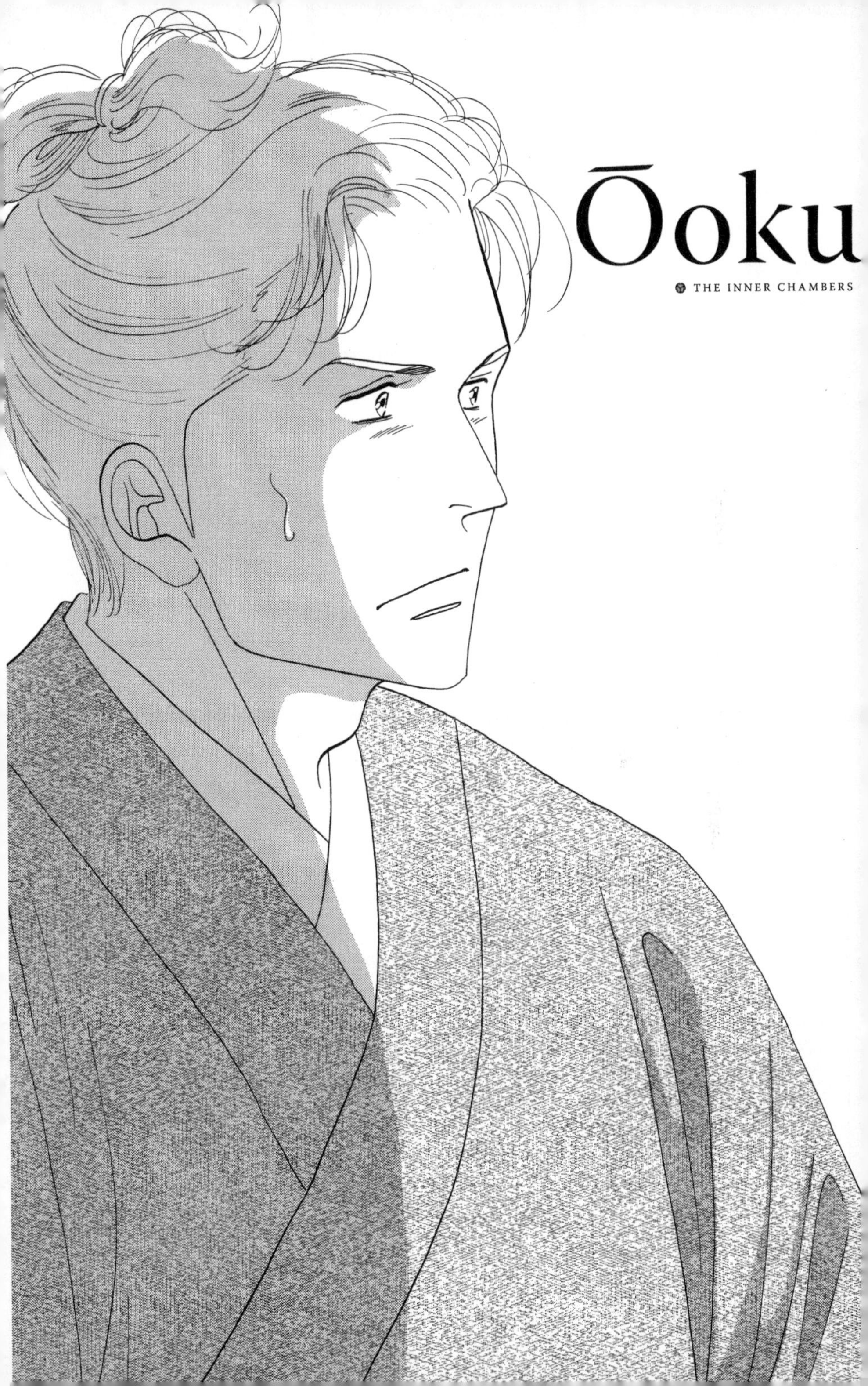

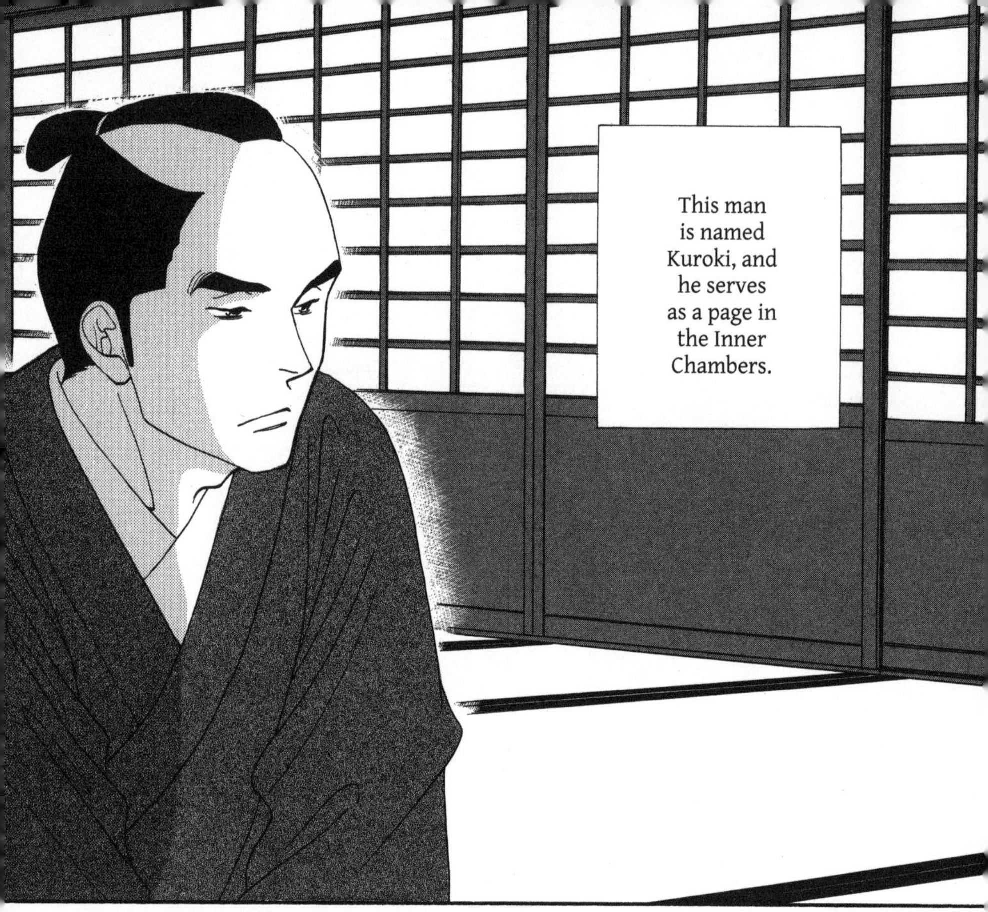
This man is named Kuroki, and he serves as a page in the Inner Chambers.

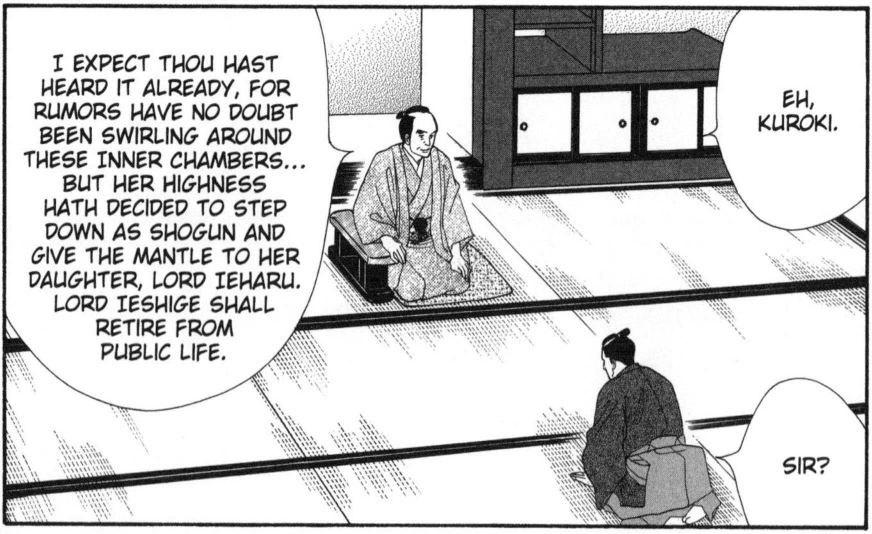
EH, KUROKI.
SIR?
I EXPECT THOU HAST HEARD IT ALREADY, FOR RUMORS HAVE NO DOUBT BEEN SWIRLING AROUND THESE INNER CHAMBERS... BUT HER HIGHNESS HATH DECIDED TO STEP DOWN AS SHOGUN AND GIVE THE MANTLE TO HER DAUGHTER, LORD IEHARU. LORD IESHIGE SHALL RETIRE FROM PUBLIC LIFE.

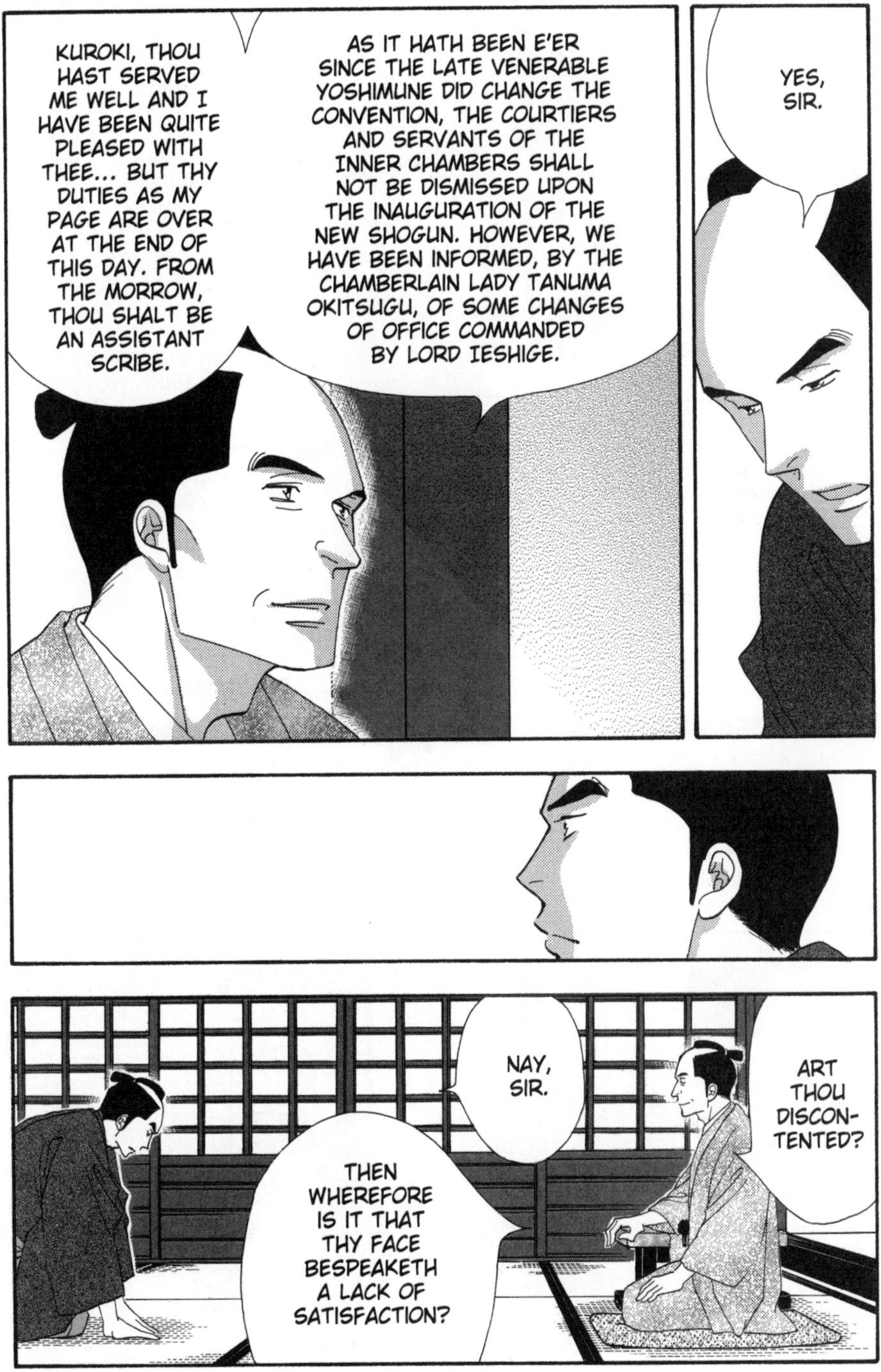
YES, SIR.
AS IT HATH BEEN E'ER SINCE THE LATE VENERABLE YOSHIMUNE DID CHANGE THE CONVENTION, THE COURTIERS AND SERVANTS OF THE INNER CHAMBERS SHALL NOT BE DISMISSED UPON THE INAUGURATION OF THE NEW SHOGUN. HOWEVER, WE HAVE BEEN INFORMED, BY THE CHAMBERLAIN LADY TANUMA OKITSUGU, OF SOME CHANGES OF OFFICE COMMANDED BY LORD IESHIGE.
KUROKI, THOU HAST SERVED ME WELL AND I HAVE BEEN QUITE PLEASED WITH THEE... BUT THY DUTIES AS MY PAGE ARE OVER AT THE END OF THIS DAY. FROM THE MORROW, THOU SHALT BE AN ASSISTANT SCRIBE.
ART THOU DISCON-TENTED?
NAY, SIR.
THEN WHEREFORE IS IT THAT THY FACE BESPEAKETH A LACK OF SATISFACTION?

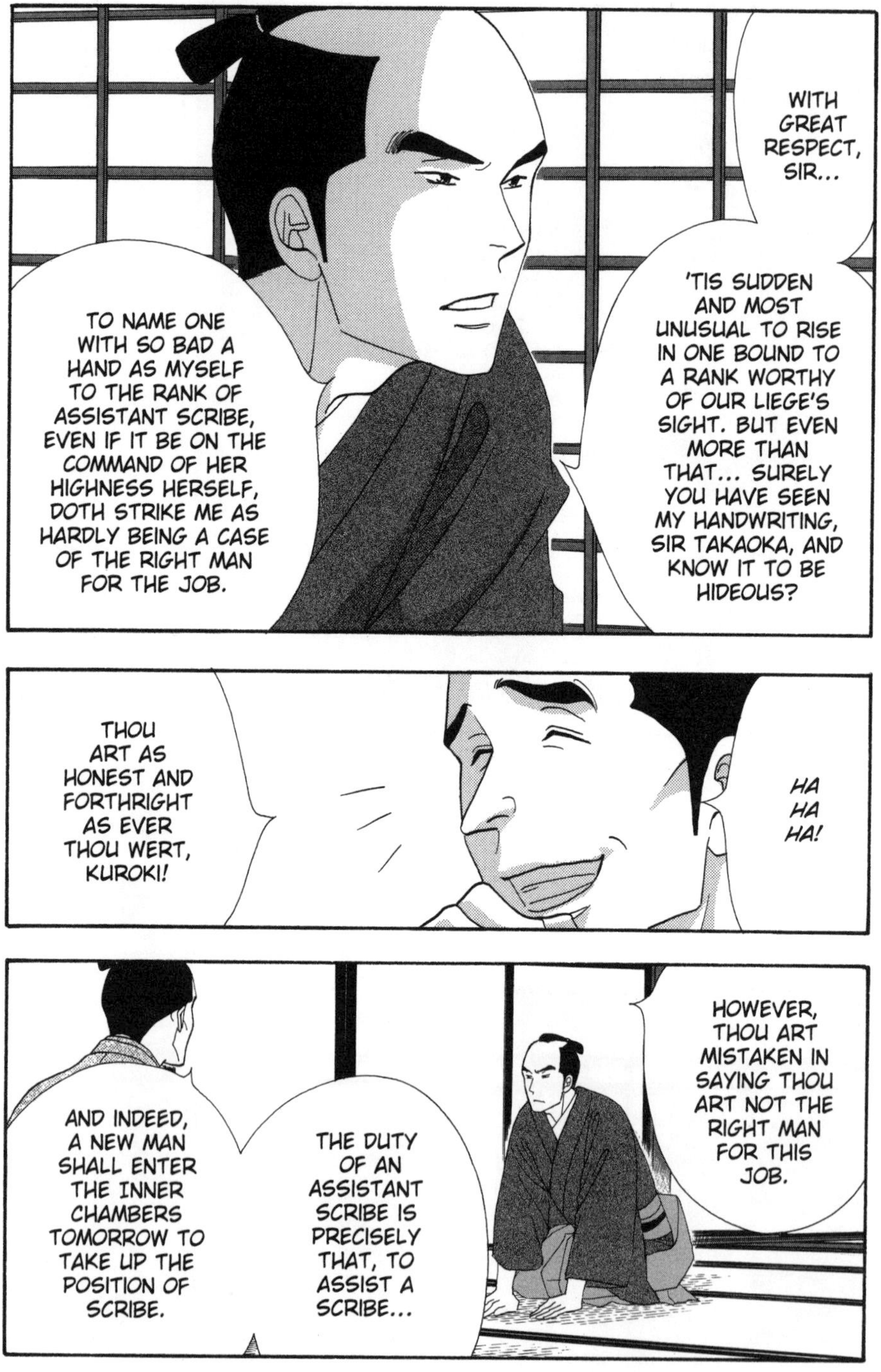
WITH GREAT RESPECT, SIR...
'TIS SUDDEN AND MOST UNUSUAL TO RISE IN ONE BOUND TO A RANK WORTHY OF OUR LIEGE'S SIGHT. BUT EVEN MORE THAN THAT... SURELY YOU HAVE SEEN MY HANDWRITING, SIR TAKAOKA, AND KNOW IT TO BE HIDEOUS?
TO NAME ONE WITH SO BAD A HAND AS MYSELF TO THE RANK OF ASSISTANT SCRIBE, EVEN IF IT BE ON THE COMMAND OF HER HIGHNESS HERSELF, DOTH STRIKE ME AS HARDLY BEING A CASE OF THE RIGHT MAN FOR THE JOB.
HA HA HA!
THOU ART AS HONEST AND FORTHRIGHT AS EVER THOU WERT, KUROKI!
HOWEVER, THOU ART MISTAKEN IN SAYING THOU ART NOT THE RIGHT MAN FOR THIS JOB.
THE DUTY OF AN ASSISTANT SCRIBE IS PRECISELY THAT, TO ASSIST A SCRIBE...
AND INDEED, A NEW MAN SHALL ENTER THE INNER CHAMBERS TOMORROW TO TAKE UP THE POSITION OF SCRIBE.

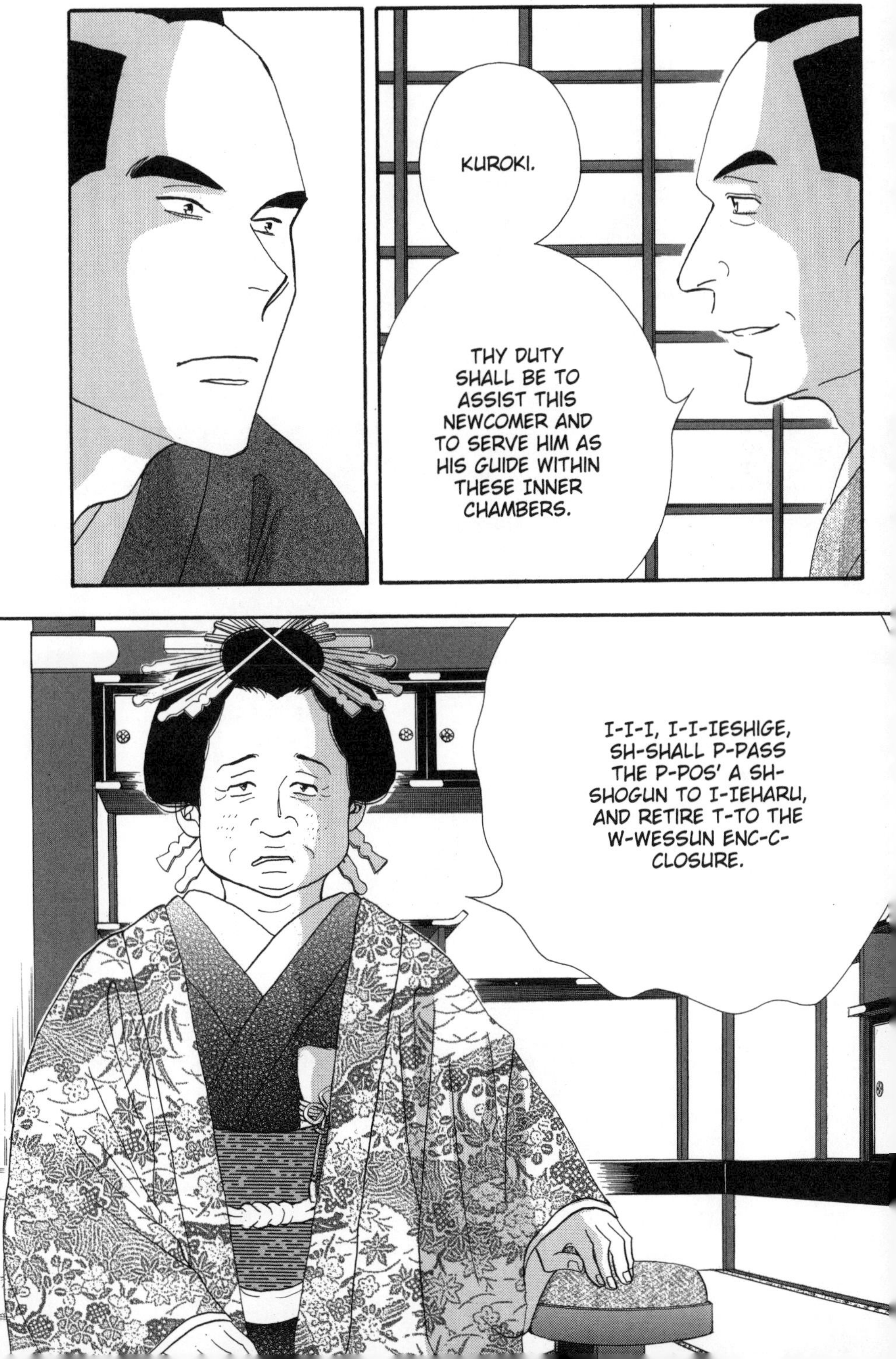
KUROKI.
THY DUTY SHALL BE TO ASSIST THIS NEWCOMER AND TO SERVE HIM AS HIS GUIDE WITHIN THESE INNER CHAMBERS.
I-I-I, I-I-IESHIGE, SH-SHALL P-PASS THE P-POS' A SH-SHOGUN TO I-IEHARU, AND RETIRE T-TO THE W-WESSUN ENC-C-CLOSURE.

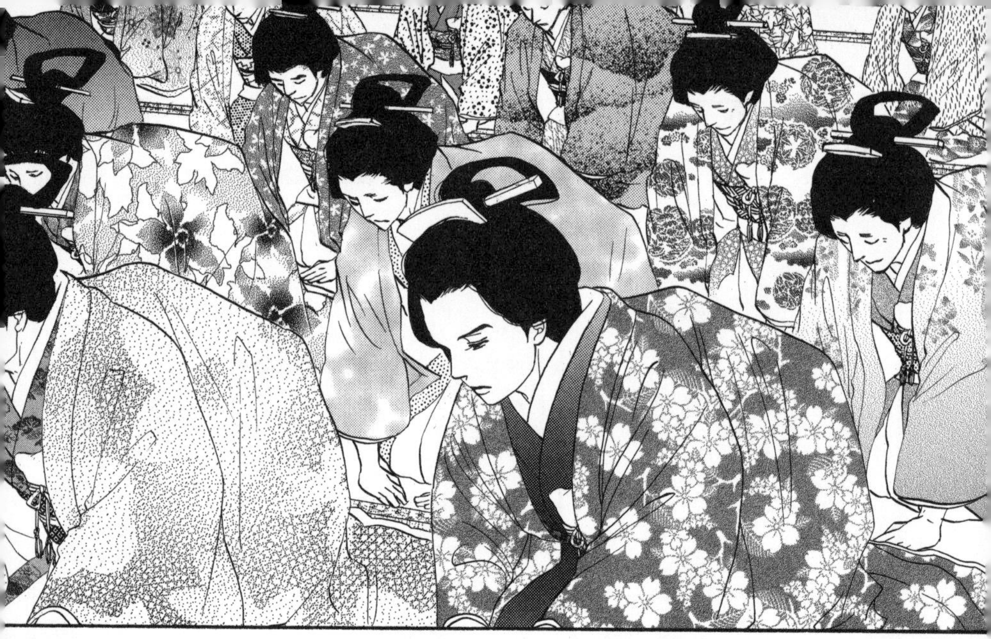

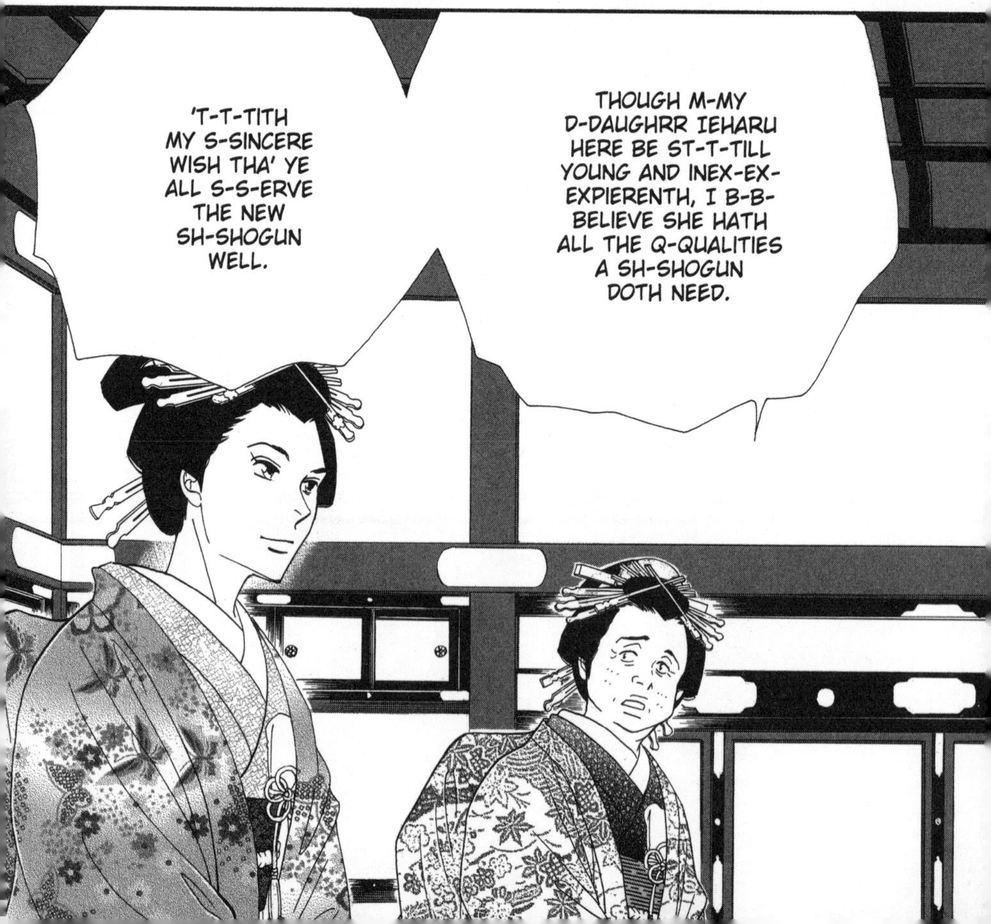
THOUGH M-MY D-DAUGHRR IEHARU HERE BE ST-T-TILL YOUNG AND INEX-EX-EXPIERENTH, I B-B-BELIEVE SHE HATH ALL THE Q-QUALITIES A SH-SHOGUN DOTH NEED.
'T-T-TITH MY S-SINCERE WISH THA' YE ALL S-S-ERVE THE NEW SH-SHOGUN WELL.

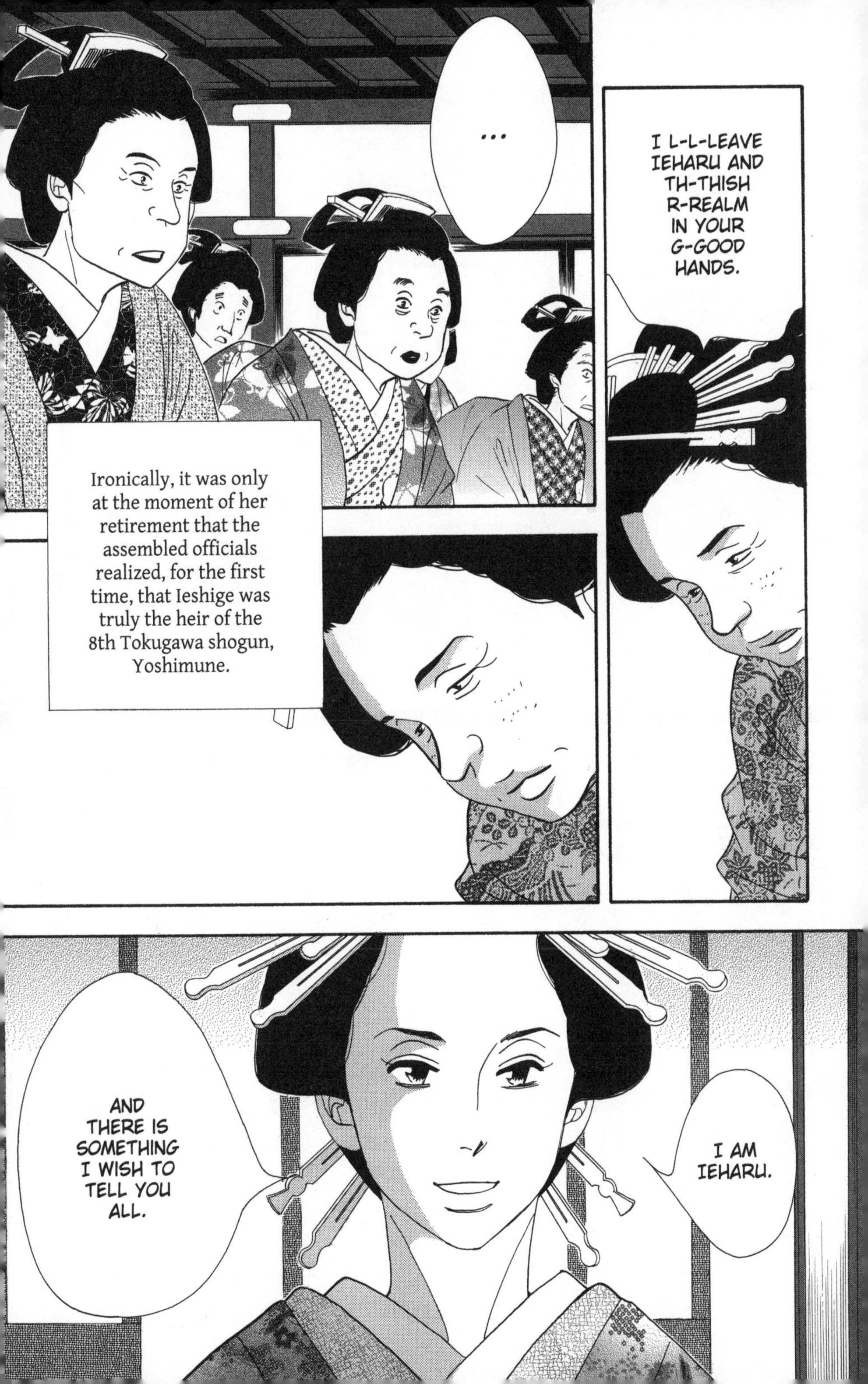
I L-L-LEAVE IEHARU AND TH-THISH R-REALM IN YOUR G-GOOD HANDS.
...
Ironically, it was only at the moment of her retirement that the assembled officials realized, for the first time, that Ieshige was truly the heir of the 8th Tokugawa shogun, Yoshimune.
I AM IEHARU.
AND THERE IS SOMETHING I WISH TO TELL YOU ALL.

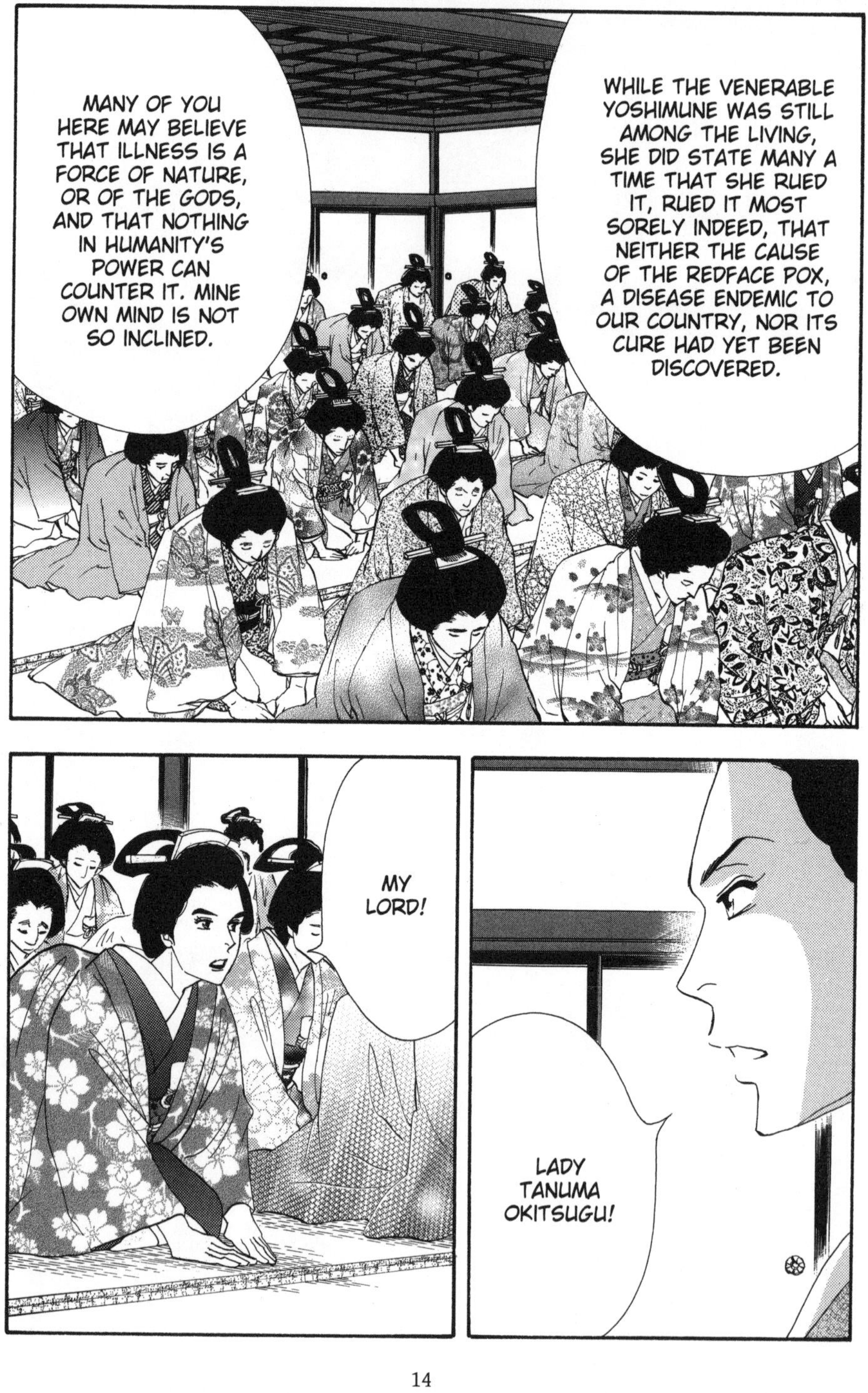
WHILE THE VENERABLE YOSHIMUNE WAS STILL AMONG THE LIVING, SHE DID STATE MANY A TIME THAT SHE RUED IT, RUED IT MOST SORELY INDEED, THAT NEITHER THE CAUSE OF THE REDFACE POX, A DISEASE ENDEMIC TO OUR COUNTRY, NOR ITS CURE HAD YET BEEN DISCOVERED.
MANY OF YOU HERE MAY BELIEVE THAT ILLNESS IS A FORCE OF NATURE, OR OF THE GODS, AND THAT NOTHING IN HUMANITY'S POWER CAN COUNTER IT. MINE OWN MIND IS NOT SO INCLINED.
LADY TANUMA OKITSUGU!
MY LORD!

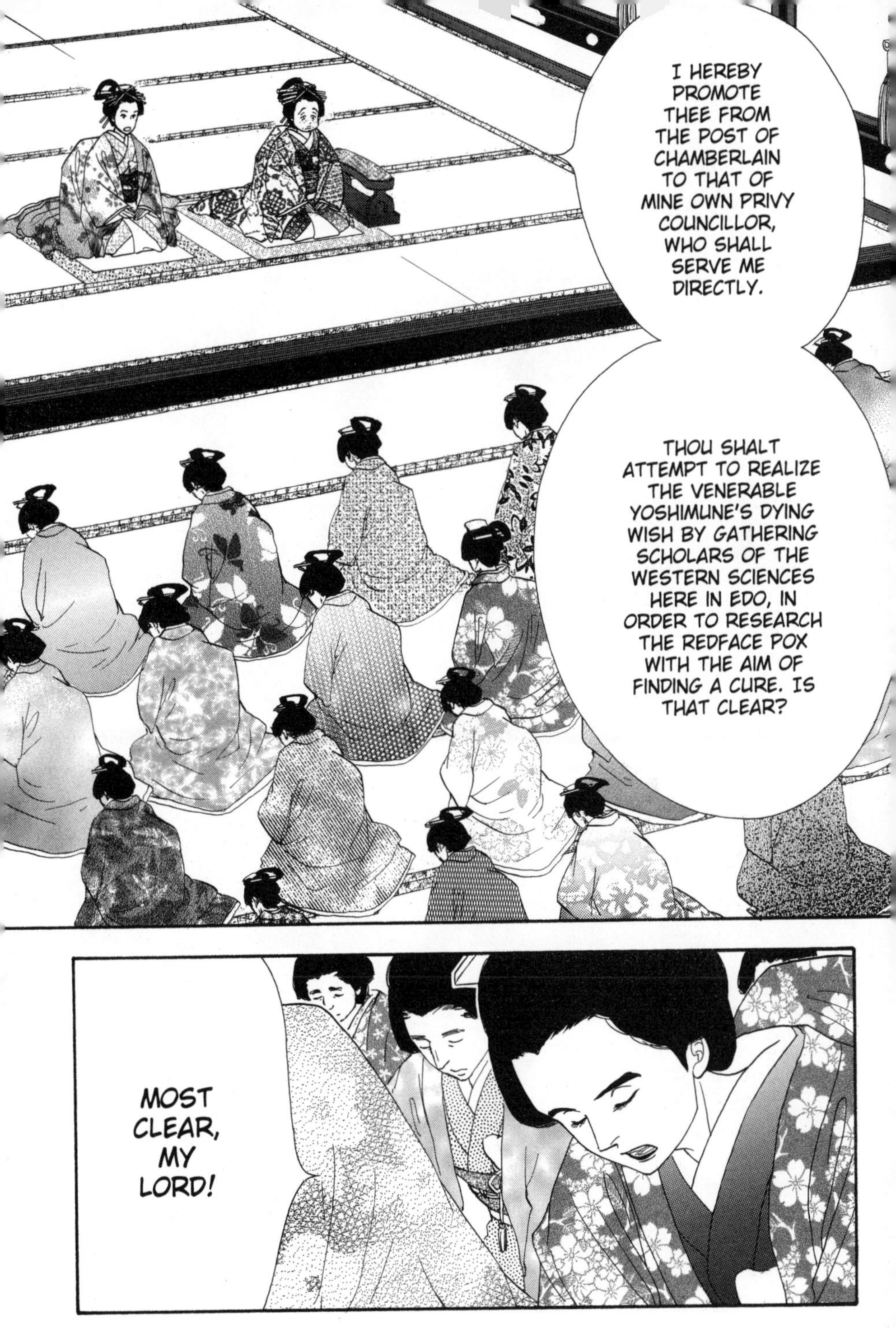
I HEREBY PROMOTE THEE FROM THE POST OF CHAMBERLAIN TO THAT OF MINE OWN PRIVY COUNCILLOR, WHO SHALL SERVE ME DIRECTLY.
THOU SHALT ATTEMPT TO REALIZE THE VENERABLE YOSHIMUNE'S DYING WISH BY GATHERING SCHOLARS OF THE WESTERN SCIENCES HERE IN EDO, IN ORDER TO RESEARCH THE REDFACE POX WITH THE AIM OF FINDING A CURE. IS THAT CLEAR?
MOST CLEAR, MY LORD!

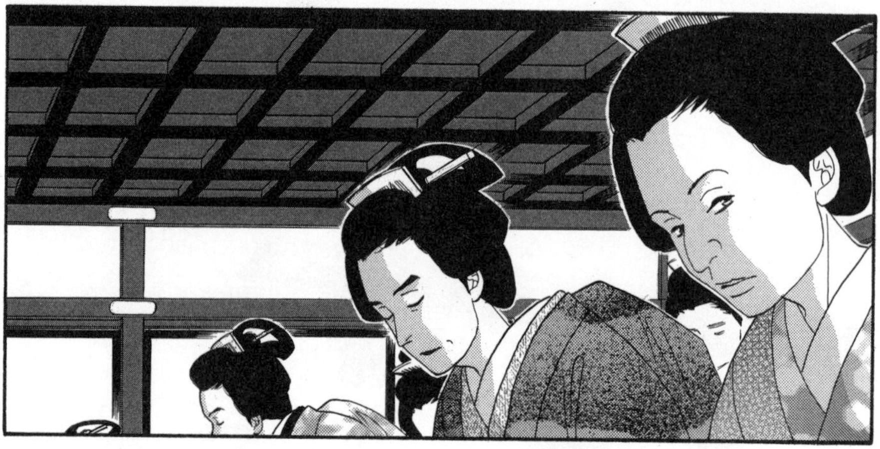

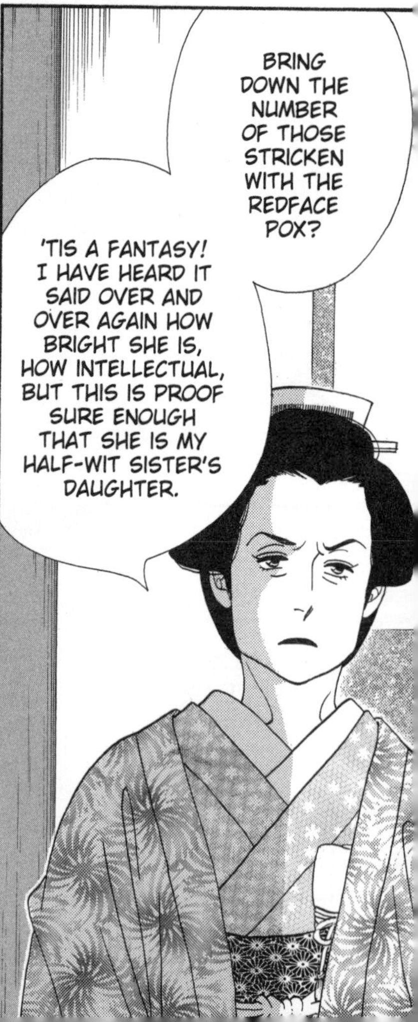
BRING DOWN THE NUMBER OF THOSE STRICKEN WITH THE REDFACE POX?
'TIS A FANTASY! I HAVE HEARD IT SAID OVER AND OVER AGAIN HOW BRIGHT SHE IS, HOW INTELLECTUAL, BUT THIS IS PROOF SURE ENOUGH THAT SHE IS MY HALF-WIT SISTER'S DAUGHTER.

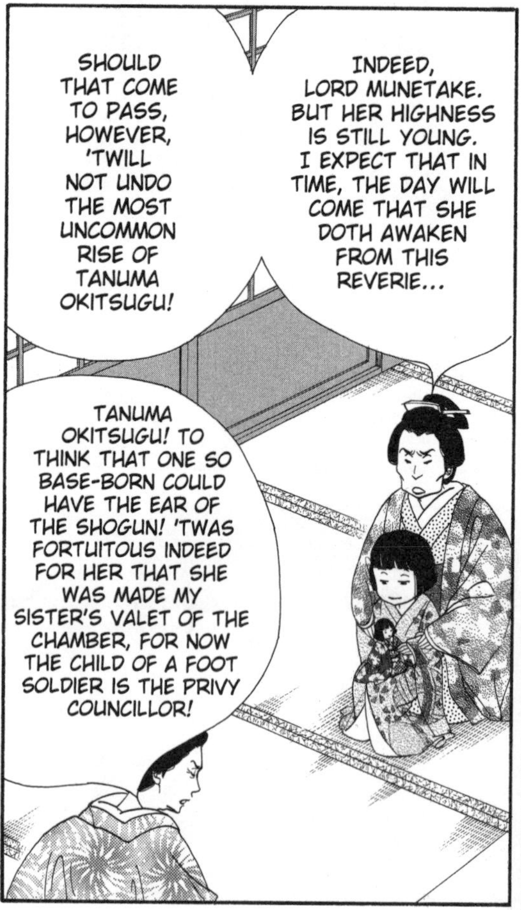
INDEED, LORD MUNETAKE. BUT HER HIGHNESS IS STILL YOUNG. I EXPECT THAT IN TIME, THE DAY WILL COME THAT SHE DOTH AWAKEN FROM THIS REVERIE...
SHOULD THAT COME TO PASS, HOWEVER, 'TWILL NOT UNDO THE MOST UNCOMMON RISE OF TANUMA OKITSUGU!
TANUMA OKITSUGU! TO THINK THAT ONE SO BASE-BORN COULD HAVE THE EAR OF THE SHOGUN! 'TWAS FORTUITOUS INDEED FOR HER THAT SHE WAS MADE MY SISTER'S VALET OF THE CHAMBER, FOR NOW THE CHILD OF A FOOT SOLDIER IS THE PRIVY COUNCILLOR!

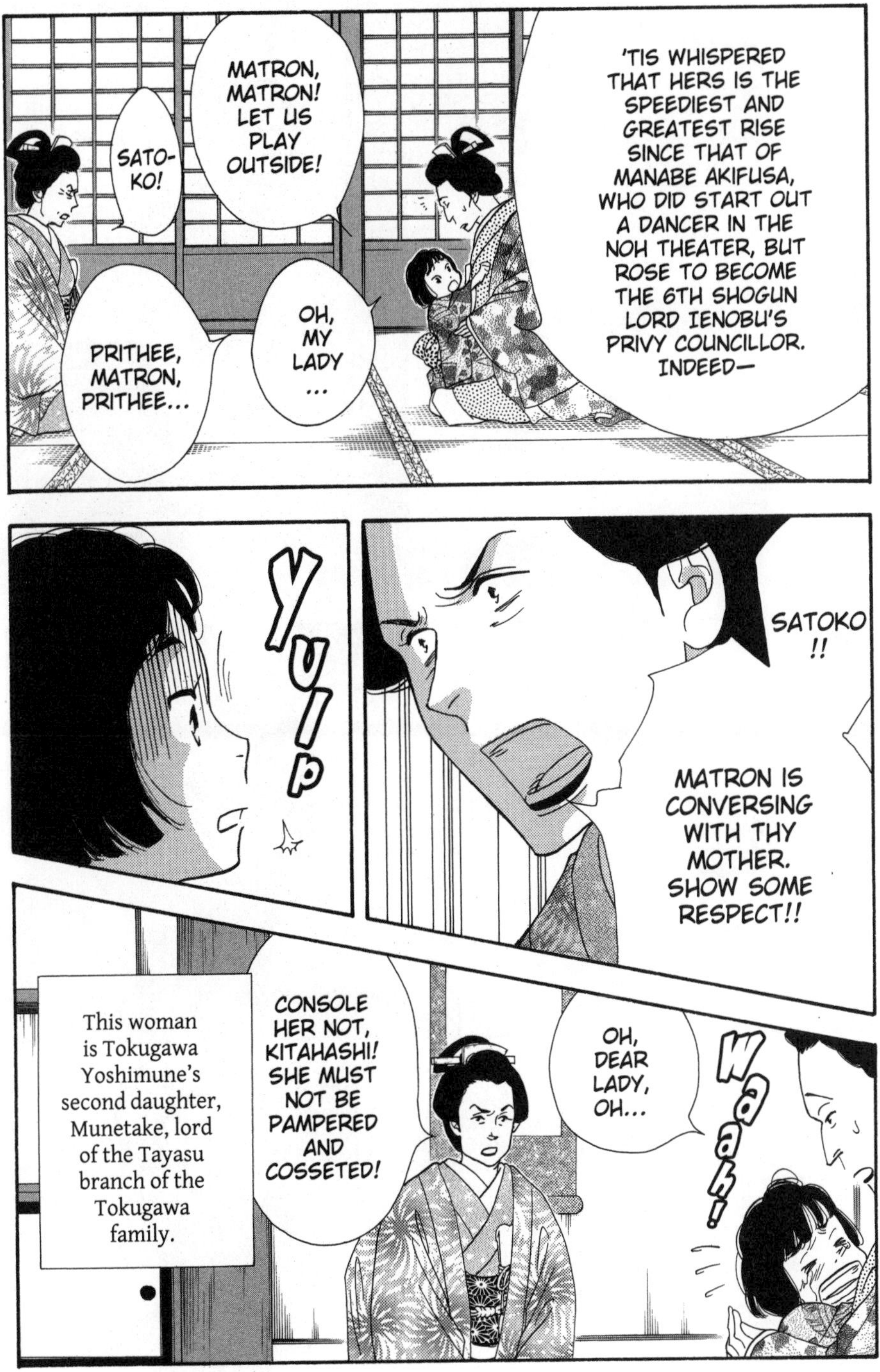
'TIS WHISPERED THAT HERS IS THE SPEEDIEST AND GREATEST RISE SINCE THAT OF MANABE AKIFUSA, WHO DID START OUT A DANCER IN THE NOH THEATER, BUT ROSE TO BECOME THE 6TH SHOGUN LORD IENOBU'S PRIVY COUNCILLOR. INDEED—
MATRON, MATRON! LET US PLAY OUTSIDE!
SATO-KO!
OH, MY LADY ...
PRITHEE, MATRON, PRITHEE...
SATOKO !!
MATRON IS CONVERSING WITH THY MOTHER. SHOW SOME RESPECT!!
Yulp
Waah!
OH, DEAR LADY, OH...
CONSOLE HER NOT, KITAHASHI! SHE MUST NOT BE PAMPERED AND COSSETED!
This woman is Tokugawa Yoshimune's second daughter, Munetake, lord of the Tayasu branch of the Tokugawa family.

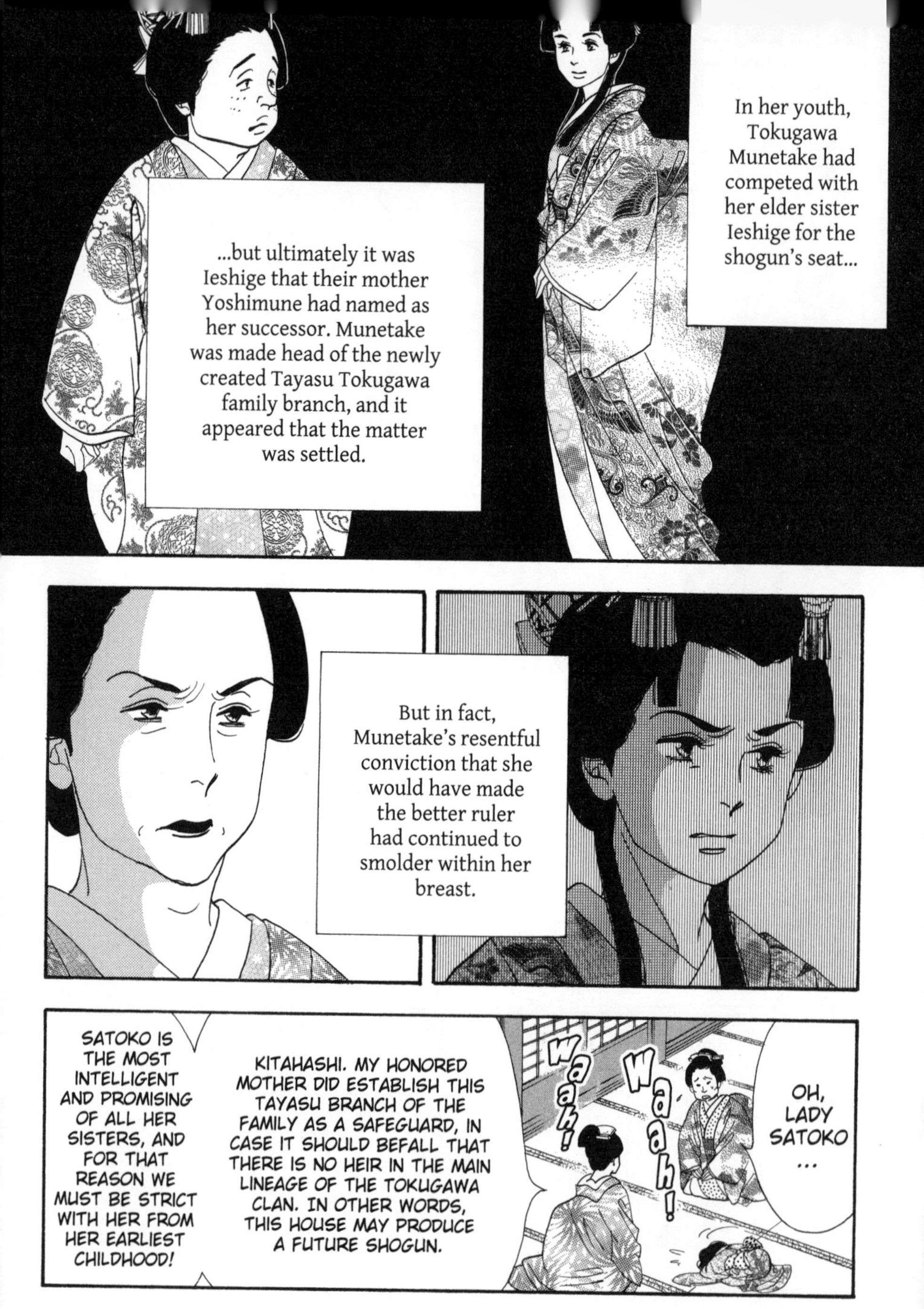
In her youth, Tokugawa Munetake had competed with her elder sister Ieshige for the shogun's seat...
...but ultimately it was Ieshige that their mother Yoshimune had named as her successor. Munetake was made head of the newly created Tayasu Tokugawa family branch, and it appeared that the matter was settled.
But in fact, Munetake's resentful conviction that she would have made the better ruler had continued to smolder within her breast.
OH, LADY SATOKO ...
WAAH!
WAAH!
KITAHASHI. MY HONORED MOTHER DID ESTABLISH THIS TAYASU BRANCH OF THE FAMILY AS A SAFEGUARD, IN CASE IT SHOULD BEFALL THAT THERE IS NO HEIR IN THE MAIN LINEAGE OF THE TOKUGAWA CLAN. IN OTHER WORDS, THIS HOUSE MAY PRODUCE A FUTURE SHOGUN.
SATOKO IS THE MOST INTELLIGENT AND PROMISING OF ALL HER SISTERS, AND FOR THAT REASON WE MUST BE STRICT WITH HER FROM HER EARLIEST CHILDHOOD!

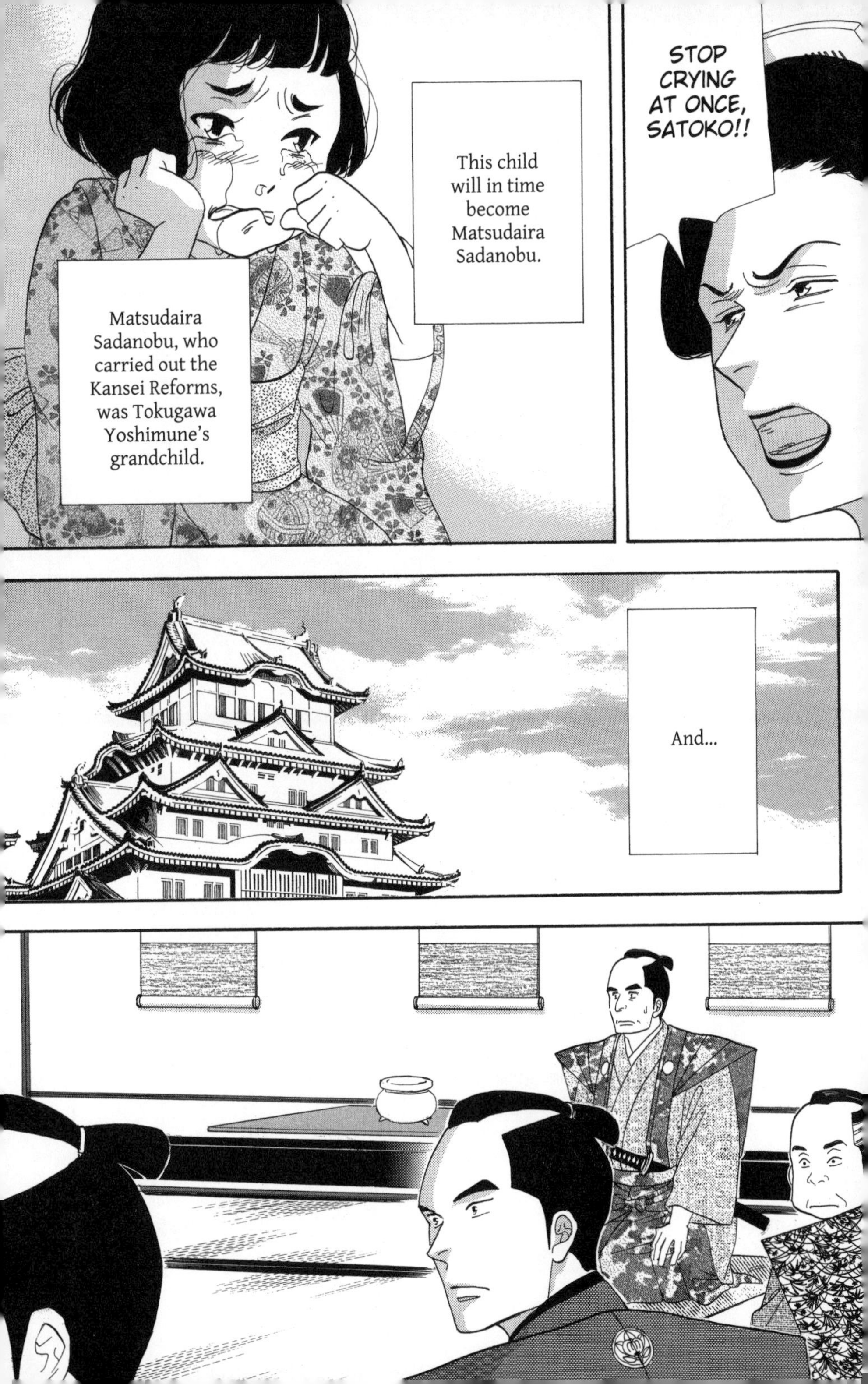
STOP CRYING AT ONCE, SATOKO!!
This child will in time become Matsudaira Sadanobu.
Matsudaira Sadanobu, who carried out the Kansei Reforms, was Tokugawa Yoshimune's grandchild.
And...

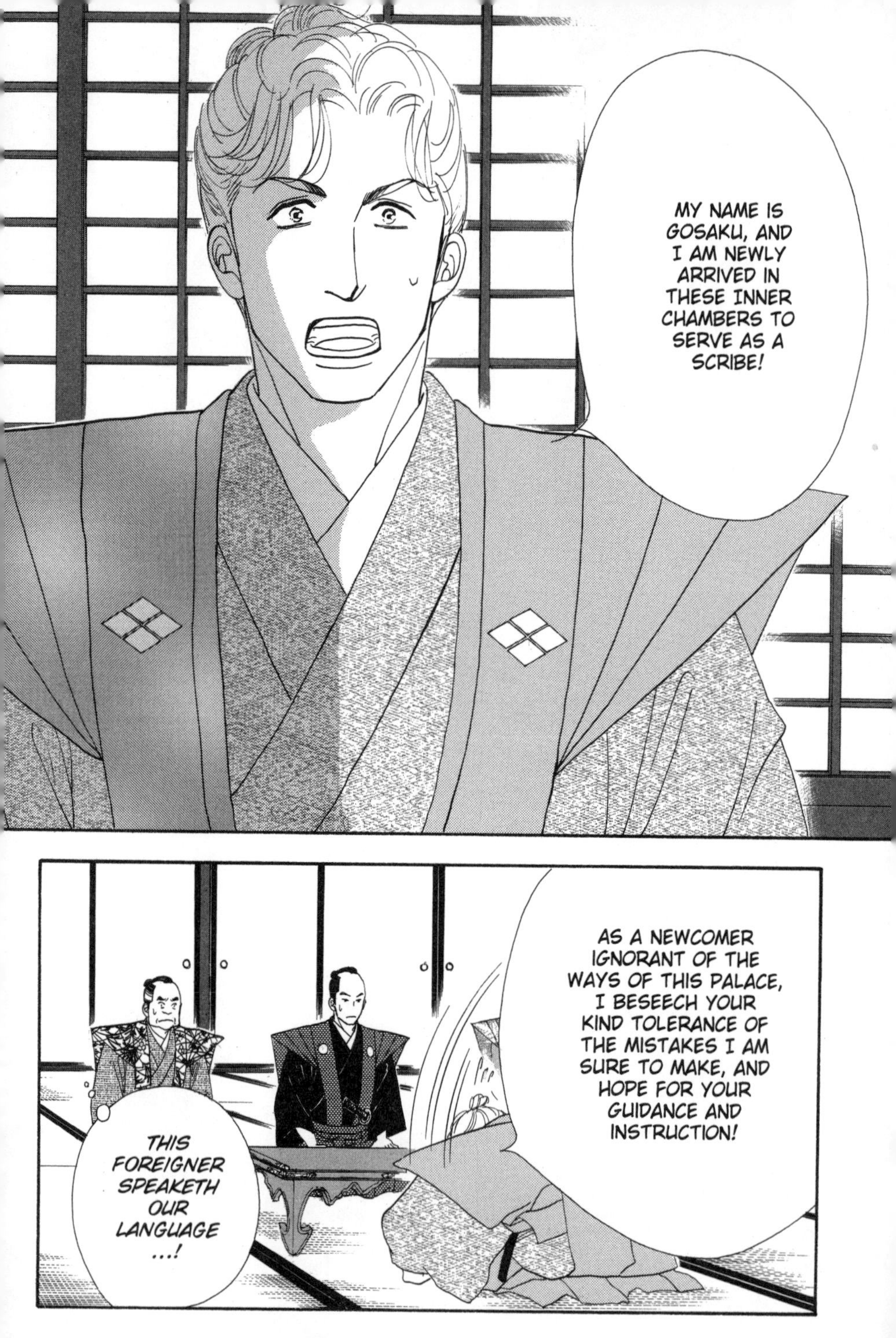
MY NAME IS GOSAKU, AND I AM NEWLY ARRIVED IN THESE INNER CHAMBERS TO SERVE AS A SCRIBE!
AS A NEWCOMER IGNORANT OF THE WAYS OF THIS PALACE, I BESEECH YOUR KIND TOLERANCE OF THE MISTAKES I AM SURE TO MAKE, AND HOPE FOR YOUR GUIDANCE AND INSTRUCTION!
THIS FOREIGNER SPEAKETH OUR LANGUAGE ...!

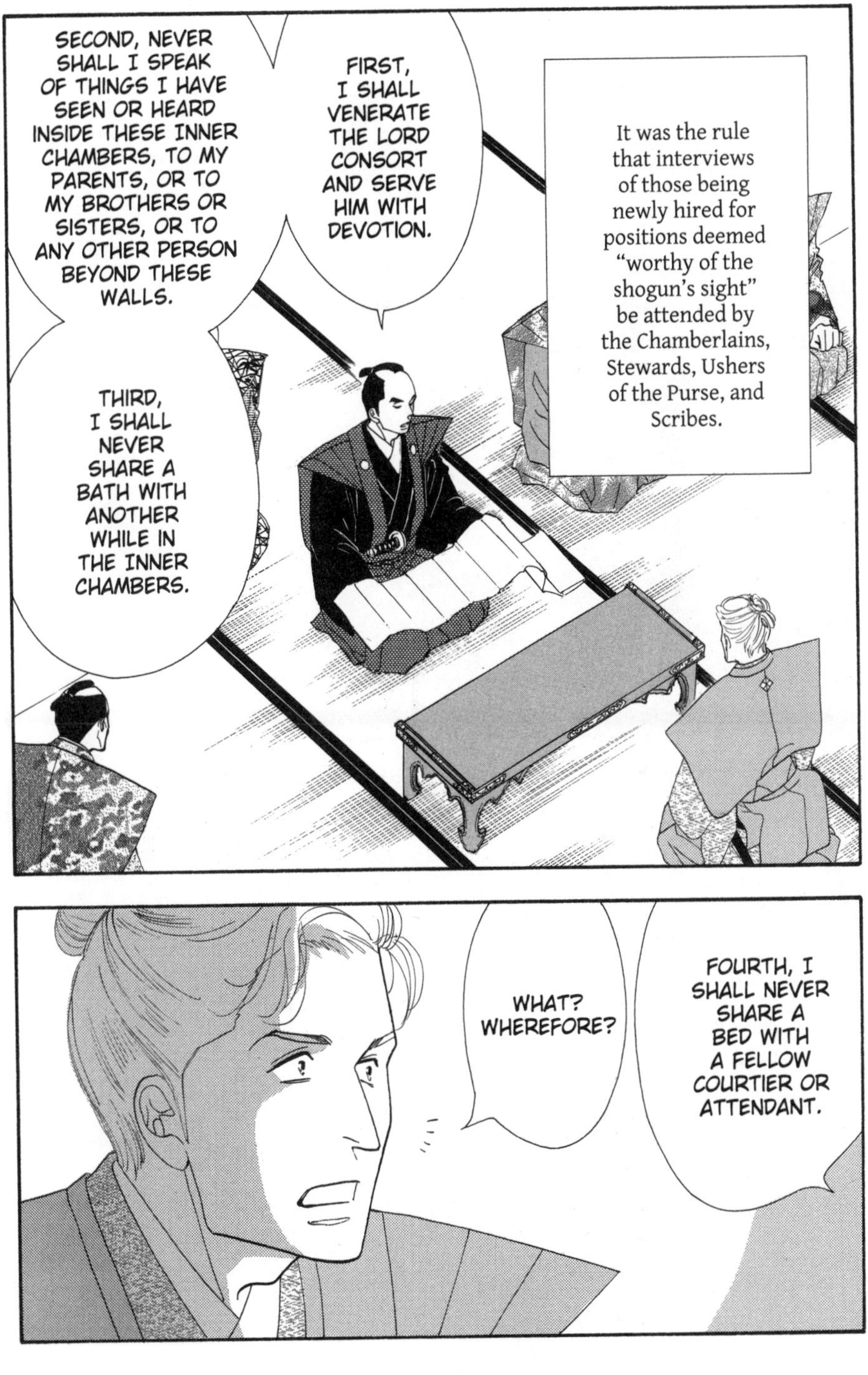
It was the rule that interviews of those being newly hired for positions deemed "worthy of the shogun's sight" be attended by the Chamberlains, Stewards, Ushers of the Purse, and Scribes.
FIRST, I SHALL VENERATE THE LORD CONSORT AND SERVE HIM WITH DEVOTION.
SECOND, NEVER SHALL I SPEAK OF THINGS I HAVE SEEN OR HEARD INSIDE THESE INNER CHAMBERS, TO MY PARENTS, OR TO MY BROTHERS OR SISTERS, OR TO ANY OTHER PERSON BEYOND THESE WALLS.
THIRD, I SHALL NEVER SHARE A BATH WITH ANOTHER WHILE IN THE INNER CHAMBERS.
FOURTH, I SHALL NEVER SHARE A BED WITH A FELLOW COURTIER OR ATTENDANT.
WHAT? WHEREFORE?

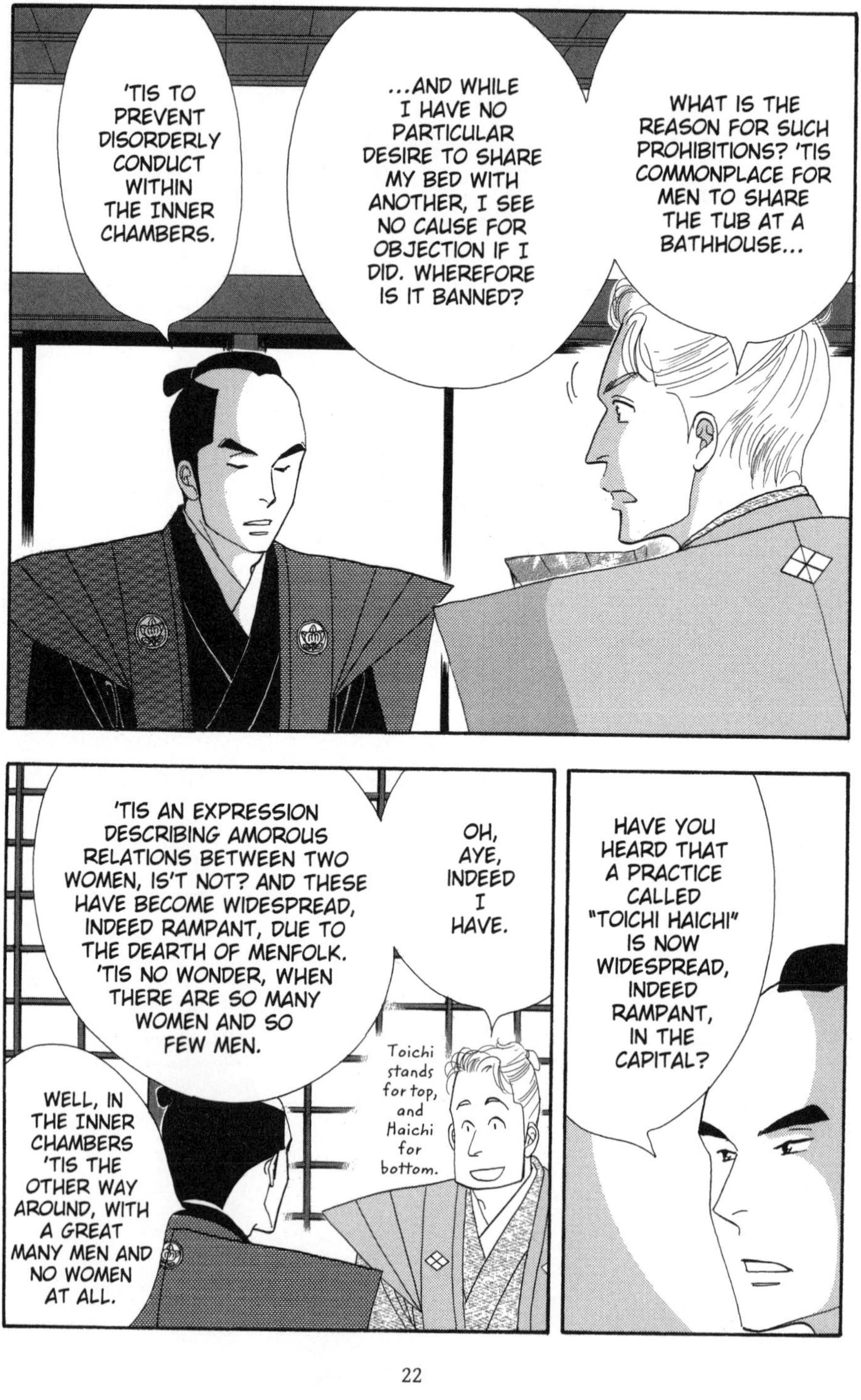
WHAT IS THE REASON FOR SUCH PROHIBITIONS? 'TIS COMMONPLACE FOR MEN TO SHARE THE TUB AT A BATHHOUSE...
...AND WHILE I HAVE NO PARTICULAR DESIRE TO SHARE MY BED WITH ANOTHER, I SEE NO CAUSE FOR OBJECTION IF I DID. WHEREFORE IS IT BANNED?
'TIS TO PREVENT DISORDERLY CONDUCT WITHIN THE INNER CHAMBERS.
HAVE YOU HEARD THAT A PRACTICE CALLED "TOICHI HAICHI" IS NOW WIDESPREAD, INDEED RAMPANT, IN THE CAPITAL?
OH, AYE, INDEED I HAVE.
'TIS AN EXPRESSION DESCRIBING AMOROUS RELATIONS BETWEEN TWO WOMEN, IS'T NOT? AND THESE HAVE BECOME WIDESPREAD, INDEED RAMPANT, DUE TO THE DEARTH OF MENFOLK. 'TIS NO WONDER, WHEN THERE ARE SO MANY WOMEN AND SO FEW MEN.
Toichi stands for top, and Haichi for bottom.
WELL, IN THE INNER CHAMBERS 'TIS THE OTHER WAY AROUND, WITH A GREAT MANY MEN AND NO WOMEN AT ALL.

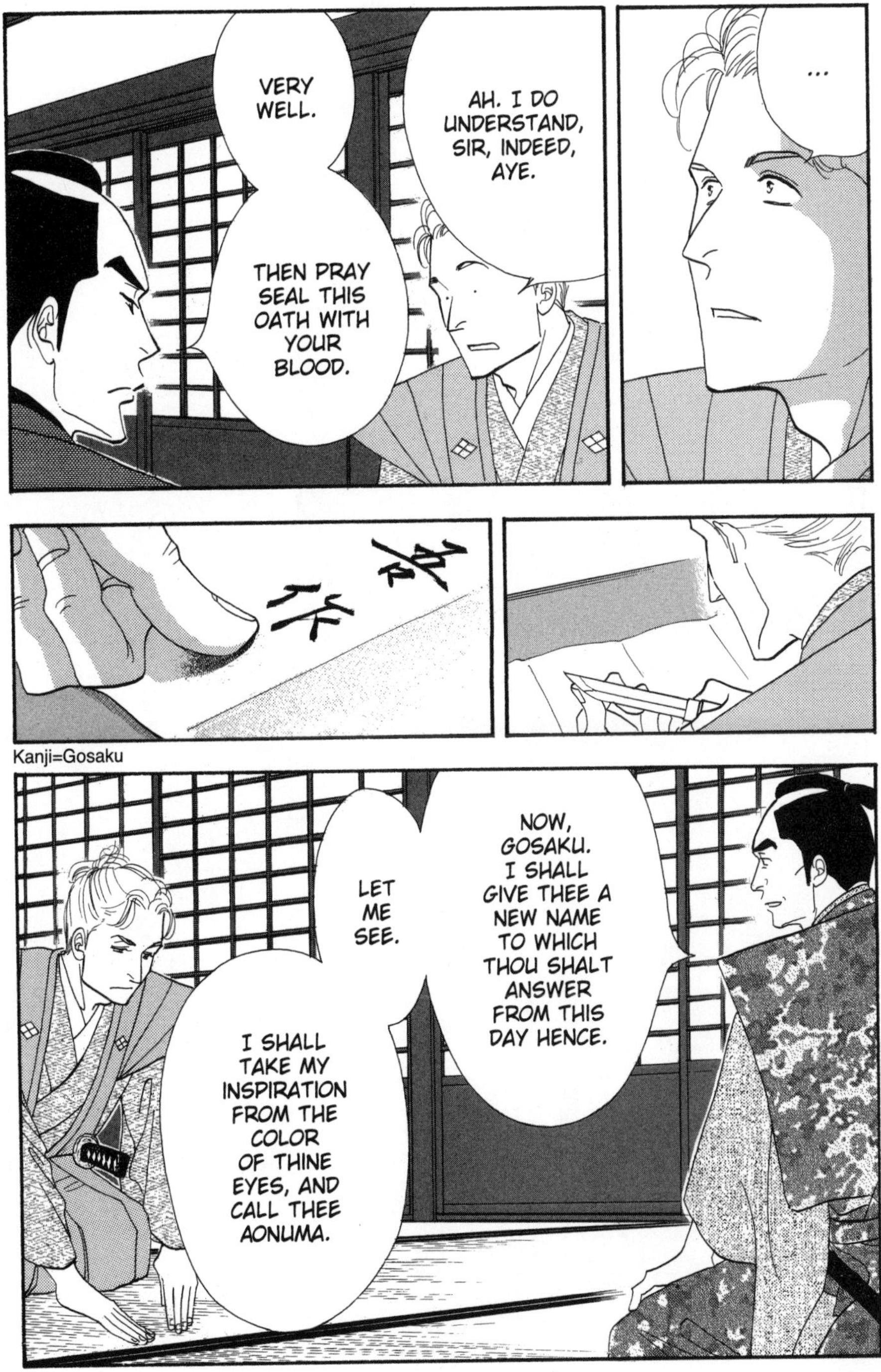
...
AH. I DO UNDERSTAND, SIR, INDEED, AYE.
VERY WELL.
THEN PRAY SEAL THIS OATH WITH YOUR BLOOD.
NOW, GOSAKU. I SHALL GIVE THEE A NEW NAME TO WHICH THOU SHALT ANSWER FROM THIS DAY HENCE.
LET ME SEE.
I SHALL TAKE MY INSPIRATION FROM THE COLOR OF THINE EYES, AND CALL THEE AONUMA.
Kanji=Gosaku

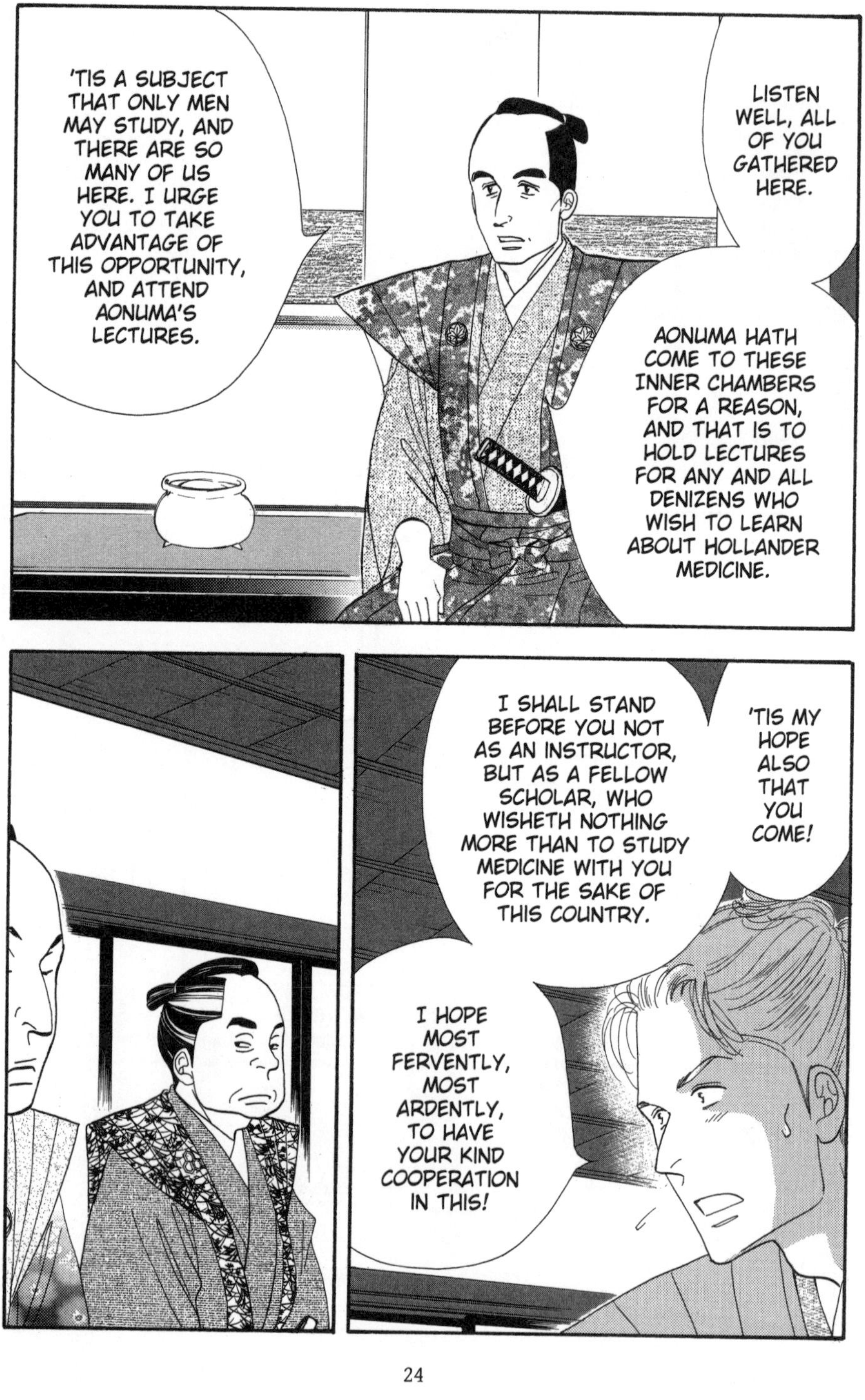
LISTEN WELL, ALL OF YOU GATHERED HERE.
AONUMA HATH COME TO THESE INNER CHAMBERS FOR A REASON, AND THAT IS TO HOLD LECTURES FOR ANY AND ALL DENIZENS WHO WISH TO LEARN ABOUT HOLLANDER MEDICINE.
'TIS A SUBJECT THAT ONLY MEN MAY STUDY, AND THERE ARE SO MANY OF US HERE. I URGE YOU TO TAKE ADVANTAGE OF THIS OPPORTUNITY, AND ATTEND AONUMA'S LECTURES.
'TIS MY HOPE ALSO THAT YOU COME!
I SHALL STAND BEFORE YOU NOT AS AN INSTRUCTOR, BUT AS A FELLOW SCHOLAR, WHO WISHETH NOTHING MORE THAN TO STUDY MEDICINE WITH YOU FOR THE SAKE OF THIS COUNTRY.
I HOPE MOST FERVENTLY, MOST ARDENTLY, TO HAVE YOUR KIND COOPERATION IN THIS!

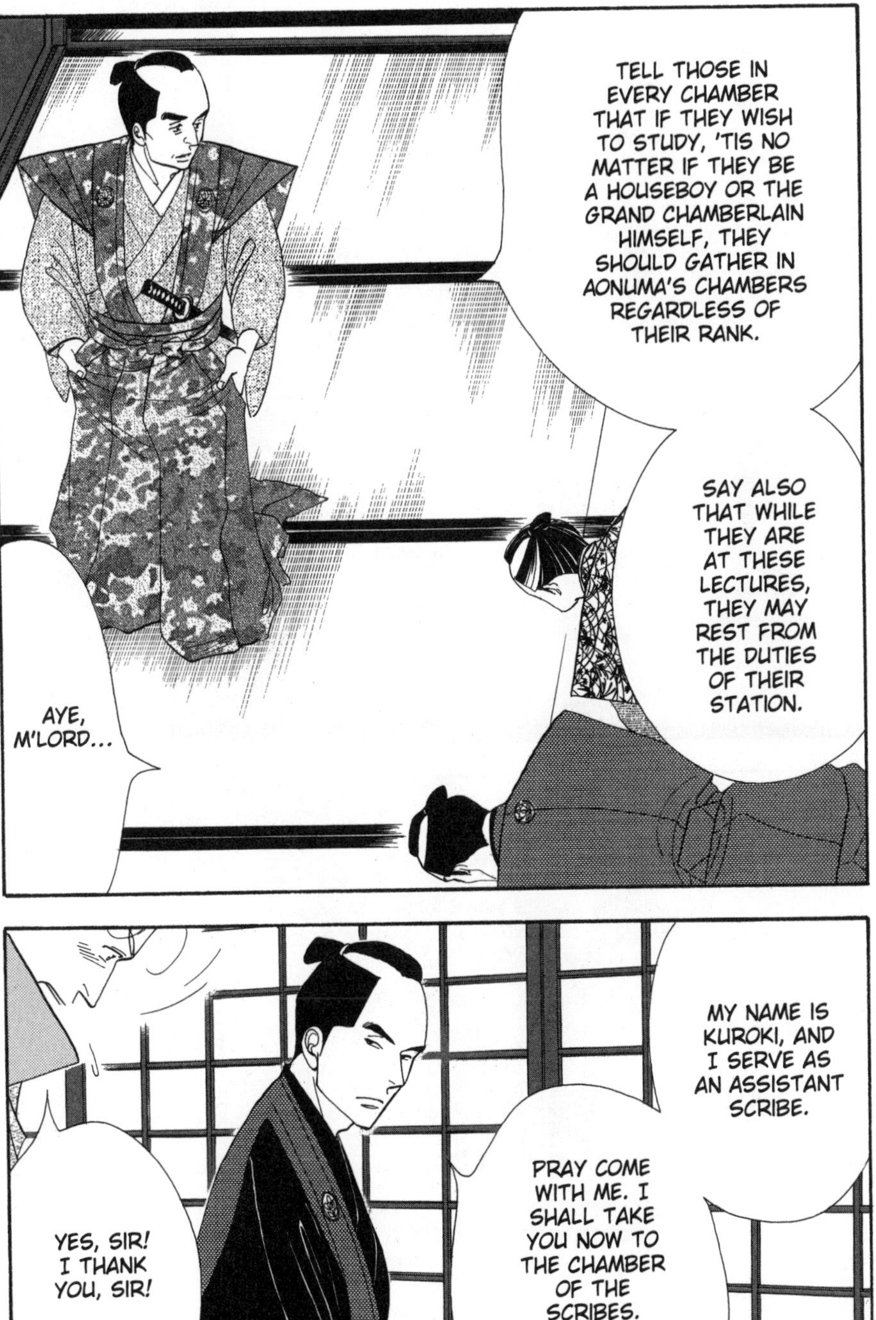
TELL THOSE IN EVERY CHAMBER THAT IF THEY WISH TO STUDY, 'TIS NO MATTER IF THEY BE A HOUSEBOY OR THE GRAND CHAMBERLAIN HIMSELF, THEY SHOULD GATHER IN AONUMA'S CHAMBERS REGARDLESS OF THEIR RANK.
SAY ALSO THAT WHILE THEY ARE AT THESE LECTURES, THEY MAY REST FROM THE DUTIES OF THEIR STATION.
AYE, M'LORD...
MY NAME IS KUROKI, AND I SERVE AS AN ASSISTANT SCRIBE.
PRAY COME WITH ME. I SHALL TAKE YOU NOW TO THE CHAMBER OF THE SCRIBES.
YES, SIR! I THANK YOU, SIR!

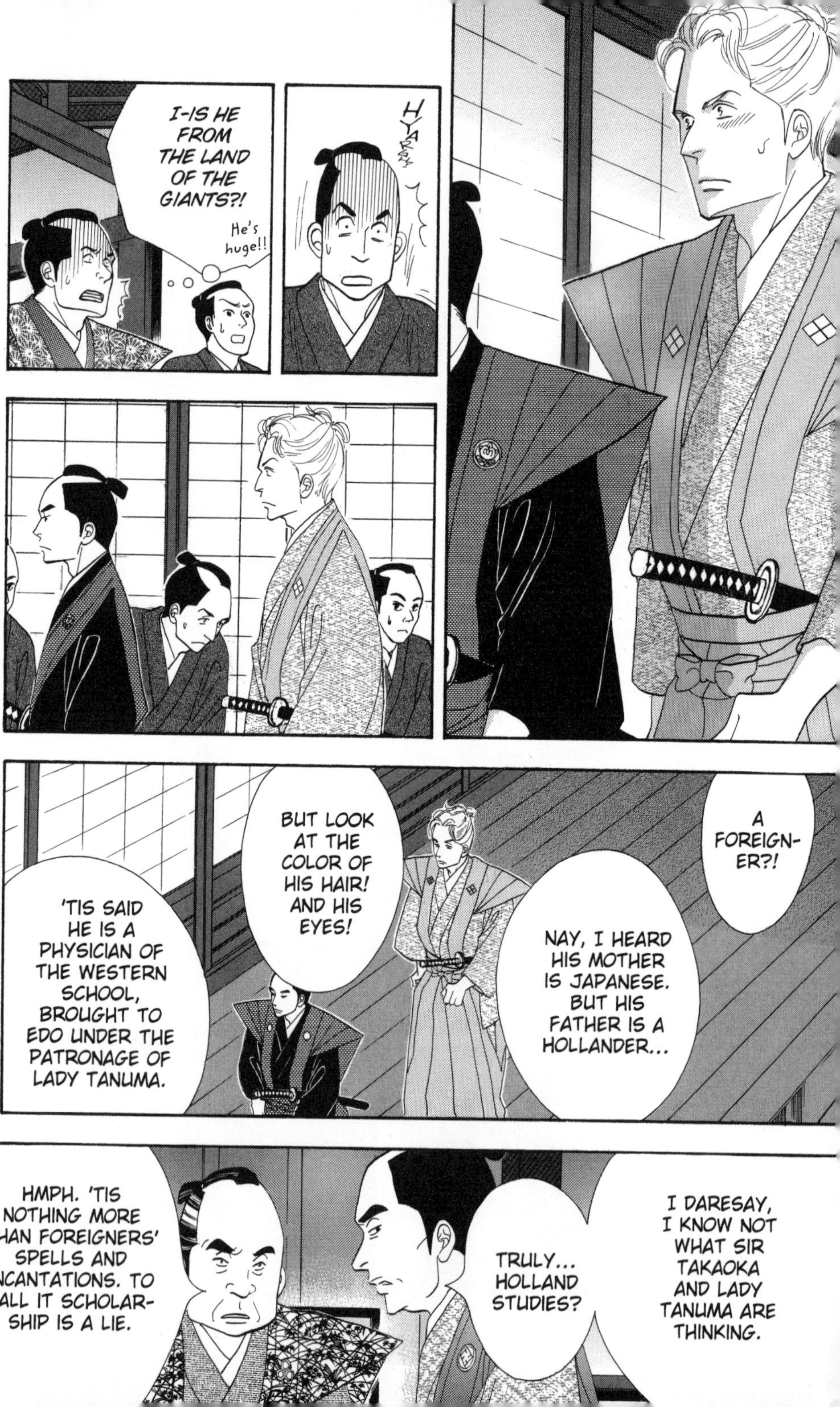
HYARGH!!
I-IS HE FROM THE LAND OF THE GIANTS?!
He's huge!!
A FOREIGNER?!
NAY, I HEARD HIS MOTHER IS JAPANESE. BUT HIS FATHER IS A HOLLANDER...
BUT LOOK AT THE COLOR OF HIS HAIR! AND HIS EYES!
'TIS SAID HE IS A PHYSICIAN OF THE WESTERN SCHOOL, BROUGHT TO EDO UNDER THE PATRONAGE OF LADY TANUMA.
I DARESAY, I KNOW NOT WHAT SIR TAKAOKA AND LADY TANUMA ARE THINKING.
TRULY... HOLLAND STUDIES?
HMPH. 'TIS NOTHING MORE THAN FOREIGNERS' SPELLS AND INCANTATIONS. TO CALL IT SCHOLARSHIP IS A LIE.

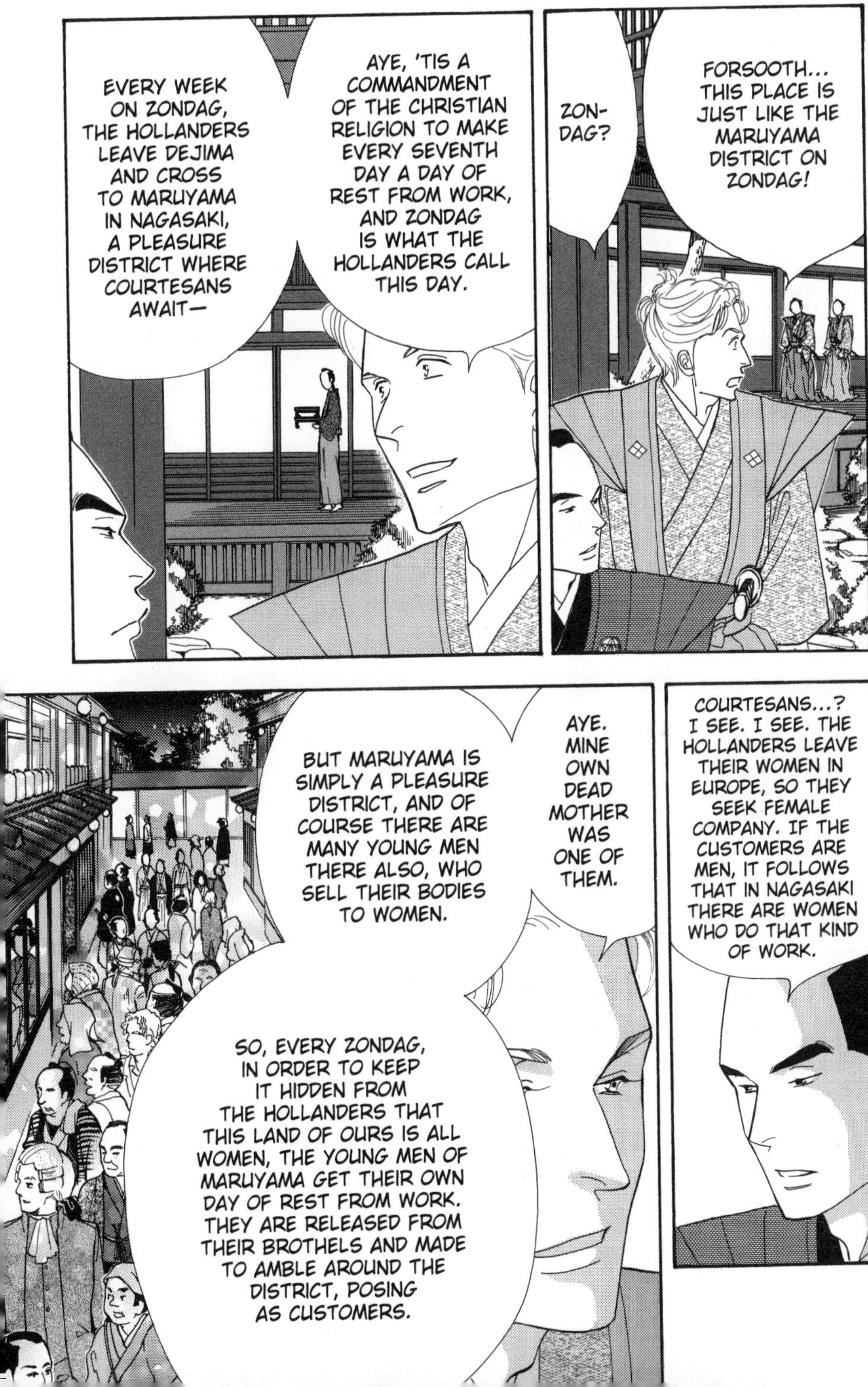
FORSOOTH... THIS PLACE IS JUST LIKE THE MARUYAMA DISTRICT ON ZONDAG!
ZON-DAG?
AYE, 'TIS A COMMANDMENT OF THE CHRISTIAN RELIGION TO MAKE EVERY SEVENTH DAY A DAY OF REST FROM WORK, AND ZONDAG IS WHAT THE HOLLANDERS CALL THIS DAY.
EVERY WEEK ON ZONDAG, THE HOLLANDERS LEAVE DEJIMA AND CROSS TO MARUYAMA IN NAGASAKI, A PLEASURE DISTRICT WHERE COURTESANS AWAIT—
COURTESANS...? I SEE. I SEE. THE HOLLANDERS LEAVE THEIR WOMEN IN EUROPE, SO THEY SEEK FEMALE COMPANY. IF THE CUSTOMERS ARE MEN, IT FOLLOWS THAT IN NAGASAKI THERE ARE WOMEN WHO DO THAT KIND OF WORK.
AYE. MINE OWN DEAD MOTHER WAS ONE OF THEM.
BUT MARUYAMA IS SIMPLY A PLEASURE DISTRICT, AND OF COURSE THERE ARE MANY YOUNG MEN THERE ALSO, WHO SELL THEIR BODIES TO WOMEN.
SO, EVERY ZONDAG, IN ORDER TO KEEP IT HIDDEN FROM THE HOLLANDERS THAT THIS LAND OF OURS IS ALL WOMEN, THE YOUNG MEN OF MARUYAMA GET THEIR OWN DAY OF REST FROM WORK. THEY ARE RELEASED FROM THEIR BROTHELS AND MADE TO AMBLE AROUND THE DISTRICT, POSING AS CUSTOMERS.

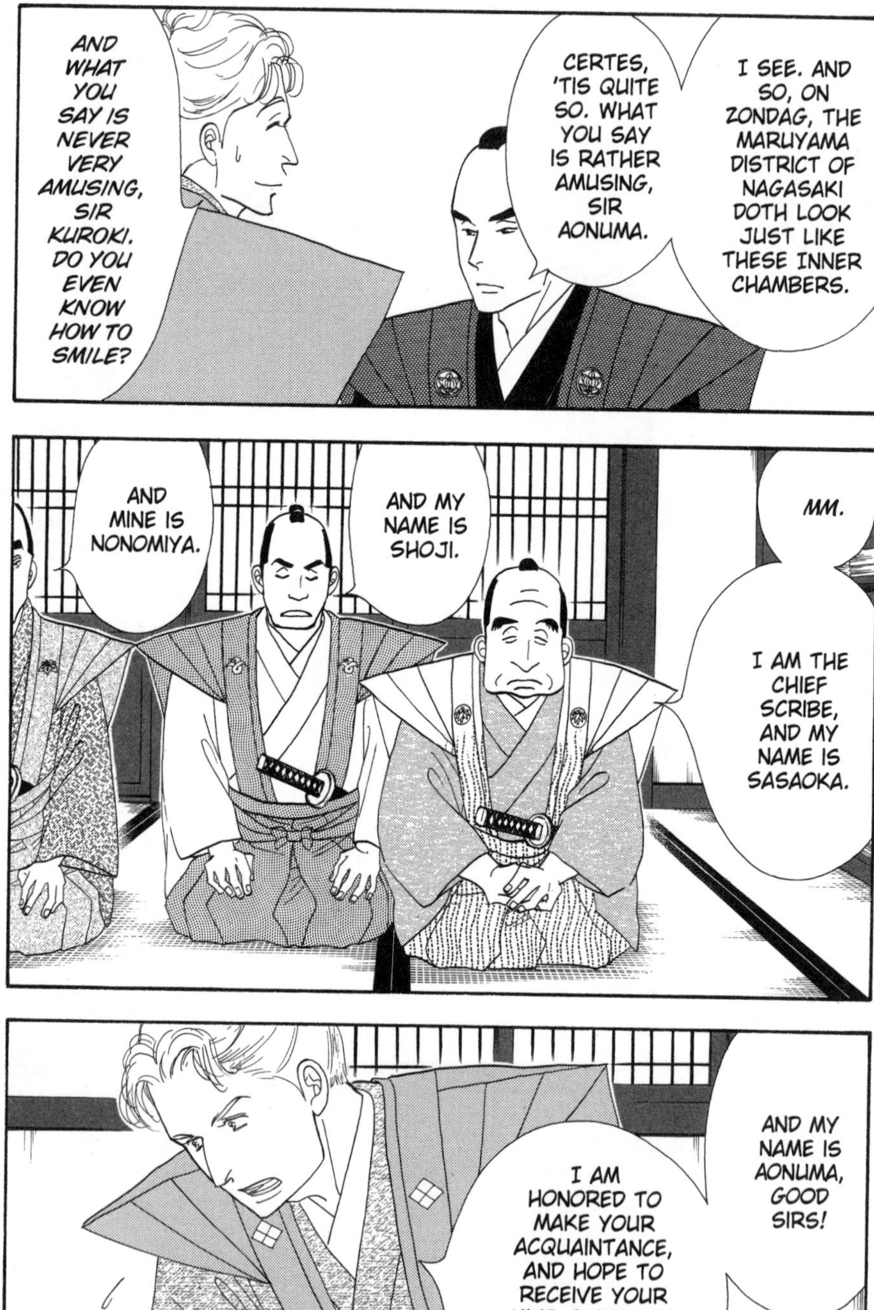
I SEE. AND SO, ON ZONDAG, THE MARUYAMA DISTRICT OF NAGASAKI DOTH LOOK JUST LIKE THESE INNER CHAMBERS.
CERTES, 'TIS QUITE SO. WHAT YOU SAY IS RATHER AMUSING, SIR AONUMA.
AND WHAT YOU SAY IS NEVER VERY AMUSING, SIR KUROKI. DO YOU EVEN KNOW HOW TO SMILE?
MM.
I AM THE CHIEF SCRIBE, AND MY NAME IS SASAOKA.
AND MY NAME IS SHOJI.
AND MINE IS NONOMIYA.
AND MY NAME IS AONUMA, GOOD SIRS!
I AM HONORED TO MAKE YOUR ACQUAINTANCE, AND HOPE TO RECEIVE YOUR KIND GUIDANCE!

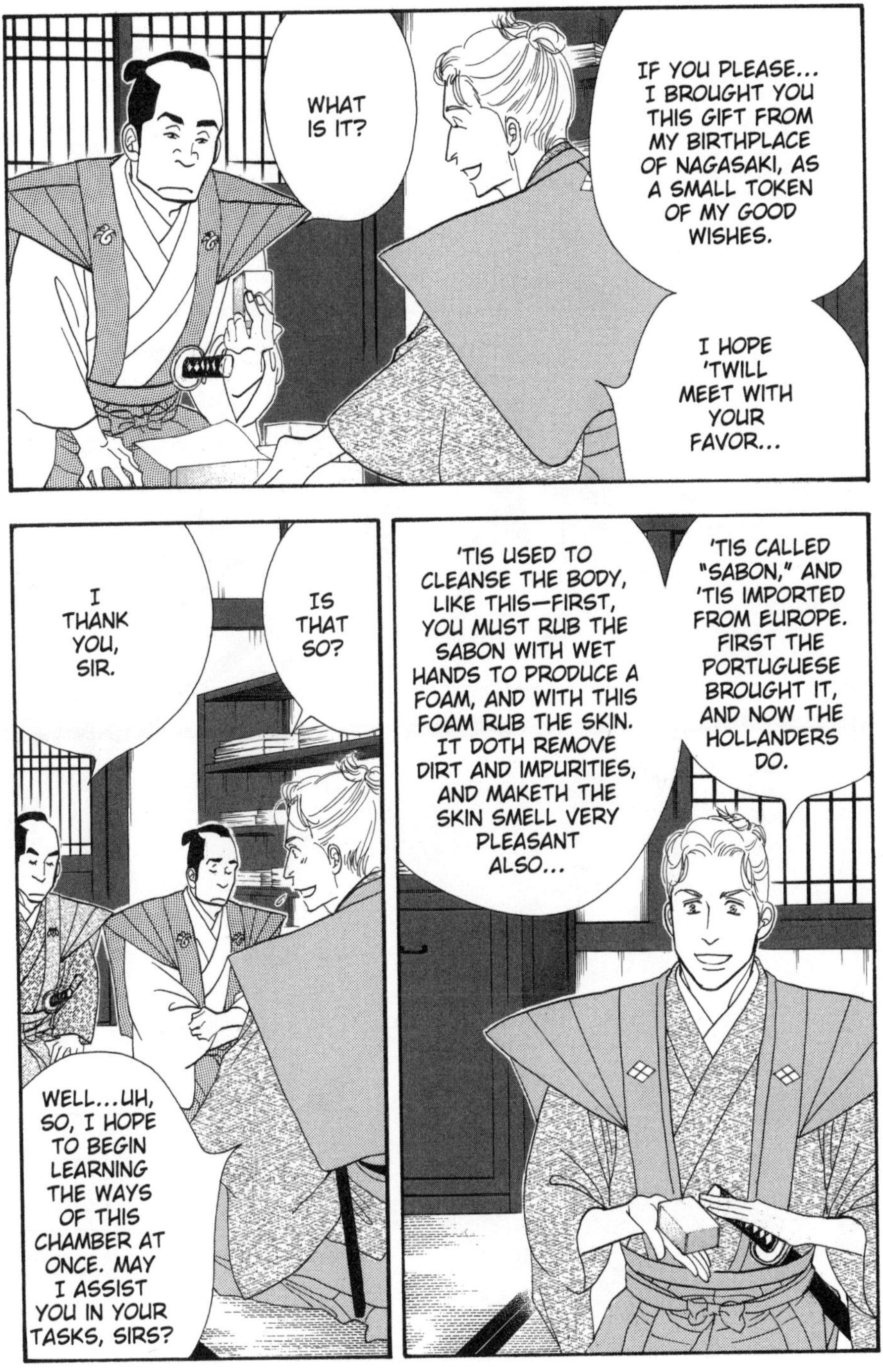
IF YOU PLEASE... I BROUGHT YOU THIS GIFT FROM MY BIRTHPLACE OF NAGASAKI, AS A SMALL TOKEN OF MY GOOD WISHES.
I HOPE 'TWILL MEET WITH YOUR FAVOR...
WHAT IS IT?
'TIS CALLED "SABON," AND 'TIS IMPORTED FROM EUROPE. FIRST THE PORTUGUESE BROUGHT IT, AND NOW THE HOLLANDERS DO.
'TIS USED TO CLEANSE THE BODY, LIKE THIS—FIRST, YOU MUST RUB THE SABON WITH WET HANDS TO PRODUCE A FOAM, AND WITH THIS FOAM RUB THE SKIN. IT DOTH REMOVE DIRT AND IMPURITIES, AND MAKETH THE SKIN SMELL VERY PLEASANT ALSO...
IS THAT SO?
I THANK YOU, SIR.
WELL...UH, SO, I HOPE TO BEGIN LEARNING THE WAYS OF THIS CHAMBER AT ONCE. MAY I ASSIST YOU IN YOUR TASKS, SIRS?

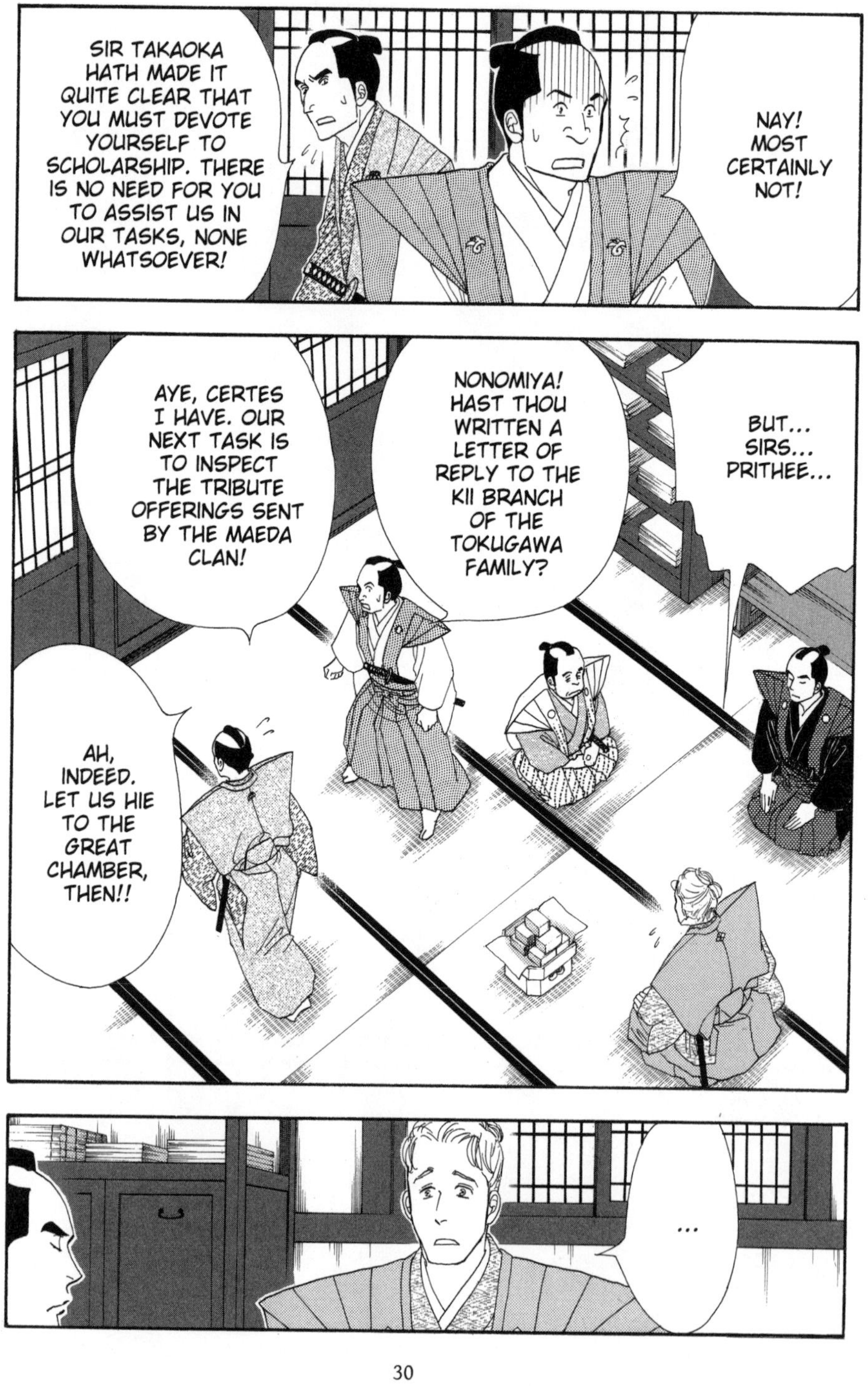
NAY! MOST CERTAINLY NOT!
SIR TAKAOKA HATH MADE IT QUITE CLEAR THAT YOU MUST DEVOTE YOURSELF TO SCHOLARSHIP. THERE IS NO NEED FOR YOU TO ASSIST US IN OUR TASKS, NONE WHATSOEVER!
BUT... SIRS... PRITHEE...
NONOMIYA! HAST THOU WRITTEN A LETTER OF REPLY TO THE KII BRANCH OF THE TOKUGAWA FAMILY?
AYE, CERTES I HAVE. OUR NEXT TASK IS TO INSPECT THE TRIBUTE OFFERINGS SENT BY THE MAEDA CLAN!
AH, INDEED. LET US HIE TO THE GREAT CHAMBER, THEN!!
...

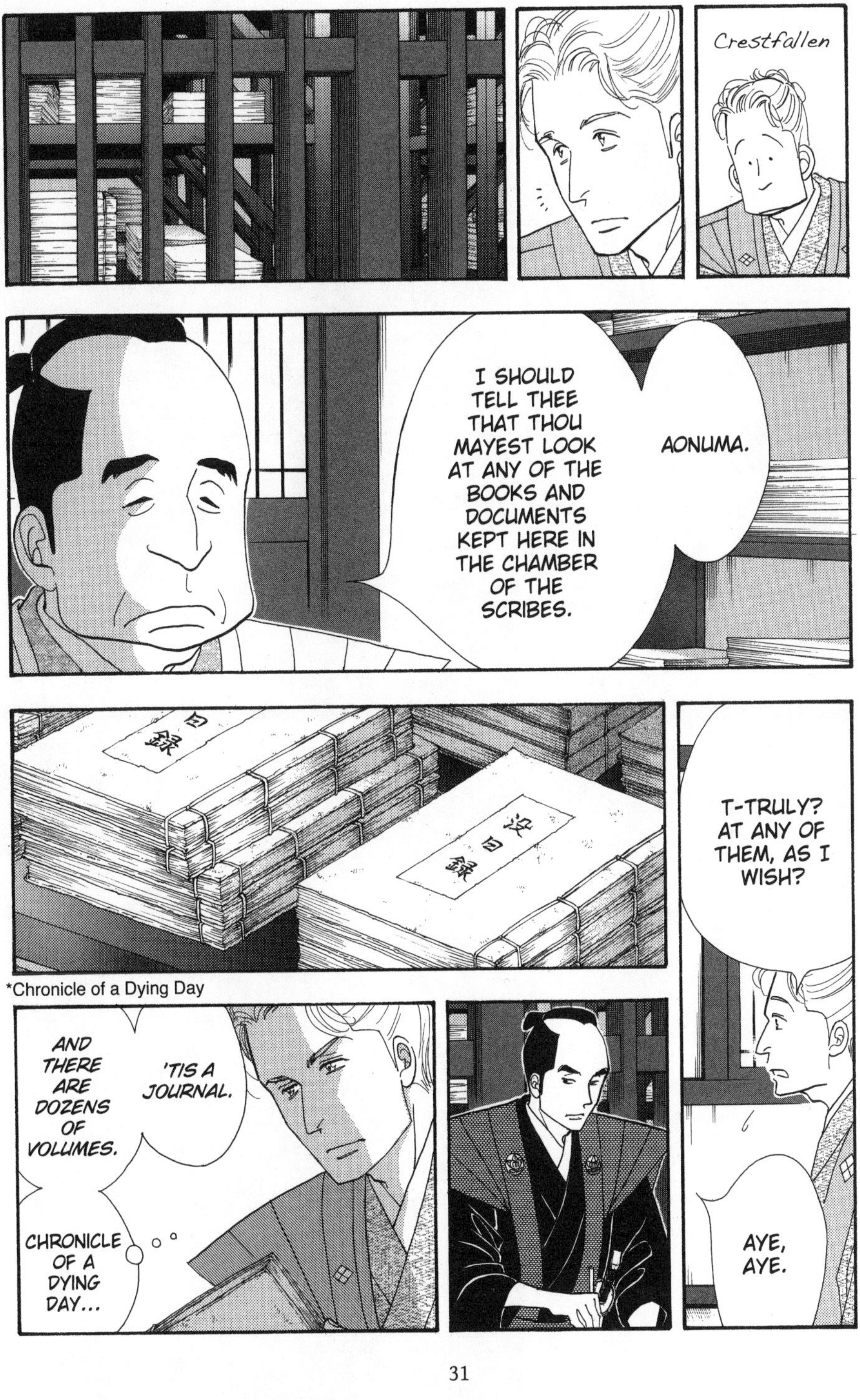
Crestfallen
AONUMA.
I SHOULD TELL THEE THAT THOU MAYEST LOOK AT ANY OF THE BOOKS AND DOCUMENTS KEPT HERE IN THE CHAMBER OF THE SCRIBES.
T-TRULY? AT ANY OF THEM, AS I WISH?
AYE, AYE.
日録
没日録
'TIS A JOURNAL.
AND THERE ARE DOZENS OF VOLUMES.
CHRONICLE OF A DYING DAY...

*Chronicle of a Dying Day

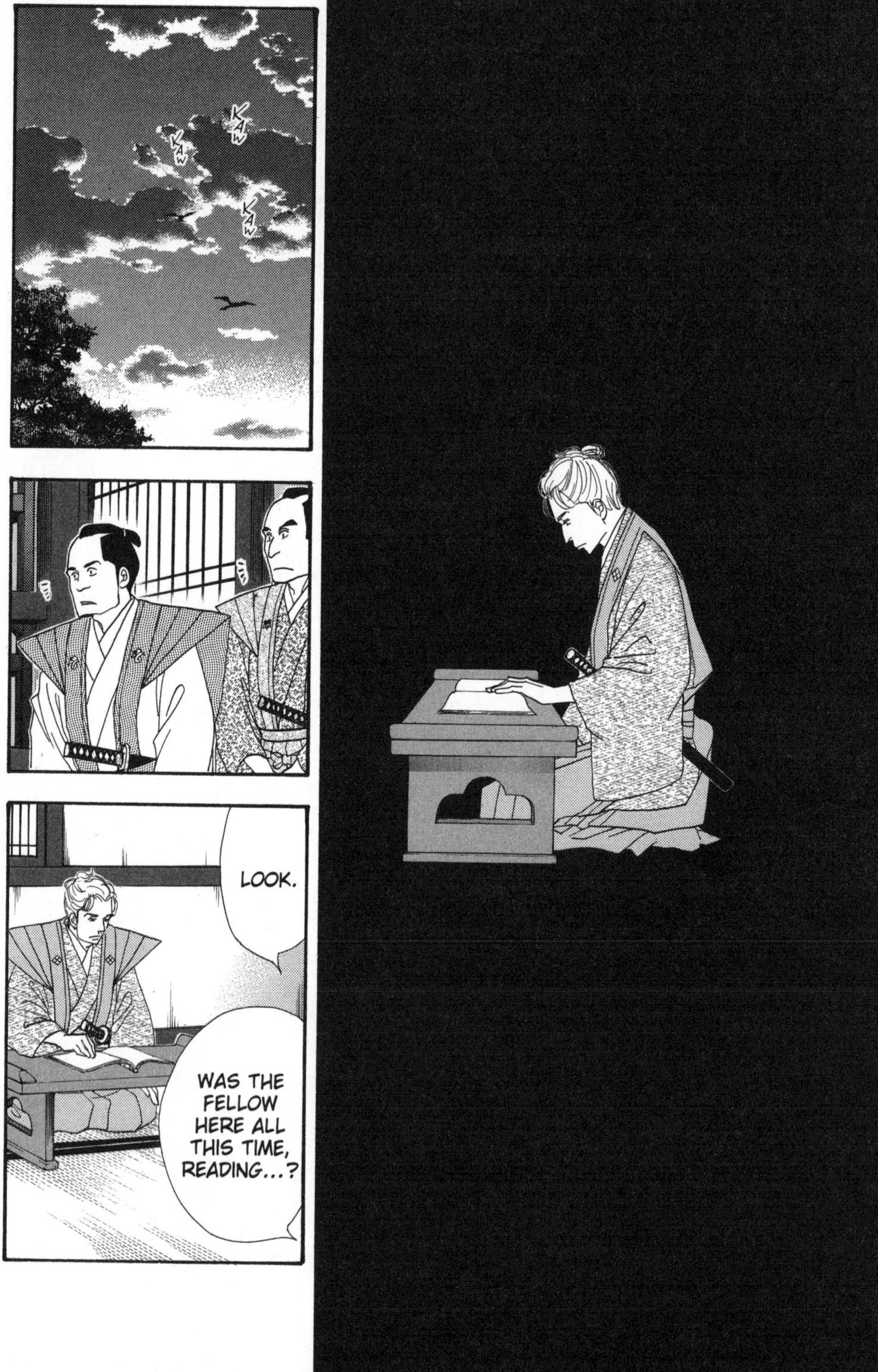
KAW
KAW
KAW
LOOK.
WAS THE FELLOW HERE ALL THIS TIME, READING...?

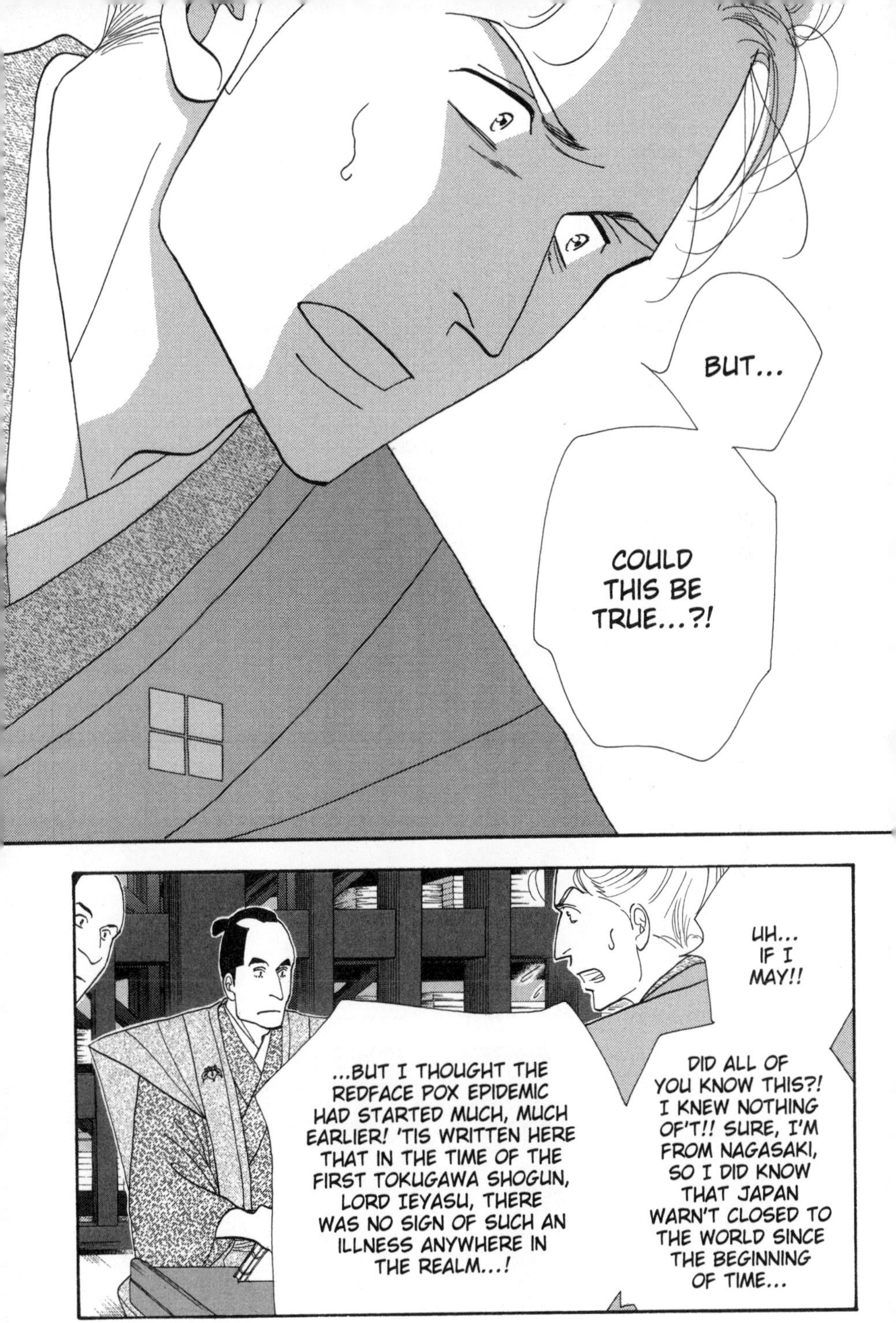
BUT...
COULD THIS BE TRUE...?!
UH... IF I MAY!!
DID ALL OF YOU KNOW THIS?! I KNEW NOTHING OF'T!! SURE, I'M FROM NAGASAKI, SO I DID KNOW THAT JAPAN WARN'T CLOSED TO THE WORLD SINCE THE BEGINNING OF TIME...
...BUT I THOUGHT THE REDFACE POX EPIDEMIC HAD STARTED MUCH, MUCH EARLIER! 'TIS WRITTEN HERE THAT IN THE TIME OF THE FIRST TOKUGAWA SHOGUN, LORD IEYASU, THERE WAS NO SIGN OF SUCH AN ILLNESS ANYWHERE IN THE REALM...!

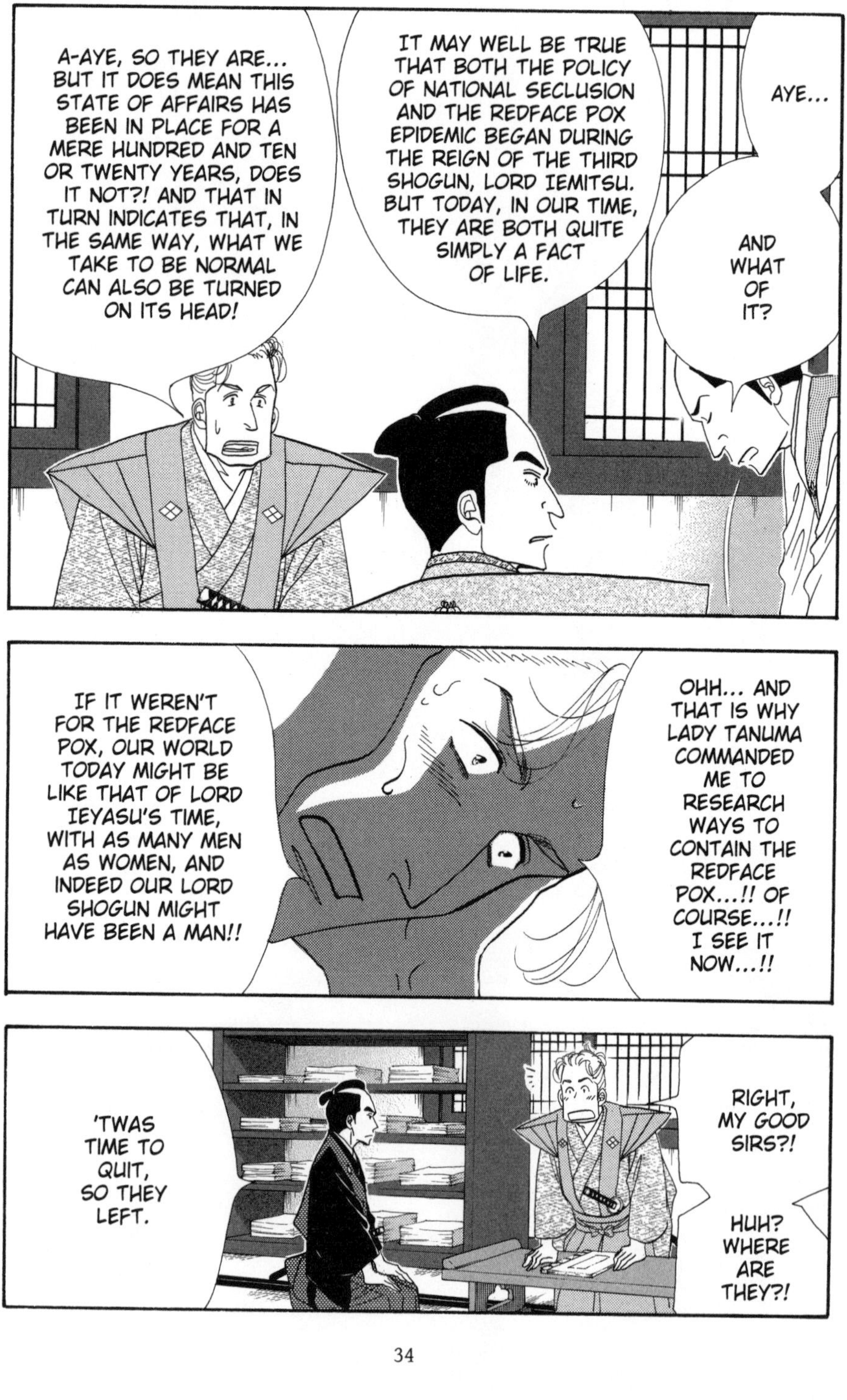
AYE...
AND WHAT OF IT?
IT MAY WELL BE TRUE THAT BOTH THE POLICY OF NATIONAL SECLUSION AND THE REDFACE POX EPIDEMIC BEGAN DURING THE REIGN OF THE THIRD SHOGUN, LORD IEMITSU. BUT TODAY, IN OUR TIME, THEY ARE BOTH QUITE SIMPLY A FACT OF LIFE.
A-AYE, SO THEY ARE... BUT IT DOES MEAN THIS STATE OF AFFAIRS HAS BEEN IN PLACE FOR A MERE HUNDRED AND TEN OR TWENTY YEARS, DOES IT NOT?! AND THAT IN TURN INDICATES THAT, IN THE SAME WAY, WHAT WE TAKE TO BE NORMAL CAN ALSO BE TURNED ON ITS HEAD!
OHH... AND THAT IS WHY LADY TANUMA COMMANDED ME TO RESEARCH WAYS TO CONTAIN THE REDFACE POX...!! OF COURSE...!! I SEE IT NOW...!!
IF IT WEREN'T FOR THE REDFACE POX, OUR WORLD TODAY MIGHT BE LIKE THAT OF LORD IEYASU'S TIME, WITH AS MANY MEN AS WOMEN, AND INDEED OUR LORD SHOGUN MIGHT HAVE BEEN A MAN!!
RIGHT, MY GOOD SIRS?!
HUH? WHERE ARE THEY?!
'TWAS TIME TO QUIT, SO THEY LEFT.

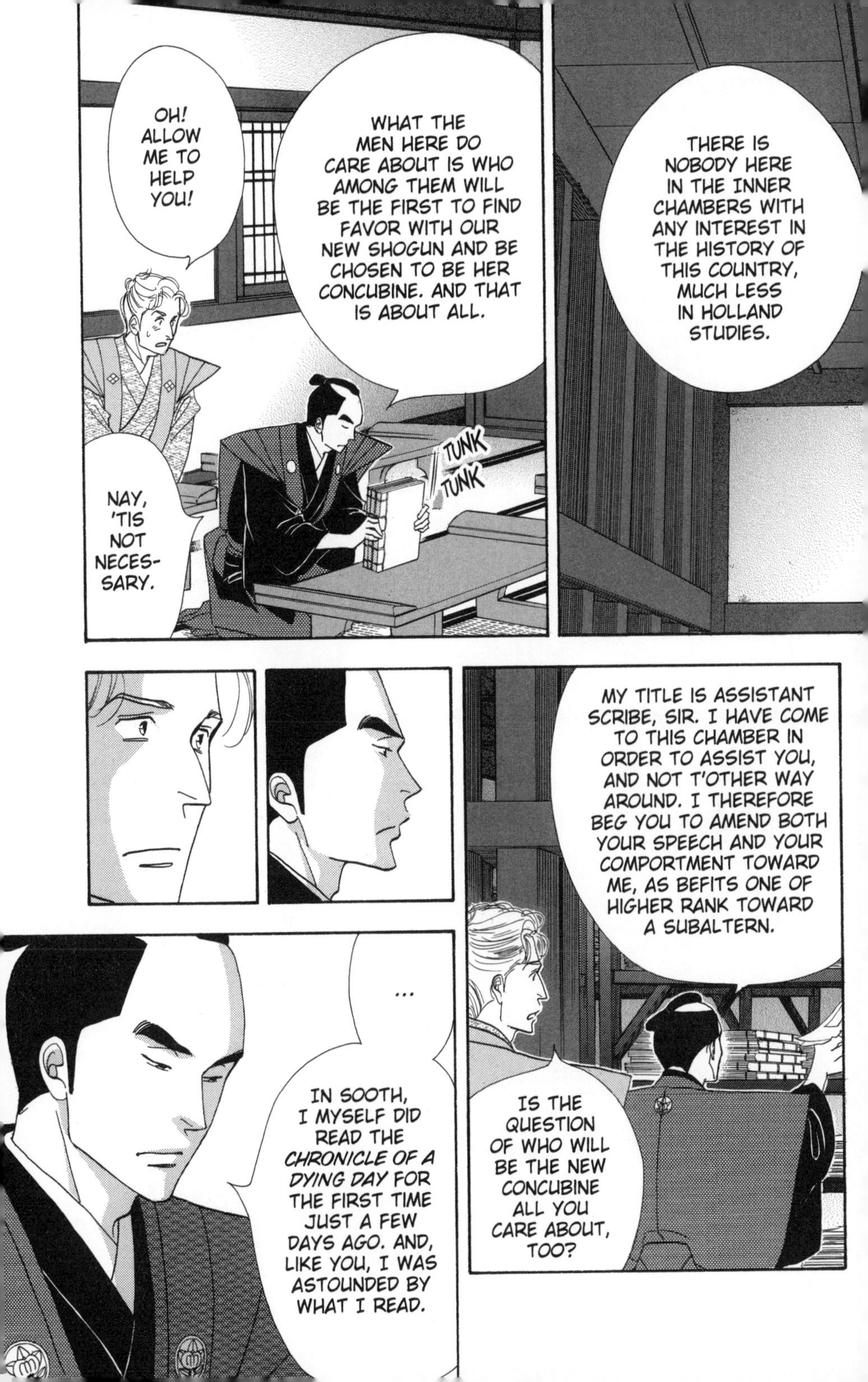
THERE IS NOBODY HERE IN THE INNER CHAMBERS WITH ANY INTEREST IN THE HISTORY OF THIS COUNTRY, MUCH LESS IN HOLLAND STUDIES.
WHAT THE MEN HERE DO CARE ABOUT IS WHO AMONG THEM WILL BE THE FIRST TO FIND FAVOR WITH OUR NEW SHOGUN AND BE CHOSEN TO BE HER CONCUBINE. AND THAT IS ABOUT ALL.
OH! ALLOW ME TO HELP YOU!
TUNK
TUNK
NAY, 'TIS NOT NECES-SARY.
MY TITLE IS ASSISTANT SCRIBE, SIR. I HAVE COME TO THIS CHAMBER IN ORDER TO ASSIST YOU, AND NOT T'OTHER WAY AROUND. I THEREFORE BEG YOU TO AMEND BOTH YOUR SPEECH AND YOUR COMPORTMENT TOWARD ME, AS BEFITS ONE OF HIGHER RANK TOWARD A SUBALTERN.
IS THE QUESTION OF WHO WILL BE THE NEW CONCUBINE ALL YOU CARE ABOUT, TOO?
...
IN SOOTH, I MYSELF DID READ THE *CHRONICLE OF A DYING DAY* FOR THE FIRST TIME JUST A FEW DAYS AGO. AND, LIKE YOU, I WAS ASTOUNDED BY WHAT I READ.

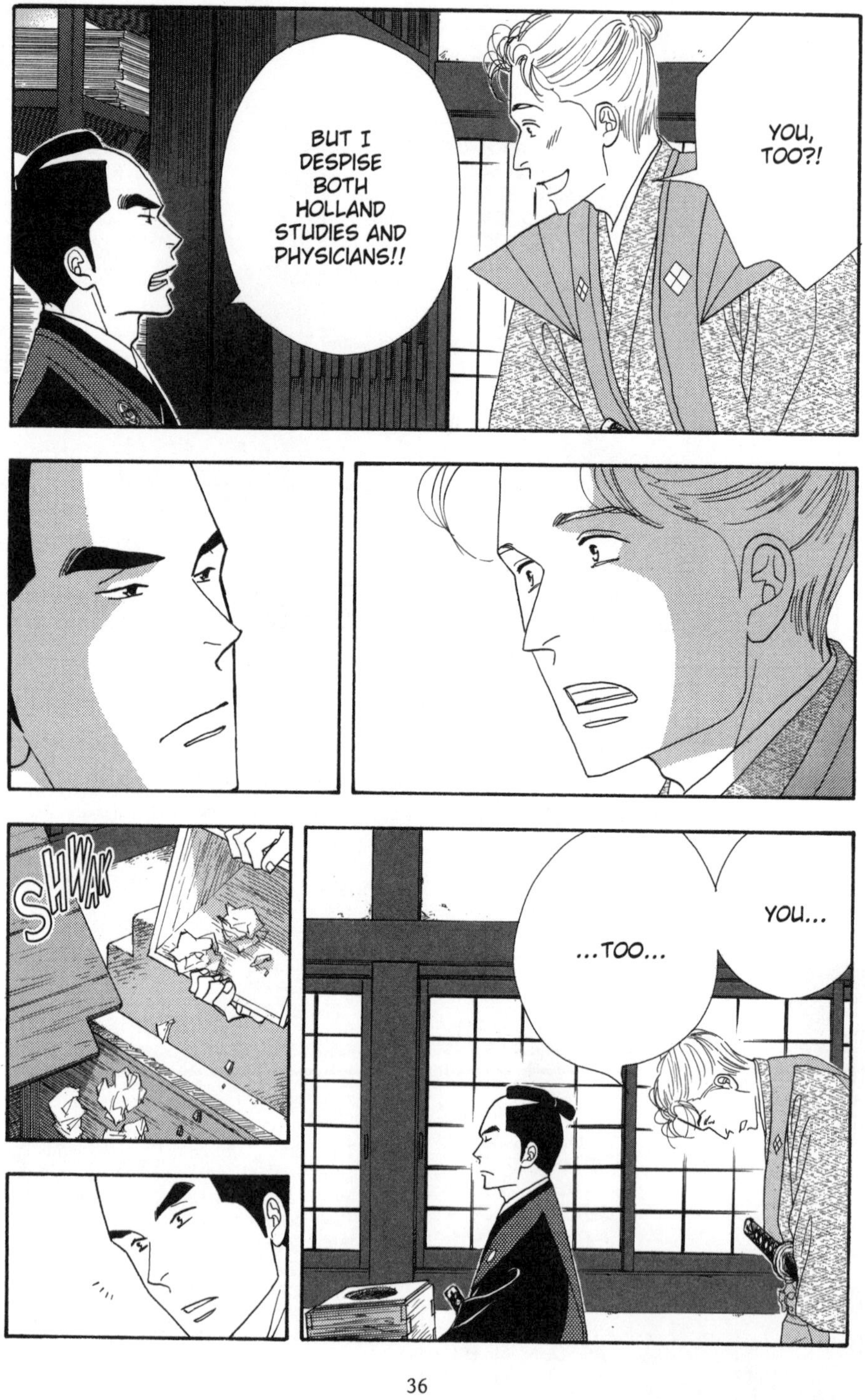
BUT I DESPISE BOTH HOLLAND STUDIES AND PHYSICIANS!!
YOU, TOO?!
YOU...
...TOO...
SHWAK

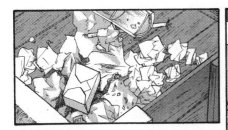

OH!

A SABON...

WHILE I HAVE BROUGHT MANY OF THEM TO EDO, 'TIS A PRECIOUS COMMODITY... SO I SHALL KEEP THIS ONE FOR MINE OWN USE.

Kuroki came from a family of doctors in town, and his father was a general practitioner of great repute in their neighborhood.

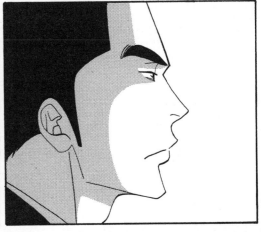

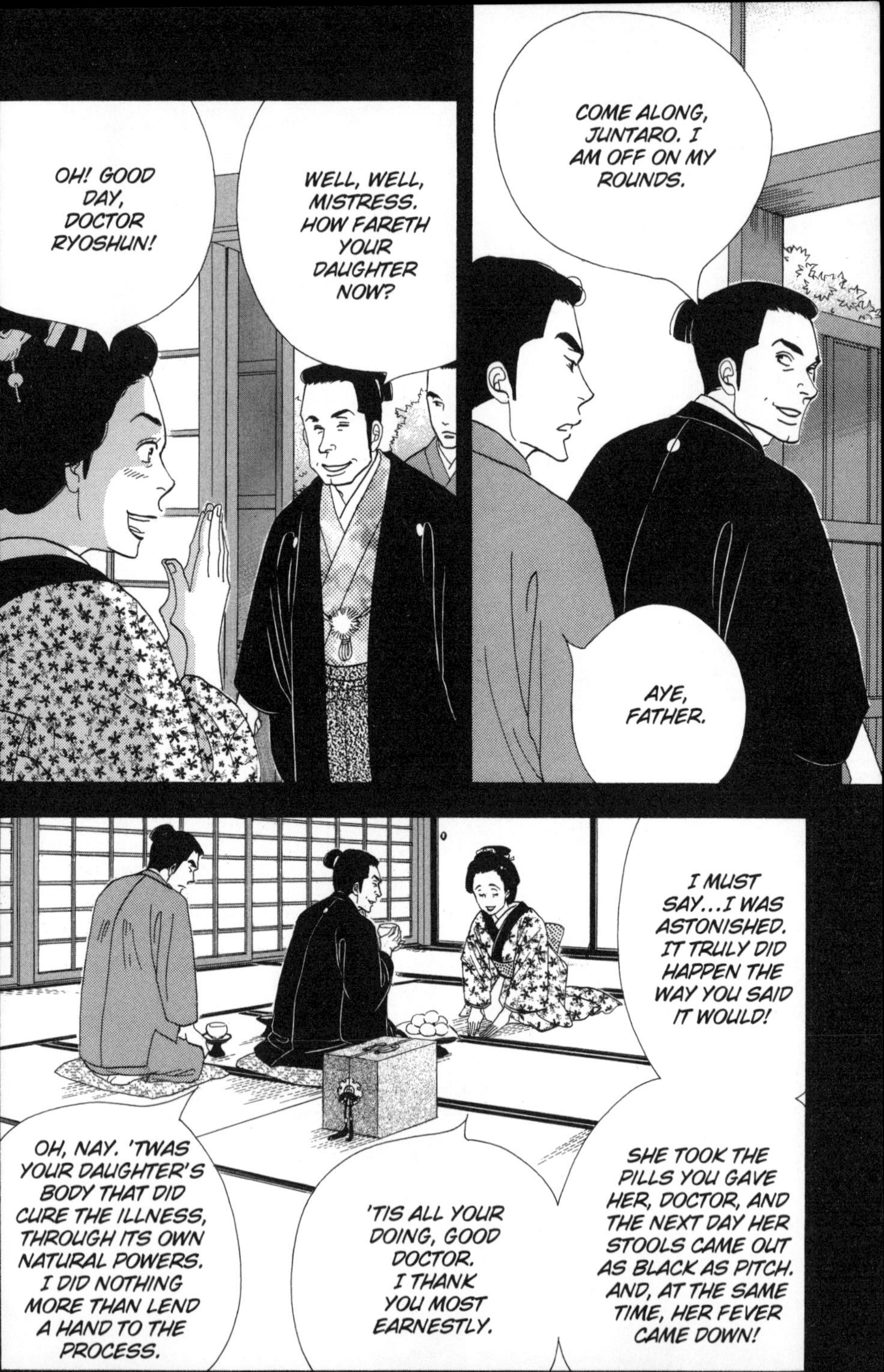
COME ALONG, JUNTARO. I AM OFF ON MY ROUNDS.
AYE, FATHER.
OH! GOOD DAY, DOCTOR RYOSHUN!
WELL, WELL, MISTRESS. HOW FARETH YOUR DAUGHTER NOW?
I MUST SAY...I WAS ASTONISHED. IT TRULY DID HAPPEN THE WAY YOU SAID IT WOULD!
SHE TOOK THE PILLS YOU GAVE HER, DOCTOR, AND THE NEXT DAY HER STOOLS CAME OUT AS BLACK AS PITCH. AND, AT THE SAME TIME, HER FEVER CAME DOWN!
'TIS ALL YOUR DOING, GOOD DOCTOR. I THANK YOU MOST EARNESTLY.
OH, NAY. 'TWAS YOUR DAUGHTER'S BODY THAT DID CURE THE ILLNESS, THROUGH ITS OWN NATURAL POWERS. I DID NOTHING MORE THAN LEND A HAND TO THE PROCESS.

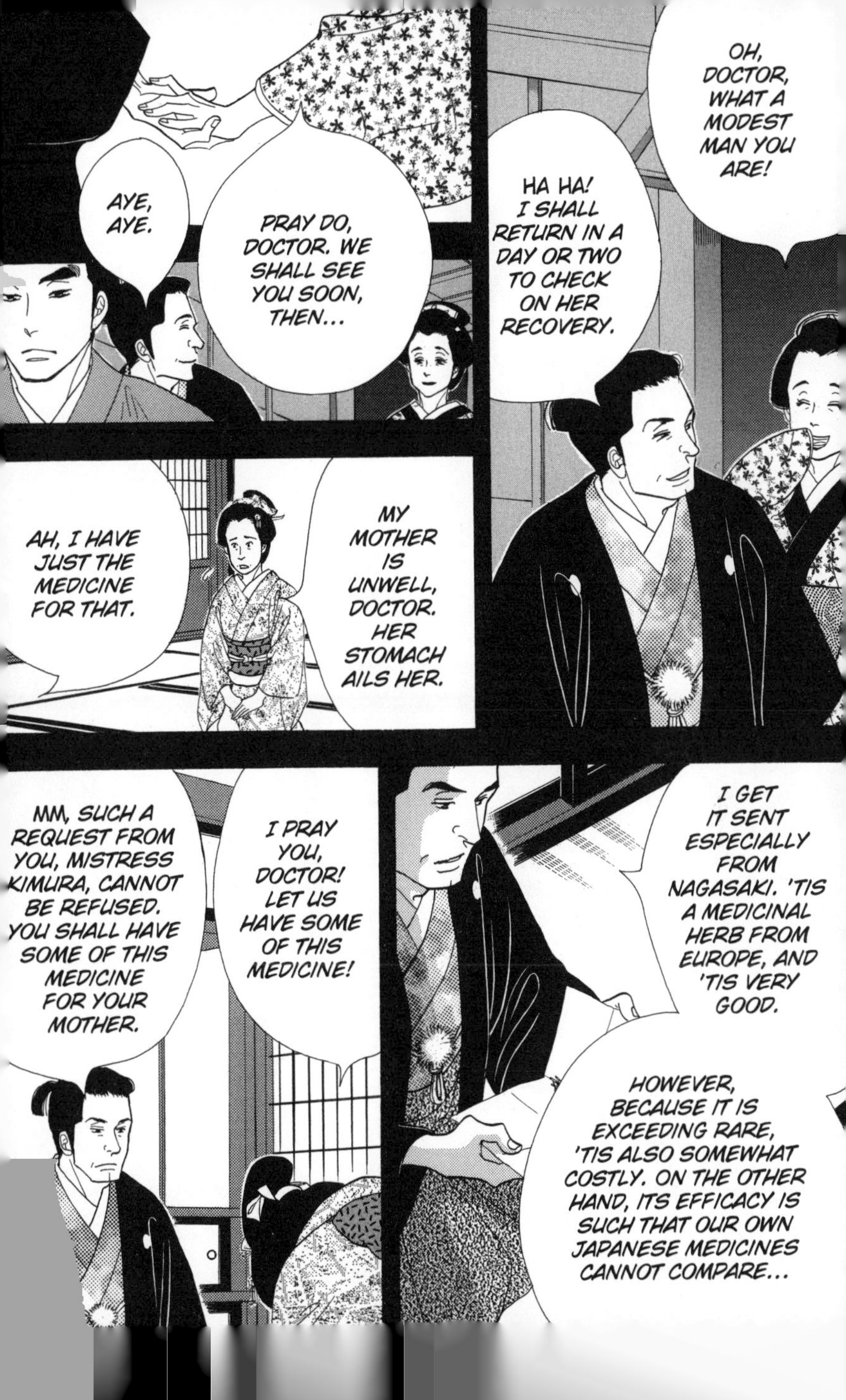
OH, DOCTOR, WHAT A MODEST MAN YOU ARE!
HA HA! I SHALL RETURN IN A DAY OR TWO TO CHECK ON HER RECOVERY.
PRAY DO, DOCTOR. WE SHALL SEE YOU SOON, THEN...
AYE, AYE.
MY MOTHER IS UNWELL, DOCTOR. HER STOMACH AILS HER.
AH, I HAVE JUST THE MEDICINE FOR THAT.
I GET IT SENT ESPECIALLY FROM NAGASAKI. 'TIS A MEDICINAL HERB FROM EUROPE, AND 'TIS VERY GOOD.
HOWEVER, BECAUSE IT IS EXCEEDING RARE, 'TIS ALSO SOMEWHAT COSTLY. ON THE OTHER HAND, ITS EFFICACY IS SUCH THAT OUR OWN JAPANESE MEDICINES CANNOT COMPARE...
I PRAY YOU, DOCTOR! LET US HAVE SOME OF THIS MEDICINE!
MM, SUCH A REQUEST FROM YOU, MISTRESS KIMURA, CANNOT BE REFUSED. YOU SHALL HAVE SOME OF THIS MEDICINE FOR YOUR MOTHER.

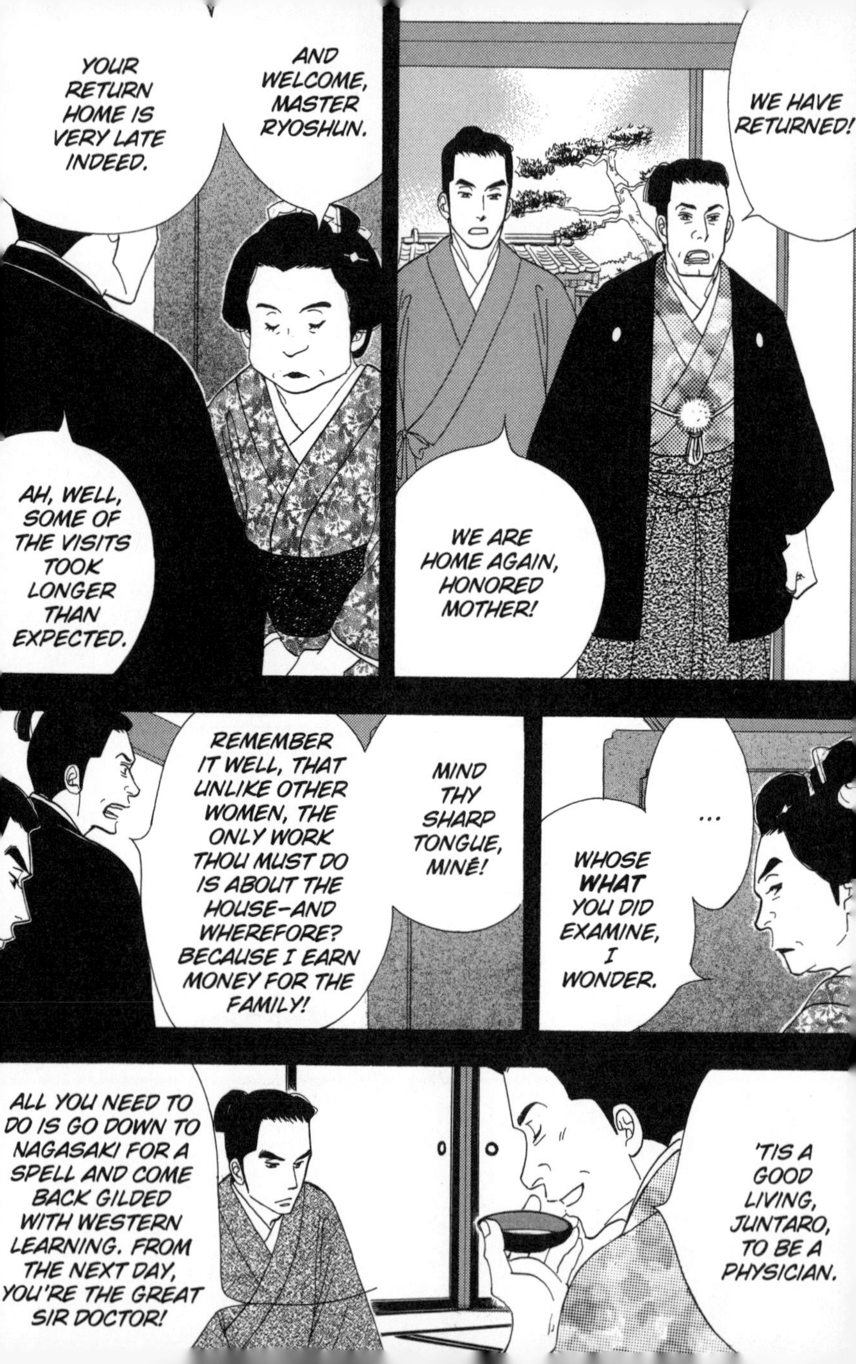
WE HAVE RETURNED!
WE ARE HOME AGAIN, HONORED MOTHER!
AND WELCOME, MASTER RYOSHUN.
YOUR RETURN HOME IS VERY LATE INDEED.
AH, WELL, SOME OF THE VISITS TOOK LONGER THAN EXPECTED.
...
WHOSE **WHAT** YOU DID EXAMINE, I WONDER.
MIND THY SHARP TONGUE, MINÉ!
REMEMBER IT WELL, THAT UNLIKE OTHER WOMEN, THE ONLY WORK THOU MUST DO IS ABOUT THE HOUSE—AND WHEREFORE? BECAUSE I EARN MONEY FOR THE FAMILY!
'TIS A GOOD LIVING, JUNTARO, TO BE A PHYSICIAN.
ALL YOU NEED TO DO IS GO DOWN TO NAGASAKI FOR A SPELL AND COME BACK GILDED WITH WESTERN LEARNING. FROM THE NEXT DAY, YOU'RE THE GREAT SIR DOCTOR!

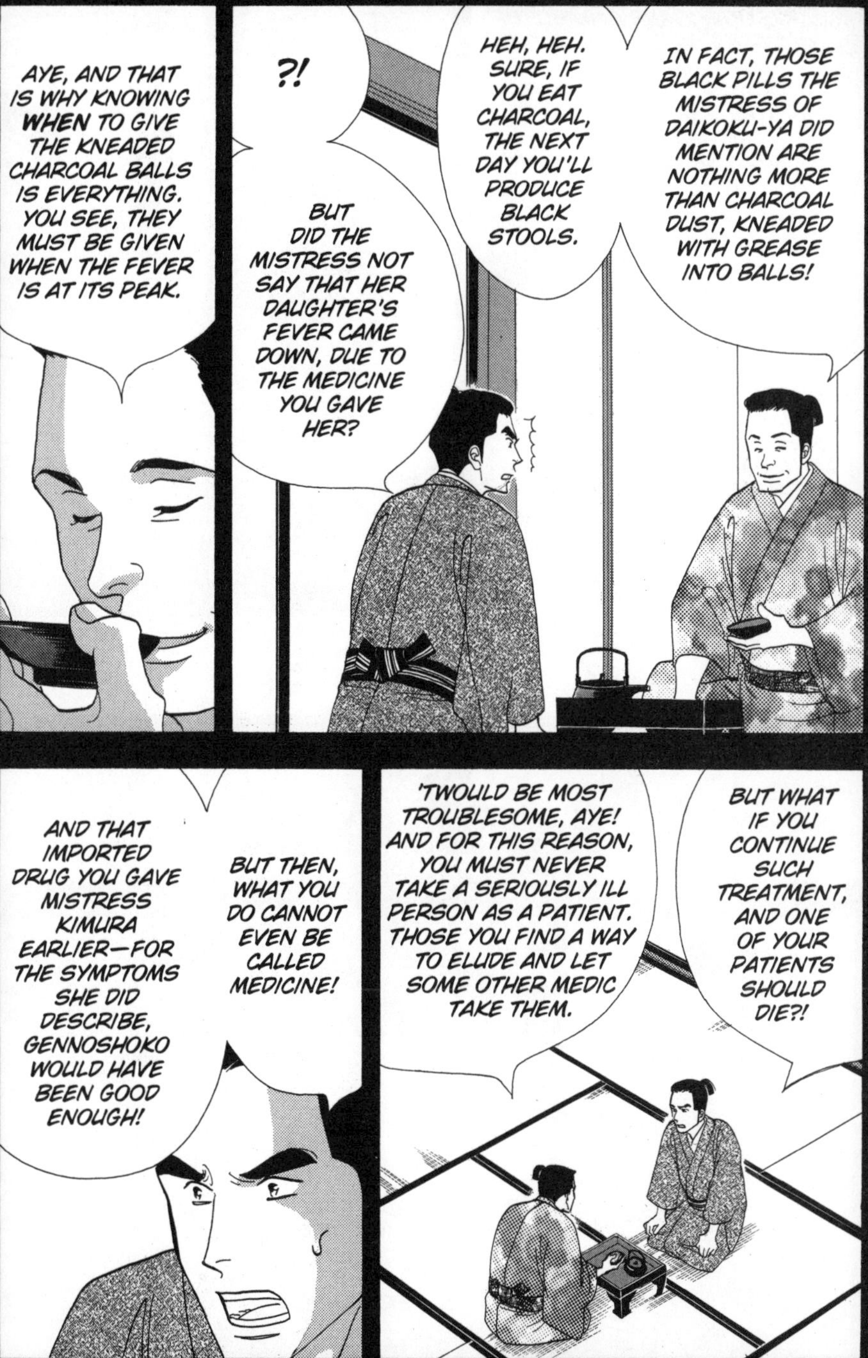
IN FACT, THOSE BLACK PILLS THE MISTRESS OF DAIKOKU-YA DID MENTION ARE NOTHING MORE THAN CHARCOAL DUST, KNEADED WITH GREASE INTO BALLS!
HEH, HEH. SURE, IF YOU EAT CHARCOAL, THE NEXT DAY YOU'LL PRODUCE BLACK STOOLS.
?!
BUT DID THE MISTRESS NOT SAY THAT HER DAUGHTER'S FEVER CAME DOWN, DUE TO THE MEDICINE YOU GAVE HER?
AYE, AND THAT IS WHY KNOWING **WHEN** TO GIVE THE KNEADED CHARCOAL BALLS IS EVERYTHING. YOU SEE, THEY MUST BE GIVEN WHEN THE FEVER IS AT ITS PEAK.
BUT WHAT IF YOU CONTINUE SUCH TREATMENT, AND ONE OF YOUR PATIENTS SHOULD DIE?!
'TWOULD BE MOST TROUBLESOME, AYE! AND FOR THIS REASON, YOU MUST NEVER TAKE A SERIOUSLY ILL PERSON AS A PATIENT. THOSE YOU FIND A WAY TO ELUDE AND LET SOME OTHER MEDIC TAKE THEM.
BUT THEN, WHAT YOU DO CANNOT EVEN BE CALLED MEDICINE!
AND THAT IMPORTED DRUG YOU GAVE MISTRESS KIMURA EARLIER—FOR THE SYMPTOMS SHE DID DESCRIBE, GENNOSHOKO WOULD HAVE BEEN GOOD ENOUGH!

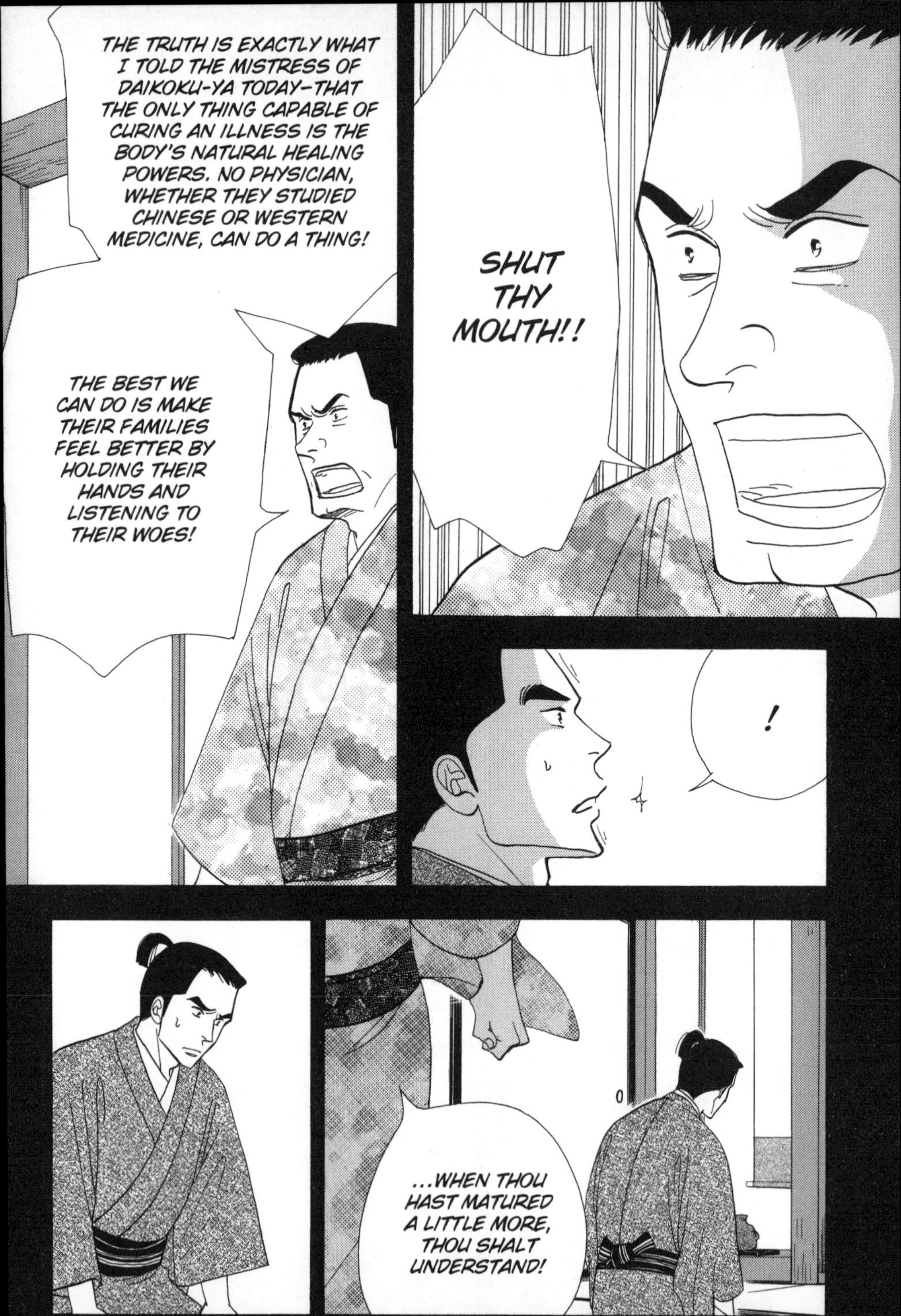
SHUT THY MOUTH!!
!
THE TRUTH IS EXACTLY WHAT I TOLD THE MISTRESS OF DAIKOKU-YA TODAY—THAT THE ONLY THING CAPABLE OF CURING AN ILLNESS IS THE BODY'S NATURAL HEALING POWERS. NO PHYSICIAN, WHETHER THEY STUDIED CHINESE OR WESTERN MEDICINE, CAN DO A THING!
THE BEST WE CAN DO IS MAKE THEIR FAMILIES FEEL BETTER BY HOLDING THEIR HANDS AND LISTENING TO THEIR WOES!
...WHEN THOU HAST MATURED A LITTLE MORE, THOU SHALT UNDERSTAND!

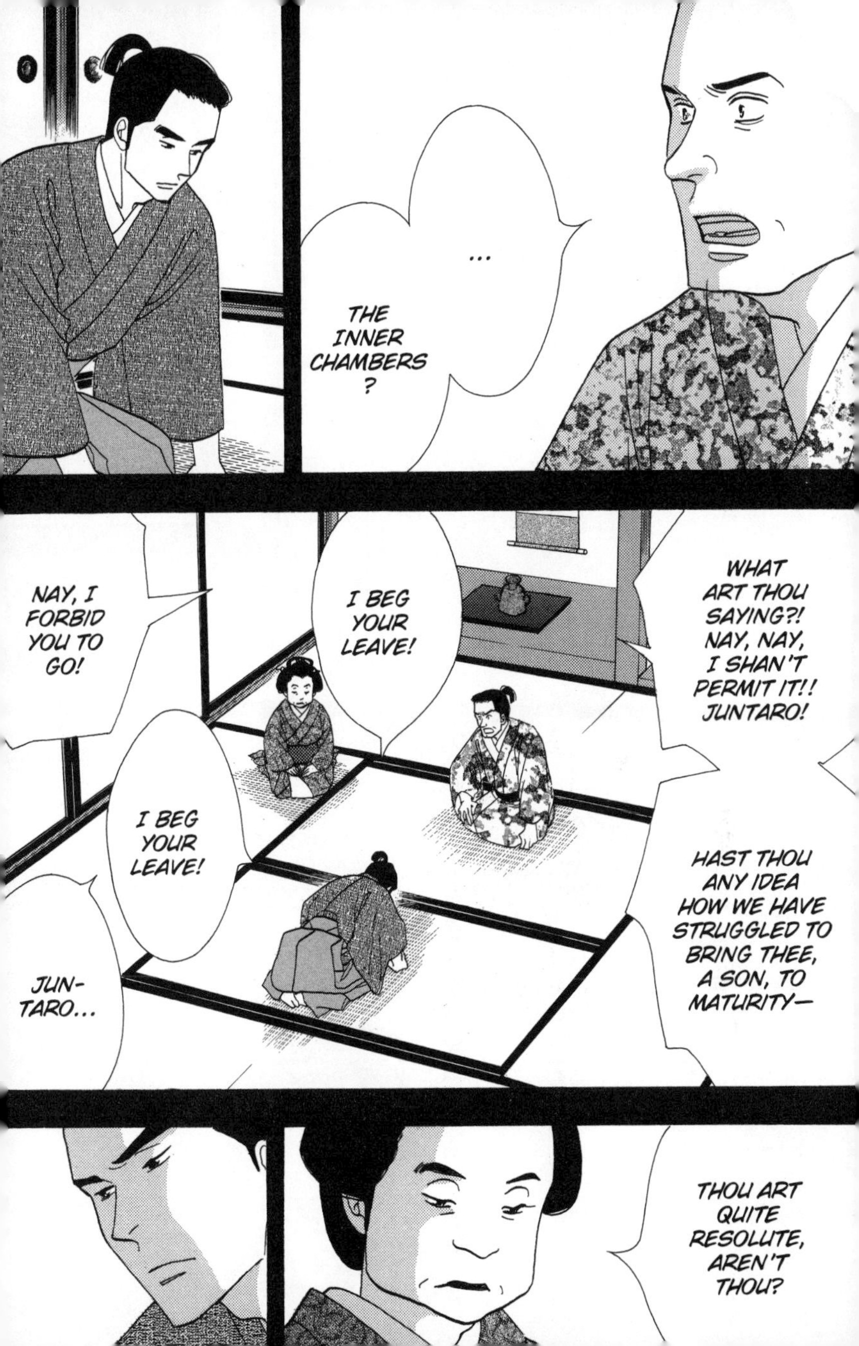
...
THE INNER CHAMBERS?
WHAT ART THOU SAYING?! NAY, NAY, I SHAN'T PERMIT IT!! JUNTARO!
HAST THOU ANY IDEA HOW WE HAVE STRUGGLED TO BRING THEE, A SON, TO MATURITY—
I BEG YOUR LEAVE!
NAY, I FORBID YOU TO GO!
I BEG YOUR LEAVE!
JUN-TARO...
THOU ART QUITE RESOLUTE, AREN'T THOU?

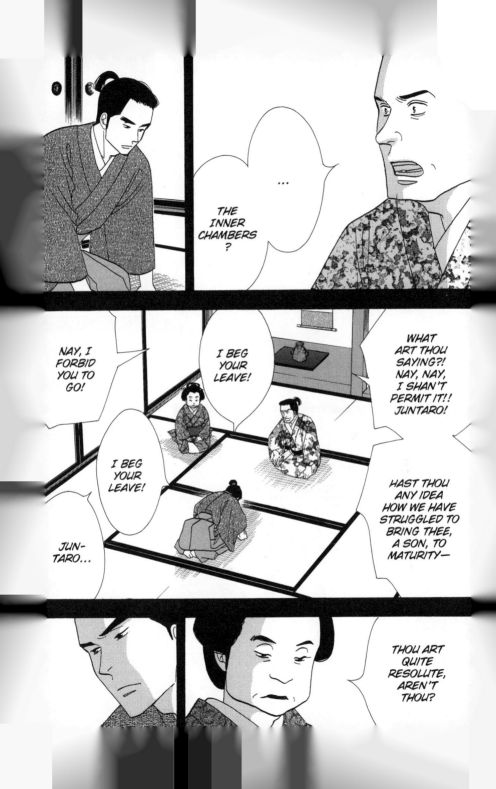

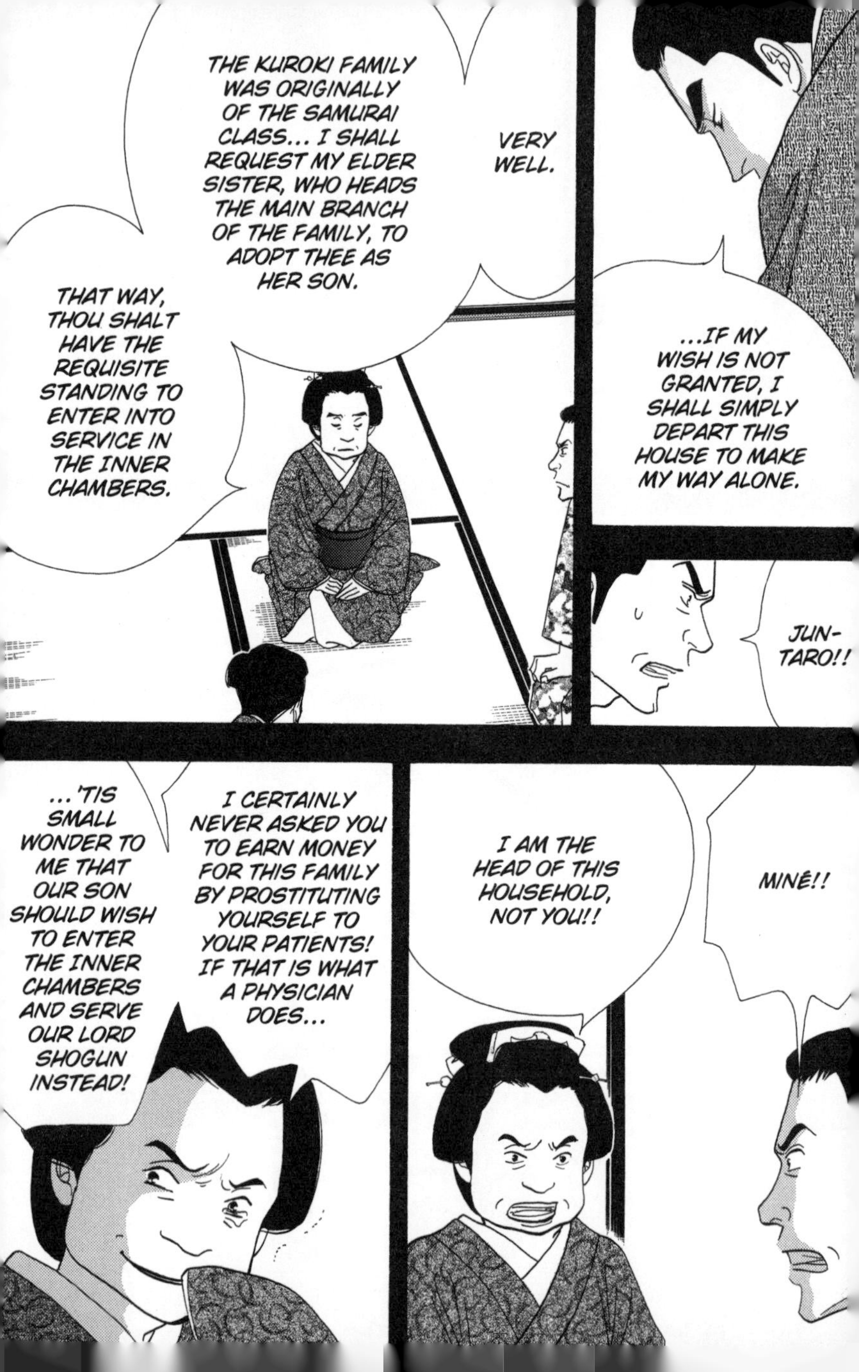
...IF MY WISH IS NOT GRANTED, I SHALL SIMPLY DEPART THIS HOUSE TO MAKE MY WAY ALONE.
JUN-TARO!!
VERY WELL.
THE KUROKI FAMILY WAS ORIGINALLY OF THE SAMURAI CLASS... I SHALL REQUEST MY ELDER SISTER, WHO HEADS THE MAIN BRANCH OF THE FAMILY, TO ADOPT THEE AS HER SON.
THAT WAY, THOU SHALT HAVE THE REQUISITE STANDING TO ENTER INTO SERVICE IN THE INNER CHAMBERS.
MINÉ!!
I AM THE HEAD OF THIS HOUSEHOLD, NOT YOU!!
I CERTAINLY NEVER ASKED YOU TO EARN MONEY FOR THIS FAMILY BY PROSTITUTING YOURSELF TO YOUR PATIENTS! IF THAT IS WHAT A PHYSICIAN DOES...
...'TIS SMALL WONDER TO ME THAT OUR SON SHOULD WISH TO ENTER THE INNER CHAMBERS AND SERVE OUR LORD SHOGUN INSTEAD!

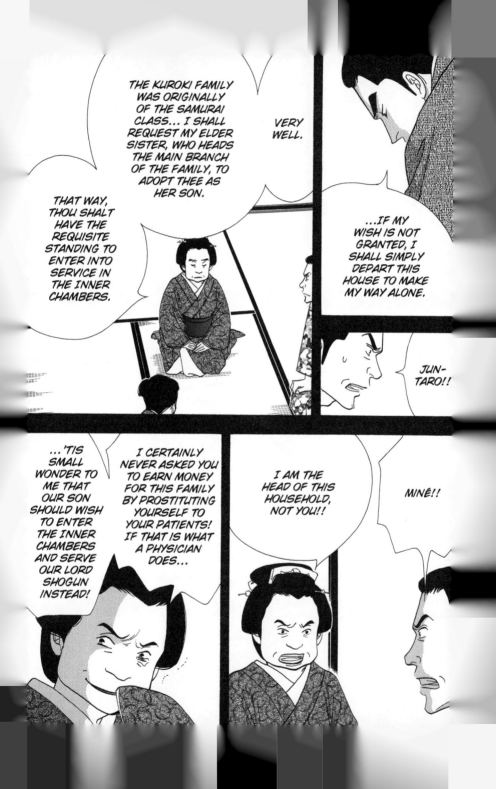

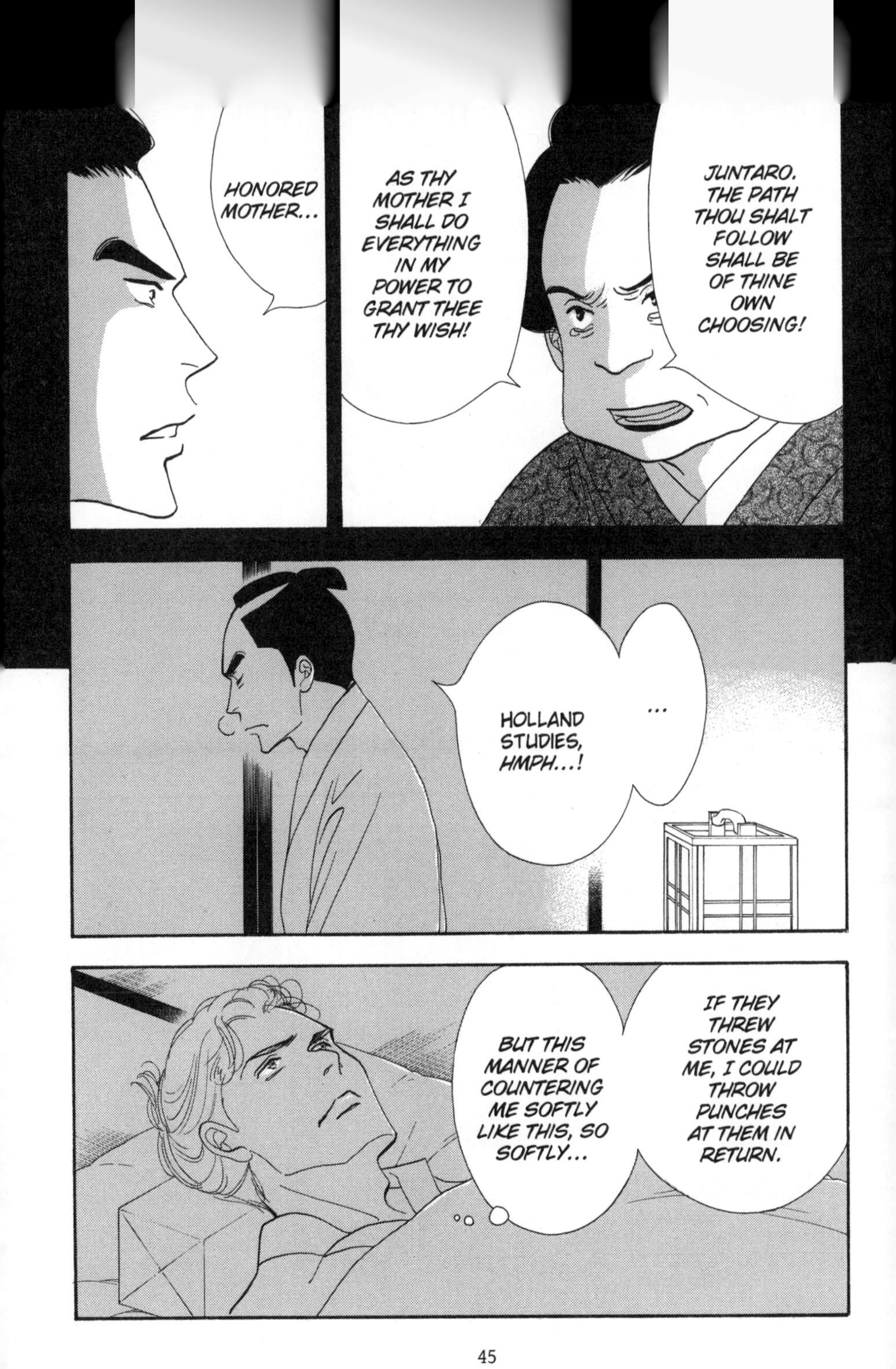
JUNTARO. THE PATH THOU SHALT FOLLOW SHALL BE OF THINE OWN CHOOSING!
AS THY MOTHER I SHALL DO EVERYTHING IN MY POWER TO GRANT THEE THY WISH!
HONORED MOTHER...
...
HOLLAND STUDIES, HMPH...!
IF THEY THREW STONES AT ME, I COULD THROW PUNCHES AT THEM IN RETURN.
BUT THIS MANNER OF COUNTERING ME SOFTLY LIKE THIS, SO SOFTLY...

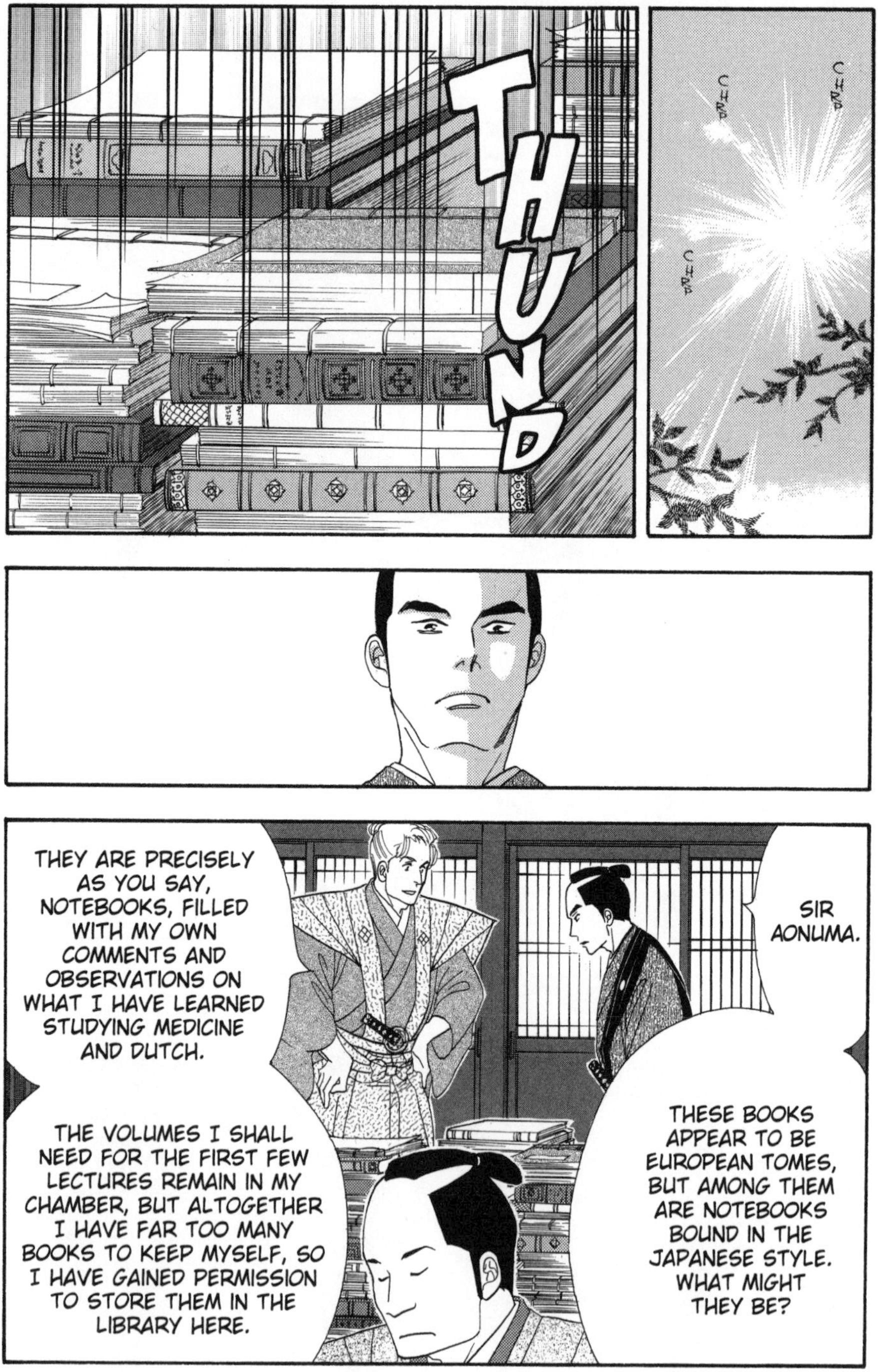

CHIRP
CHIRP
CHIRP
THUND
SIR AONUMA.
THESE BOOKS APPEAR TO BE EUROPEAN TOMES, BUT AMONG THEM ARE NOTEBOOKS BOUND IN THE JAPANESE STYLE. WHAT MIGHT THEY BE?
THEY ARE PRECISELY AS YOU SAY, NOTEBOOKS, FILLED WITH MY OWN COMMENTS AND OBSERVATIONS ON WHAT I HAVE LEARNED STUDYING MEDICINE AND DUTCH.
THE VOLUMES I SHALL NEED FOR THE FIRST FEW LECTURES REMAIN IN MY CHAMBER, BUT ALTOGETHER I HAVE FAR TOO MANY BOOKS TO KEEP MYSELF, SO I HAVE GAINED PERMISSION TO STORE THEM IN THE LIBRARY HERE.

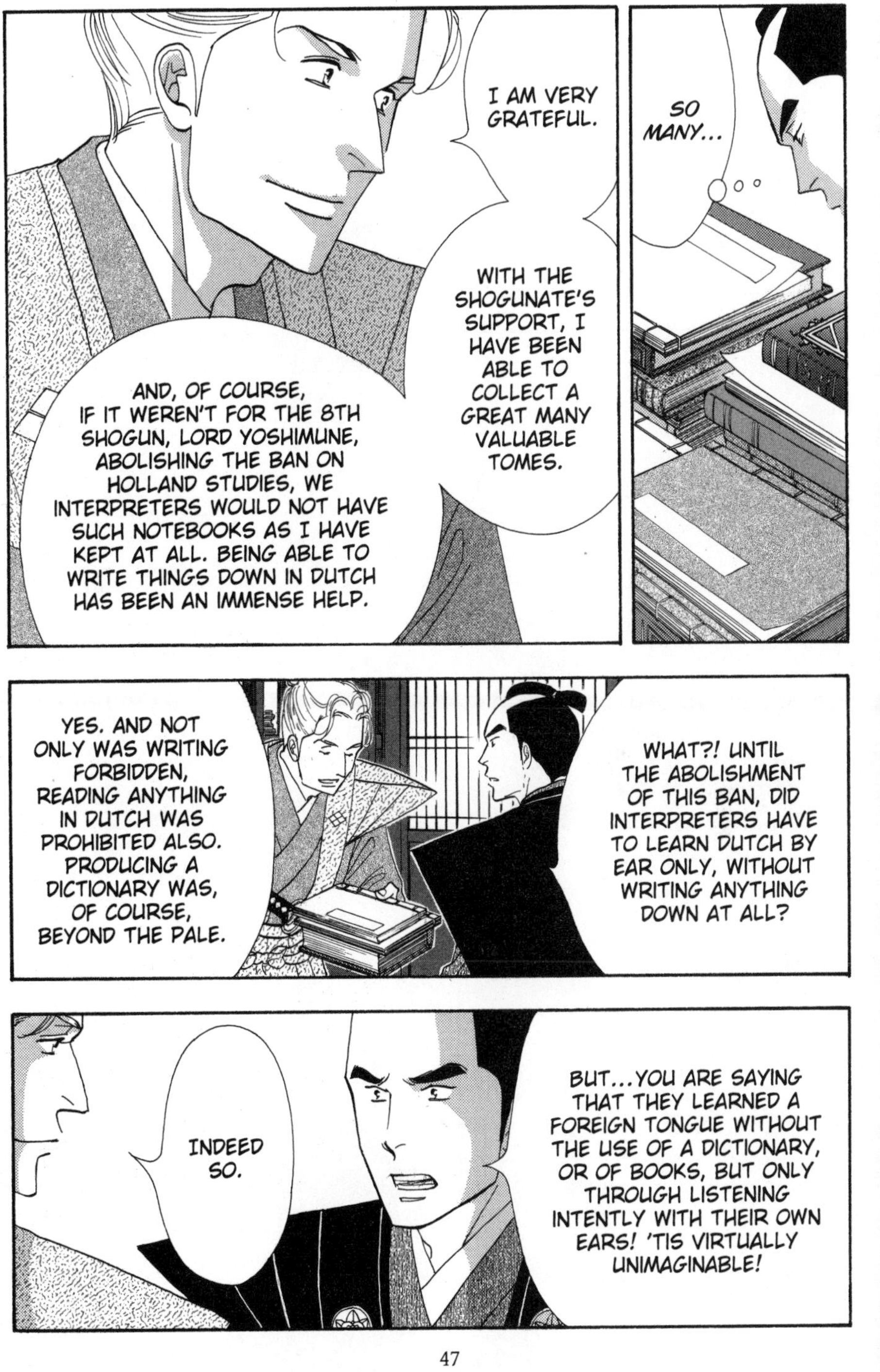
SO MANY...
I AM VERY GRATEFUL.
WITH THE SHOGUNATE'S SUPPORT, I HAVE BEEN ABLE TO COLLECT A GREAT MANY VALUABLE TOMES.
AND, OF COURSE, IF IT WEREN'T FOR THE 8TH SHOGUN, LORD YOSHIMUNE, ABOLISHING THE BAN ON HOLLAND STUDIES, WE INTERPRETERS WOULD NOT HAVE SUCH NOTEBOOKS AS I HAVE KEPT AT ALL. BEING ABLE TO WRITE THINGS DOWN IN DUTCH HAS BEEN AN IMMENSE HELP.
WHAT?! UNTIL THE ABOLISHMENT OF THIS BAN, DID INTERPRETERS HAVE TO LEARN DUTCH BY EAR ONLY, WITHOUT WRITING ANYTHING DOWN AT ALL?
YES. AND NOT ONLY WAS WRITING FORBIDDEN, READING ANYTHING IN DUTCH WAS PROHIBITED ALSO. PRODUCING A DICTIONARY WAS, OF COURSE, BEYOND THE PALE.
BUT...YOU ARE SAYING THAT THEY LEARNED A FOREIGN TONGUE WITHOUT THE USE OF A DICTIONARY, OR OF BOOKS, BUT ONLY THROUGH LISTENING INTENTLY WITH THEIR OWN EARS! 'TIS VIRTUALLY UNIMAGINABLE!
INDEED SO.

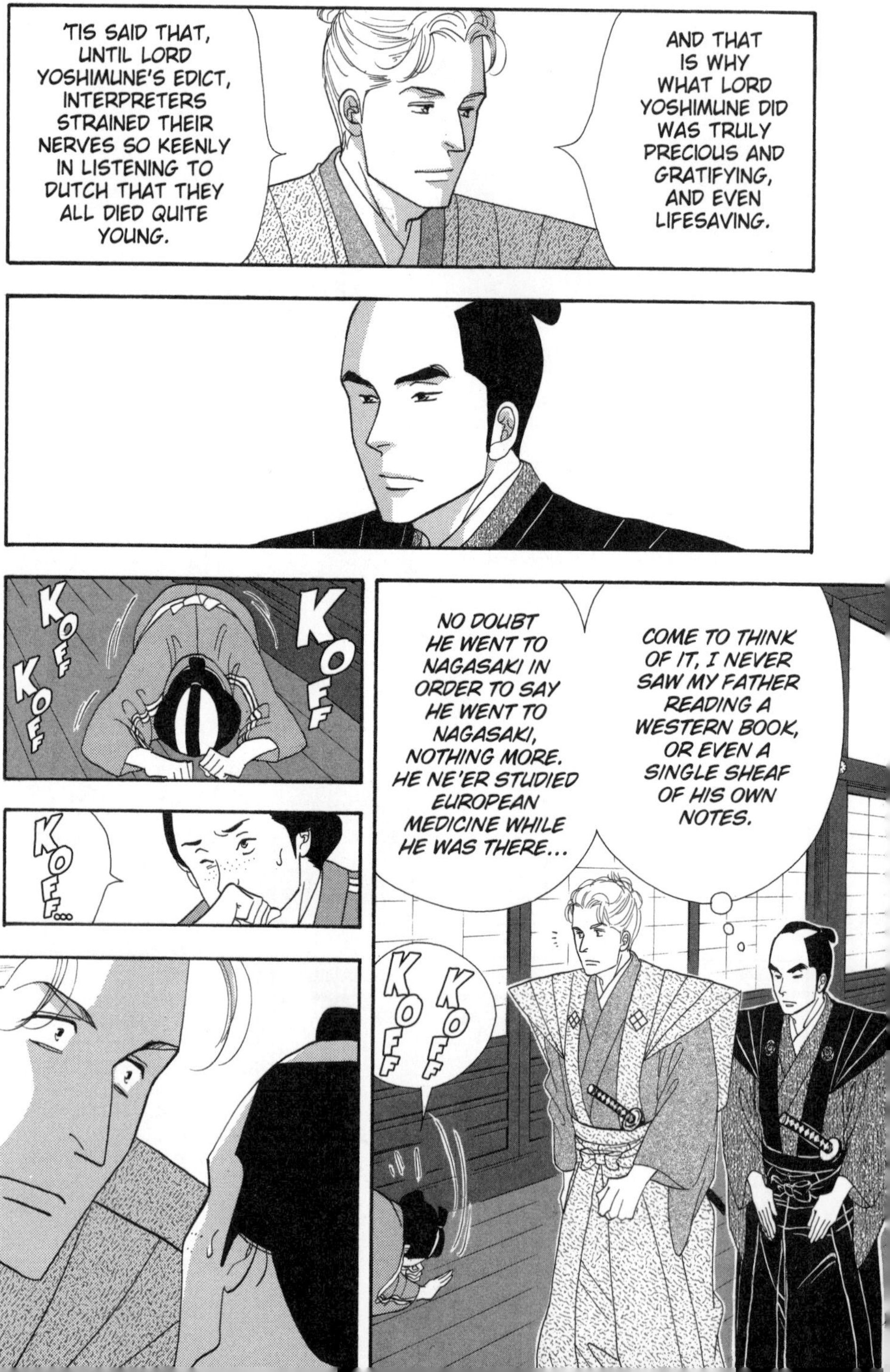
'TIS SAID THAT, UNTIL LORD YOSHIMUNE'S EDICT, INTERPRETERS STRAINED THEIR NERVES SO KEENLY IN LISTENING TO DUTCH THAT THEY ALL DIED QUITE YOUNG.
AND THAT IS WHY WHAT LORD YOSHIMUNE DID WAS TRULY PRECIOUS AND GRATIFYING, AND EVEN LIFESAVING.
COME TO THINK OF IT, I NEVER SAW MY FATHER READING A WESTERN BOOK, OR EVEN A SINGLE SHEAF OF HIS OWN NOTES.
NO DOUBT HE WENT TO NAGASAKI IN ORDER TO SAY HE WENT TO NAGASAKI, NOTHING MORE. HE NE'ER STUDIED EUROPEAN MEDICINE WHILE HE WAS THERE...
KOFF KOFF
KOFF KOFF KOFF KOFF
KOFF...

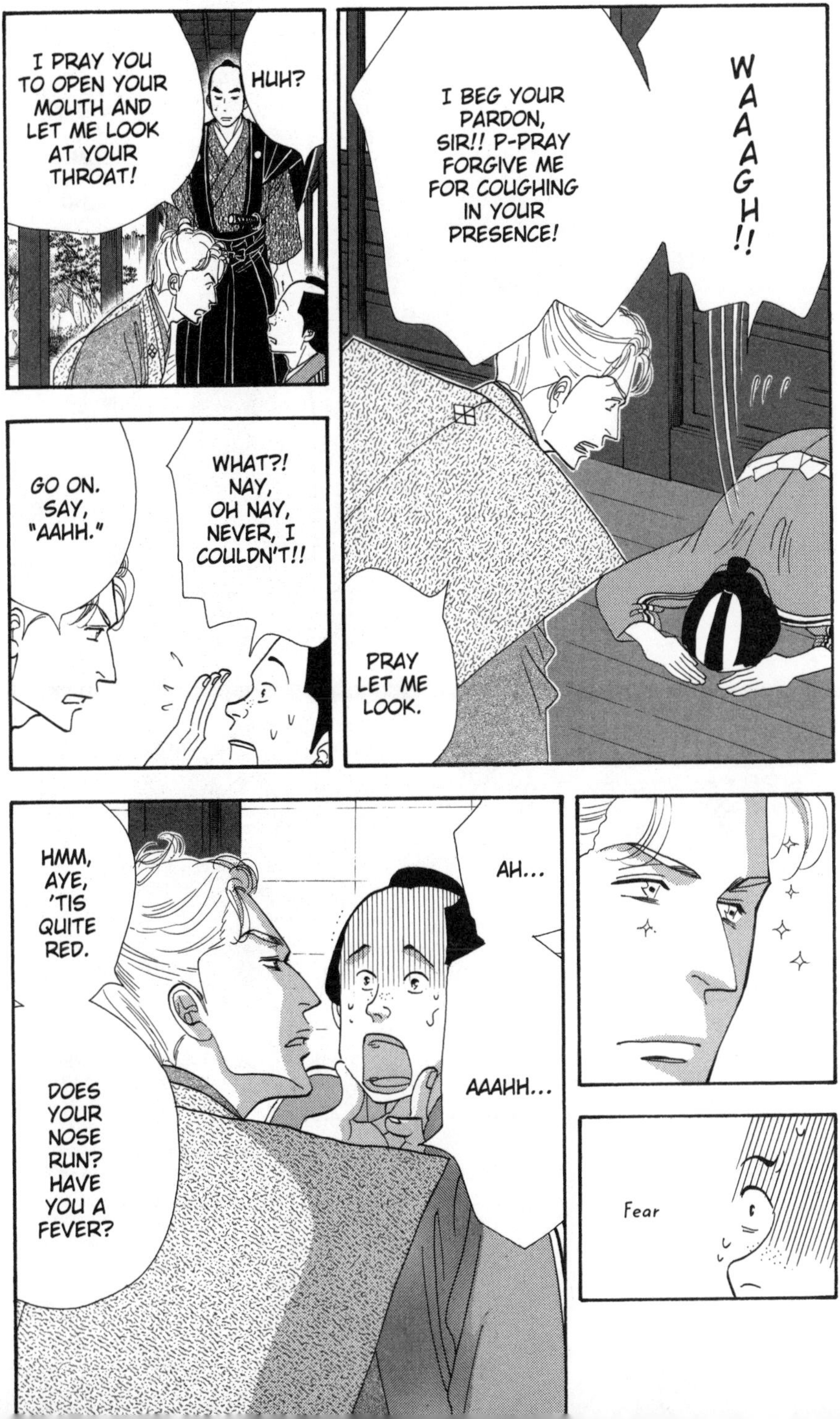
WAAAGH!!
I BEG YOUR PARDON, SIR!! P-PRAY FORGIVE ME FOR COUGHING IN YOUR PRESENCE!
PRAY LET ME LOOK.
HUH?
I PRAY YOU TO OPEN YOUR MOUTH AND LET ME LOOK AT YOUR THROAT!
WHAT?! NAY, OH NAY, NEVER, I COULDN'T!!
GO ON. SAY, "AAHH."
Fear
AH...
AAAHH...
HMM, AYE, 'TIS QUITE RED.
DOES YOUR NOSE RUN? HAVE YOU A FEVER?

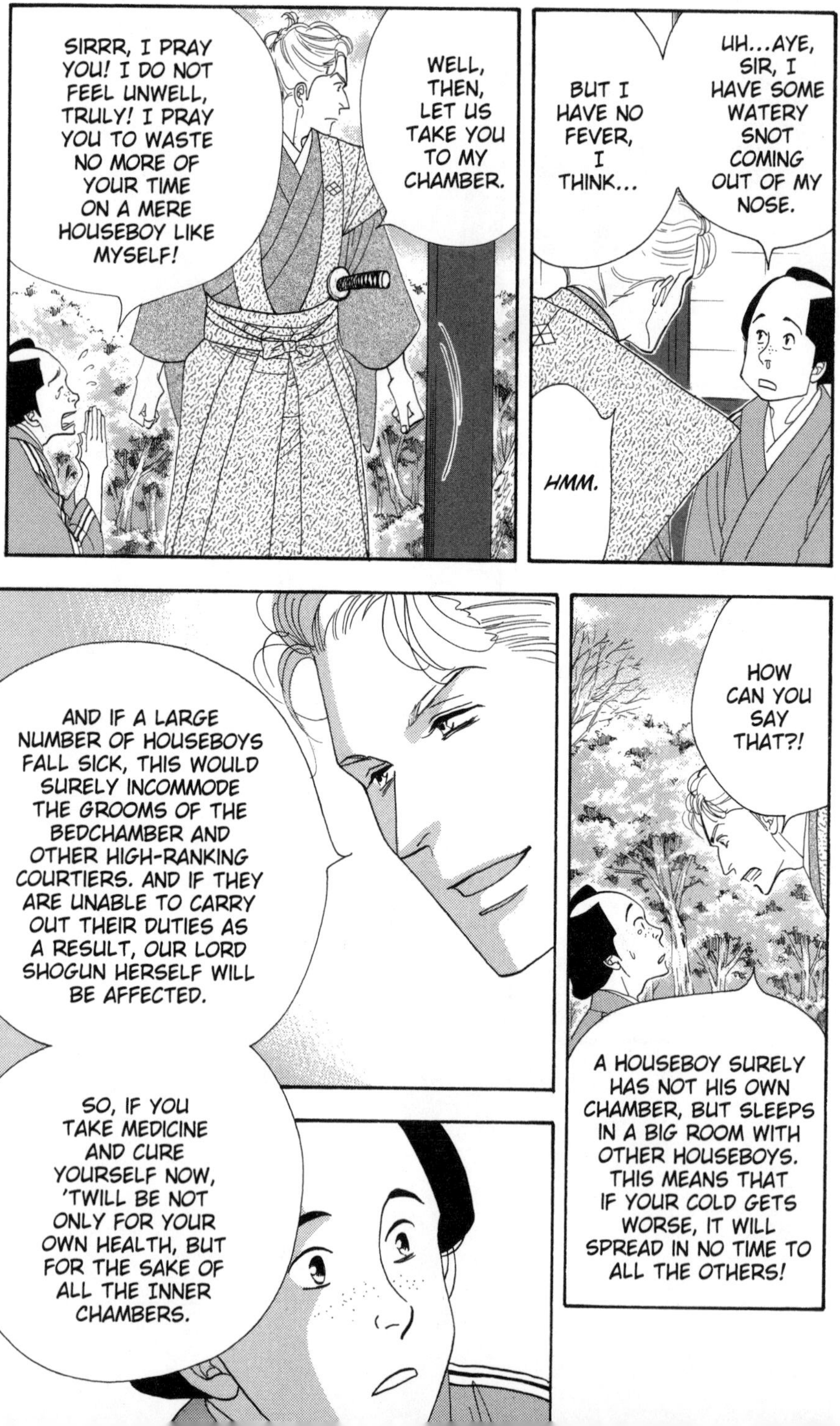
UH...AYE, SIR, I HAVE SOME WATERY SNOT COMING OUT OF MY NOSE.
BUT I HAVE NO FEVER, I THINK...
HMM.
WELL, THEN, LET US TAKE YOU TO MY CHAMBER.
SIRRR, I PRAY YOU! I DO NOT FEEL UNWELL, TRULY! I PRAY YOU TO WASTE NO MORE OF YOUR TIME ON A MERE HOUSEBOY LIKE MYSELF!
HOW CAN YOU SAY THAT?!
A HOUSEBOY SURELY HAS NOT HIS OWN CHAMBER, BUT SLEEPS IN A BIG ROOM WITH OTHER HOUSEBOYS. THIS MEANS THAT IF YOUR COLD GETS WORSE, IT WILL SPREAD IN NO TIME TO ALL THE OTHERS!
AND IF A LARGE NUMBER OF HOUSEBOYS FALL SICK, THIS WOULD SURELY INCOMMODE THE GROOMS OF THE BEDCHAMBER AND OTHER HIGH-RANKING COURTIERS. AND IF THEY ARE UNABLE TO CARRY OUT THEIR DUTIES AS A RESULT, OUR LORD SHOGUN HERSELF WILL BE AFFECTED.
SO, IF YOU TAKE MEDICINE AND CURE YOURSELF NOW, 'TWILL BE NOT ONLY FOR YOUR OWN HEALTH, BUT FOR THE SAKE OF ALL THE INNER CHAMBERS.

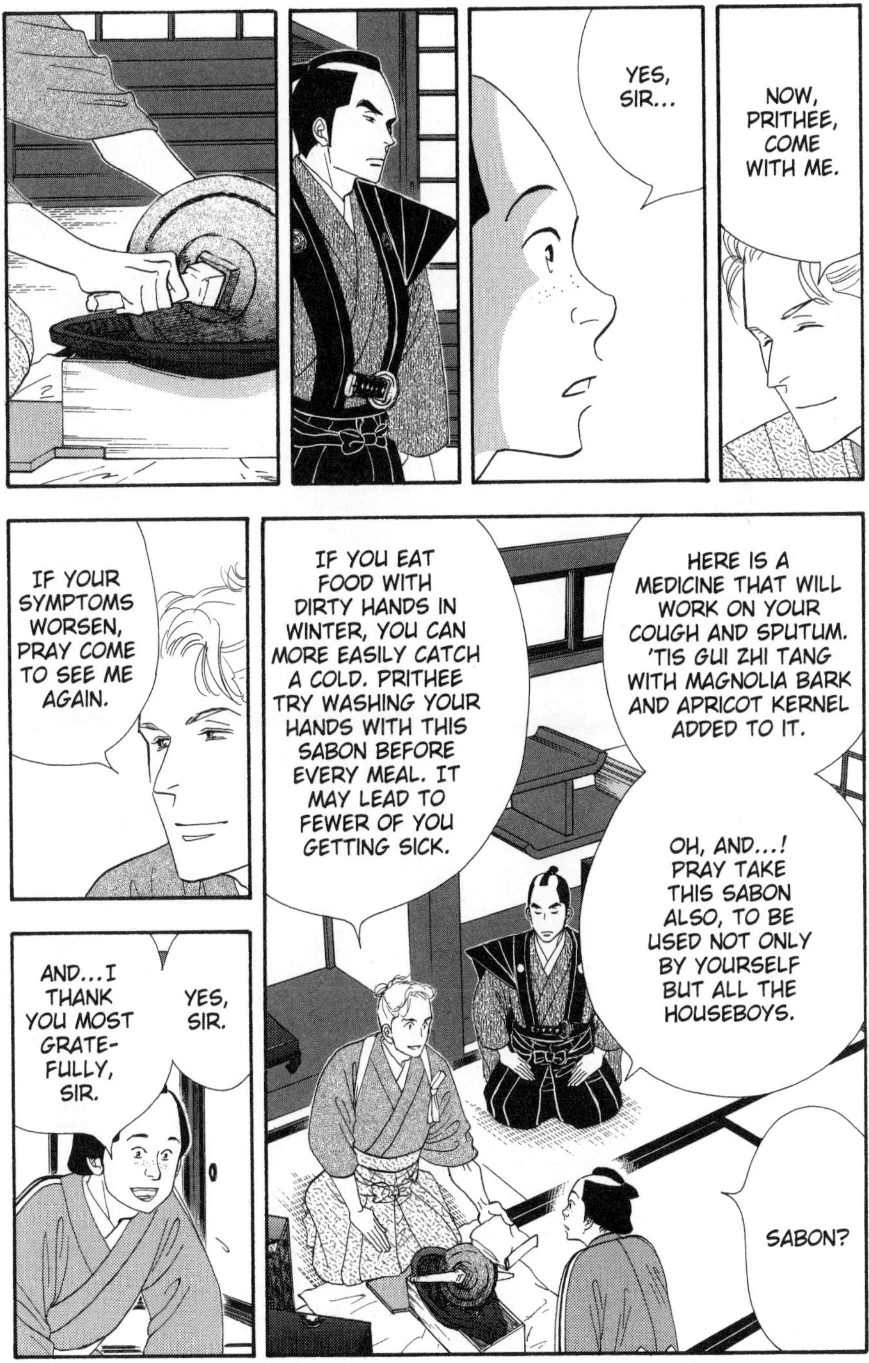

NOW, PRITHEE, COME WITH ME.
YES, SIR...
HERE IS A MEDICINE THAT WILL WORK ON YOUR COUGH AND SPUTUM. 'TIS GUI ZHI TANG WITH MAGNOLIA BARK AND APRICOT KERNEL ADDED TO IT.
OH, AND...! PRAY TAKE THIS SABON ALSO, TO BE USED NOT ONLY BY YOURSELF BUT ALL THE HOUSEBOYS.
SABON?
IF YOU EAT FOOD WITH DIRTY HANDS IN WINTER, YOU CAN MORE EASILY CATCH A COLD. PRITHEE TRY WASHING YOUR HANDS WITH THIS SABON BEFORE EVERY MEAL. IT MAY LEAD TO FEWER OF YOU GETTING SICK.
IF YOUR SYMPTOMS WORSEN, PRAY COME TO SEE ME AGAIN.
YES, SIR.
AND...I THANK YOU MOST GRATE-FULLY, SIR.

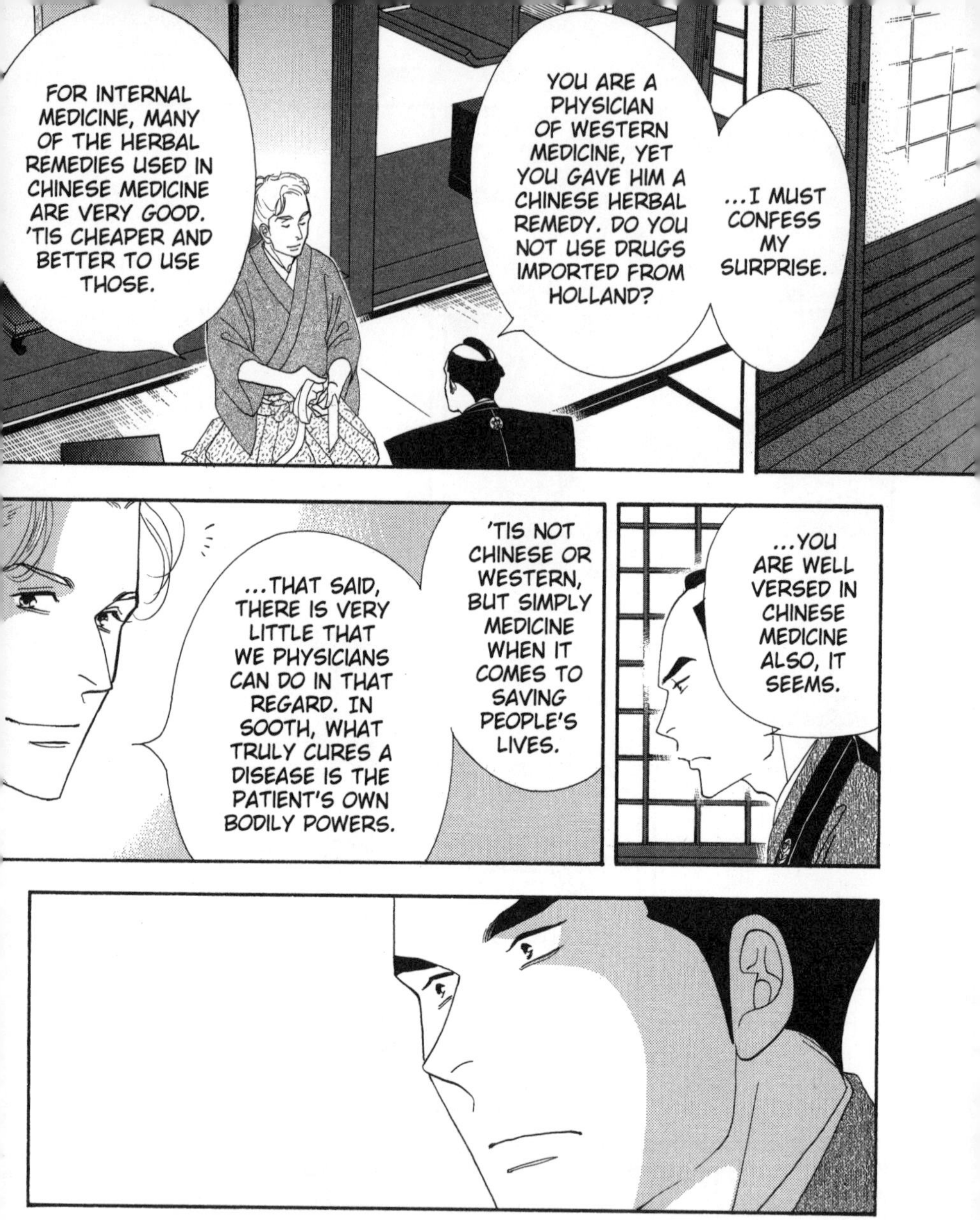
...I MUST CONFESS MY SURPRISE.
YOU ARE A PHYSICIAN OF WESTERN MEDICINE, YET YOU GAVE HIM A CHINESE HERBAL REMEDY. DO YOU NOT USE DRUGS IMPORTED FROM HOLLAND?
FOR INTERNAL MEDICINE, MANY OF THE HERBAL REMEDIES USED IN CHINESE MEDICINE ARE VERY GOOD. 'TIS CHEAPER AND BETTER TO USE THOSE.
...YOU ARE WELL VERSED IN CHINESE MEDICINE ALSO, IT SEEMS.
'TIS NOT CHINESE OR WESTERN, BUT SIMPLY MEDICINE WHEN IT COMES TO SAVING PEOPLE'S LIVES.
...THAT SAID, THERE IS VERY LITTLE THAT WE PHYSICIANS CAN DO IN THAT REGARD. IN SOOTH, WHAT TRULY CURES A DISEASE IS THE PATIENT'S OWN BODILY POWERS.

HE USED VIRTUALLY THE SAME WORDS AS MY FATHER. SO WHY DOES IT SOUND SO DIFFERENT?

And...

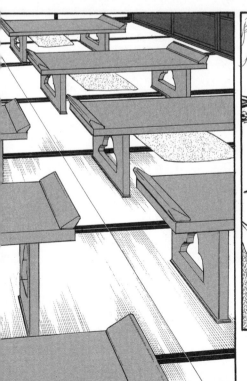

"I SHALL COMMAND THAT EVERY CHAMBER HERE SEND ONE PERSON TO THY LECTURES."

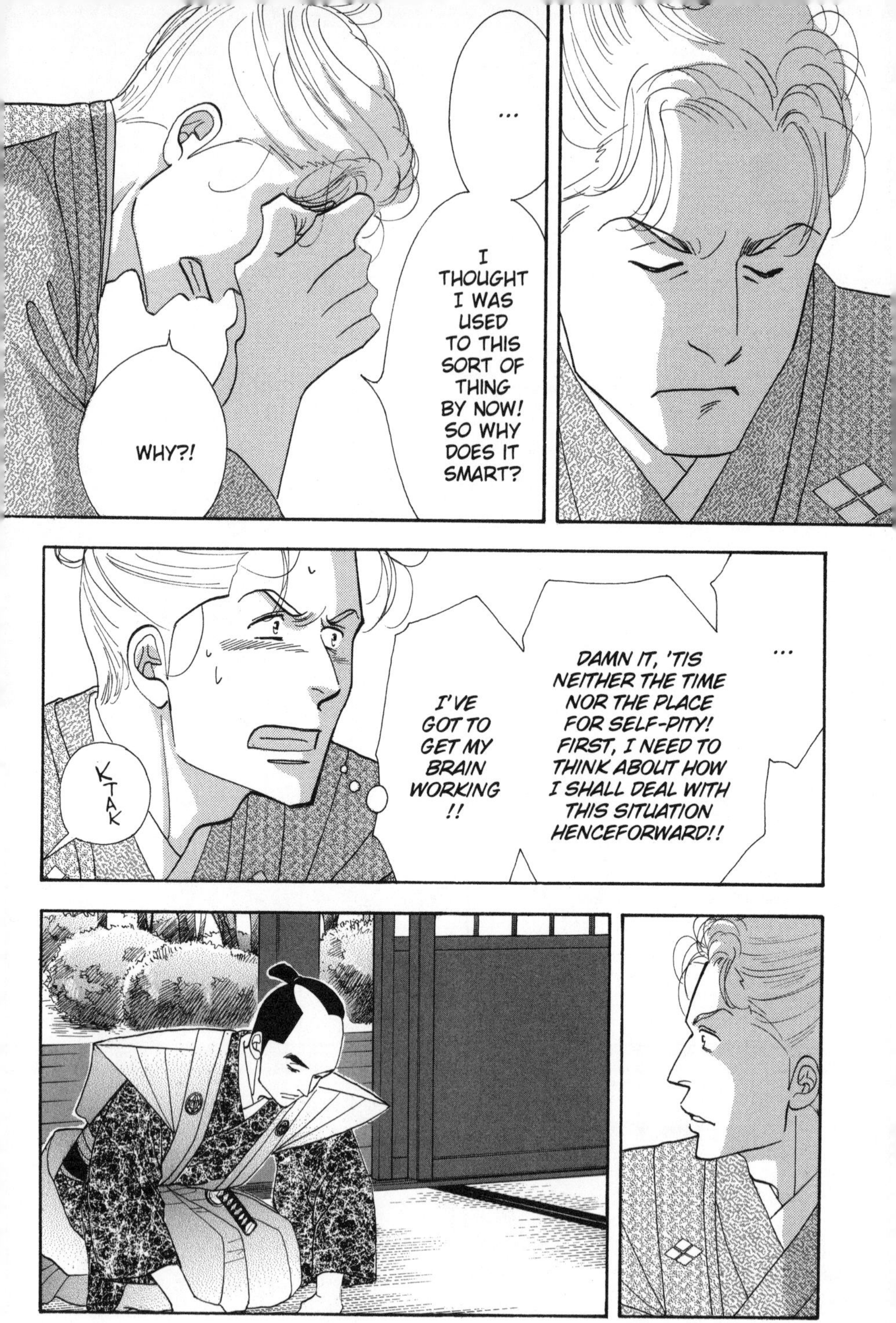
...
I THOUGHT I WAS USED TO THIS SORT OF THING BY NOW! SO WHY DOES IT SMART?
WHY?!
...
DAMN IT, 'TIS NEITHER THE TIME NOR THE PLACE FOR SELF-PITY! FIRST, I NEED TO THINK ABOUT HOW I SHALL DEAL WITH THIS SITUATION HENCEFORWARD!!
I'VE GOT TO GET MY BRAIN WORKING!!
KTAK

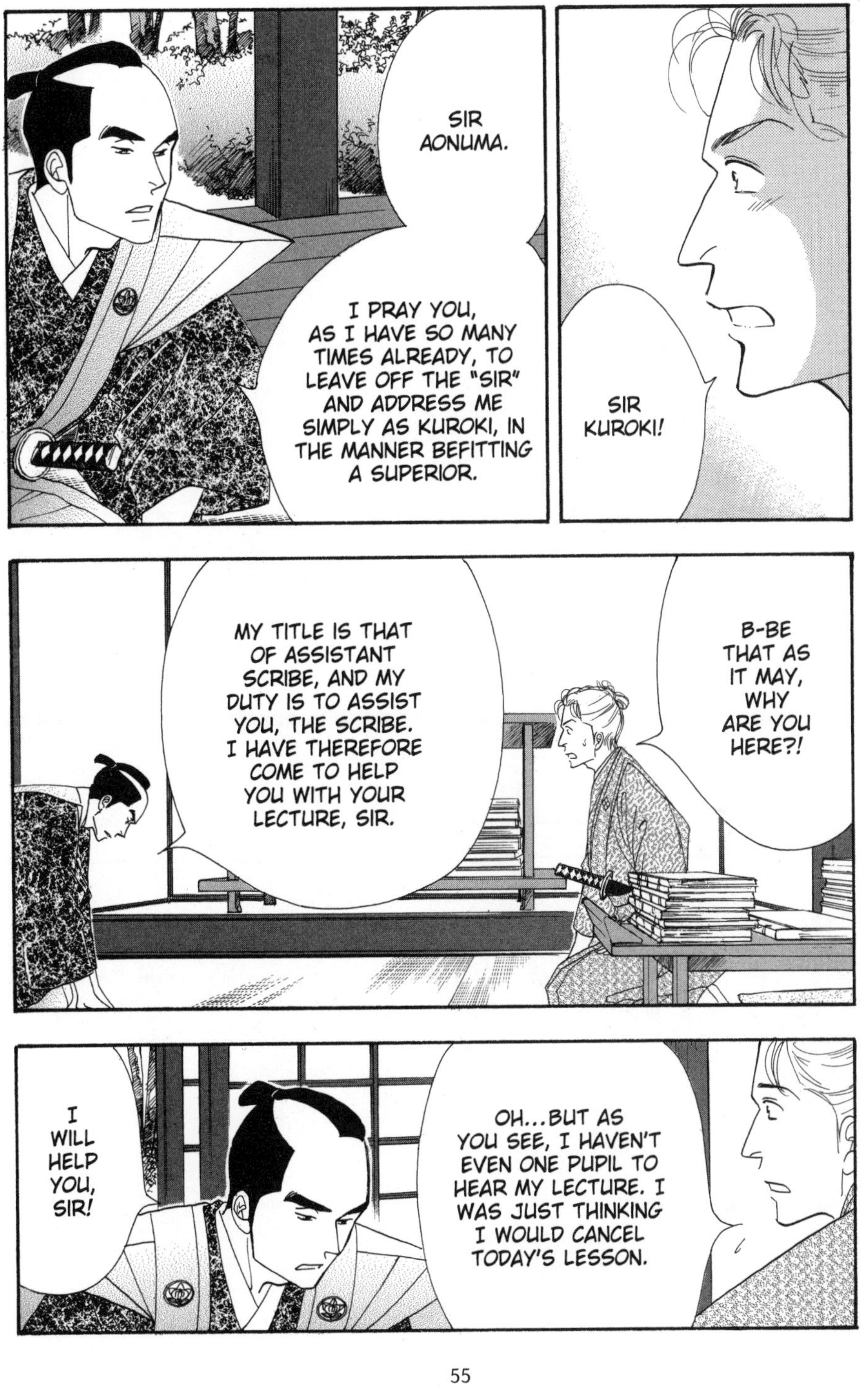
SIR KUROKI!
SIR AONUMA.
I PRAY YOU, AS I HAVE SO MANY TIMES ALREADY, TO LEAVE OFF THE "SIR" AND ADDRESS ME SIMPLY AS KUROKI, IN THE MANNER BEFITTING A SUPERIOR.
B-BE THAT AS IT MAY, WHY ARE YOU HERE?!
MY TITLE IS THAT OF ASSISTANT SCRIBE, AND MY DUTY IS TO ASSIST YOU, THE SCRIBE. I HAVE THEREFORE COME TO HELP YOU WITH YOUR LECTURE, SIR.
OH...BUT AS YOU SEE, I HAVEN'T EVEN ONE PUPIL TO HEAR MY LECTURE. I WAS JUST THINKING I WOULD CANCEL TODAY'S LESSON.
I WILL HELP YOU, SIR!

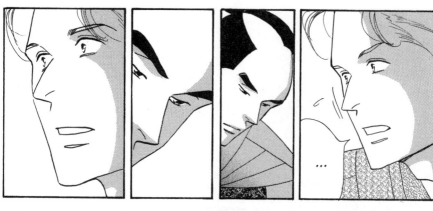

YES, SIR!

VERY WELL, THEN, KUROKI-SAN. PRAY HELP ME. I SHALL BEGIN THE LECTURE!

Ōoku
● THE INNER CHAMBERS

Ōoku

THE INNER CHAMBERS

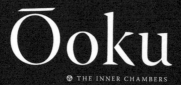

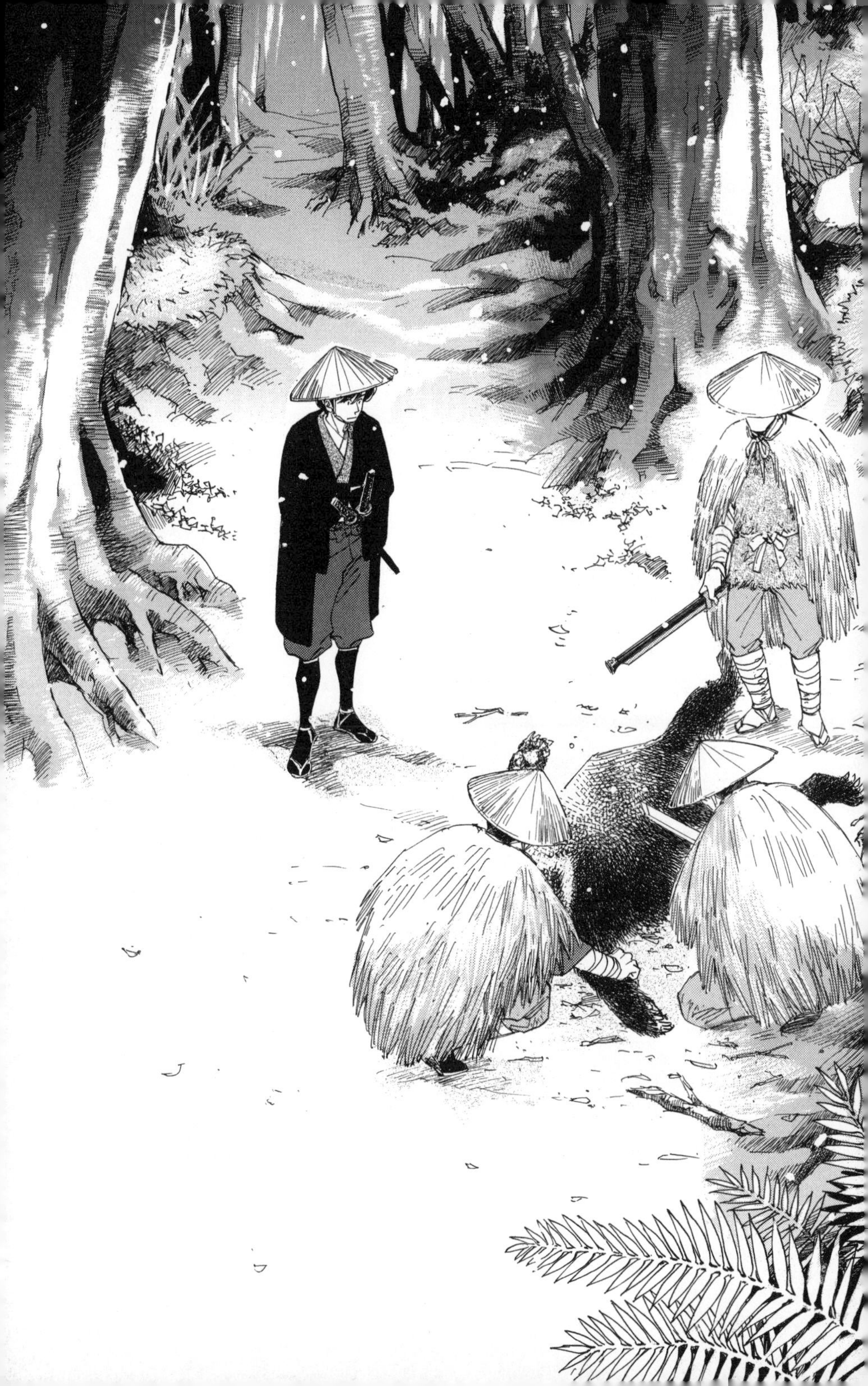

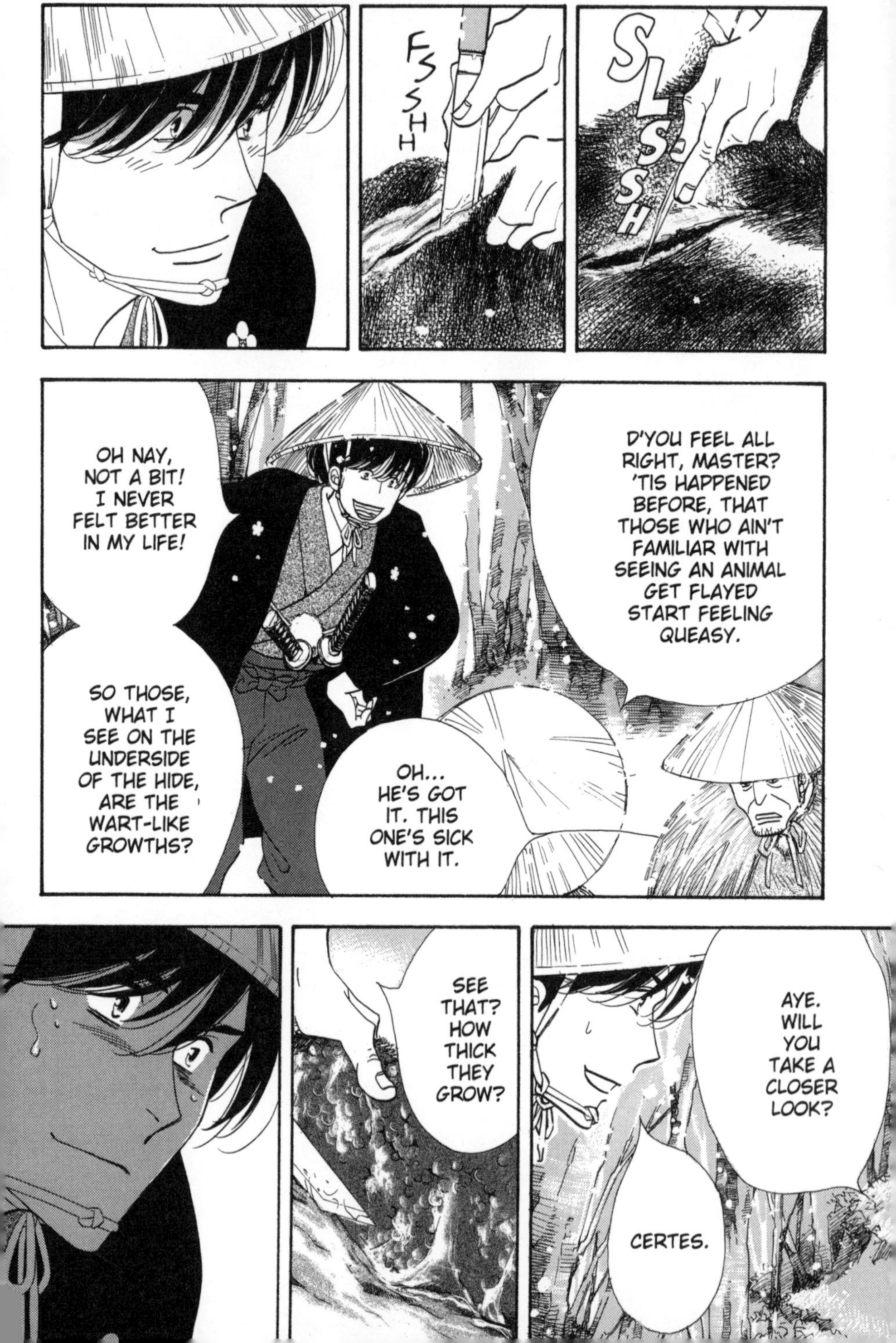
SLSSH
FSSHH
D'YOU FEEL ALL RIGHT, MASTER? 'TIS HAPPENED BEFORE, THAT THOSE WHO AIN'T FAMILIAR WITH SEEING AN ANIMAL GET FLAYED START FEELING QUEASY.
OH NAY, NOT A BIT! I NEVER FELT BETTER IN MY LIFE!
SO THOSE, WHAT I SEE ON THE UNDERSIDE OF THE HIDE, ARE THE WART-LIKE GROWTHS?
OH... HE'S GOT IT. THIS ONE'S SICK WITH IT.
AYE. WILL YOU TAKE A CLOSER LOOK?
CERTES.
SEE THAT? HOW THICK THEY GROW?

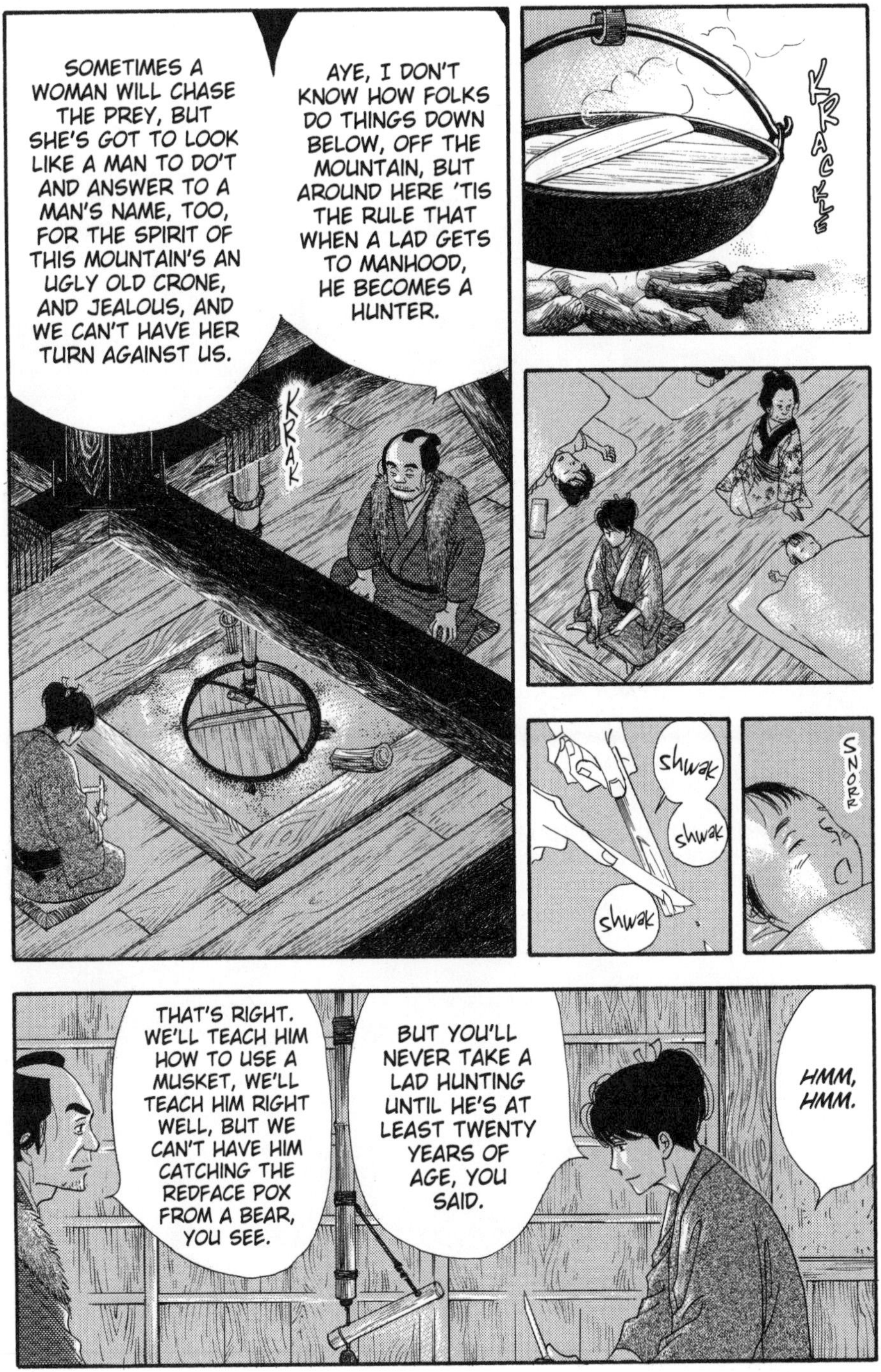
KRACKLE
SNORR
shwak
shwak
shwak
AYE, I DON'T KNOW HOW FOLKS DO THINGS DOWN BELOW, OFF THE MOUNTAIN, BUT AROUND HERE 'TIS THE RULE THAT WHEN A LAD GETS TO MANHOOD, HE BECOMES A HUNTER.
SOMETIMES A WOMAN WILL CHASE THE PREY, BUT SHE'S GOT TO LOOK LIKE A MAN TO DO'T AND ANSWER TO A MAN'S NAME, TOO, FOR THE SPIRIT OF THIS MOUNTAIN'S AN UGLY OLD CRONE, AND JEALOUS, AND WE CAN'T HAVE HER TURN AGAINST US.
KRAK
HMM, HMM.
BUT YOU'LL NEVER TAKE A LAD HUNTING UNTIL HE'S AT LEAST TWENTY YEARS OF AGE, YOU SAID.
THAT'S RIGHT. WE'LL TEACH HIM HOW TO USE A MUSKET, WE'LL TEACH HIM RIGHT WELL, BUT WE CAN'T HAVE HIM CATCHING THE REDFACE POX FROM A BEAR, YOU SEE.

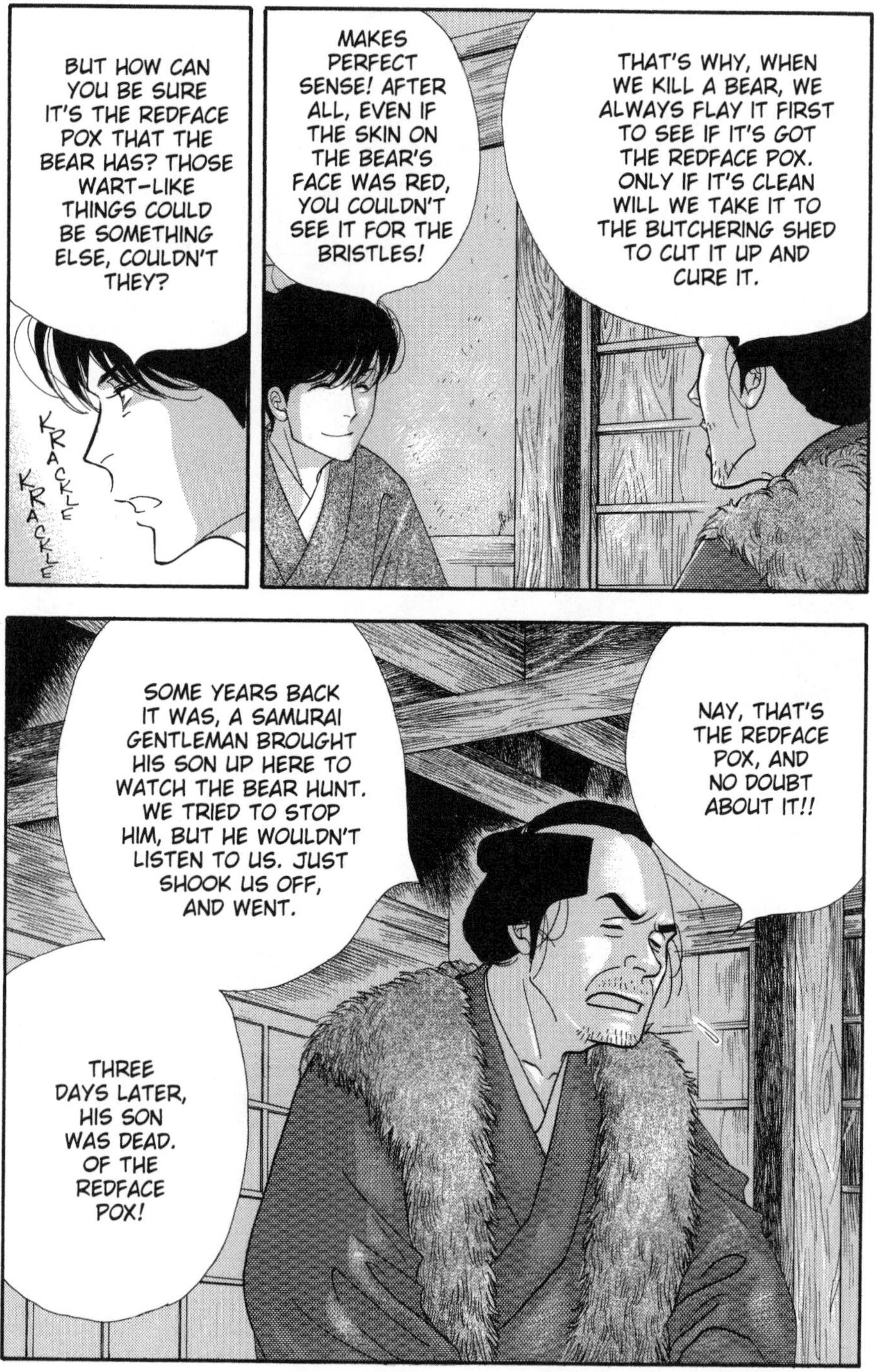
THAT'S WHY, WHEN WE KILL A BEAR, WE ALWAYS FLAY IT FIRST TO SEE IF IT'S GOT THE REDFACE POX. ONLY IF IT'S CLEAN WILL WE TAKE IT TO THE BUTCHERING SHED TO CUT IT UP AND CURE IT.
MAKES PERFECT SENSE! AFTER ALL, EVEN IF THE SKIN ON THE BEAR'S FACE WAS RED, YOU COULDN'T SEE IT FOR THE BRISTLES!
BUT HOW CAN YOU BE SURE IT'S THE REDFACE POX THAT THE BEAR HAS? THOSE WART-LIKE THINGS COULD BE SOMETHING ELSE, COULDN'T THEY?
KRACKLE
KRACKLE
NAY, THAT'S THE REDFACE POX, AND NO DOUBT ABOUT IT!!
SOME YEARS BACK IT WAS, A SAMURAI GENTLEMAN BROUGHT HIS SON UP HERE TO WATCH THE BEAR HUNT. WE TRIED TO STOP HIM, BUT HE WOULDN'T LISTEN TO US. JUST SHOOK US OFF, AND WENT.
THREE DAYS LATER, HIS SON WAS DEAD. OF THE REDFACE POX!

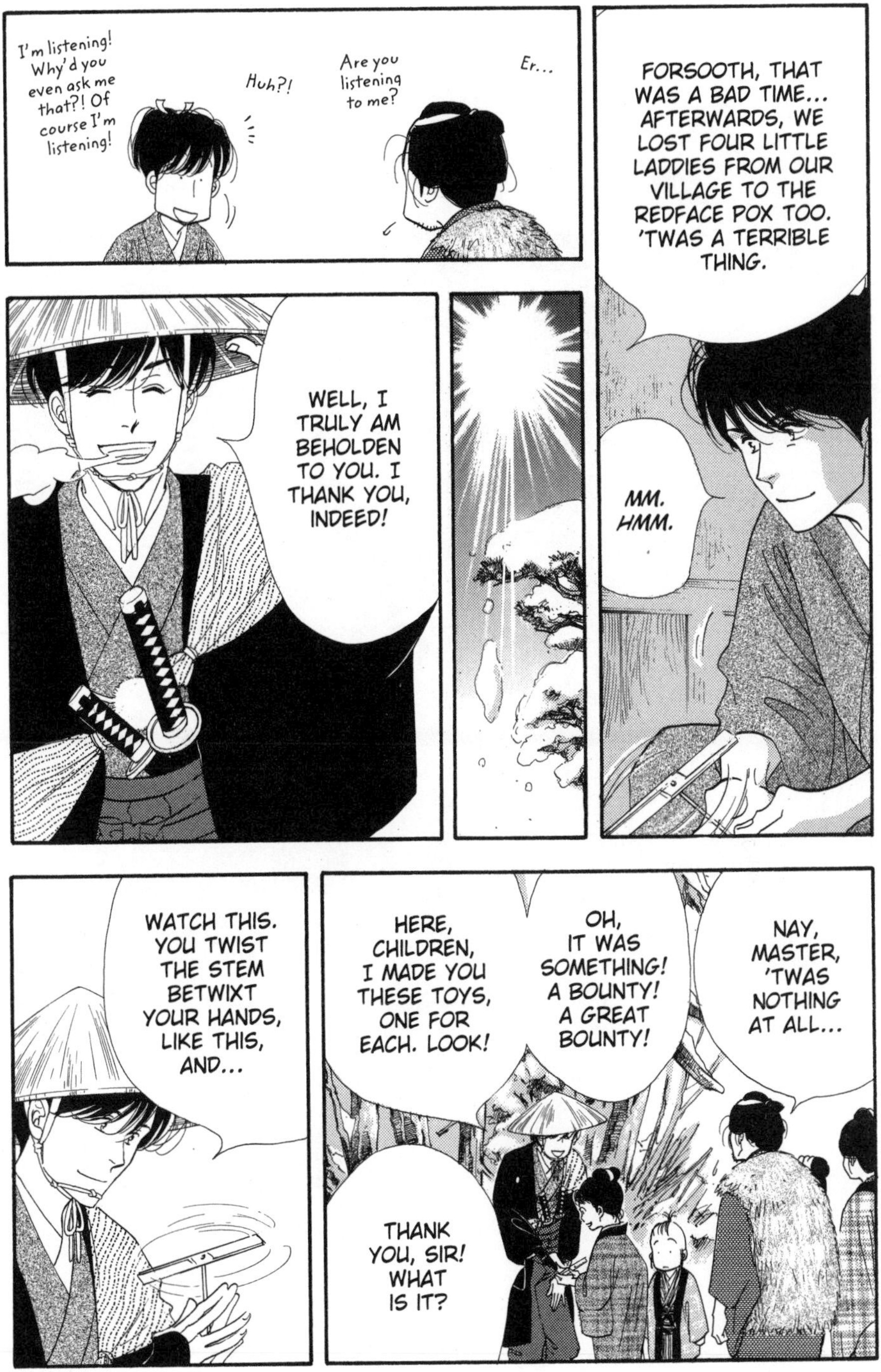
FORSOOTH, THAT WAS A BAD TIME... AFTERWARDS, WE LOST FOUR LITTLE LADDIES FROM OUR VILLAGE TO THE REDFACE POX TOO. 'TWAS A TERRIBLE THING.
MM. HMM.
Er...
Are you listening to me?
Huh?!
I'm listening! Why'd you even ask me that?! Of course I'm listening!
WELL, I TRULY AM BEHOLDEN TO YOU. I THANK YOU, INDEED!
NAY, MASTER, 'TWAS NOTHING AT ALL...
OH, IT WAS SOMETHING! A BOUNTY! A GREAT BOUNTY!
HERE, CHILDREN, I MADE YOU THESE TOYS, ONE FOR EACH. LOOK!
THANK YOU, SIR! WHAT IS IT?
WATCH THIS. YOU TWIST THE STEM BETWIXT YOUR HANDS, LIKE THIS, AND...

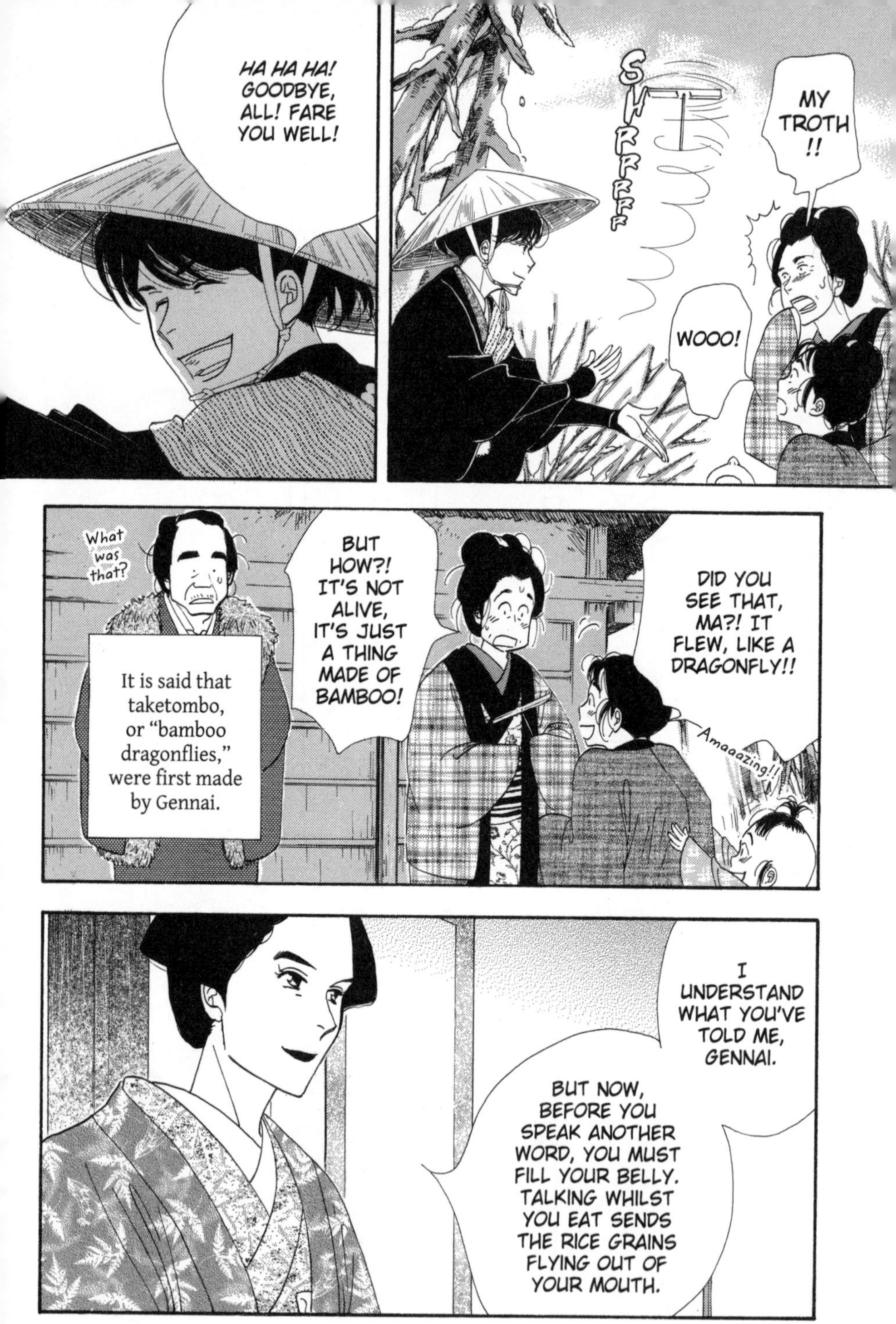
MY TROTH!!
SHRRRRR
WOOO!
HA HA HA! GOODBYE, ALL! FARE YOU WELL!
DID YOU SEE THAT, MA?! IT FLEW, LIKE A DRAGONFLY!!
Amaaazing!!
BUT HOW?! IT'S NOT ALIVE, IT'S JUST A THING MADE OF BAMBOO!
What was that?
It is said that taketombo, or "bamboo dragonflies," were first made by Gennai.
I UNDERSTAND WHAT YOU'VE TOLD ME, GENNAI.
BUT NOW, BEFORE YOU SPEAK ANOTHER WORD, YOU MUST FILL YOUR BELLY. TALKING WHILST YOU EAT SENDS THE RICE GRAINS FLYING OUT OF YOUR MOUTH.

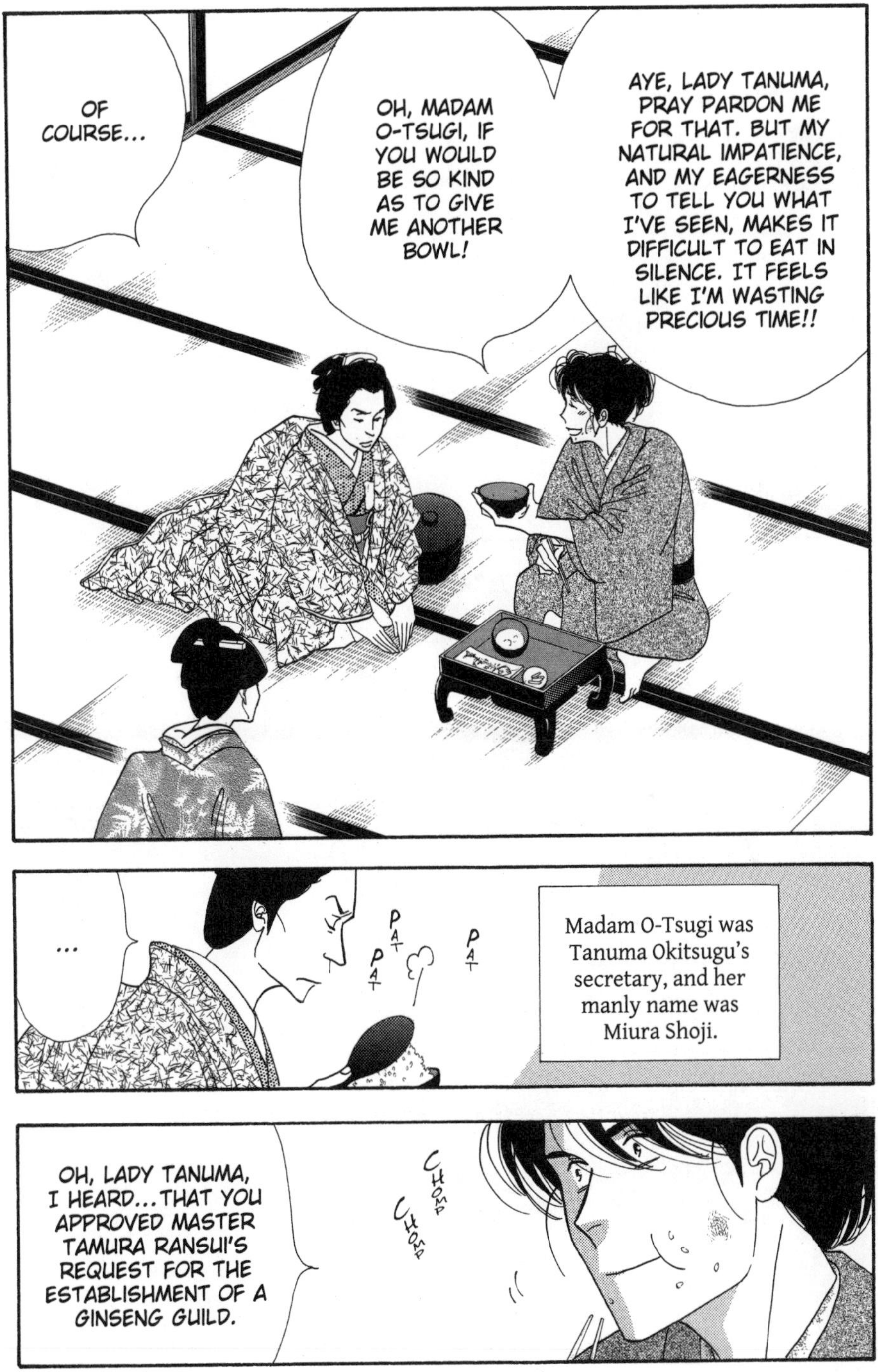
AYE, LADY TANUMA, PRAY PARDON ME FOR THAT. BUT MY NATURAL IMPATIENCE, AND MY EAGERNESS TO TELL YOU WHAT I'VE SEEN, MAKES IT DIFFICULT TO EAT IN SILENCE. IT FEELS LIKE I'M WASTING PRECIOUS TIME!!
OH, MADAM O-TSUGI, IF YOU WOULD BE SO KIND AS TO GIVE ME ANOTHER BOWL!
OF COURSE...
Madam O-Tsugi was Tanuma Okitsugu's secretary, and her manly name was Miura Shoji.
PAT
PAT
PAT
...
CHOMP
CHOMP
OH, LADY TANUMA, I HEARD...THAT YOU APPROVED MASTER TAMURA RANSUI'S REQUEST FOR THE ESTABLISHMENT OF A GINSENG GUILD.

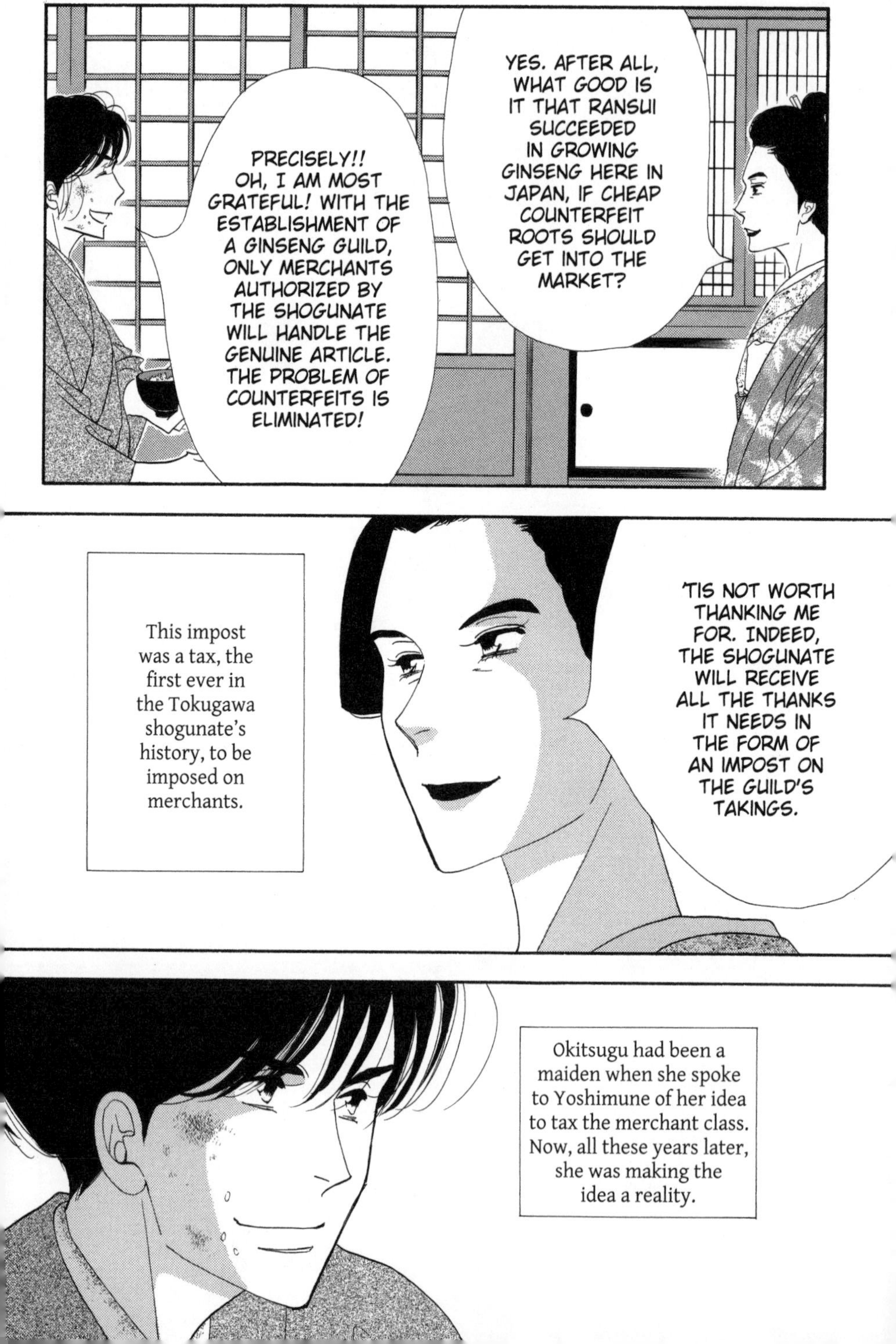
YES. AFTER ALL, WHAT GOOD IS IT THAT RANSUI SUCCEEDED IN GROWING GINSENG HERE IN JAPAN, IF CHEAP COUNTERFEIT ROOTS SHOULD GET INTO THE MARKET?
PRECISELY!! OH, I AM MOST GRATEFUL! WITH THE ESTABLISHMENT OF A GINSENG GUILD, ONLY MERCHANTS AUTHORIZED BY THE SHOGUNATE WILL HANDLE THE GENUINE ARTICLE. THE PROBLEM OF COUNTERFEITS IS ELIMINATED!
'TIS NOT WORTH THANKING ME FOR. INDEED, THE SHOGUNATE WILL RECEIVE ALL THE THANKS IT NEEDS IN THE FORM OF AN IMPOST ON THE GUILD'S TAKINGS.
This impost was a tax, the first ever in the Tokugawa shogunate's history, to be imposed on merchants.
Okitsugu had been a maiden when she spoke to Yoshimune of her idea to tax the merchant class. Now, all these years later, she was making the idea a reality.

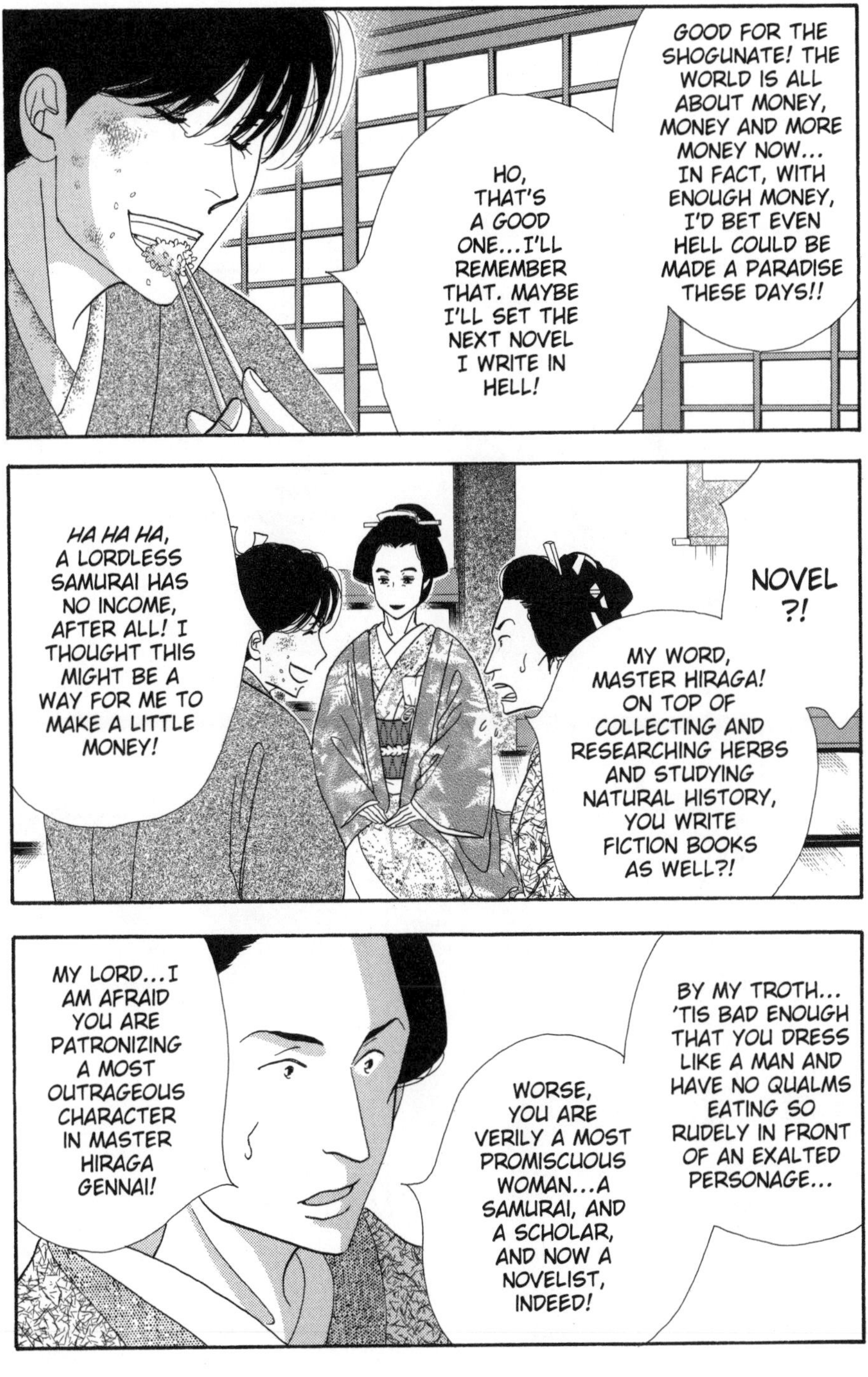
GOOD FOR THE SHOGUNATE! THE WORLD IS ALL ABOUT MONEY, MONEY AND MORE MONEY NOW... IN FACT, WITH ENOUGH MONEY, I'D BET EVEN HELL COULD BE MADE A PARADISE THESE DAYS!!
HO, THAT'S A GOOD ONE...I'LL REMEMBER THAT. MAYBE I'LL SET THE NEXT NOVEL I WRITE IN HELL!
NOVEL ?!
MY WORD, MASTER HIRAGA! ON TOP OF COLLECTING AND RESEARCHING HERBS AND STUDYING NATURAL HISTORY, YOU WRITE FICTION BOOKS AS WELL?!
HA HA HA, A LORDLESS SAMURAI HAS NO INCOME, AFTER ALL! I THOUGHT THIS MIGHT BE A WAY FOR ME TO MAKE A LITTLE MONEY!
BY MY TROTH... 'TIS BAD ENOUGH THAT YOU DRESS LIKE A MAN AND HAVE NO QUALMS EATING SO RUDELY IN FRONT OF AN EXALTED PERSONAGE...
WORSE, YOU ARE VERILY A MOST PROMISCUOUS WOMAN...A SAMURAI, AND A SCHOLAR, AND NOW A NOVELIST, INDEED!
MY LORD...I AM AFRAID YOU ARE PATRONIZING A MOST OUTRAGEOUS CHARACTER IN MASTER HIRAGA GENNAI!

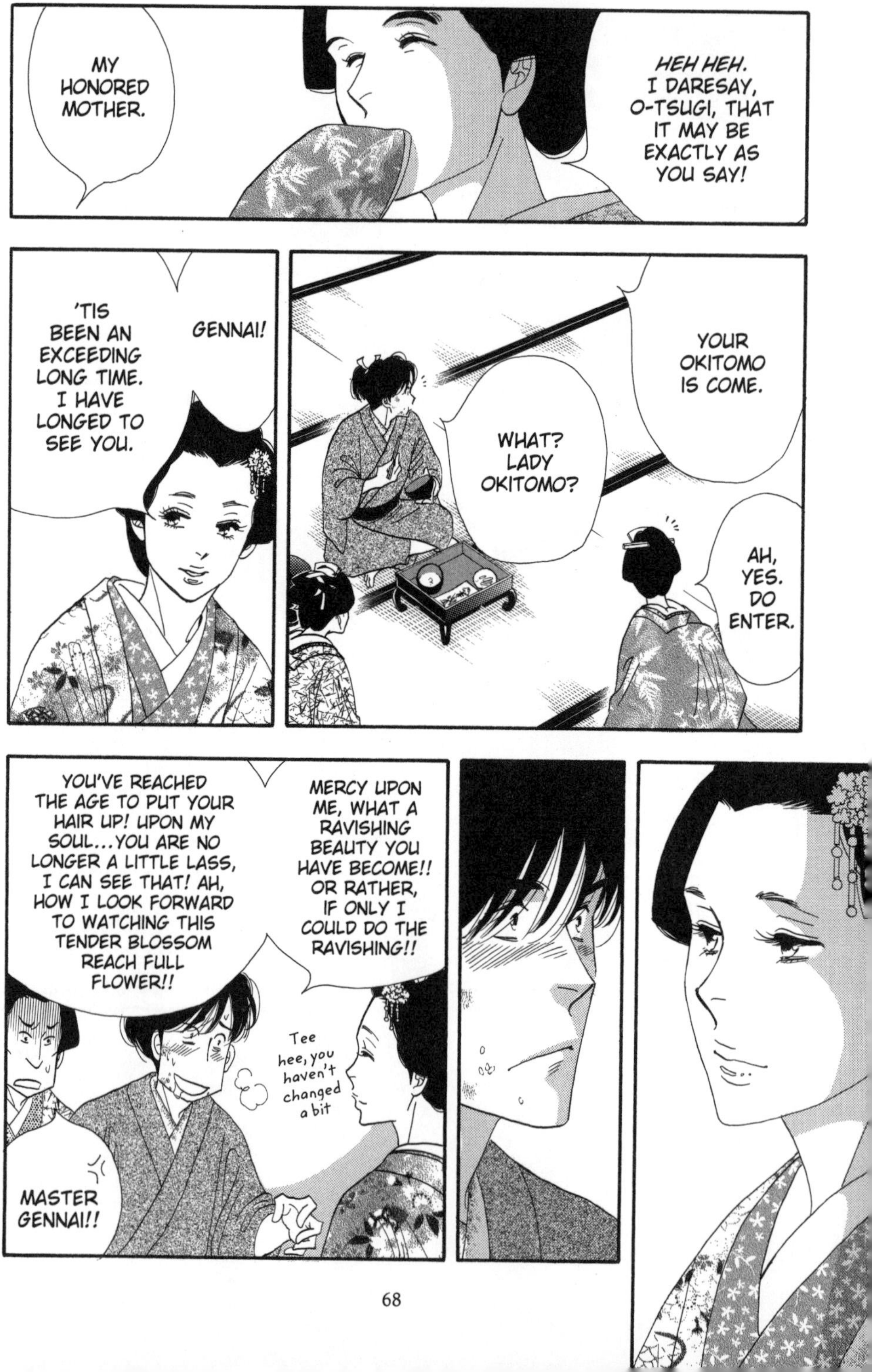
HEH HEH. I DARESAY, O-TSUGI, THAT IT MAY BE EXACTLY AS YOU SAY!
MY HONORED MOTHER.
YOUR OKITOMO IS COME.
WHAT? LADY OKITOMO?
AH, YES. DO ENTER.
GENNAI!
'TIS BEEN AN EXCEEDING LONG TIME. I HAVE LONGED TO SEE YOU.
MERCY UPON ME, WHAT A RAVISHING BEAUTY YOU HAVE BECOME!! OR RATHER, IF ONLY I COULD DO THE RAVISHING!!
YOU'VE REACHED THE AGE TO PUT YOUR HAIR UP! UPON MY SOUL...YOU ARE NO LONGER A LITTLE LASS, I CAN SEE THAT! AH, HOW I LOOK FORWARD TO WATCHING THIS TENDER BLOSSOM REACH FULL FLOWER!!
Tee hee, you haven't changed a bit
MASTER GENNAI!!

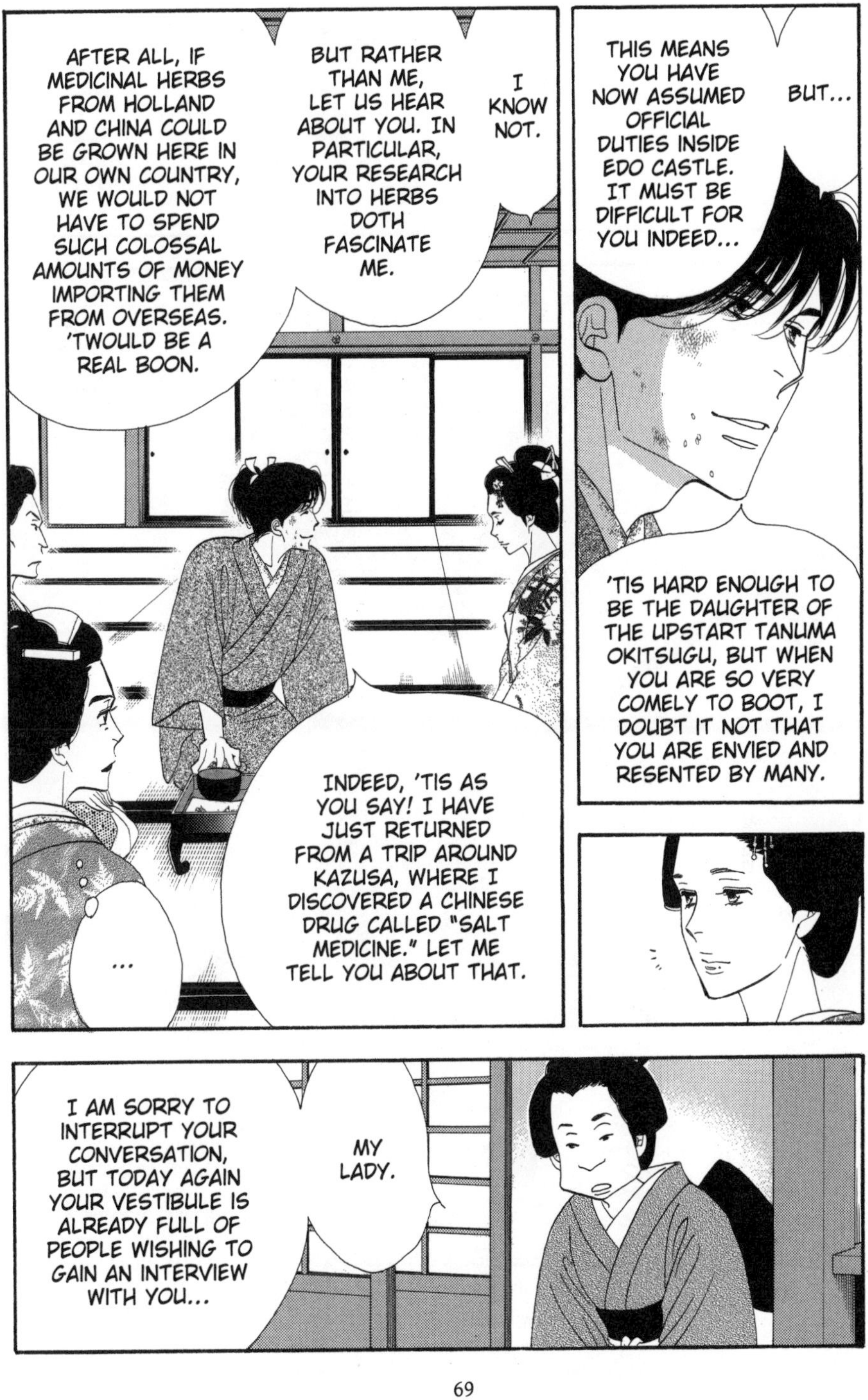
BUT...
THIS MEANS YOU HAVE NOW ASSUMED OFFICIAL DUTIES INSIDE EDO CASTLE. IT MUST BE DIFFICULT FOR YOU INDEED...
'TIS HARD ENOUGH TO BE THE DAUGHTER OF THE UPSTART TANUMA OKITSUGU, BUT WHEN YOU ARE SO VERY COMELY TO BOOT, I DOUBT IT NOT THAT YOU ARE ENVIED AND RESENTED BY MANY.
I KNOW NOT.
BUT RATHER THAN ME, LET US HEAR ABOUT YOU. IN PARTICULAR, YOUR RESEARCH INTO HERBS DOTH FASCINATE ME.
AFTER ALL, IF MEDICINAL HERBS FROM HOLLAND AND CHINA COULD BE GROWN HERE IN OUR OWN COUNTRY, WE WOULD NOT HAVE TO SPEND SUCH COLOSSAL AMOUNTS OF MONEY IMPORTING THEM FROM OVERSEAS. 'TWOULD BE A REAL BOON.
INDEED, 'TIS AS YOU SAY! I HAVE JUST RETURNED FROM A TRIP AROUND KAZUSA, WHERE I DISCOVERED A CHINESE DRUG CALLED "SALT MEDICINE." LET ME TELL YOU ABOUT THAT.
...
MY LADY.
I AM SORRY TO INTERRUPT YOUR CONVERSATION, BUT TODAY AGAIN YOUR VESTIBULE IS ALREADY FULL OF PEOPLE WISHING TO GAIN AN INTERVIEW WITH YOU...

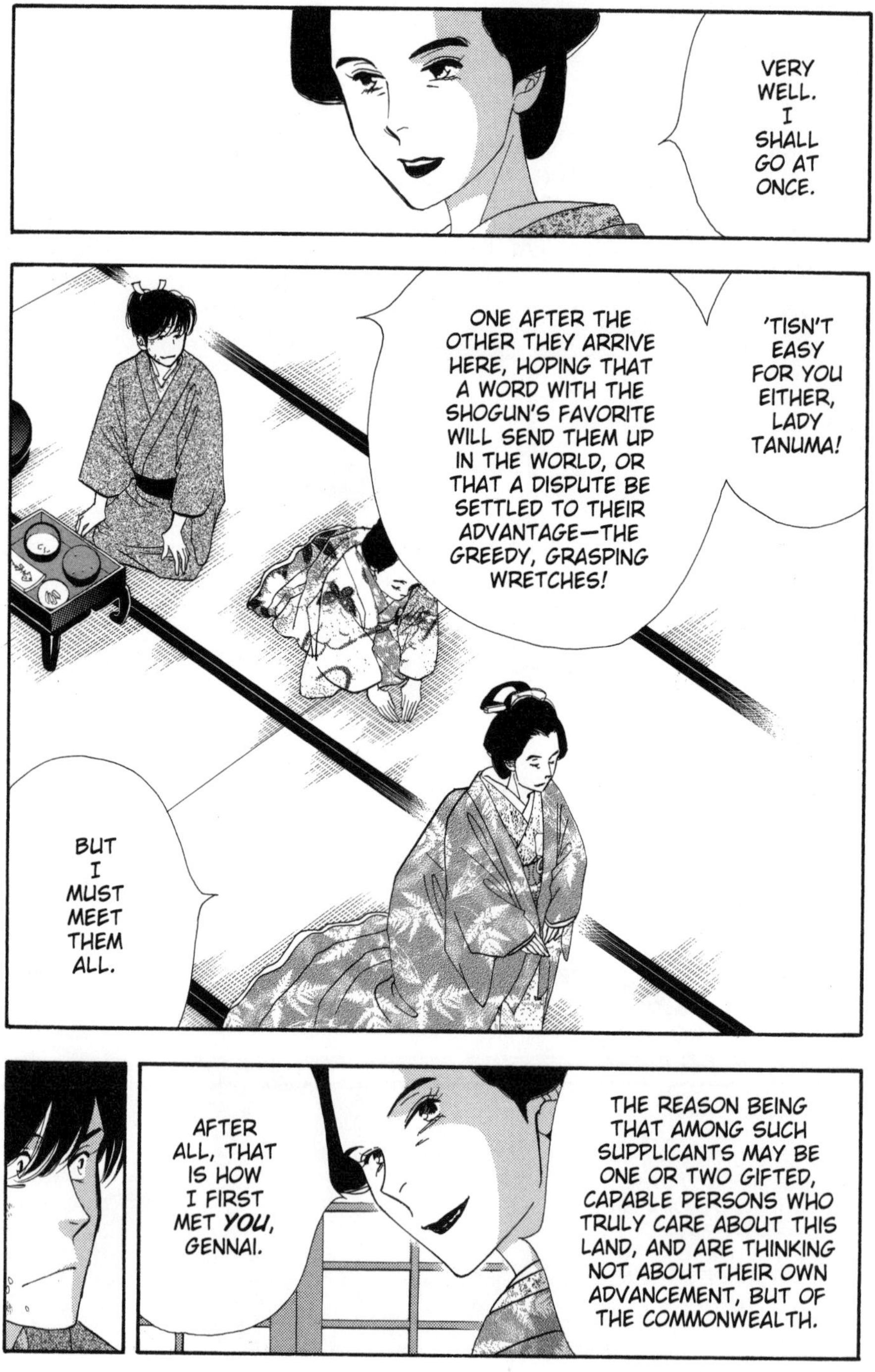
VERY WELL. I SHALL GO AT ONCE.
'TISN'T EASY FOR YOU EITHER, LADY TANUMA!
ONE AFTER THE OTHER THEY ARRIVE HERE, HOPING THAT A WORD WITH THE SHOGUN'S FAVORITE WILL SEND THEM UP IN THE WORLD, OR THAT A DISPUTE BE SETTLED TO THEIR ADVANTAGE—THE GREEDY, GRASPING WRETCHES!
BUT I MUST MEET THEM ALL.
THE REASON BEING THAT AMONG SUCH SUPPLICANTS MAY BE ONE OR TWO GIFTED, CAPABLE PERSONS WHO TRULY CARE ABOUT THIS LAND, AND ARE THINKING NOT ABOUT THEIR OWN ADVANCEMENT, BUT OF THE COMMONWEALTH.
AFTER ALL, THAT IS HOW I FIRST MET *YOU*, GENNAI.

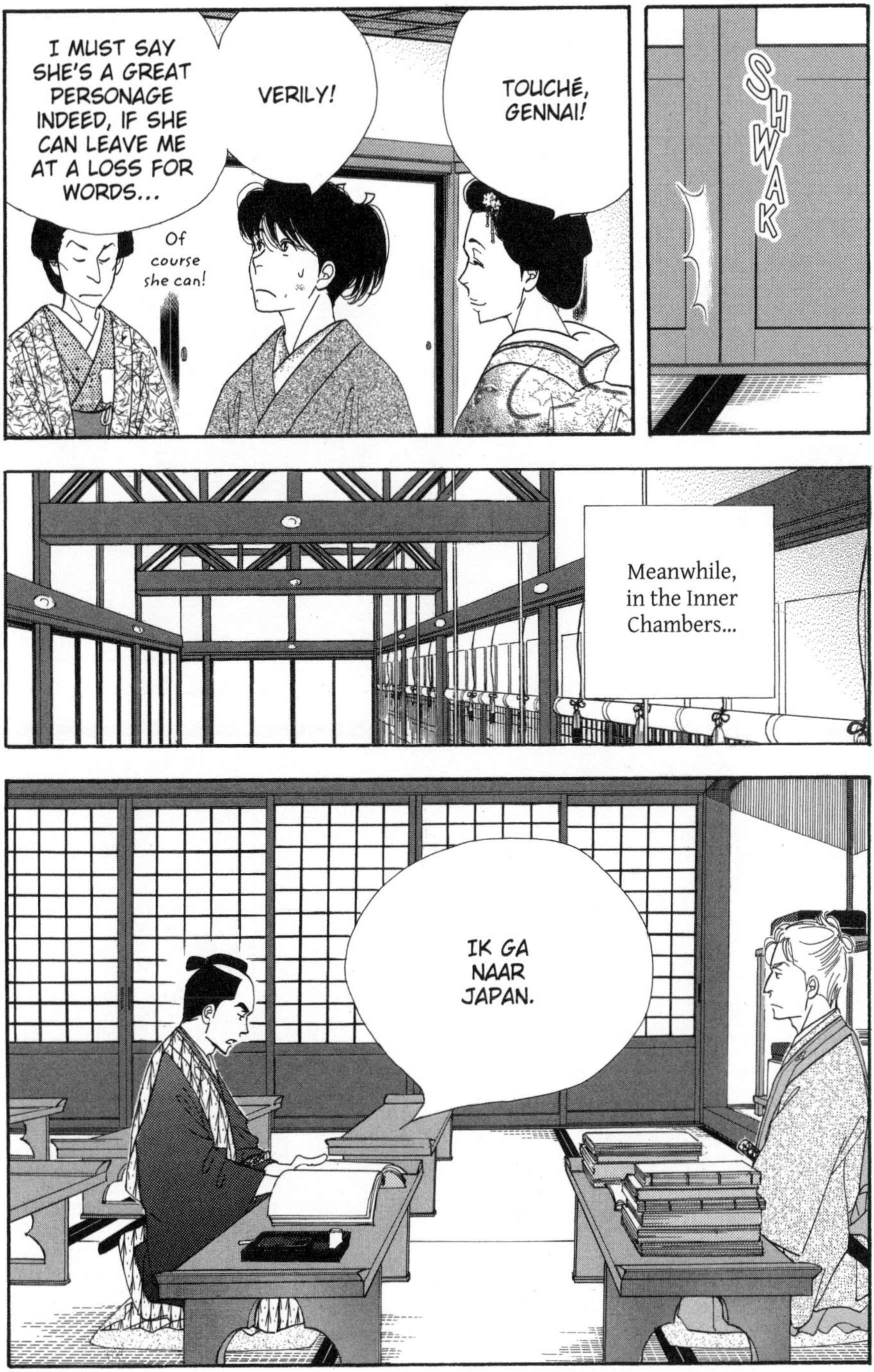
SHWAK
TOUCHÉ, GENNAI!
VERILY!
I MUST SAY SHE'S A GREAT PERSONAGE INDEED, IF SHE CAN LEAVE ME AT A LOSS FOR WORDS...
Of course she can!
Meanwhile, in the Inner Chambers...
IK GA NAAR JAPAN.

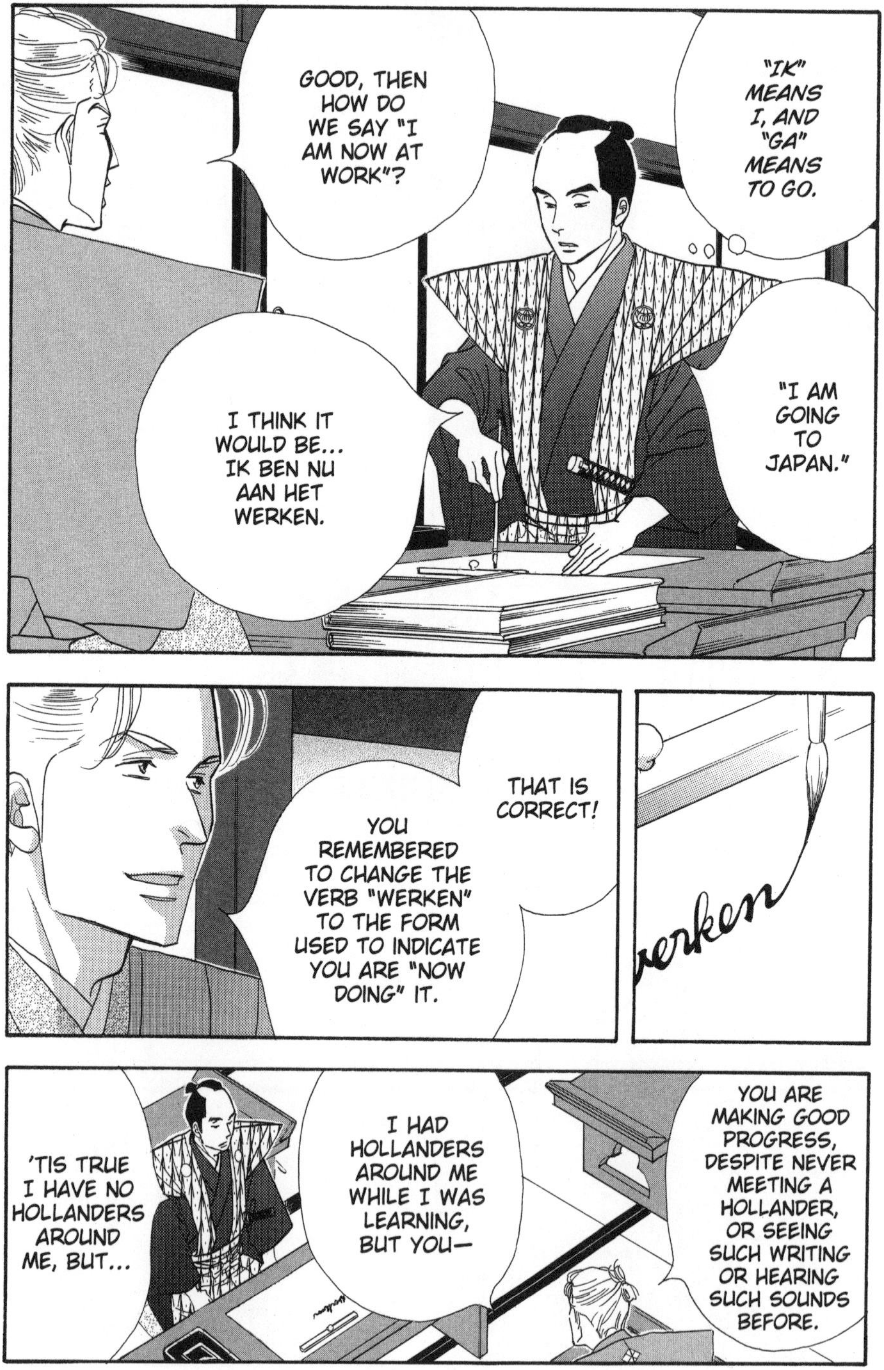

"IK" MEANS I, AND "GA" MEANS TO GO.
"I AM GOING TO JAPAN."
GOOD, THEN HOW DO WE SAY "I AM NOW AT WORK"?
I THINK IT WOULD BE... IK BEN NU AAN HET WERKEN.
erken
THAT IS CORRECT!
YOU REMEMBERED TO CHANGE THE VERB "WERKEN" TO THE FORM USED TO INDICATE YOU ARE "NOW DOING" IT.
YOU ARE MAKING GOOD PROGRESS, DESPITE NEVER MEETING A HOLLANDER, OR SEEING SUCH WRITING OR HEARING SUCH SOUNDS BEFORE.
I HAD HOLLANDERS AROUND ME WHILE I WAS LEARNING, BUT YOU—
'TIS TRUE I HAVE NO HOLLANDERS AROUND ME, BUT...

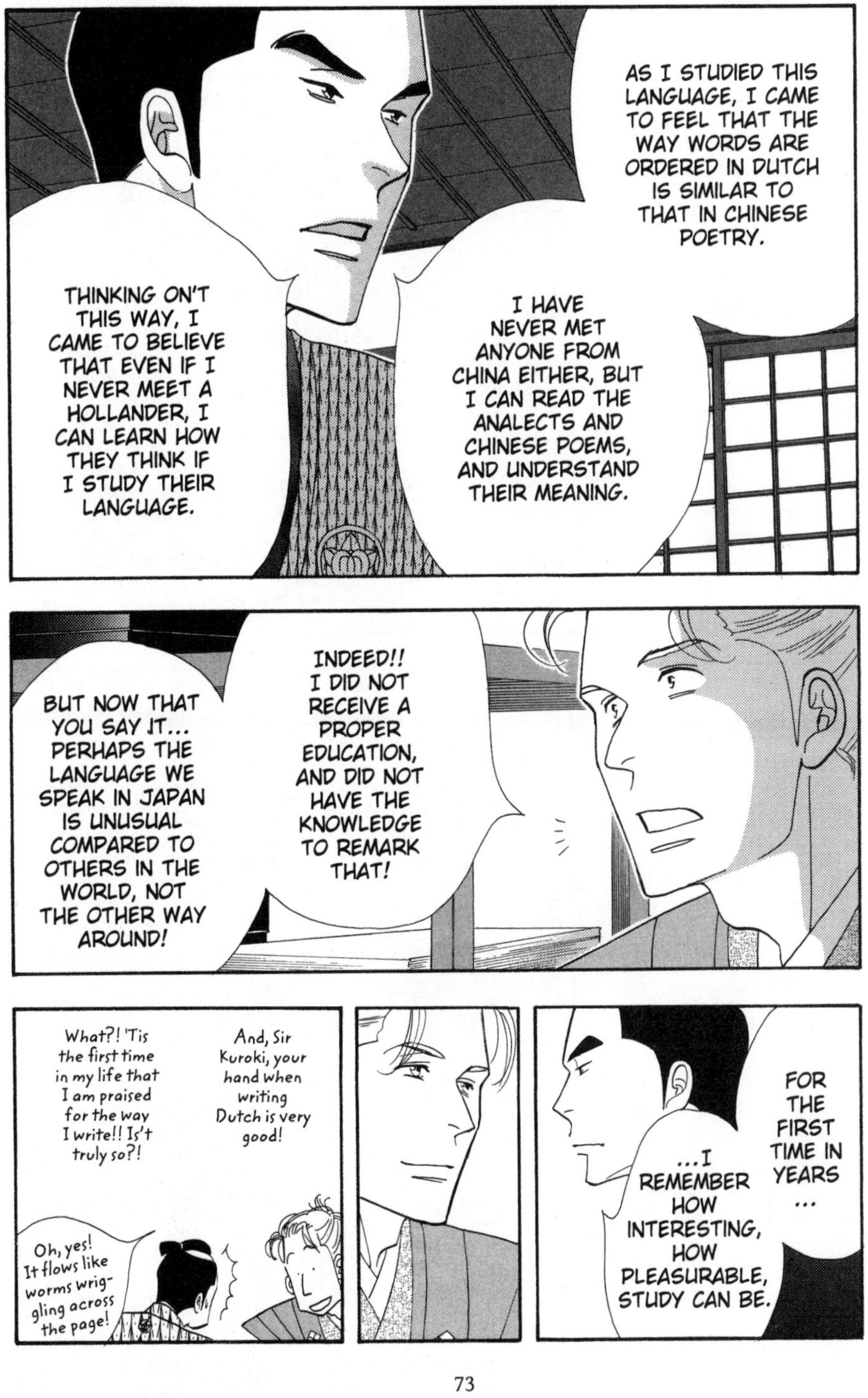
AS I STUDIED THIS LANGUAGE, I CAME TO FEEL THAT THE WAY WORDS ARE ORDERED IN DUTCH IS SIMILAR TO THAT IN CHINESE POETRY.
I HAVE NEVER MET ANYONE FROM CHINA EITHER, BUT I CAN READ THE ANALECTS AND CHINESE POEMS, AND UNDERSTAND THEIR MEANING.
THINKING ON'T THIS WAY, I CAME TO BELIEVE THAT EVEN IF I NEVER MEET A HOLLANDER, I CAN LEARN HOW THEY THINK IF I STUDY THEIR LANGUAGE.
INDEED!! I DID NOT RECEIVE A PROPER EDUCATION, AND DID NOT HAVE THE KNOWLEDGE TO REMARK THAT!
BUT NOW THAT YOU SAY IT... PERHAPS THE LANGUAGE WE SPEAK IN JAPAN IS UNUSUAL COMPARED TO OTHERS IN THE WORLD, NOT THE OTHER WAY AROUND!
FOR THE FIRST TIME IN YEARS...
...I REMEMBER HOW INTERESTING, HOW PLEASURABLE, STUDY CAN BE.
And, Sir Kuroki, your hand when writing Dutch is very good!
What?! 'Tis the first time in my life that I am praised for the way I write!! Is't truly so?!
Oh, yes! It flows like worms wriggling across the page!

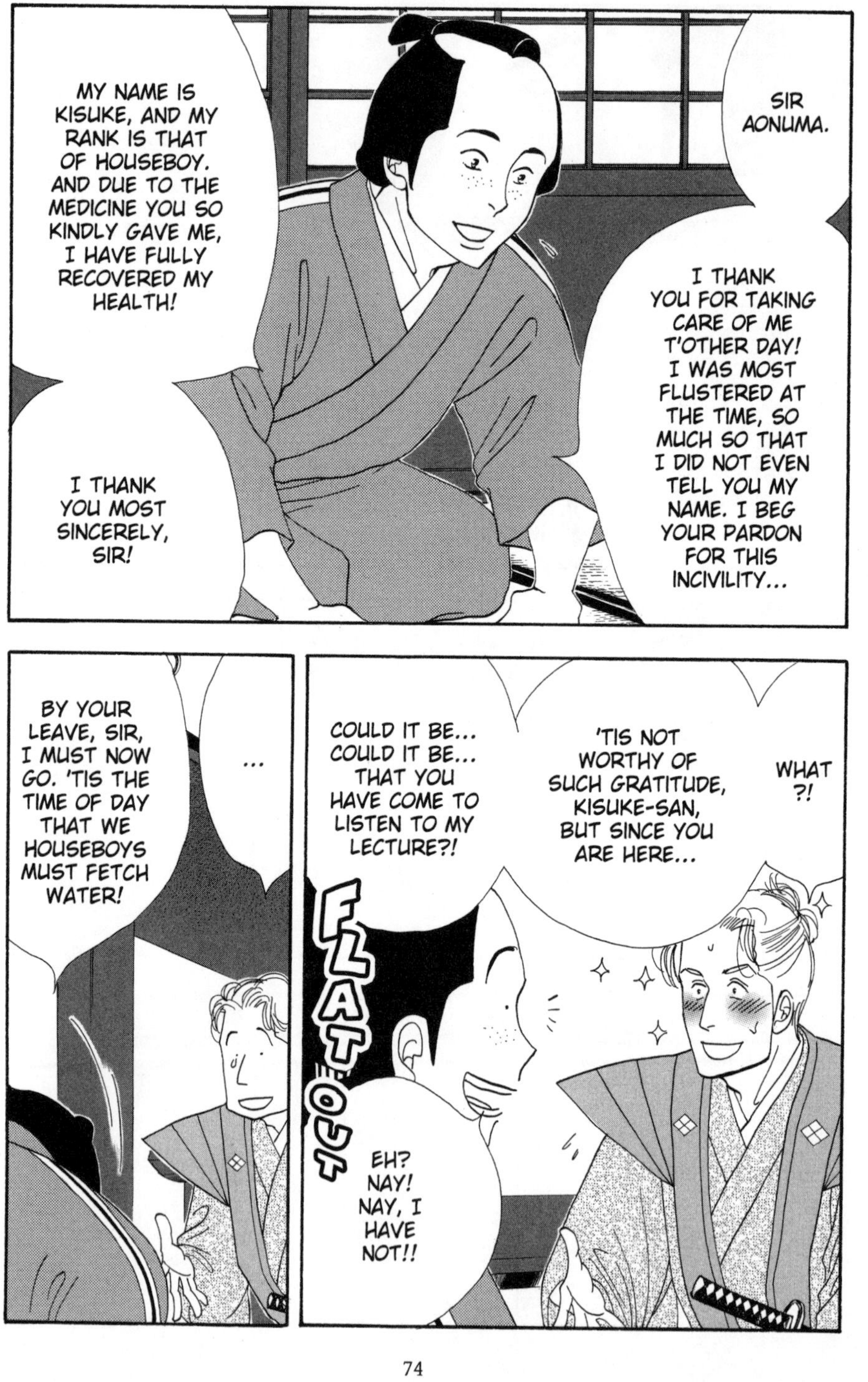
SIR AONUMA.
MY NAME IS KISUKE, AND MY RANK IS THAT OF HOUSEBOY. AND DUE TO THE MEDICINE YOU SO KINDLY GAVE ME, I HAVE FULLY RECOVERED MY HEALTH!
I THANK YOU FOR TAKING CARE OF ME T'OTHER DAY! I WAS MOST FLUSTERED AT THE TIME, SO MUCH SO THAT I DID NOT EVEN TELL YOU MY NAME. I BEG YOUR PARDON FOR THIS INCIVILITY...
I THANK YOU MOST SINCERELY, SIR!
WHAT ?!
'TIS NOT WORTHY OF SUCH GRATITUDE, KISUKE-SAN, BUT SINCE YOU ARE HERE...
COULD IT BE... COULD IT BE... THAT YOU HAVE COME TO LISTEN TO MY LECTURE?!
FLAT OUT
EH? NAY! NAY, I HAVE NOT!!
...
BY YOUR LEAVE, SIR, I MUST NOW GO. 'TIS THE TIME OF DAY THAT WE HOUSEBOYS MUST FETCH WATER!

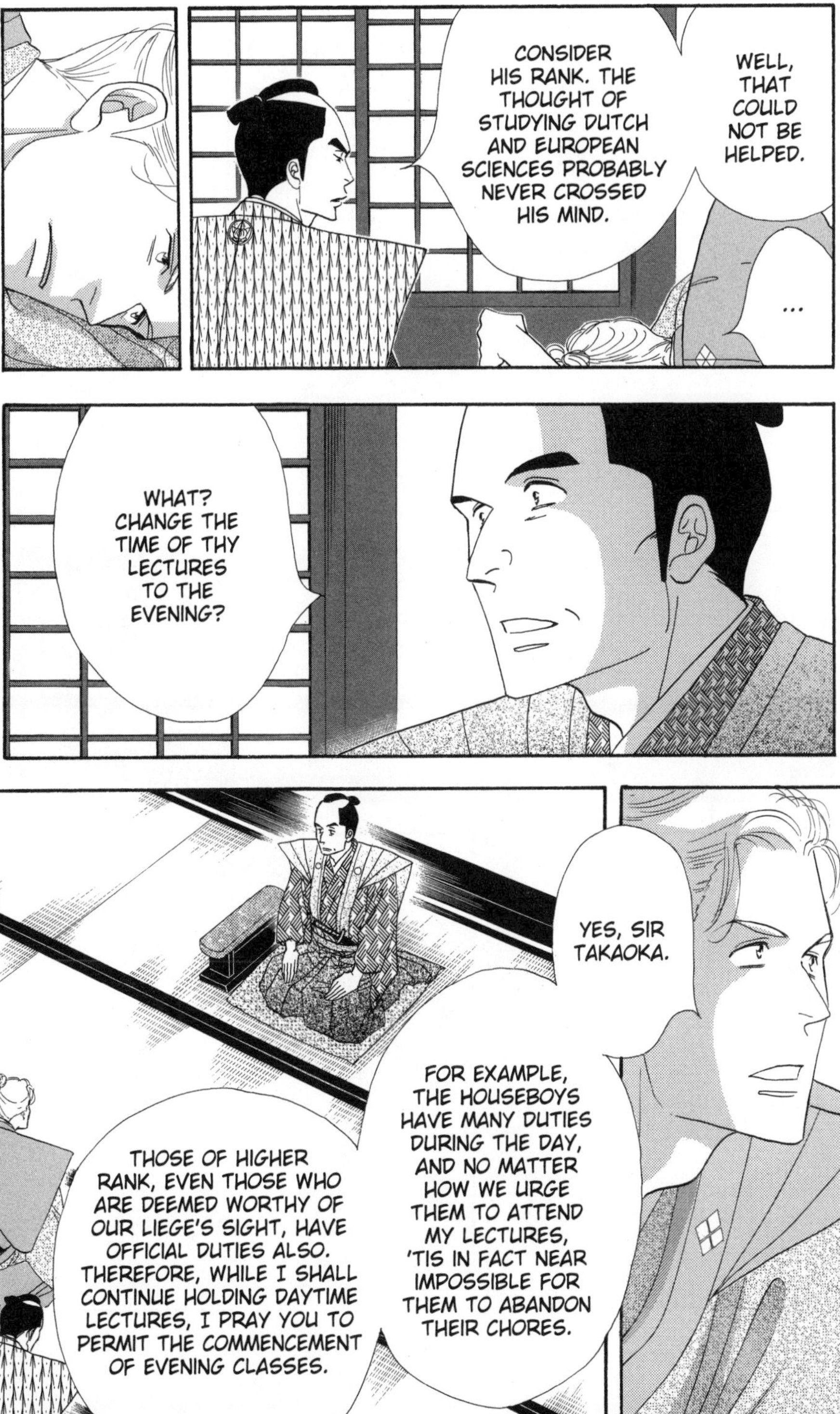
WELL, THAT COULD NOT BE HELPED.
CONSIDER HIS RANK. THE THOUGHT OF STUDYING DUTCH AND EUROPEAN SCIENCES PROBABLY NEVER CROSSED HIS MIND.
...
WHAT? CHANGE THE TIME OF THY LECTURES TO THE EVENING?
YES, SIR TAKAOKA.
FOR EXAMPLE, THE HOUSEBOYS HAVE MANY DUTIES DURING THE DAY, AND NO MATTER HOW WE URGE THEM TO ATTEND MY LECTURES, 'TIS IN FACT NEAR IMPOSSIBLE FOR THEM TO ABANDON THEIR CHORES.
THOSE OF HIGHER RANK, EVEN THOSE WHO ARE DEEMED WORTHY OF OUR LIEGE'S SIGHT, HAVE OFFICIAL DUTIES ALSO. THEREFORE, WHILE I SHALL CONTINUE HOLDING DAYTIME LECTURES, I PRAY YOU TO PERMIT THE COMMENCEMENT OF EVENING CLASSES.

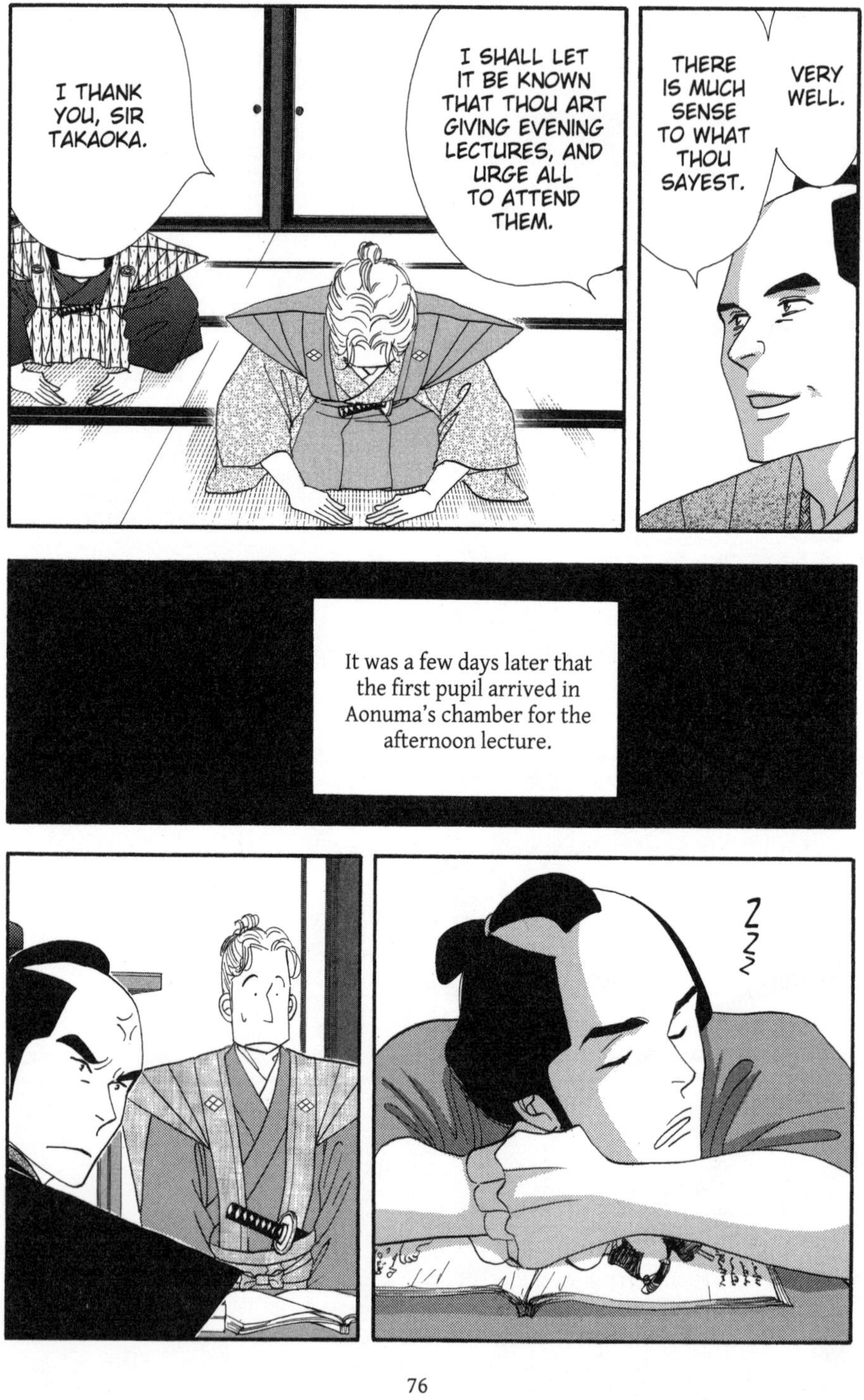
VERY WELL.
THERE IS MUCH SENSE TO WHAT THOU SAYEST.
I SHALL LET IT BE KNOWN THAT THOU ART GIVING EVENING LECTURES, AND URGE ALL TO ATTEND THEM.
I THANK YOU, SIR TAKAOKA.
It was a few days later that the first pupil arrived in Aonuma's chamber for the afternoon lecture.
ZZZ

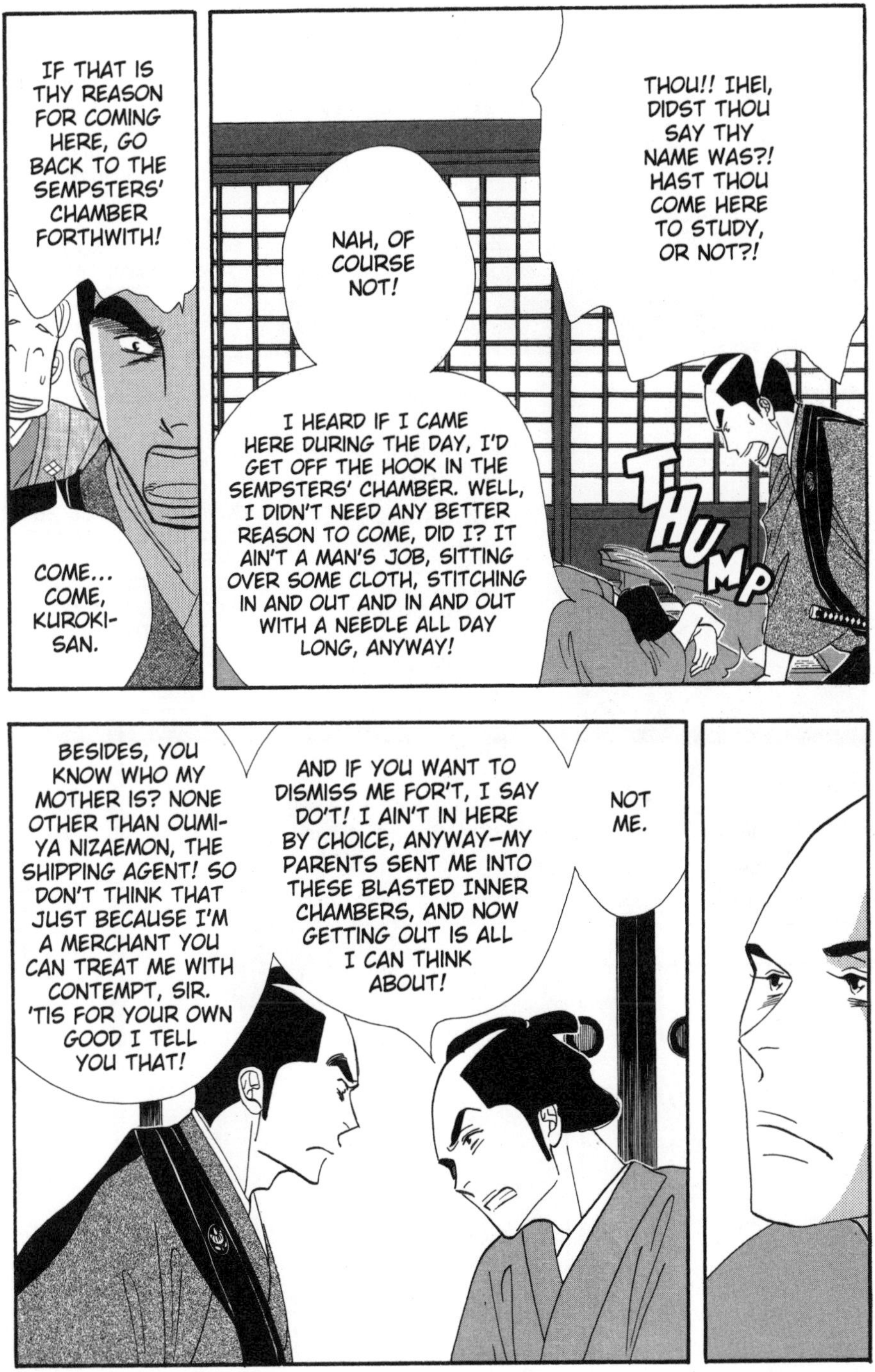
THOU!! IHEI, DIDST THOU SAY THY NAME WAS?! HAST THOU COME HERE TO STUDY, OR NOT?!
NAH, OF COURSE NOT!
THUMP
I HEARD IF I CAME HERE DURING THE DAY, I'D GET OFF THE HOOK IN THE SEMPSTERS' CHAMBER. WELL, I DIDN'T NEED ANY BETTER REASON TO COME, DID I? IT AIN'T A MAN'S JOB, SITTING OVER SOME CLOTH, STITCHING IN AND OUT AND IN AND OUT WITH A NEEDLE ALL DAY LONG, ANYWAY!
IF THAT IS THY REASON FOR COMING HERE, GO BACK TO THE SEMPSTERS' CHAMBER FORTHWITH!
COME... COME, KUROKI-SAN.
NOT ME.
AND IF YOU WANT TO DISMISS ME FOR'T, I SAY DO'T! I AIN'T IN HERE BY CHOICE, ANYWAY—MY PARENTS SENT ME INTO THESE BLASTED INNER CHAMBERS, AND NOW GETTING OUT IS ALL I CAN THINK ABOUT!
BESIDES, YOU KNOW WHO MY MOTHER IS? NONE OTHER THAN OUMI-YA NIZAEMON, THE SHIPPING AGENT! SO DON'T THINK THAT JUST BECAUSE I'M A MERCHANT YOU CAN TREAT ME WITH CONTEMPT, SIR. 'TIS FOR YOUR OWN GOOD I TELL YOU THAT!

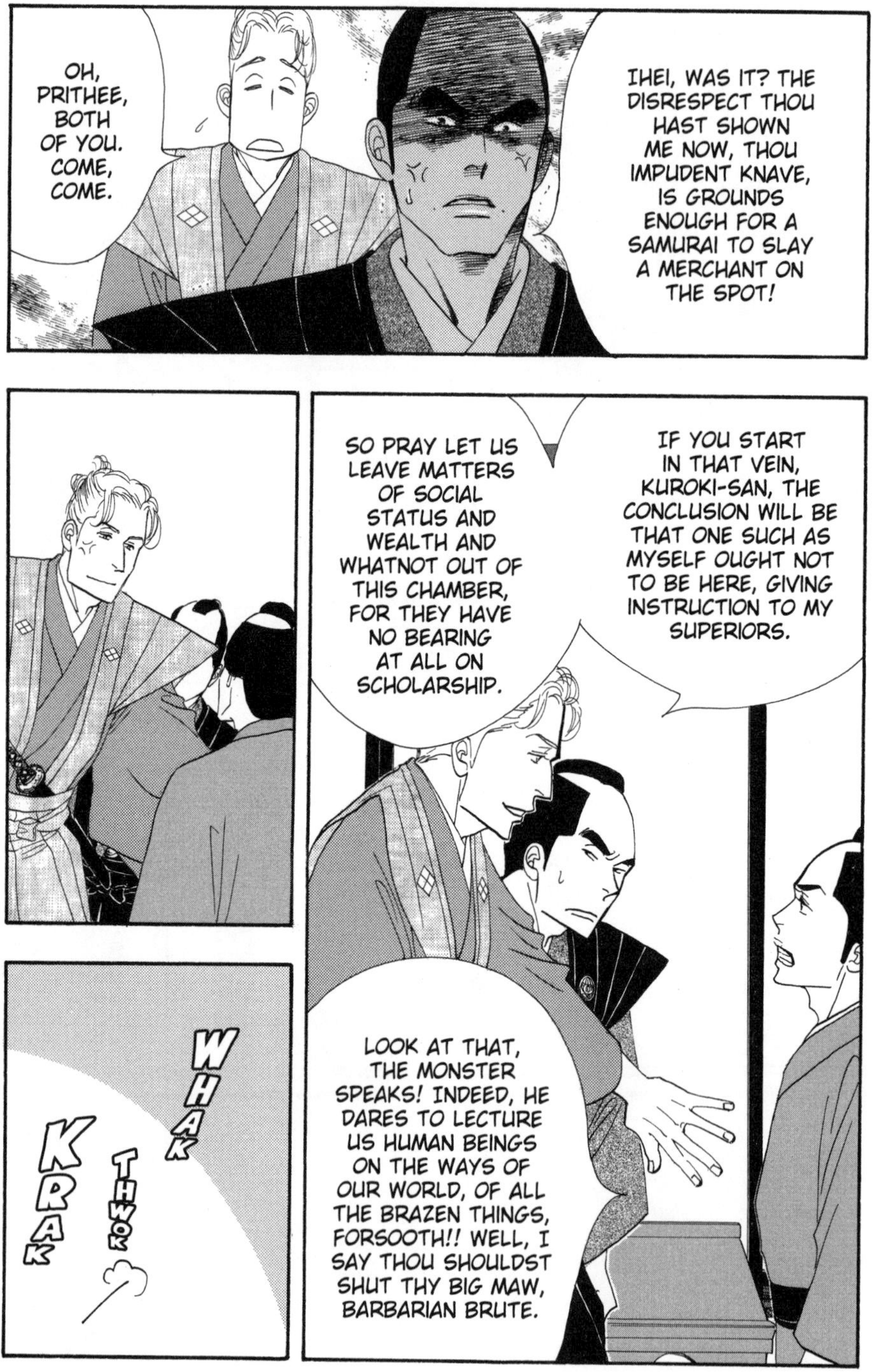
IHEI, WAS IT? THE DISRESPECT THOU HAST SHOWN ME NOW, THOU IMPUDENT KNAVE, IS GROUNDS ENOUGH FOR A SAMURAI TO SLAY A MERCHANT ON THE SPOT!
OH, PRITHEE, BOTH OF YOU. COME, COME.
IF YOU START IN THAT VEIN, KUROKI-SAN, THE CONCLUSION WILL BE THAT ONE SUCH AS MYSELF OUGHT NOT TO BE HERE, GIVING INSTRUCTION TO MY SUPERIORS.
SO PRAY LET US LEAVE MATTERS OF SOCIAL STATUS AND WEALTH AND WHATNOT OUT OF THIS CHAMBER, FOR THEY HAVE NO BEARING AT ALL ON SCHOLARSHIP.
LOOK AT THAT, THE MONSTER SPEAKS! INDEED, HE DARES TO LECTURE US HUMAN BEINGS ON THE WAYS OF OUR WORLD, OF ALL THE BRAZEN THINGS, FORSOOTH!! WELL, I SAY THOU SHOULDST SHUT THY BIG MAW, BARBARIAN BRUTE.
WHAK
THWOK
KRAK

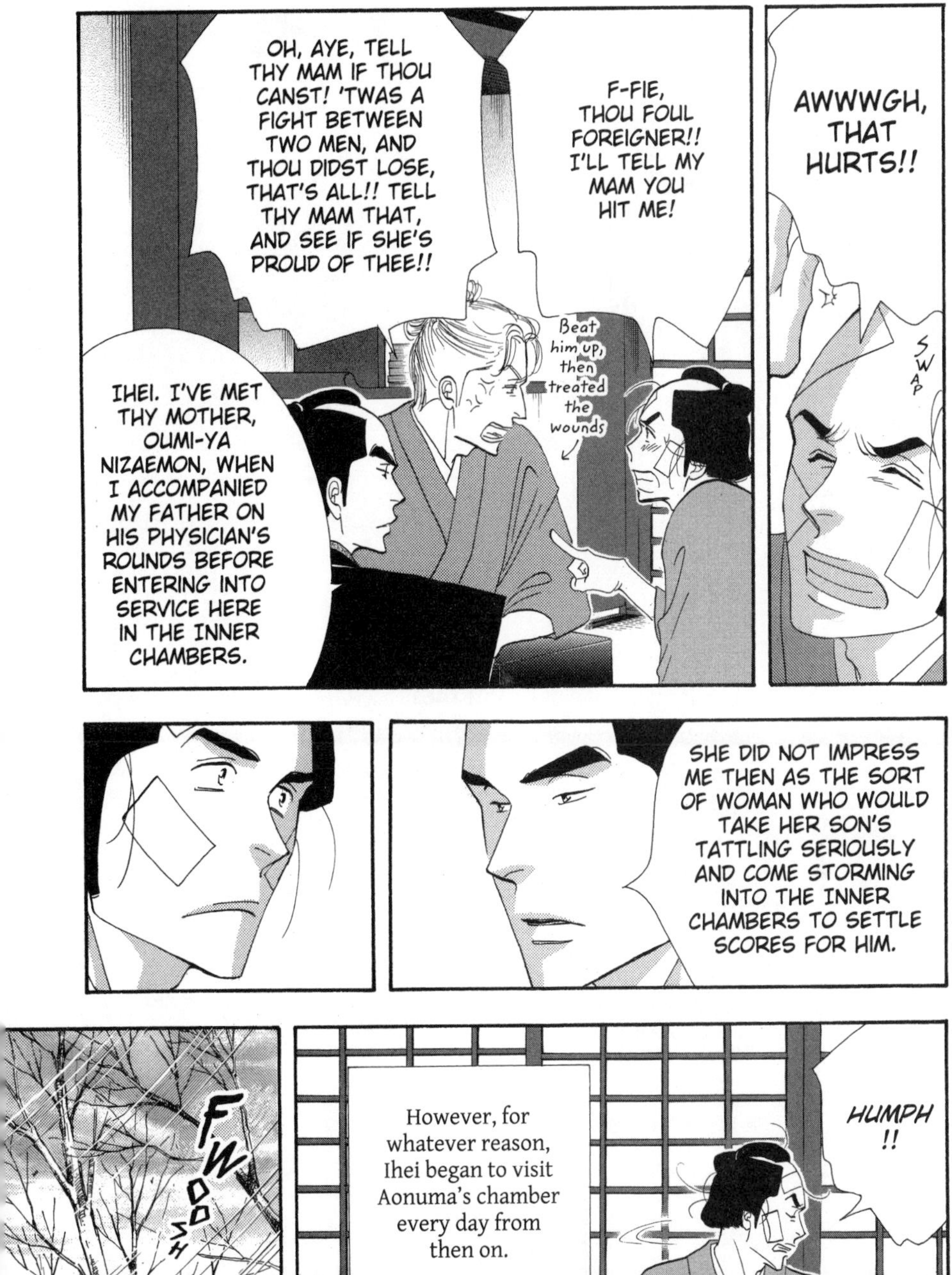
AWWWGH, THAT HURTS!!
SWAP
F-FIE, THOU FOUL FOREIGNER!! I'LL TELL MY MAM YOU HIT ME!
OH, AYE, TELL THY MAM IF THOU CANST! 'TWAS A FIGHT BETWEEN TWO MEN, AND THOU DIDST LOSE, THAT'S ALL!! TELL THY MAM THAT, AND SEE IF SHE'S PROUD OF THEE!!
Beat him up, then treated the wounds
IHEI. I'VE MET THY MOTHER, OUMI-YA NIZAEMON, WHEN I ACCOMPANIED MY FATHER ON HIS PHYSICIAN'S ROUNDS BEFORE ENTERING INTO SERVICE HERE IN THE INNER CHAMBERS.
SHE DID NOT IMPRESS ME THEN AS THE SORT OF WOMAN WHO WOULD TAKE HER SON'S TATTLING SERIOUSLY AND COME STORMING INTO THE INNER CHAMBERS TO SETTLE SCORES FOR HIM.
HUMPH!!
However, for whatever reason, Ihei began to visit Aonuma's chamber every day from then on.
FWOOSH

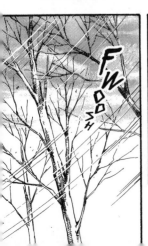

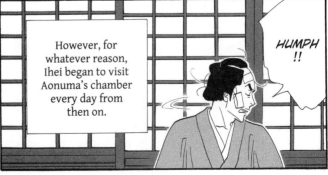

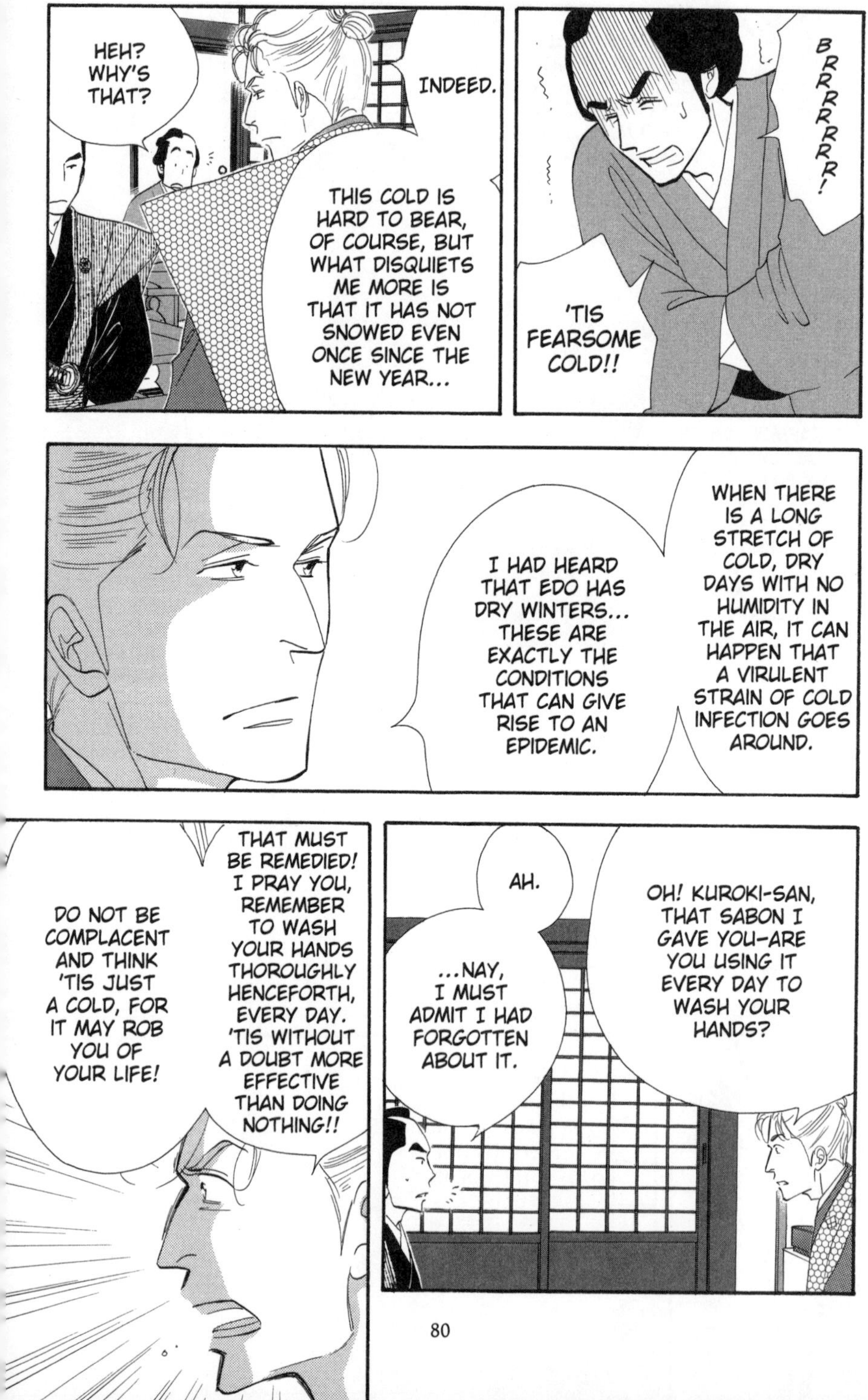
BRRRRRR!
'TIS FEARSOME COLD!!
INDEED.
THIS COLD IS HARD TO BEAR, OF COURSE, BUT WHAT DISQUIETS ME MORE IS THAT IT HAS NOT SNOWED EVEN ONCE SINCE THE NEW YEAR...
HEH? WHY'S THAT?
WHEN THERE IS A LONG STRETCH OF COLD, DRY DAYS WITH NO HUMIDITY IN THE AIR, IT CAN HAPPEN THAT A VIRULENT STRAIN OF COLD INFECTION GOES AROUND.
I HAD HEARD THAT EDO HAS DRY WINTERS... THESE ARE EXACTLY THE CONDITIONS THAT CAN GIVE RISE TO AN EPIDEMIC.
OH! KUROKI-SAN, THAT SABON I GAVE YOU—ARE YOU USING IT EVERY DAY TO WASH YOUR HANDS?
AH.
...NAY, I MUST ADMIT I HAD FORGOTTEN ABOUT IT.
THAT MUST BE REMEDIED! I PRAY YOU, REMEMBER TO WASH YOUR HANDS THOROUGHLY HENCEFORTH, EVERY DAY. 'TIS WITHOUT A DOUBT MORE EFFECTIVE THAN DOING NOTHING!!
DO NOT BE COMPLACENT AND THINK 'TIS JUST A COLD, FOR IT MAY ROB YOU OF YOUR LIFE!

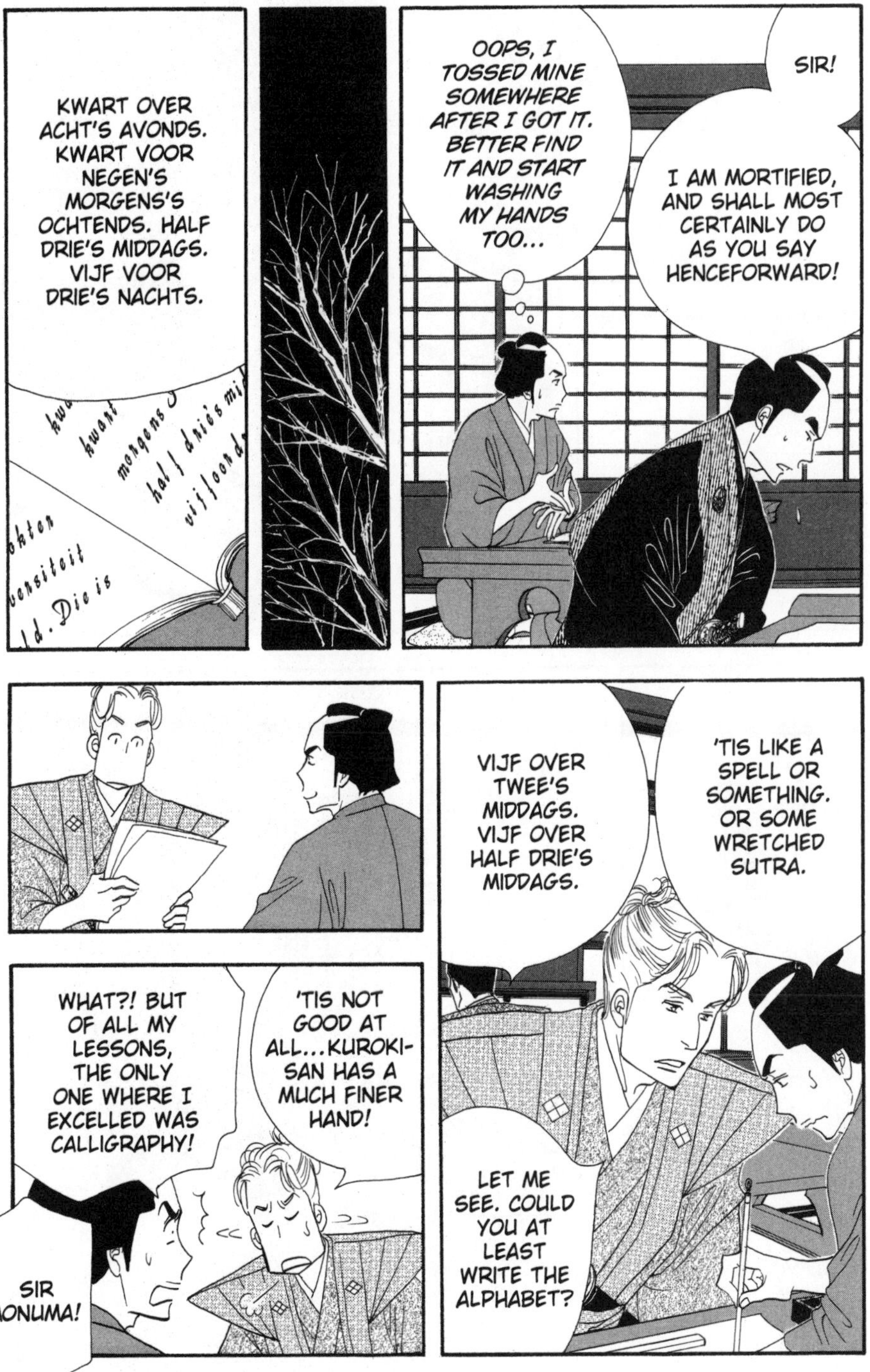

SIR!
I AM MORTIFIED, AND SHALL MOST CERTAINLY DO AS YOU SAY HENCEFORWARD!
OOPS, I TOSSED MINE SOMEWHERE AFTER I GOT IT. BETTER FIND IT AND START WASHING MY HANDS TOO...
KWART OVER ACHT'S AVONDS. KWART VOOR NEGEN'S MORGENS'S OCHTENDS. HALF DRIE'S MIDDAGS. VIJF VOOR DRIE'S NACHTS.
'TIS LIKE A SPELL OR SOMETHING. OR SOME WRETCHED SUTRA.
VIJF OVER TWEE'S MIDDAGS. VIJF OVER HALF DRIE'S MIDDAGS.
LET ME SEE. COULD YOU AT LEAST WRITE THE ALPHABET?
'TIS NOT GOOD AT ALL...KUROKI-SAN HAS A MUCH FINER HAND!
WHAT?! BUT OF ALL MY LESSONS, THE ONLY ONE WHERE I EXCELLED WAS CALLIGRAPHY!
SIR AONUMA!

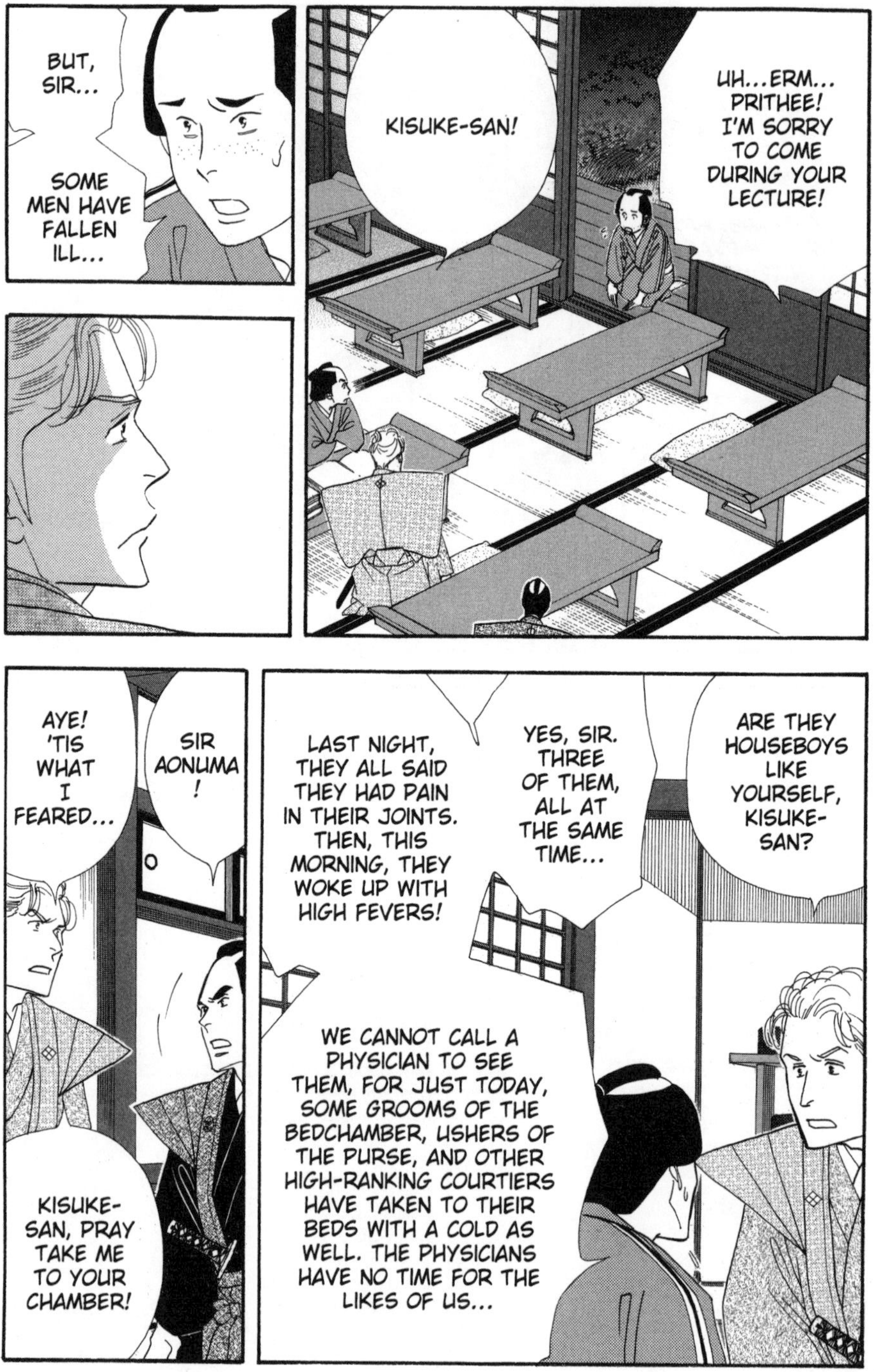
KISUKE-SAN!
UH...ERM... PRITHEE! I'M SORRY TO COME DURING YOUR LECTURE!
BUT, SIR...
SOME MEN HAVE FALLEN ILL...
ARE THEY HOUSEBOYS LIKE YOURSELF, KISUKE-SAN?
YES, SIR. THREE OF THEM, ALL AT THE SAME TIME...
LAST NIGHT, THEY ALL SAID THEY HAD PAIN IN THEIR JOINTS. THEN, THIS MORNING, THEY WOKE UP WITH HIGH FEVERS!
WE CANNOT CALL A PHYSICIAN TO SEE THEM, FOR JUST TODAY, SOME GROOMS OF THE BEDCHAMBER, USHERS OF THE PURSE, AND OTHER HIGH-RANKING COURTIERS HAVE TAKEN TO THEIR BEDS WITH A COLD AS WELL. THE PHYSICIANS HAVE NO TIME FOR THE LIKES OF US...
SIR AONUMA!
AYE! 'TIS WHAT I FEARED...
KISUKE-SAN, PRAY TAKE ME TO YOUR CHAMBER!

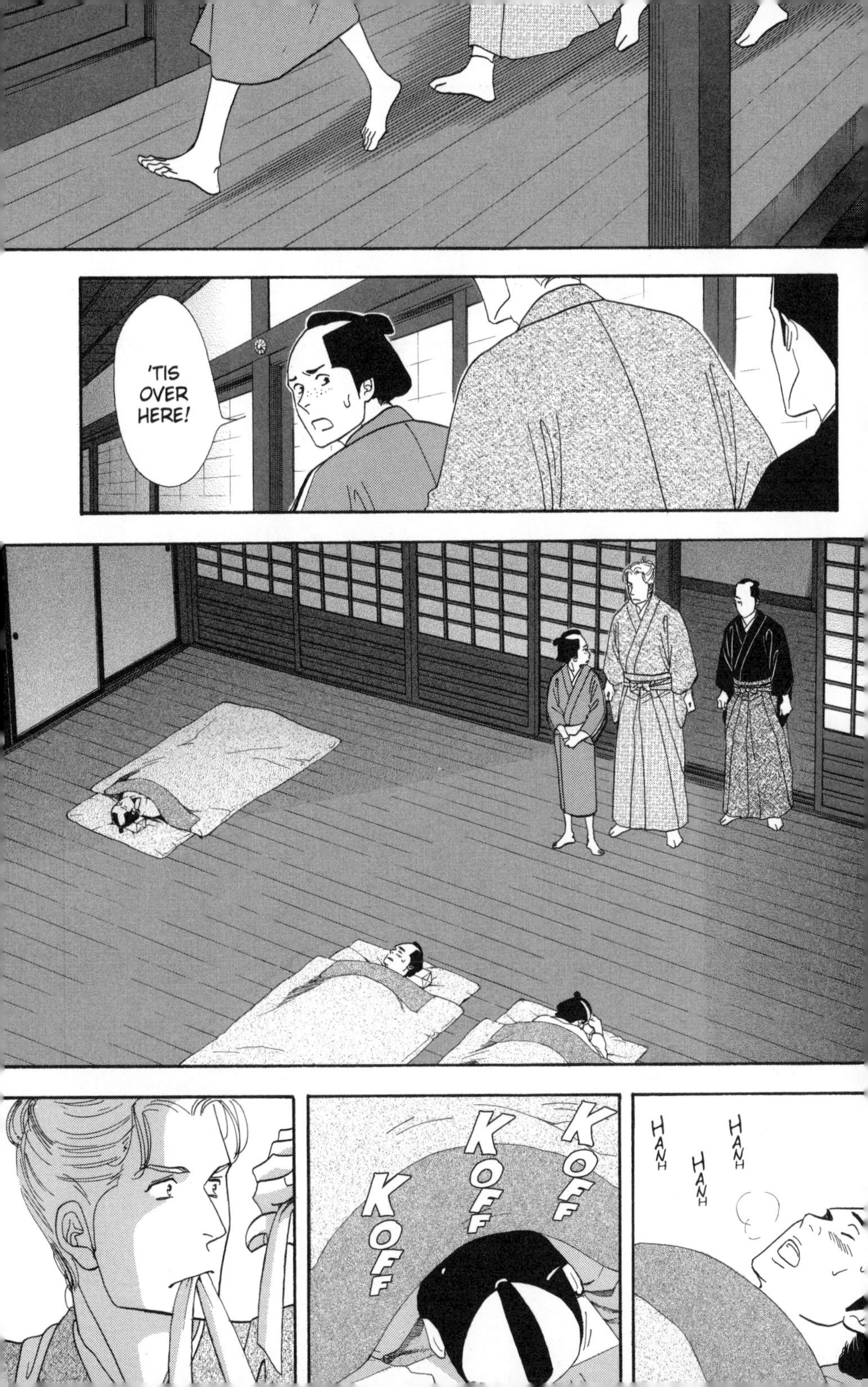
'TIS OVER HERE!
HANH HANH HANH
KOFF KOFF KOFF

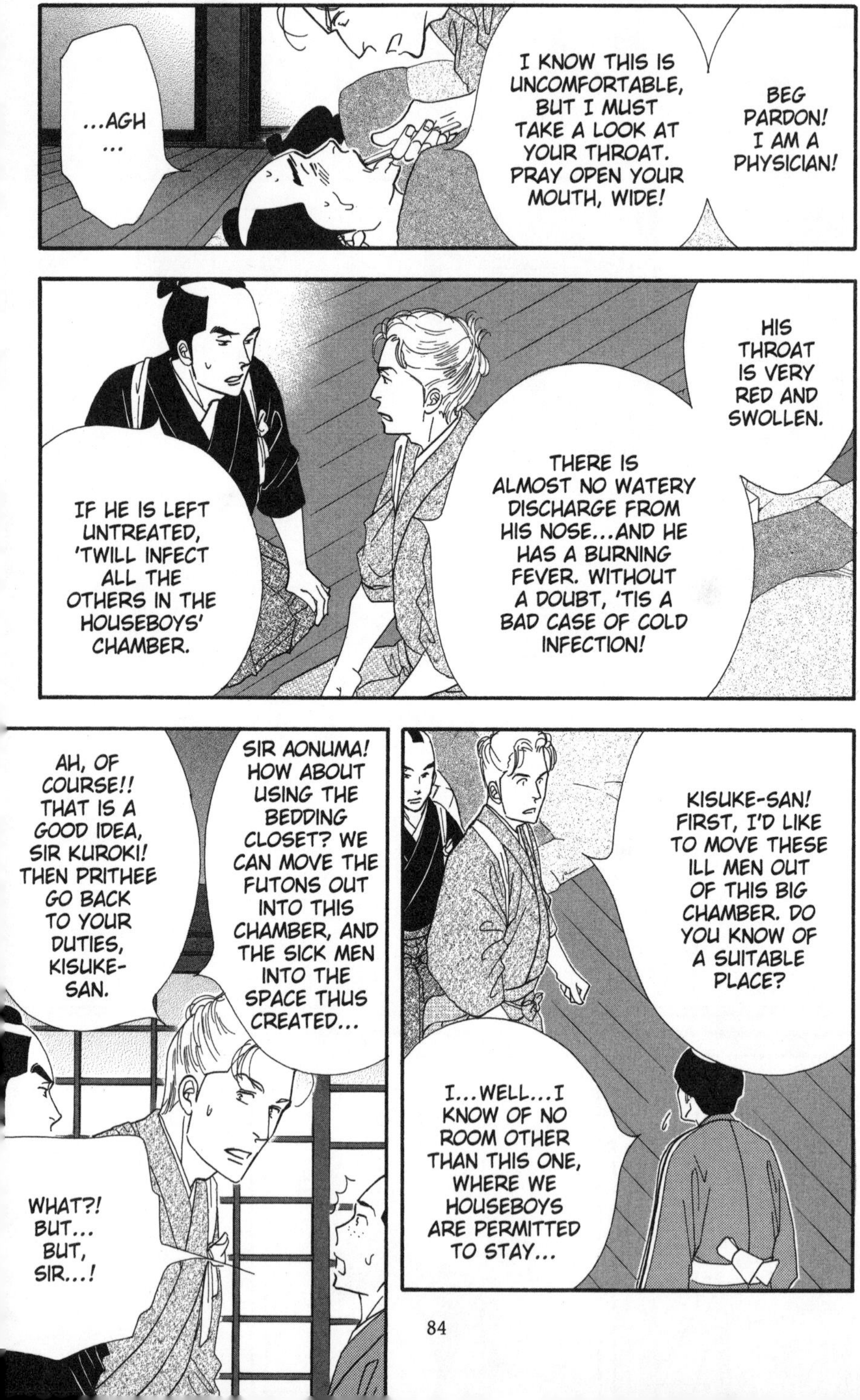
BEG PARDON! I AM A PHYSICIAN!
I KNOW THIS IS UNCOMFORTABLE, BUT I MUST TAKE A LOOK AT YOUR THROAT. PRAY OPEN YOUR MOUTH, WIDE!
...AGH ...
HIS THROAT IS VERY RED AND SWOLLEN.
THERE IS ALMOST NO WATERY DISCHARGE FROM HIS NOSE...AND HE HAS A BURNING FEVER. WITHOUT A DOUBT, 'TIS A BAD CASE OF COLD INFECTION!
IF HE IS LEFT UNTREATED, 'TWILL INFECT ALL THE OTHERS IN THE HOUSEBOYS' CHAMBER.
KISUKE-SAN! FIRST, I'D LIKE TO MOVE THESE ILL MEN OUT OF THIS BIG CHAMBER. DO YOU KNOW OF A SUITABLE PLACE?
I...WELL...I KNOW OF NO ROOM OTHER THAN THIS ONE, WHERE WE HOUSEBOYS ARE PERMITTED TO STAY...
SIR AONUMA! HOW ABOUT USING THE BEDDING CLOSET? WE CAN MOVE THE FUTONS OUT INTO THIS CHAMBER, AND THE SICK MEN INTO THE SPACE THUS CREATED...
AH, OF COURSE!! THAT IS A GOOD IDEA, SIR KUROKI! THEN PRITHEE GO BACK TO YOUR DUTIES, KISUKE-SAN.
WHAT?! BUT... BUT, SIR...!

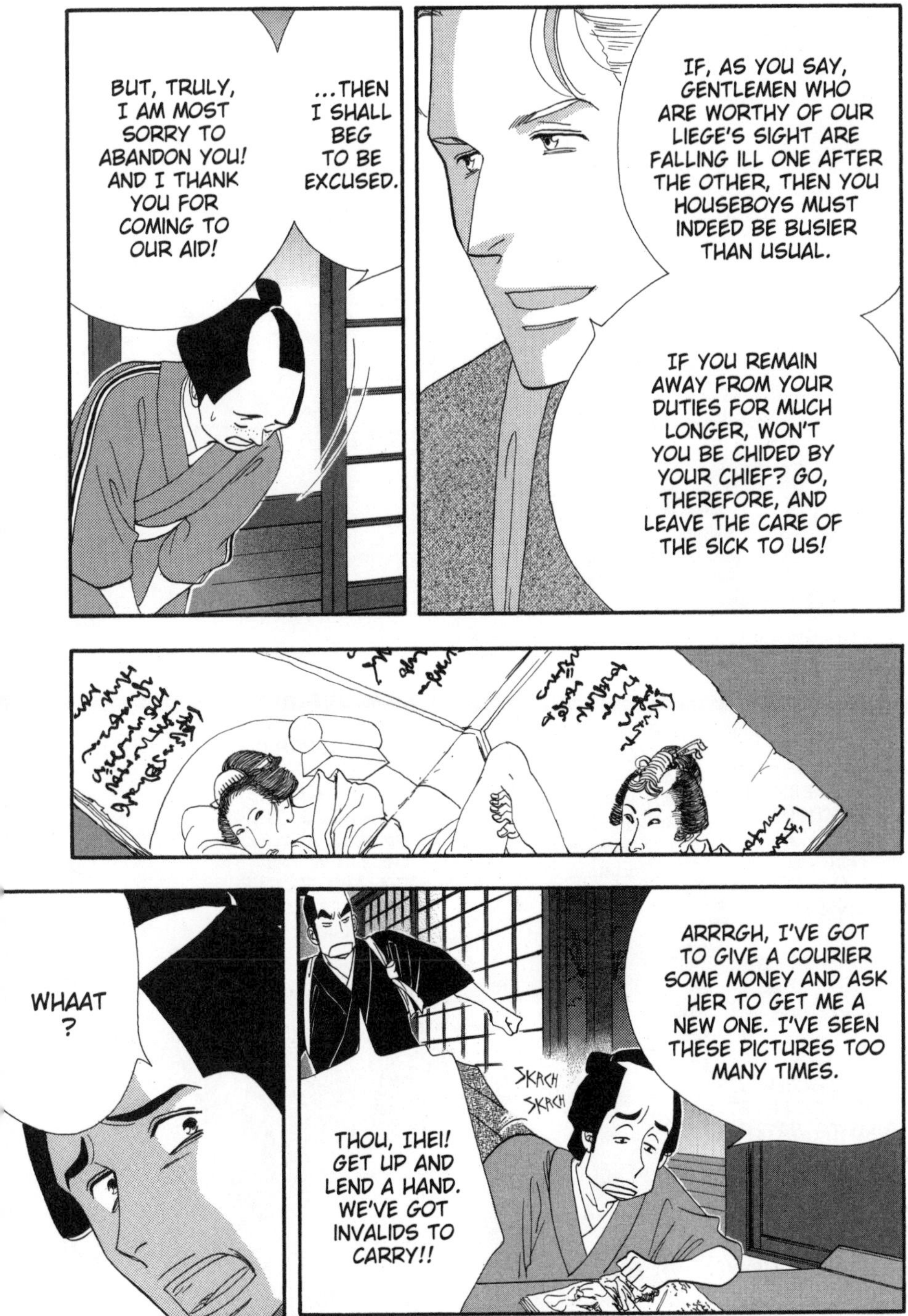
IF, AS YOU SAY, GENTLEMEN WHO ARE WORTHY OF OUR LIEGE'S SIGHT ARE FALLING ILL ONE AFTER THE OTHER, THEN YOU HOUSEBOYS MUST INDEED BE BUSIER THAN USUAL.
IF YOU REMAIN AWAY FROM YOUR DUTIES FOR MUCH LONGER, WON'T YOU BE CHIDED BY YOUR CHIEF? GO, THEREFORE, AND LEAVE THE CARE OF THE SICK TO US!
...THEN I SHALL BEG TO BE EXCUSED.
BUT, TRULY, I AM MOST SORRY TO ABANDON YOU! AND I THANK YOU FOR COMING TO OUR AID!
ARRRGH, I'VE GOT TO GIVE A COURIER SOME MONEY AND ASK HER TO GET ME A NEW ONE. I'VE SEEN THESE PICTURES TOO MANY TIMES.
SKRCH SKRCH
THOU, IHEI! GET UP AND LEND A HAND. WE'VE GOT INVALIDS TO CARRY!!
WHAAT ?

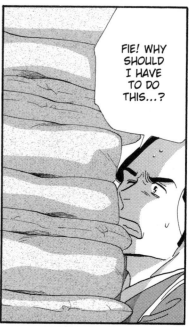

FIE! WHY SHOULD I HAVE TO DO THIS...?

WE MUST PUT A BRAZIER IN THE SICK ROOM, AND UPON IT A KETTLE FILLED WITH WATER. WHEN THE WATER BOILS, THE STEAM WILL MOISTEN THE AIR IN THE ROOM, AND SOOTHE THE MEN'S SORE THROATS.

BRING ALSO A PITCHER OF WATER FOR EACH MAN, AND FRESH NIGHT-GOWNS AS WELL!

HOW'RE WE TO REMEMBER EVERYTHING WHEN YOU TELL US IT ALL AT ONCE?!

NOW!

A BRAZIER, A KETTLE FILLED WITH WATER, PITCHERS OF WATER, AND NIGHT-GOWNS. I SHALL PROCURE THEM STRAIGHTAWAY!

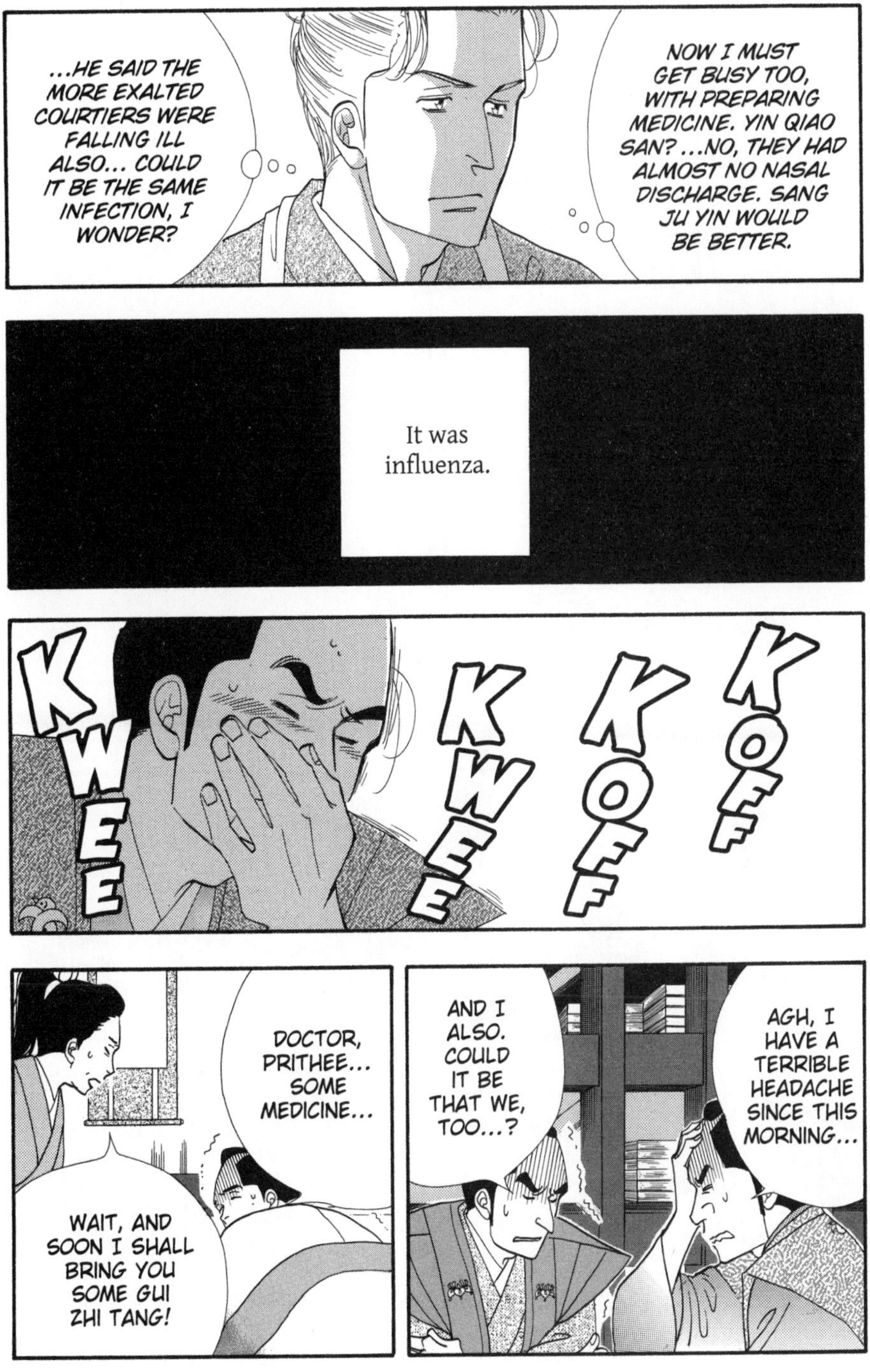
NOW I MUST GET BUSY TOO, WITH PREPARING MEDICINE. YIN QIAO SAN? ...NO, THEY HAD ALMOST NO NASAL DISCHARGE. SANG JU YIN WOULD BE BETTER.
...HE SAID THE MORE EXALTED COURTIERS WERE FALLING ILL ALSO... COULD IT BE THE SAME INFECTION, I WONDER?
It was influenza.
KOFF
KOFF
KWEE
KWEE
AGH, I HAVE A TERRIBLE HEADACHE SINCE THIS MORNING...
AND I ALSO. COULD IT BE THAT WE, TOO...?
DOCTOR, PRITHEE... SOME MEDICINE...
WAIT, AND SOON I SHALL BRING YOU SOME GUI ZHI TANG!

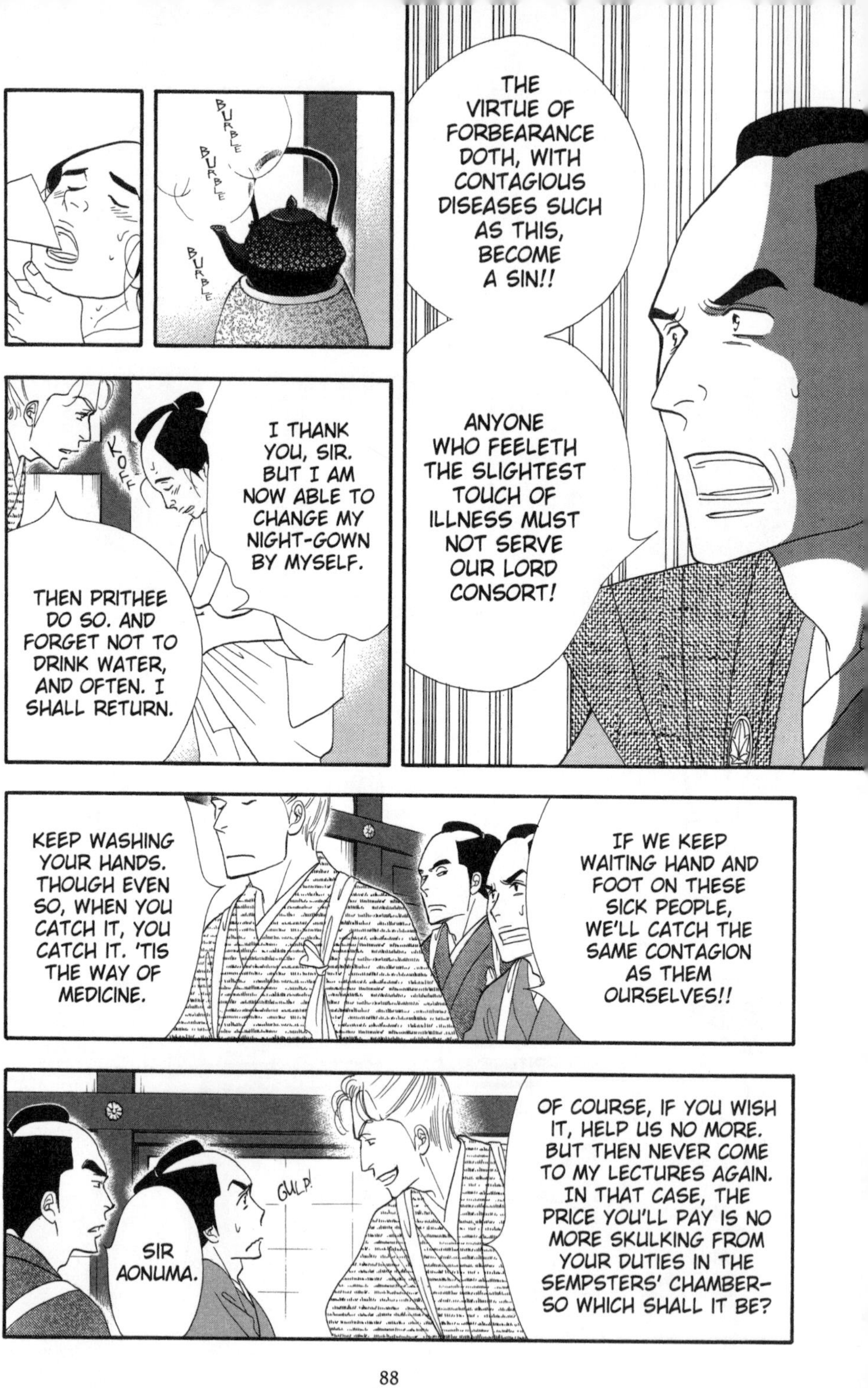
THE VIRTUE OF FORBEARANCE DOTH, WITH CONTAGIOUS DISEASES SUCH AS THIS, BECOME A SIN!!
ANYONE WHO FEELETH THE SLIGHTEST TOUCH OF ILLNESS MUST NOT SERVE OUR LORD CONSORT!
BURBLE BURBLE
BURBLE
KOFF
I THANK YOU, SIR. BUT I AM NOW ABLE TO CHANGE MY NIGHT-GOWN BY MYSELF.
THEN PRITHEE DO SO. AND FORGET NOT TO DRINK WATER, AND OFTEN. I SHALL RETURN.
IF WE KEEP WAITING HAND AND FOOT ON THESE SICK PEOPLE, WE'LL CATCH THE SAME CONTAGION AS THEM OURSELVES!!
KEEP WASHING YOUR HANDS. THOUGH EVEN SO, WHEN YOU CATCH IT, YOU CATCH IT. 'TIS THE WAY OF MEDICINE.
OF COURSE, IF YOU WISH IT, HELP US NO MORE. BUT THEN NEVER COME TO MY LECTURES AGAIN. IN THAT CASE, THE PRICE YOU'LL PAY IS NO MORE SKULKING FROM YOUR DUTIES IN THE SEMPSTERS' CHAMBER-SO WHICH SHALL IT BE?
GULP!
SIR AONUMA.

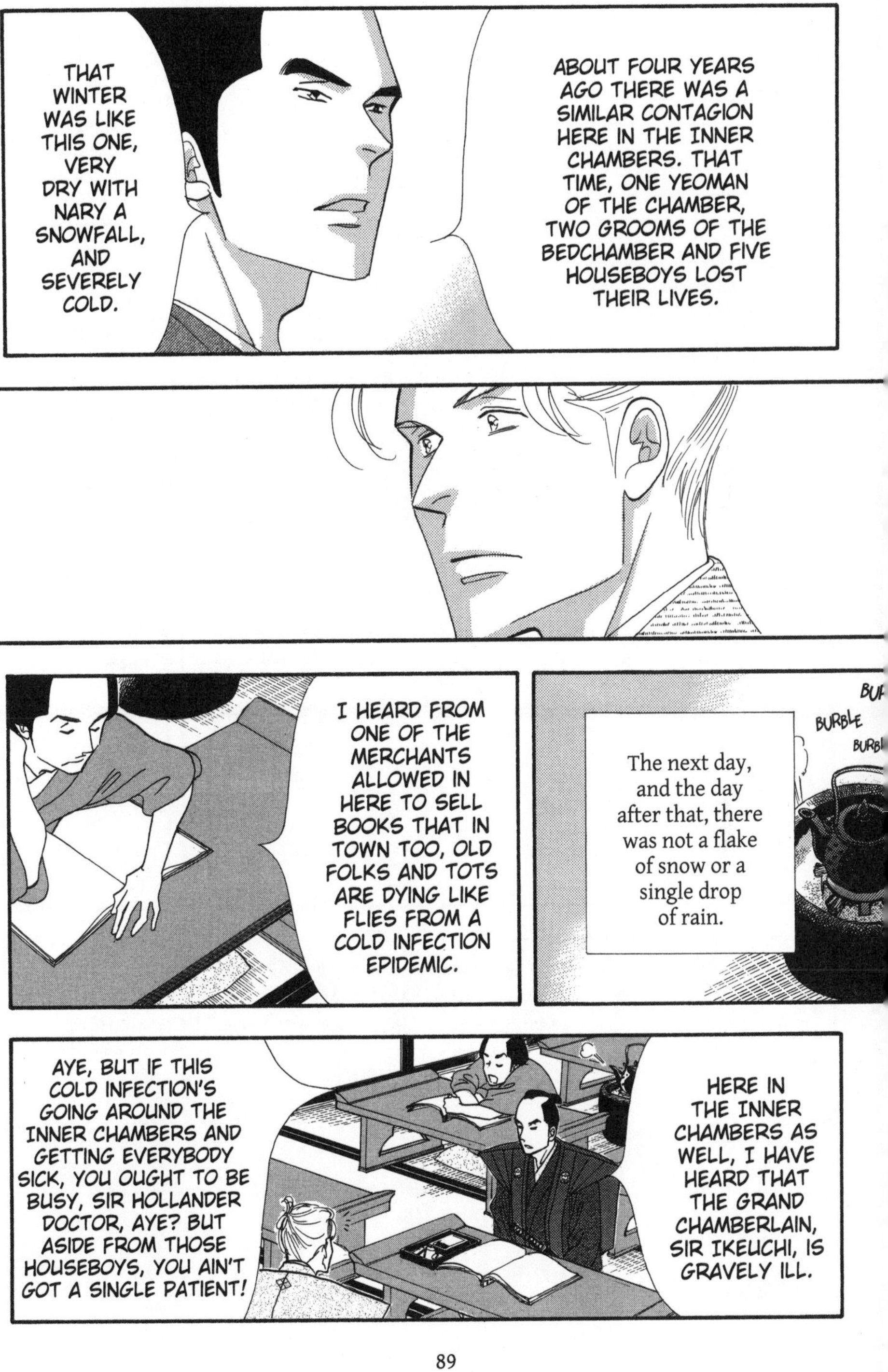
ABOUT FOUR YEARS AGO THERE WAS A SIMILAR CONTAGION HERE IN THE INNER CHAMBERS. THAT TIME, ONE YEOMAN OF THE CHAMBER, TWO GROOMS OF THE BEDCHAMBER AND FIVE HOUSEBOYS LOST THEIR LIVES.
THAT WINTER WAS LIKE THIS ONE, VERY DRY WITH NARY A SNOWFALL, AND SEVERELY COLD.
BURBLE
The next day, and the day after that, there was not a flake of snow or a single drop of rain.
I HEARD FROM ONE OF THE MERCHANTS ALLOWED IN HERE TO SELL BOOKS THAT IN TOWN TOO, OLD FOLKS AND TOTS ARE DYING LIKE FLIES FROM A COLD INFECTION EPIDEMIC.
HERE IN THE INNER CHAMBERS AS WELL, I HAVE HEARD THAT THE GRAND CHAMBERLAIN, SIR IKEUCHI, IS GRAVELY ILL.
AYE, BUT IF THIS COLD INFECTION'S GOING AROUND THE INNER CHAMBERS AND GETTING EVERYBODY SICK, YOU OUGHT TO BE BUSY, SIR HOLLANDER DOCTOR, AYE? BUT ASIDE FROM THOSE HOUSEBOYS, YOU AIN'T GOT A SINGLE PATIENT!

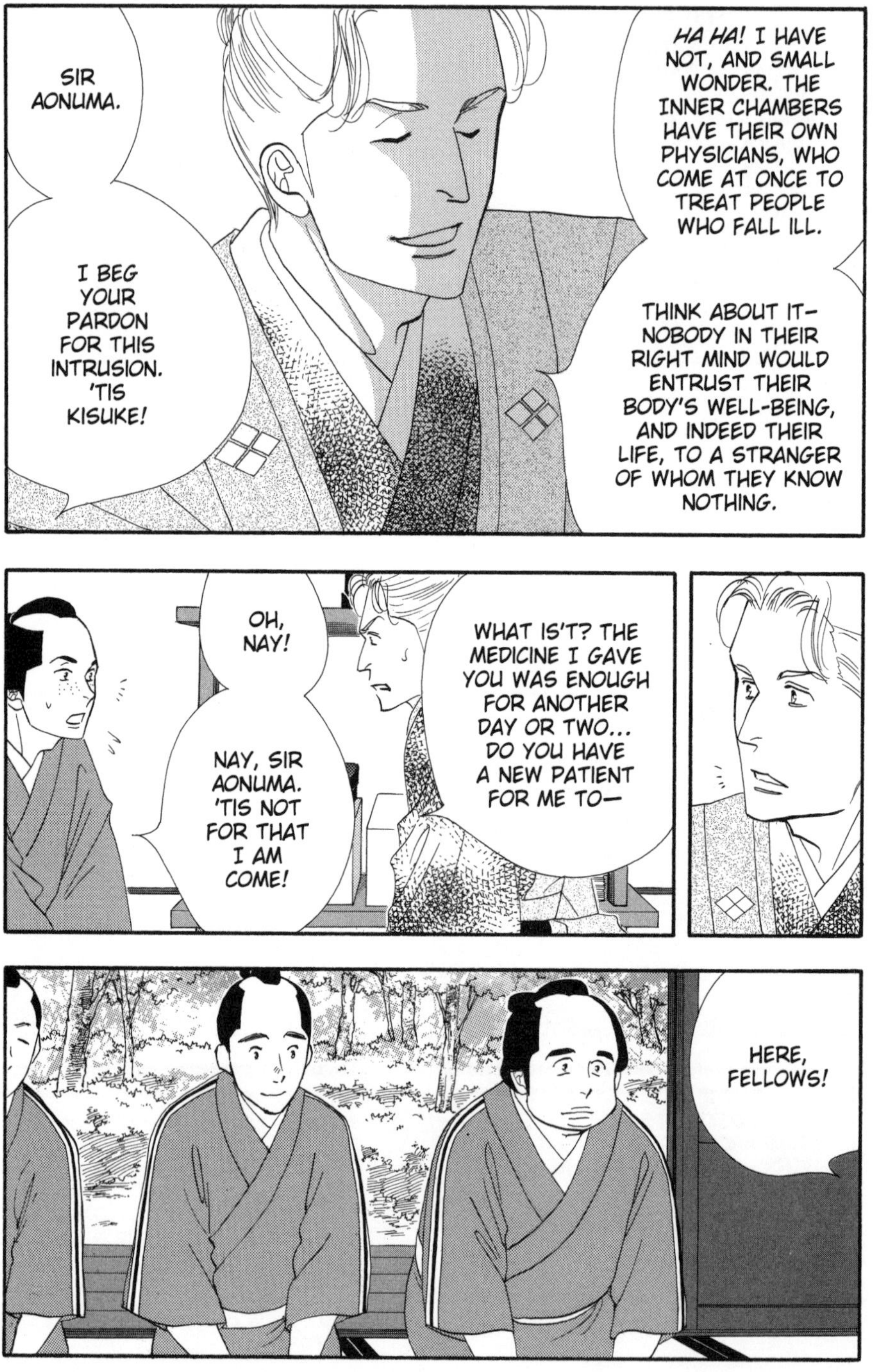
HA HA! I HAVE NOT, AND SMALL WONDER. THE INNER CHAMBERS HAVE THEIR OWN PHYSICIANS, WHO COME AT ONCE TO TREAT PEOPLE WHO FALL ILL.
THINK ABOUT IT–NOBODY IN THEIR RIGHT MIND WOULD ENTRUST THEIR BODY'S WELL-BEING, AND INDEED THEIR LIFE, TO A STRANGER OF WHOM THEY KNOW NOTHING.
SIR AONUMA.
I BEG YOUR PARDON FOR THIS INTRUSION. 'TIS KISUKE!
WHAT IS'T? THE MEDICINE I GAVE YOU WAS ENOUGH FOR ANOTHER DAY OR TWO... DO YOU HAVE A NEW PATIENT FOR ME TO—
OH, NAY!
NAY, SIR AONUMA. 'TIS NOT FOR THAT I AM COME!
HERE, FELLOWS!

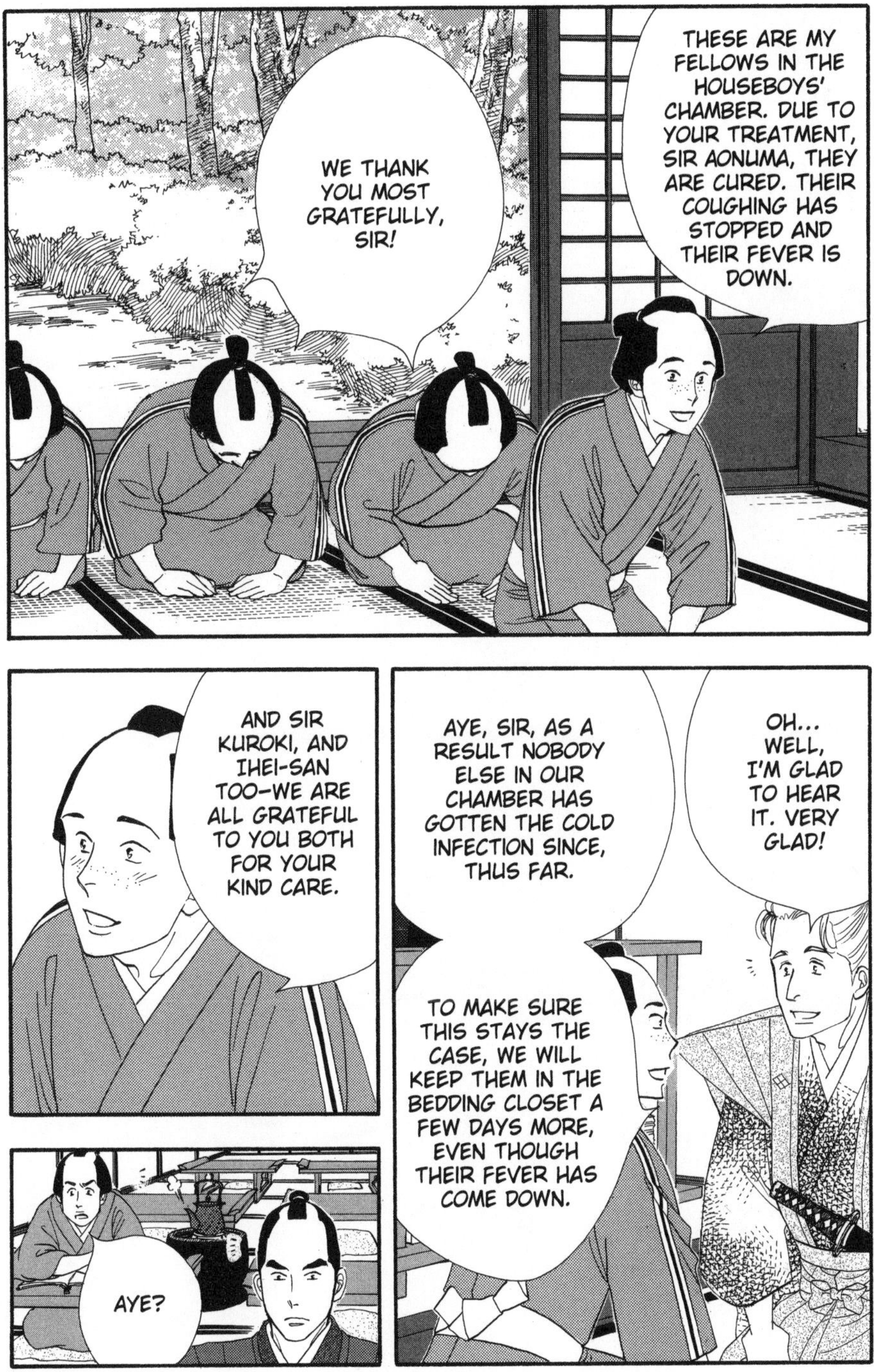
THESE ARE MY FELLOWS IN THE HOUSEBOYS' CHAMBER. DUE TO YOUR TREATMENT, SIR AONUMA, THEY ARE CURED. THEIR COUGHING HAS STOPPED AND THEIR FEVER IS DOWN.
WE THANK YOU MOST GRATEFULLY, SIR!
OH... WELL, I'M GLAD TO HEAR IT. VERY GLAD!
AYE, SIR, AS A RESULT NOBODY ELSE IN OUR CHAMBER HAS GOTTEN THE COLD INFECTION SINCE, THUS FAR.
TO MAKE SURE THIS STAYS THE CASE, WE WILL KEEP THEM IN THE BEDDING CLOSET A FEW DAYS MORE, EVEN THOUGH THEIR FEVER HAS COME DOWN.
AND SIR KUROKI, AND IHEI-SAN TOO—WE ARE ALL GRATEFUL TO YOU BOTH FOR YOUR KIND CARE.
AYE?

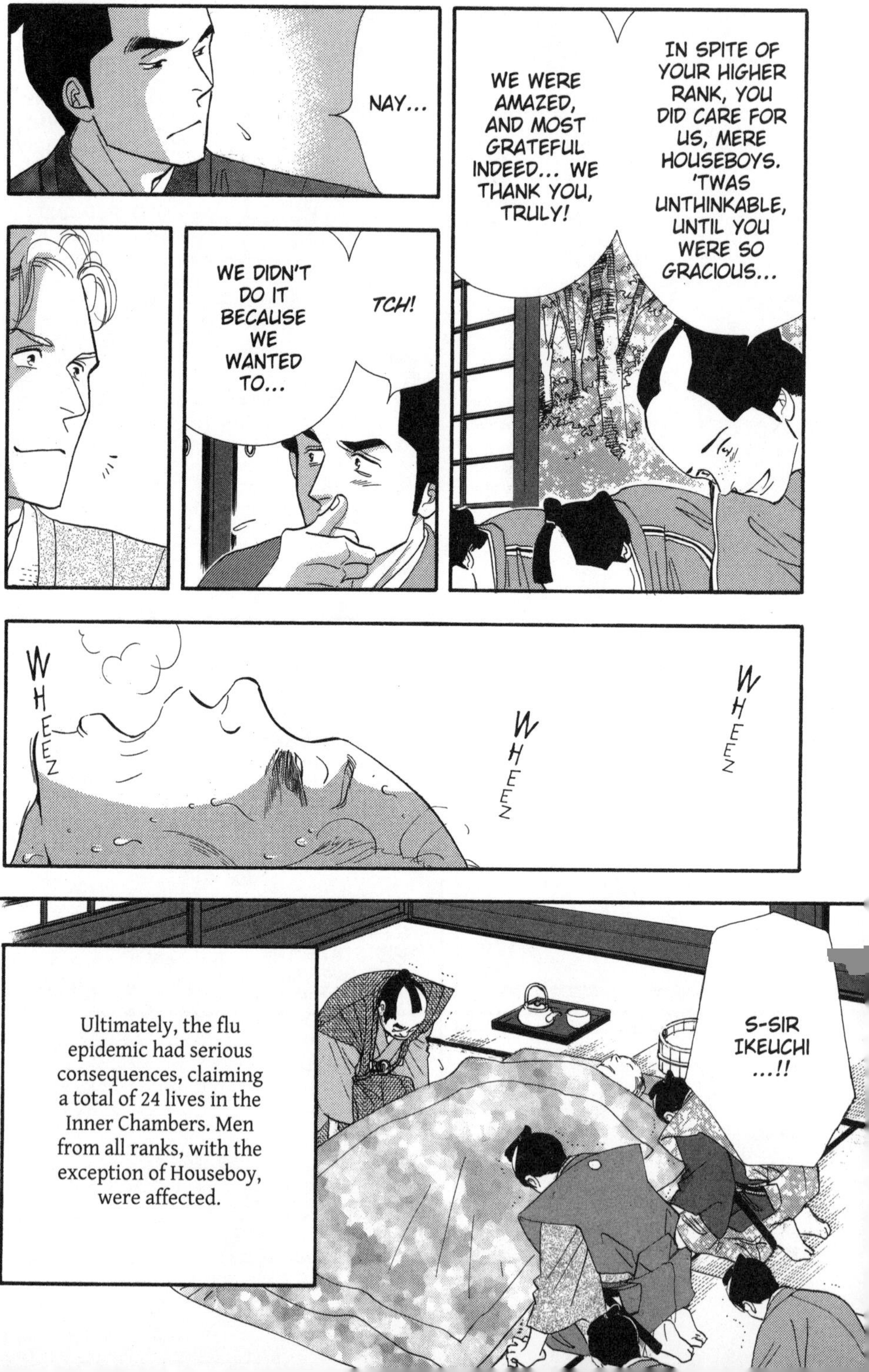
IN SPITE OF YOUR HIGHER RANK, YOU DID CARE FOR US, MERE HOUSEBOYS. 'TWAS UNTHINKABLE, UNTIL YOU WERE SO GRACIOUS...
WE WERE AMAZED, AND MOST GRATEFUL INDEED... WE THANK YOU, TRULY!
NAY...
TCH!
WE DIDN'T DO IT BECAUSE WE WANTED TO...
WHEEZ
WHEEZ
WHEEZ
S-SIR IKEUCHI ...!!
Ultimately, the flu epidemic had serious consequences, claiming a total of 24 lives in the Inner Chambers. Men from all ranks, with the exception of Houseboy, were affected.

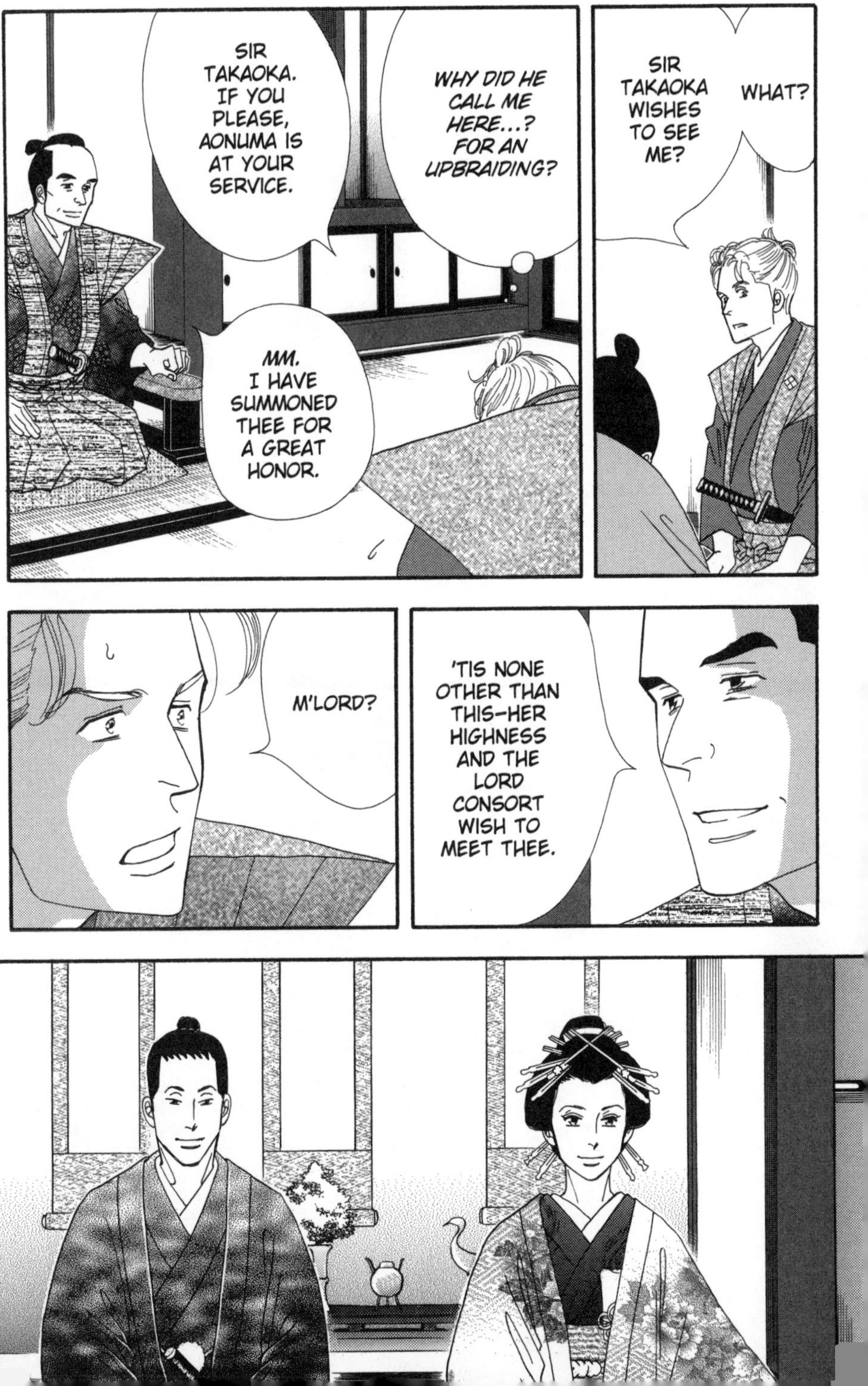
WHAT?
SIR TAKAOKA WISHES TO SEE ME?
WHY DID HE CALL ME HERE...? FOR AN UPBRAIDING?
SIR TAKAOKA. IF YOU PLEASE, AONUMA IS AT YOUR SERVICE.
MM. I HAVE SUMMONED THEE FOR A GREAT HONOR.
'TIS NONE OTHER THAN THIS–HER HIGHNESS AND THE LORD CONSORT WISH TO MEET THEE.
M'LORD?

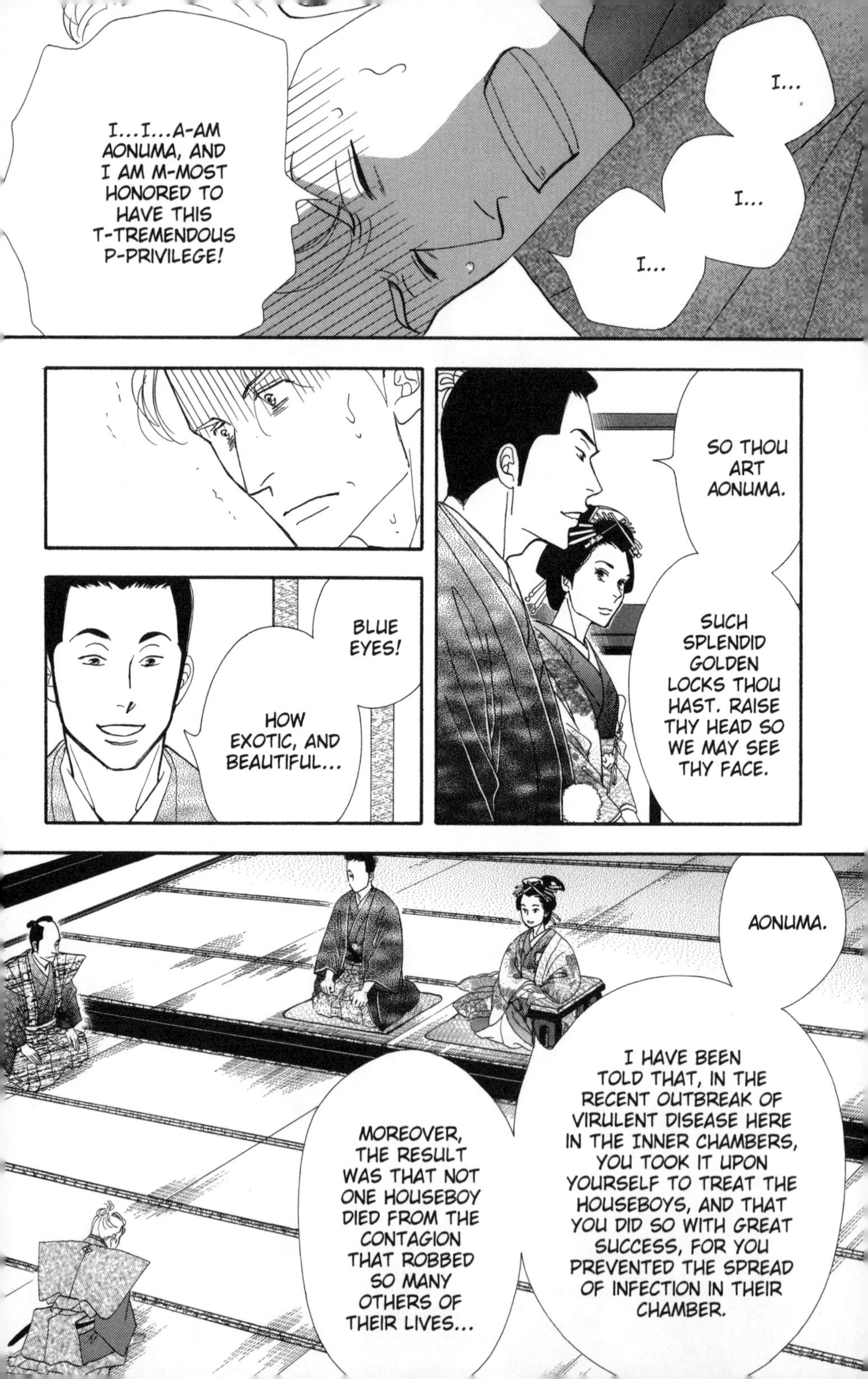
I...
I...
I...
I...I...A-AM AONUMA, AND I AM M-MOST HONORED TO HAVE THIS T-TREMENDOUS P-PRIVILEGE!
SO THOU ART AONUMA.
SUCH SPLENDID GOLDEN LOCKS THOU HAST. RAISE THY HEAD SO WE MAY SEE THY FACE.
BLUE EYES!
HOW EXOTIC, AND BEAUTIFUL...
AONUMA.
I HAVE BEEN TOLD THAT, IN THE RECENT OUTBREAK OF VIRULENT DISEASE HERE IN THE INNER CHAMBERS, YOU TOOK IT UPON YOURSELF TO TREAT THE HOUSEBOYS, AND THAT YOU DID SO WITH GREAT SUCCESS, FOR YOU PREVENTED THE SPREAD OF INFECTION IN THEIR CHAMBER.
MOREOVER, THE RESULT WAS THAT NOT ONE HOUSEBOY DIED FROM THE CONTAGION THAT ROBBED SO MANY OTHERS OF THEIR LIVES...

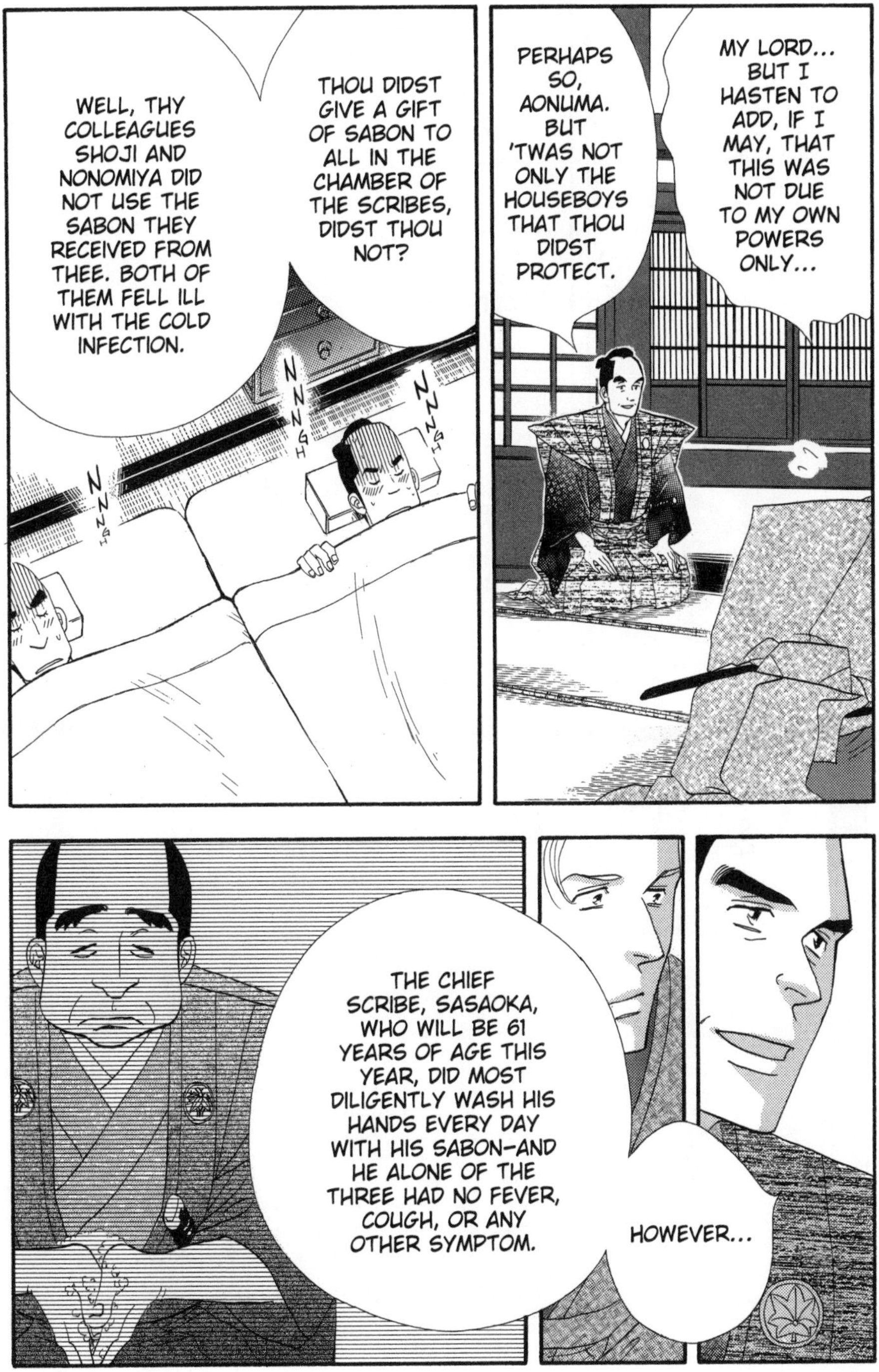
MY LORD... BUT I HASTEN TO ADD, IF I MAY, THAT THIS WAS NOT DUE TO MY OWN POWERS ONLY...
PERHAPS SO, AONUMA. BUT 'TWAS NOT ONLY THE HOUSEBOYS THAT THOU DIDST PROTECT.
THOU DIDST GIVE A GIFT OF SABON TO ALL IN THE CHAMBER OF THE SCRIBES, DIDST THOU NOT?
NNNGH
NNNGH
WELL, THY COLLEAGUES SHOJI AND NONOMIYA DID NOT USE THE SABON THEY RECEIVED FROM THEE. BOTH OF THEM FELL ILL WITH THE COLD INFECTION.
NNNGH
THE CHIEF SCRIBE, SASAOKA, WHO WILL BE 61 YEARS OF AGE THIS YEAR, DID MOST DILIGENTLY WASH HIS HANDS EVERY DAY WITH HIS SABON—AND HE ALONE OF THE THREE HAD NO FEVER, COUGH, OR ANY OTHER SYMPTOM.
HOWEVER...

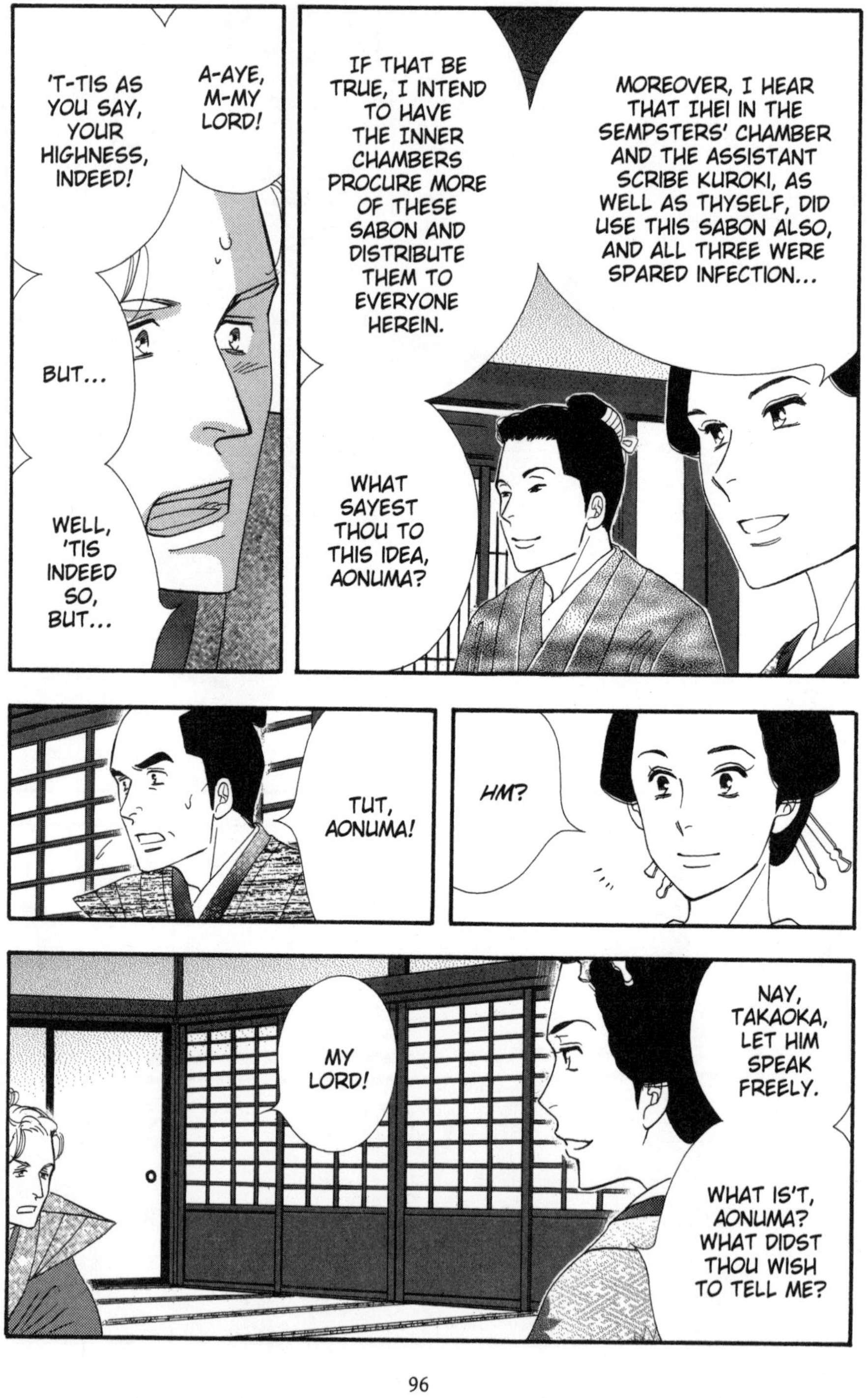
MOREOVER, I HEAR THAT IHEI IN THE SEMPSTERS' CHAMBER AND THE ASSISTANT SCRIBE KUROKI, AS WELL AS THYSELF, DID USE THIS SABON ALSO, AND ALL THREE WERE SPARED INFECTION...
IF THAT BE TRUE, I INTEND TO HAVE THE INNER CHAMBERS PROCURE MORE OF THESE SABON AND DISTRIBUTE THEM TO EVERYONE HEREIN.
WHAT SAYEST THOU TO THIS IDEA, AONUMA?
A-AYE, M-MY LORD!
'T-TIS AS YOU SAY, YOUR HIGHNESS, INDEED!
BUT...
WELL, 'TIS INDEED SO, BUT...
HM?
TUT, AONUMA!
NAY, TAKAOKA, LET HIM SPEAK FREELY.
MY LORD!
WHAT IS'T, AONUMA? WHAT DIDST THOU WISH TO TELL ME?

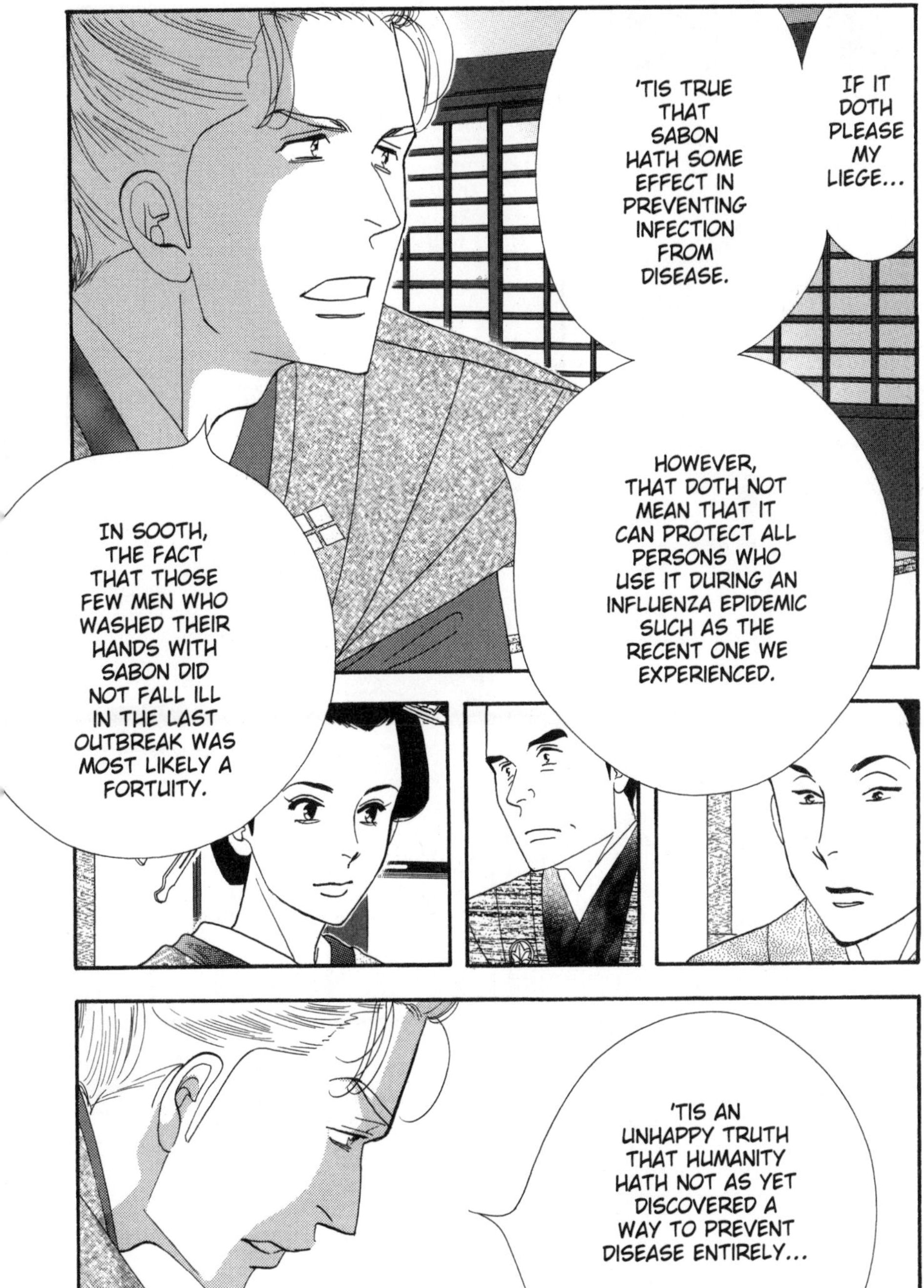
IF IT DOTH PLEASE MY LIEGE...
'TIS TRUE THAT SABON HATH SOME EFFECT IN PREVENTING INFECTION FROM DISEASE.
HOWEVER, THAT DOTH NOT MEAN THAT IT CAN PROTECT ALL PERSONS WHO USE IT DURING AN INFLUENZA EPIDEMIC SUCH AS THE RECENT ONE WE EXPERIENCED.
IN SOOTH, THE FACT THAT THOSE FEW MEN WHO WASHED THEIR HANDS WITH SABON DID NOT FALL ILL IN THE LAST OUTBREAK WAS MOST LIKELY A FORTUITY.
'TIS AN UNHAPPY TRUTH THAT HUMANITY HATH NOT AS YET DISCOVERED A WAY TO PREVENT DISEASE ENTIRELY...

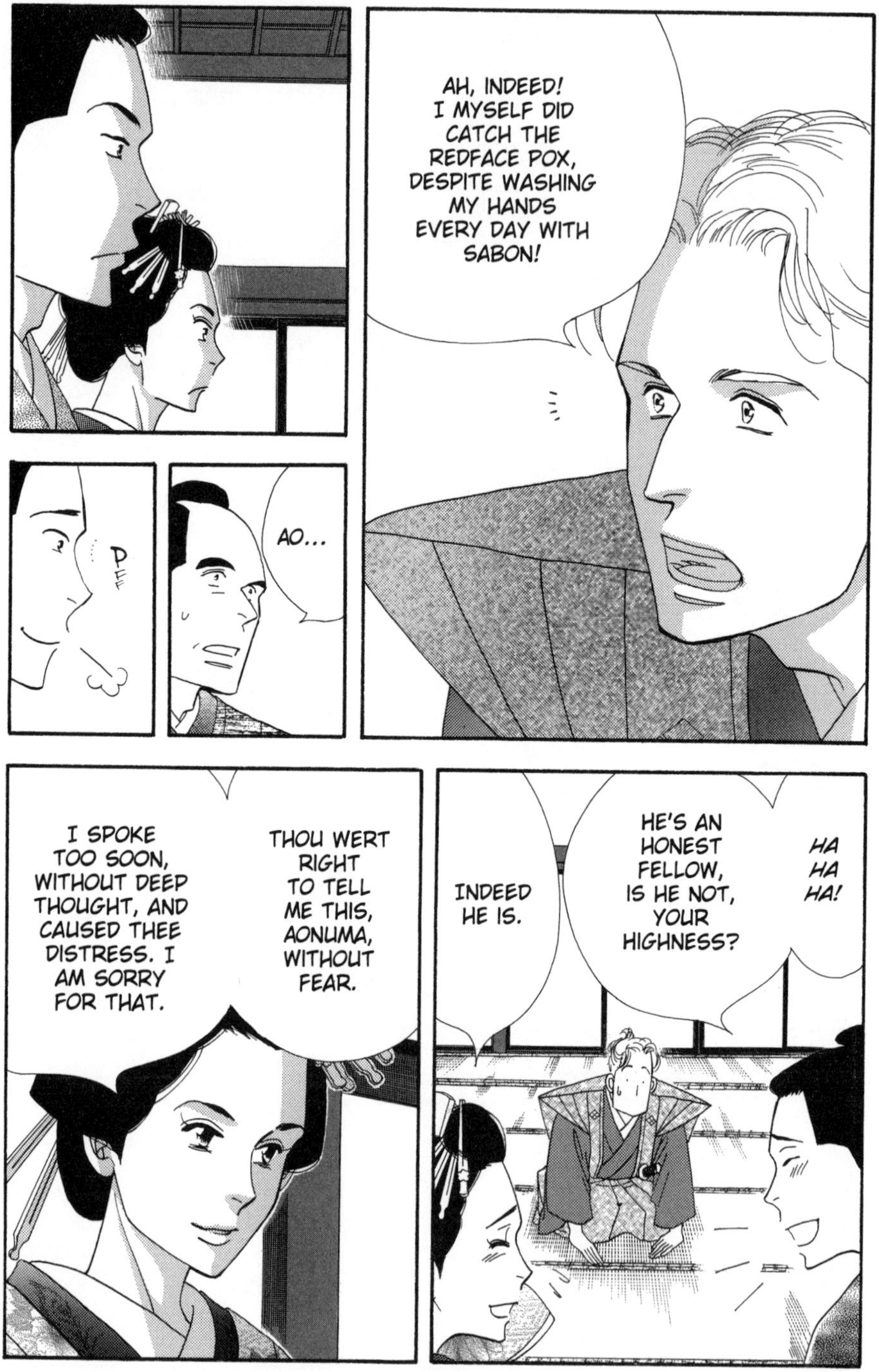
AH, INDEED! I MYSELF DID CATCH THE REDFACE POX, DESPITE WASHING MY HANDS EVERY DAY WITH SABON!
AO...
PFF
HA HA HA!
HE'S AN HONEST FELLOW, IS HE NOT, YOUR HIGHNESS?
INDEED HE IS.
THOU WERT RIGHT TO TELL ME THIS, AONUMA, WITHOUT FEAR.
I SPOKE TOO SOON, WITHOUT DEEP THOUGHT, AND CAUSED THEE DISTRESS. I AM SORRY FOR THAT.

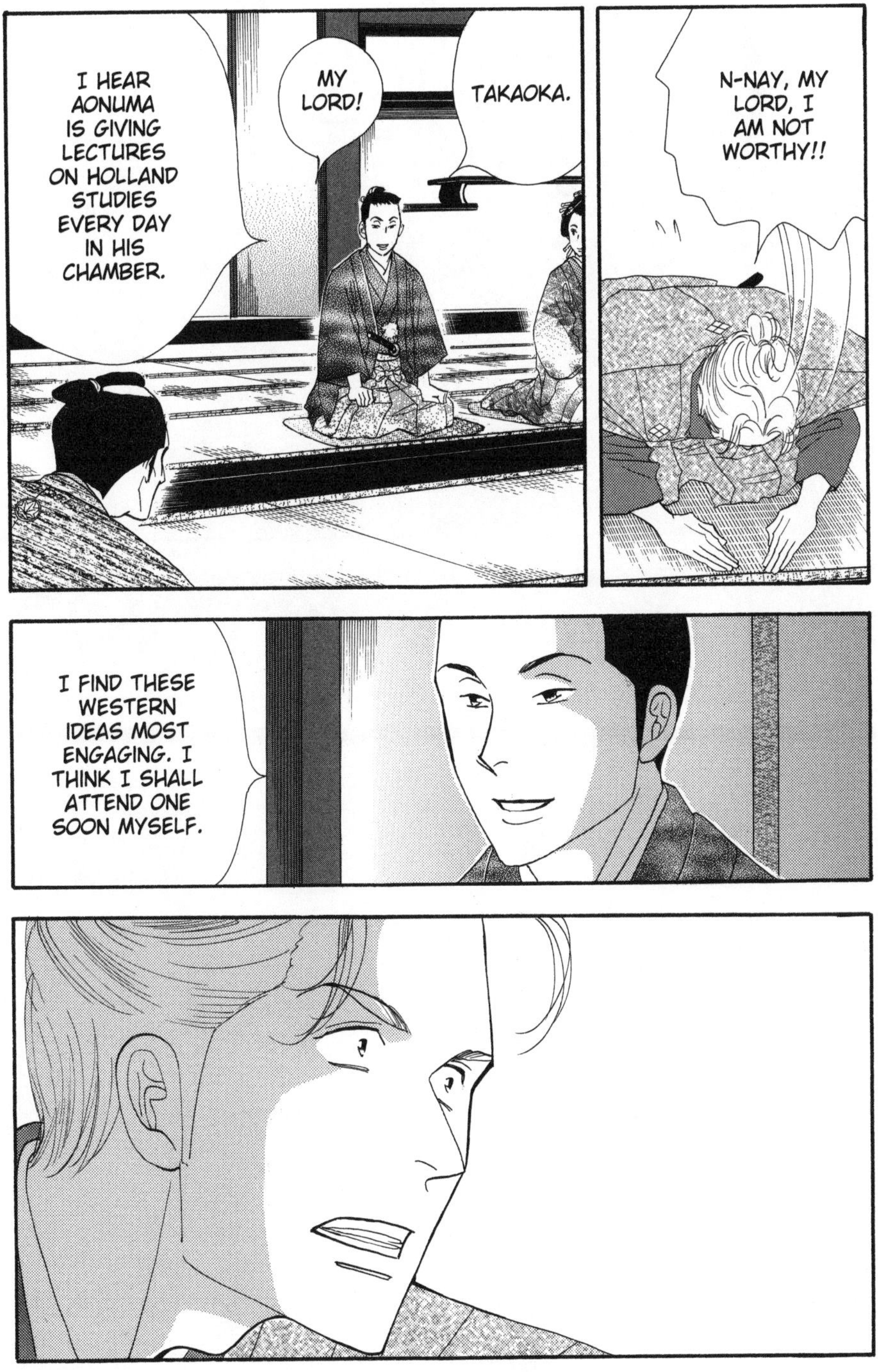
TAKAOKA.
MY LORD!
I HEAR AONUMA IS GIVING LECTURES ON HOLLAND STUDIES EVERY DAY IN HIS CHAMBER.
N-NAY, MY LORD, I AM NOT WORTHY!!
I FIND THESE WESTERN IDEAS MOST ENGAGING. I THINK I SHALL ATTEND ONE SOON MYSELF.

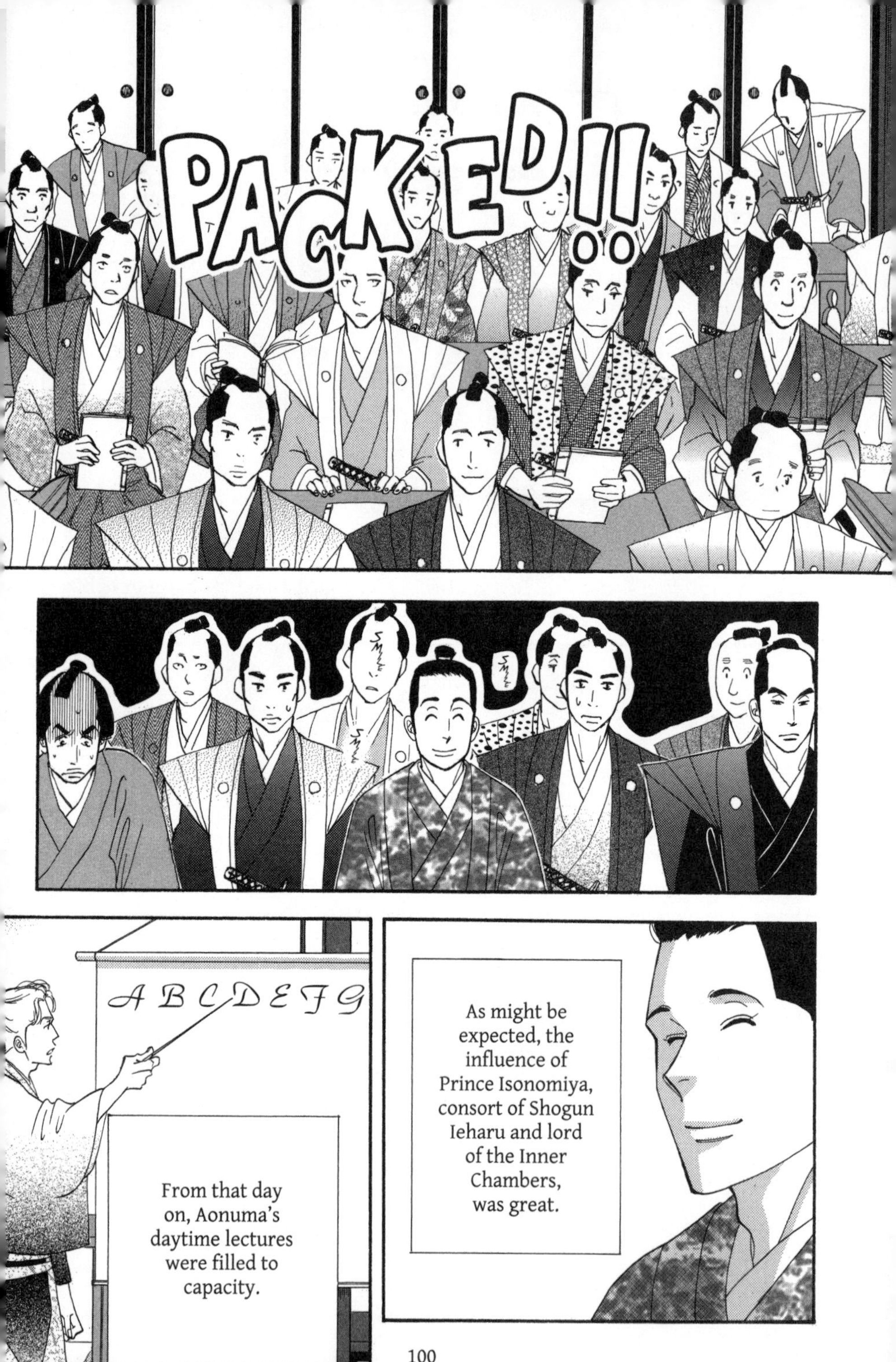
PACKED!!
As might be expected, the influence of Prince Isonomiya, consort of Shogun Ieharu and lord of the Inner Chambers, was great.
A B C D E F G
From that day on, Aonuma's daytime lectures were filled to capacity.

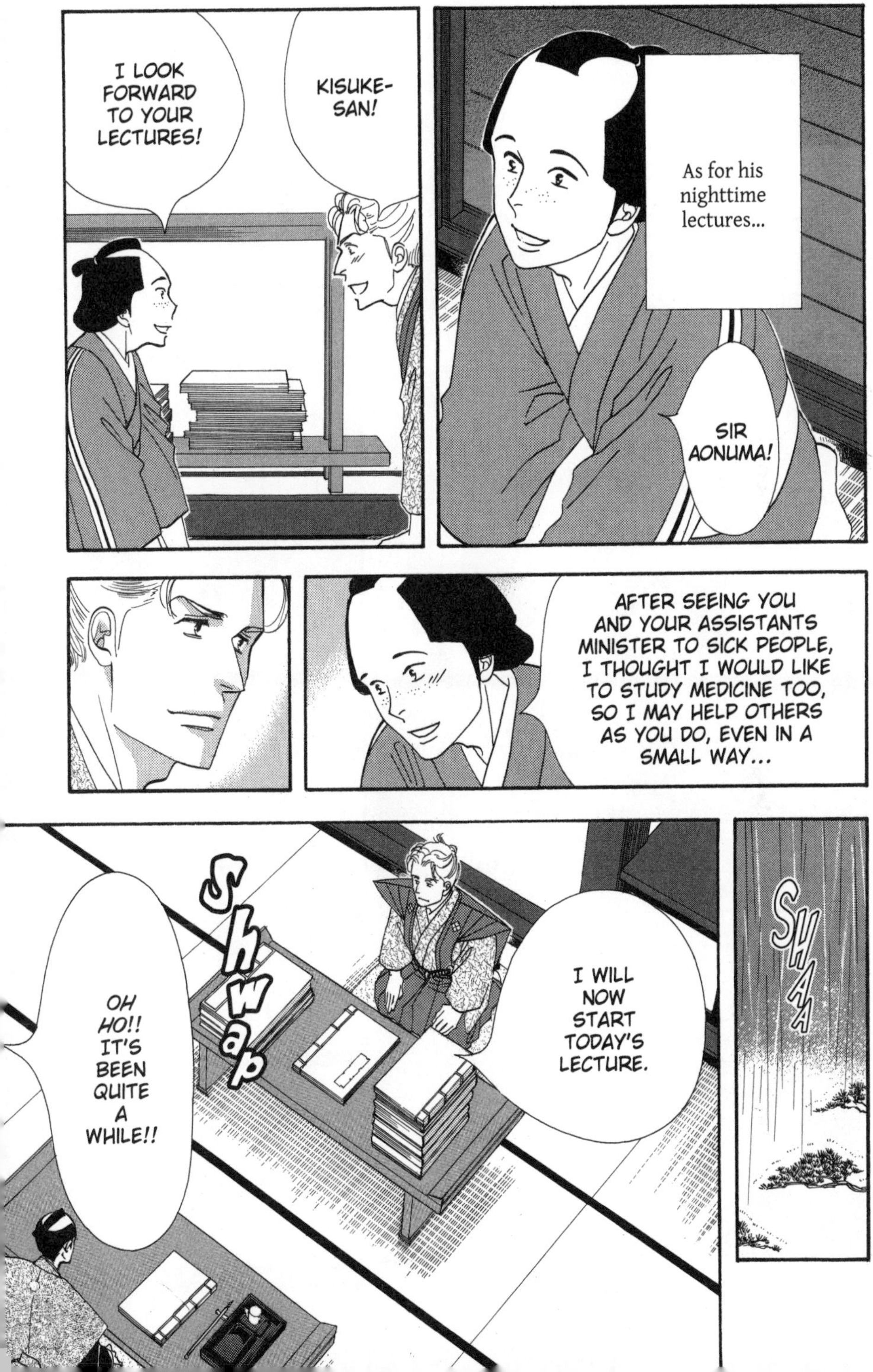
As for his nighttime lectures...
SIR AONUMA!
KISUKE-SAN!
I LOOK FORWARD TO YOUR LECTURES!
AFTER SEEING YOU AND YOUR ASSISTANTS MINISTER TO SICK PEOPLE, I THOUGHT I WOULD LIKE TO STUDY MEDICINE TOO, SO I MAY HELP OTHERS AS YOU DO, EVEN IN A SMALL WAY...
SHAA
I WILL NOW START TODAY'S LECTURE.
Shwap
OH HO!! IT'S BEEN QUITE A WHILE!!

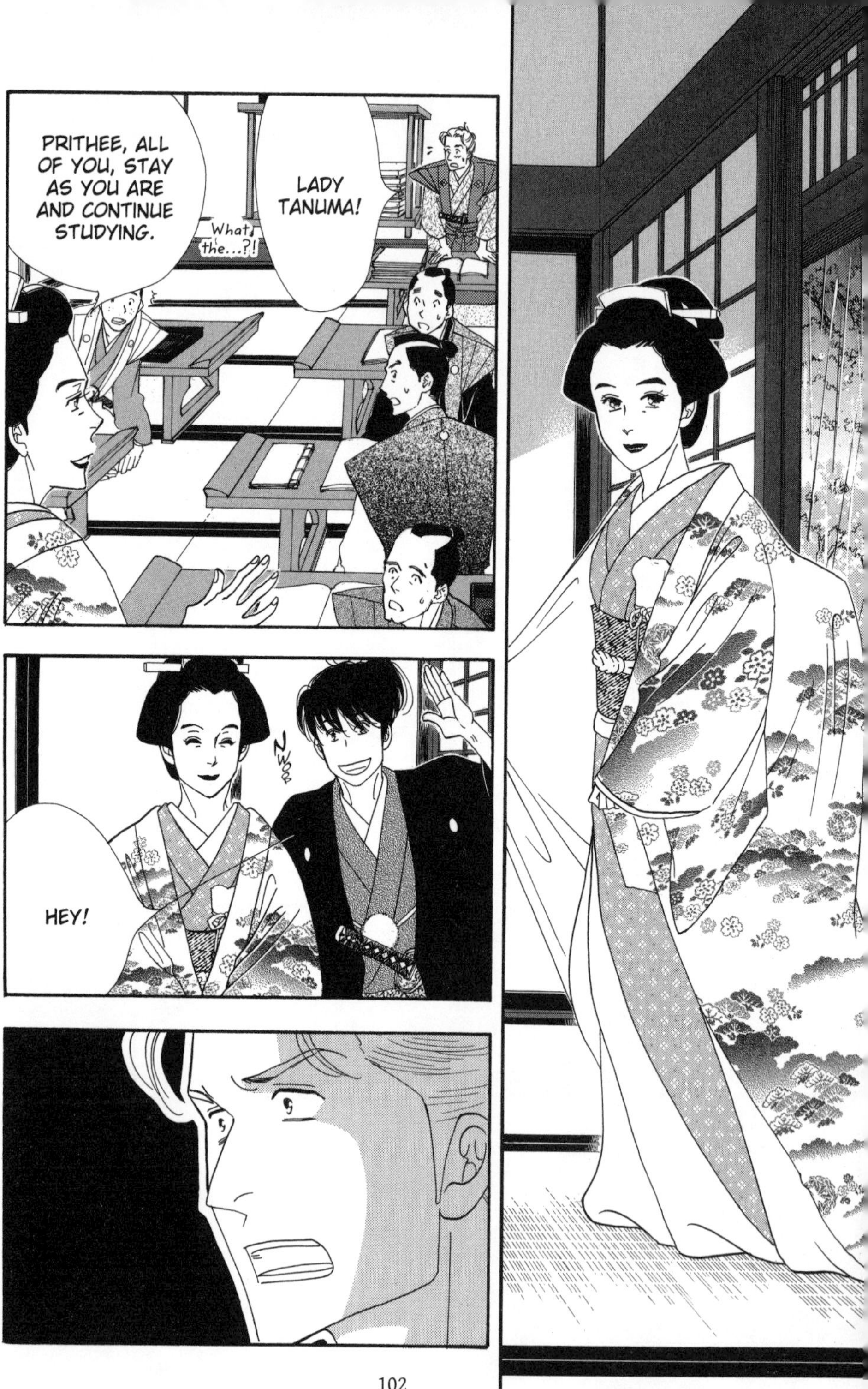
LADY TANUMA!
What the...?!
PRITHEE, ALL OF YOU, STAY AS YOU ARE AND CONTINUE STUDYING.
NWOOP
HEY!

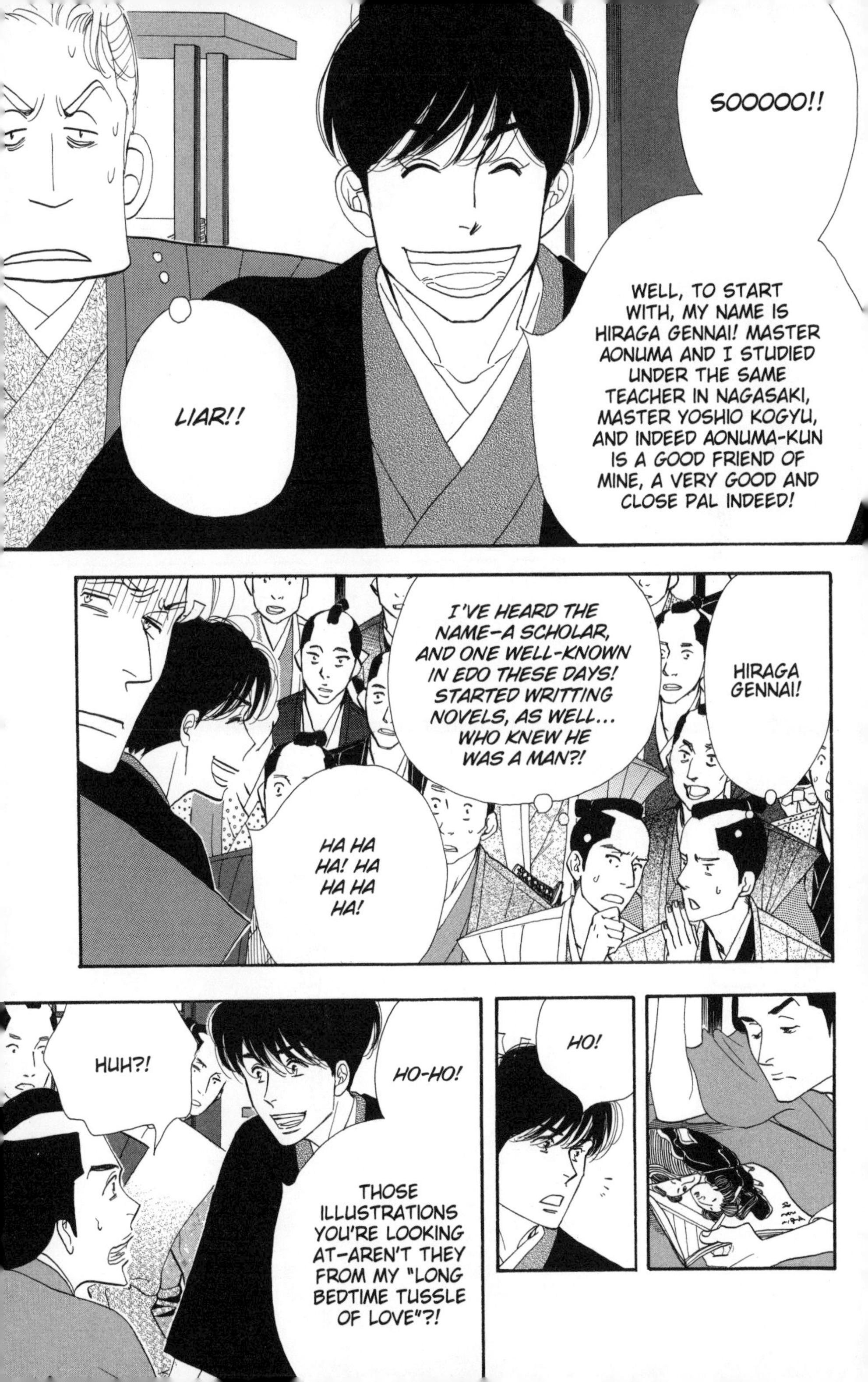
SOOOOO!!
WELL, TO START WITH, MY NAME IS HIRAGA GENNAI! MASTER AONUMA AND I STUDIED UNDER THE SAME TEACHER IN NAGASAKI, MASTER YOSHIO KOGYU, AND INDEED AONUMA-KUN IS A GOOD FRIEND OF MINE, A VERY GOOD AND CLOSE PAL INDEED!
LIAR!!
HIRAGA GENNAI!
I'VE HEARD THE NAME–A SCHOLAR, AND ONE WELL-KNOWN IN EDO THESE DAYS! STARTED WRITTING NOVELS, AS WELL... WHO KNEW HE WAS A MAN?!
HA HA HA! HA HA HA HA!
HO!
HO-HO!
THOSE ILLUSTRATIONS YOU'RE LOOKING AT–AREN'T THEY FROM MY "LONG BEDTIME TUSSLE OF LOVE"?!
HUH?!

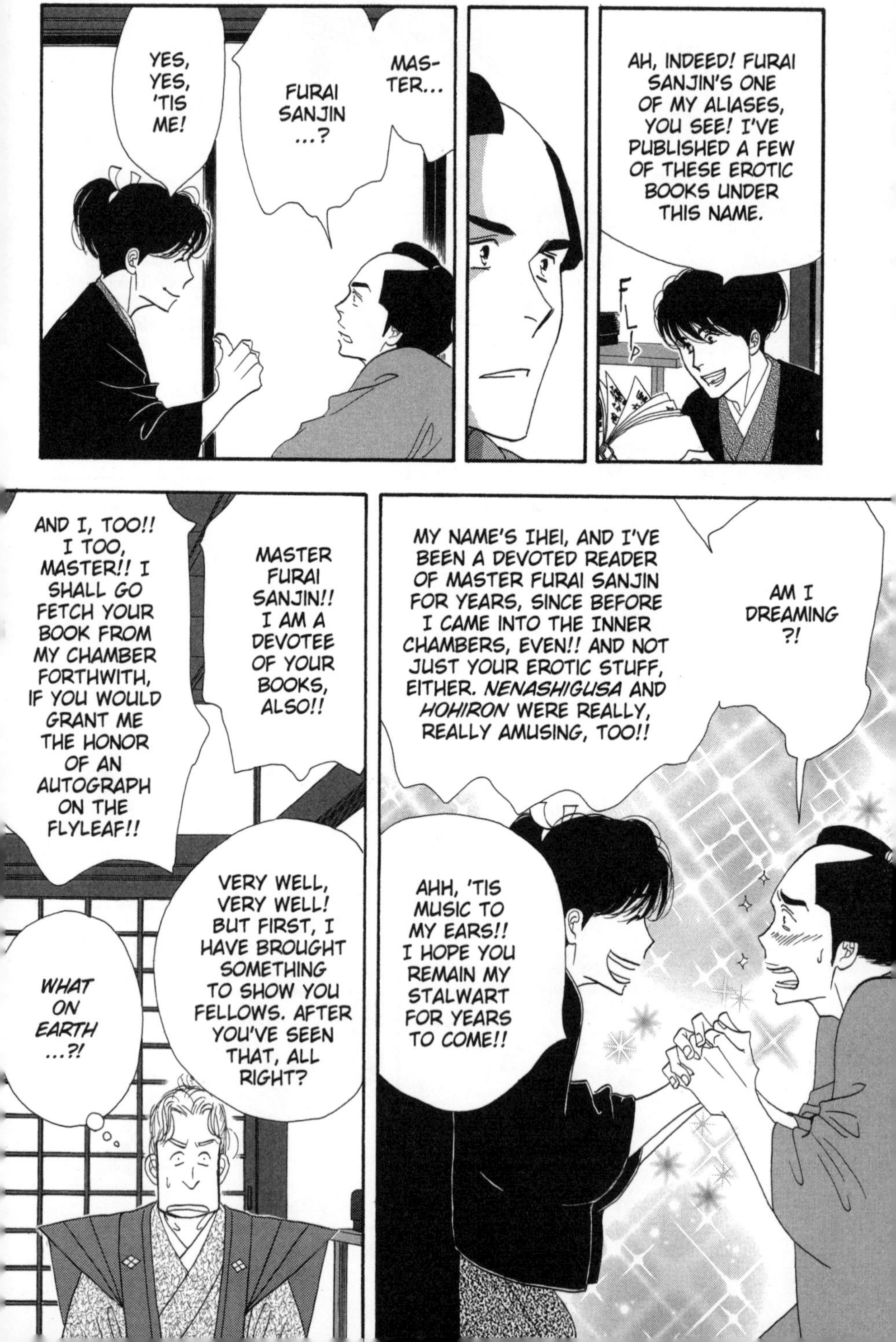
AH, INDEED! FURAI SANJIN'S ONE OF MY ALIASES, YOU SEE! I'VE PUBLISHED A FEW OF THESE EROTIC BOOKS UNDER THIS NAME.
FLIP
MASTER...
FURAI SANJIN ...?
YES, YES, 'TIS ME!
AM I DREAMING ?!
MY NAME'S IHEI, AND I'VE BEEN A DEVOTED READER OF MASTER FURAI SANJIN FOR YEARS, SINCE BEFORE I CAME INTO THE INNER CHAMBERS, EVEN!! AND NOT JUST YOUR EROTIC STUFF, EITHER. *NENASHIGUSA* AND *HOHIRON* WERE REALLY, REALLY AMUSING, TOO!!
AHH, 'TIS MUSIC TO MY EARS!! I HOPE YOU REMAIN MY STALWART FOR YEARS TO COME!!
MASTER FURAI SANJIN!! I AM A DEVOTEE OF YOUR BOOKS, ALSO!!
AND I, TOO!! I TOO, MASTER!! I SHALL GO FETCH YOUR BOOK FROM MY CHAMBER FORTHWITH, IF YOU WOULD GRANT ME THE HONOR OF AN AUTOGRAPH ON THE FLYLEAF!!
VERY WELL, VERY WELL! BUT FIRST, I HAVE BROUGHT SOMETHING TO SHOW YOU FELLOWS. AFTER YOU'VE SEEN THAT, ALL RIGHT?
WHAT ON EARTH ...?!

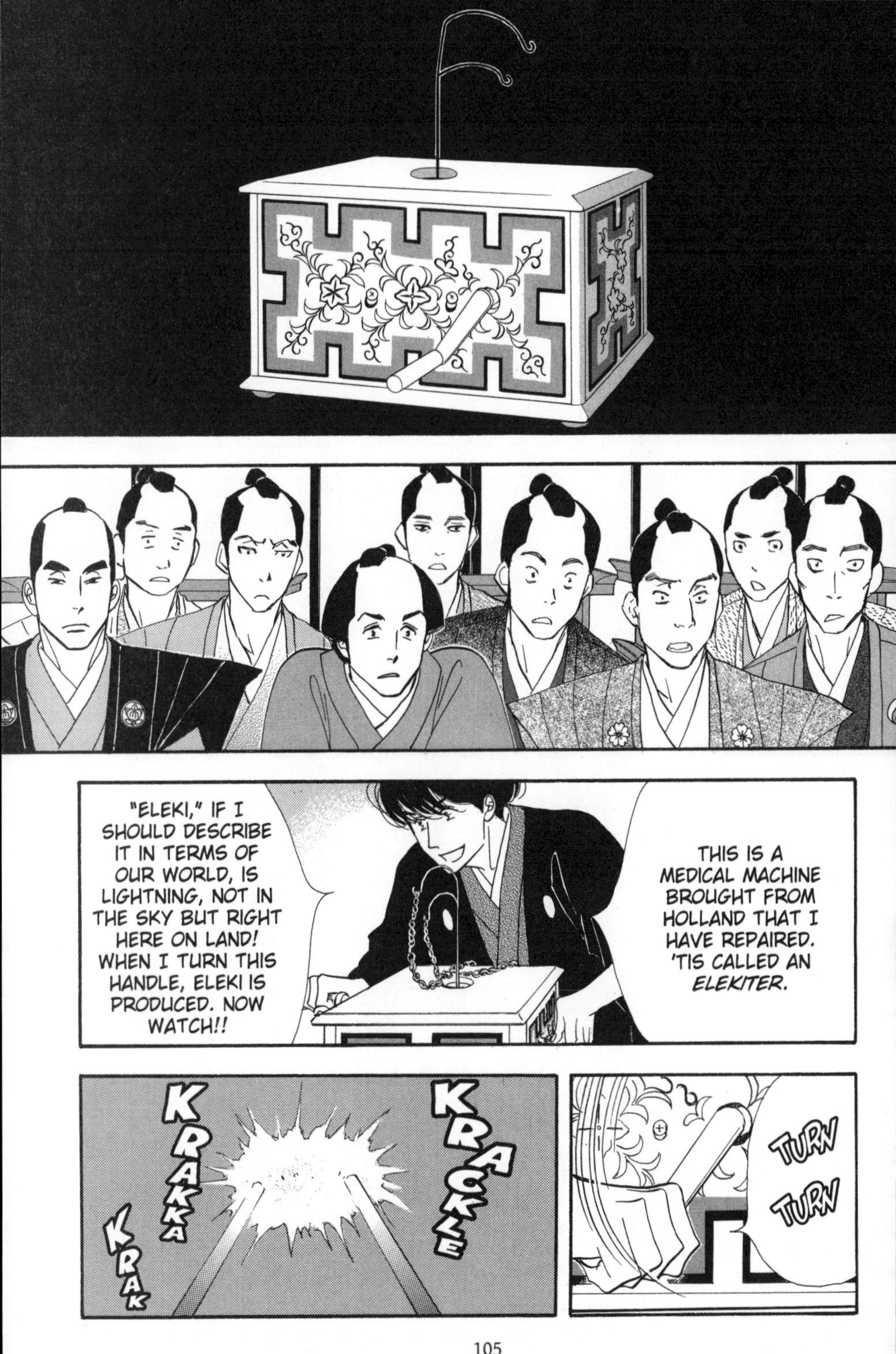
THIS IS A MEDICAL MACHINE BROUGHT FROM HOLLAND THAT I HAVE REPAIRED. 'TIS CALLED AN *ELEKITER*.
"ELEKI," IF I SHOULD DESCRIBE IT IN TERMS OF OUR WORLD, IS LIGHTNING, NOT IN THE SKY BUT RIGHT HERE ON LAND! WHEN I TURN THIS HANDLE, ELEKI IS PRODUCED. NOW WATCH!!
TURN TURN
KRACKLE
KRAKKA
KRAK

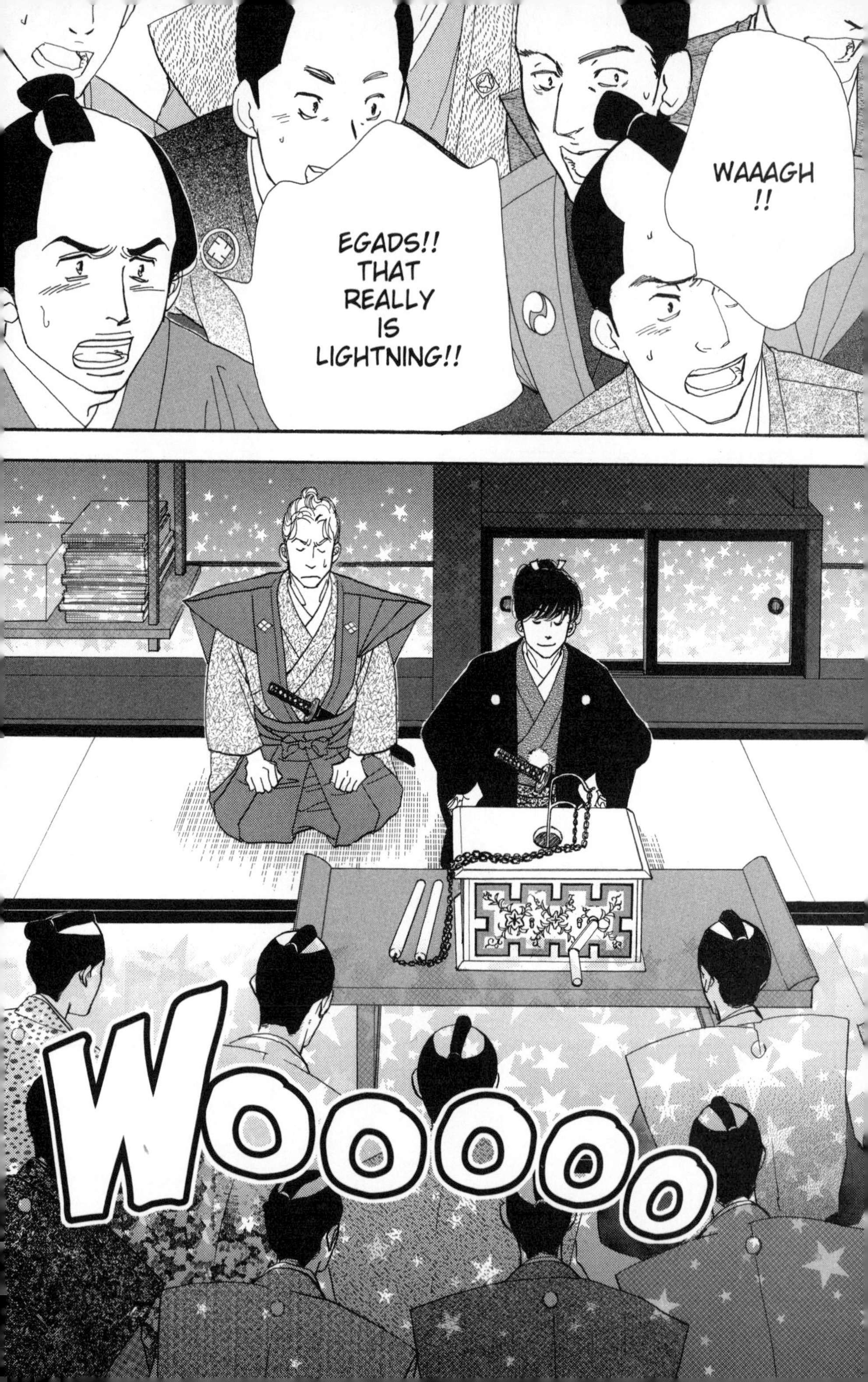
WAAAGH !!
EGADS!! THAT REALLY IS LIGHTNING!!
WOOOOO

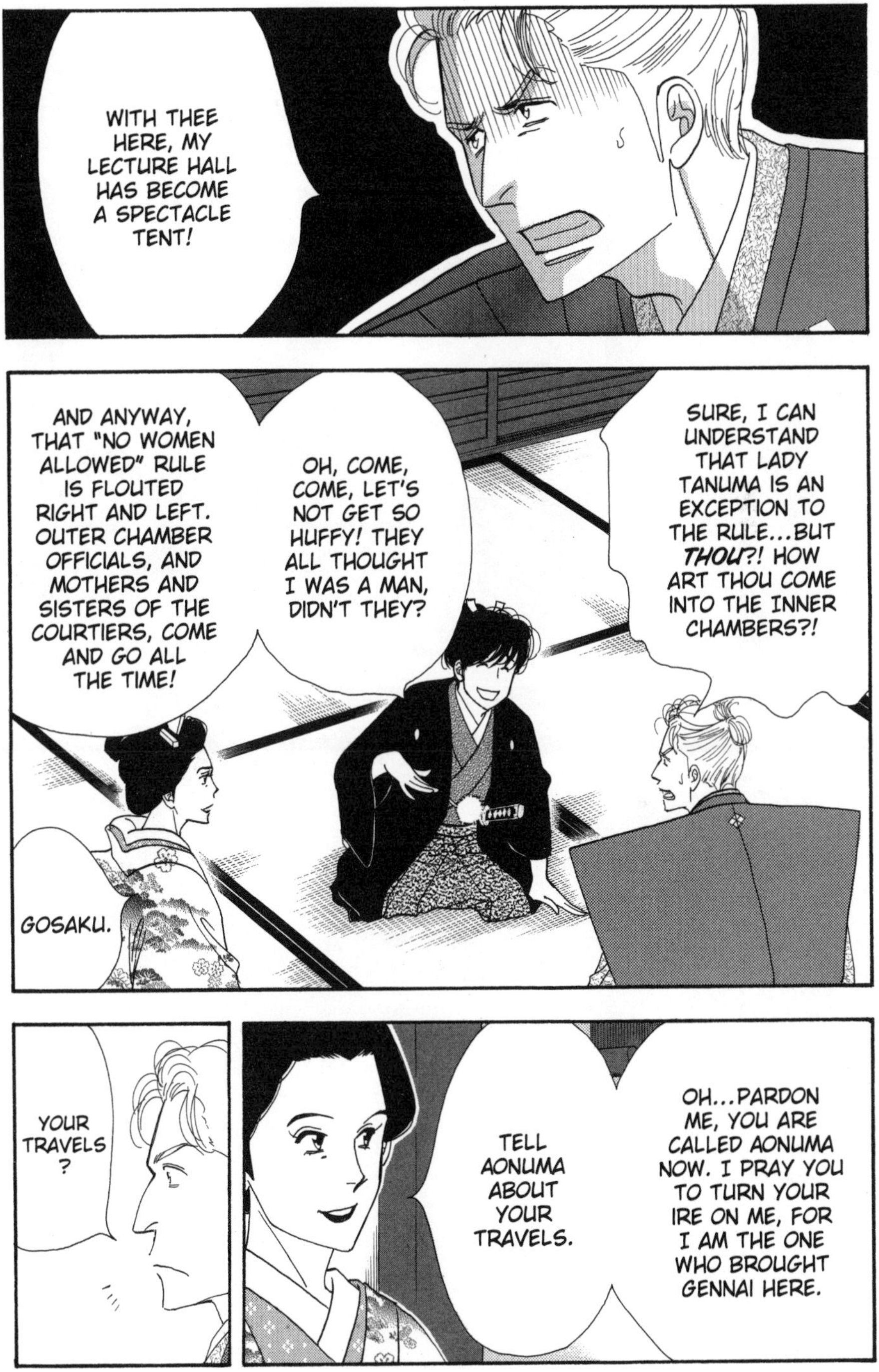
WITH THEE HERE, MY LECTURE HALL HAS BECOME A SPECTACLE TENT!
SURE, I CAN UNDERSTAND THAT LADY TANUMA IS AN EXCEPTION TO THE RULE...BUT *THOU*?! HOW ART THOU COME INTO THE INNER CHAMBERS?!
OH, COME, COME, LET'S NOT GET SO HUFFY! THEY ALL THOUGHT I WAS A MAN, DIDN'T THEY?
AND ANYWAY, THAT "NO WOMEN ALLOWED" RULE IS FLOUTED RIGHT AND LEFT. OUTER CHAMBER OFFICIALS, AND MOTHERS AND SISTERS OF THE COURTIERS, COME AND GO ALL THE TIME!
GOSAKU.
OH...PARDON ME, YOU ARE CALLED AONUMA NOW. I PRAY YOU TO TURN YOUR IRE ON ME, FOR I AM THE ONE WHO BROUGHT GENNAI HERE.
TELL AONUMA ABOUT YOUR TRAVELS.
YOUR TRAVELS?

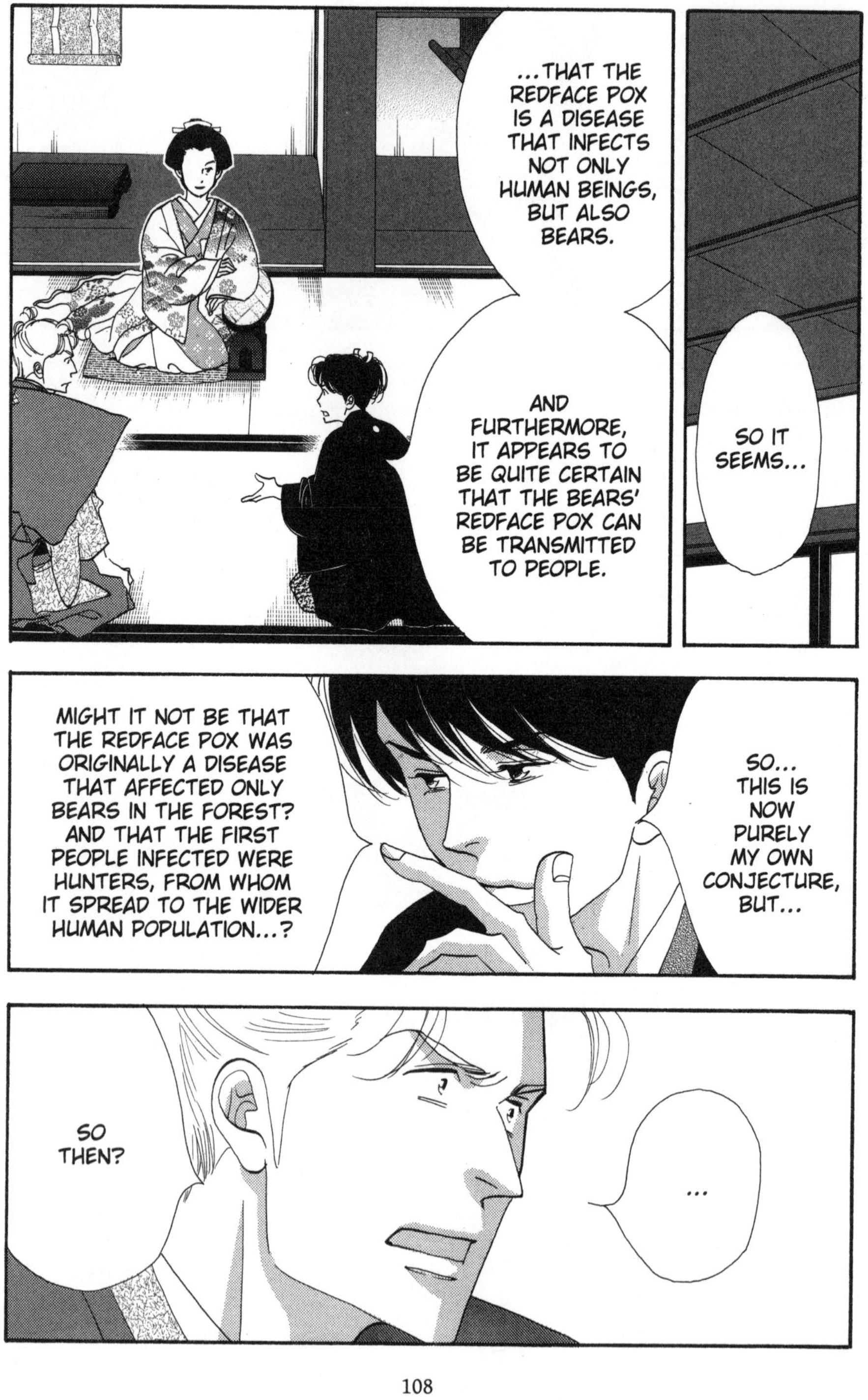
SO IT SEEMS...
...THAT THE REDFACE POX IS A DISEASE THAT INFECTS NOT ONLY HUMAN BEINGS, BUT ALSO BEARS.
AND FURTHERMORE, IT APPEARS TO BE QUITE CERTAIN THAT THE BEARS' REDFACE POX CAN BE TRANSMITTED TO PEOPLE.
SO... THIS IS NOW PURELY MY OWN CONJECTURE, BUT...
MIGHT IT NOT BE THAT THE REDFACE POX WAS ORIGINALLY A DISEASE THAT AFFECTED ONLY BEARS IN THE FOREST? AND THAT THE FIRST PEOPLE INFECTED WERE HUNTERS, FROM WHOM IT SPREAD TO THE WIDER HUMAN POPULATION...?
...
SO THEN?

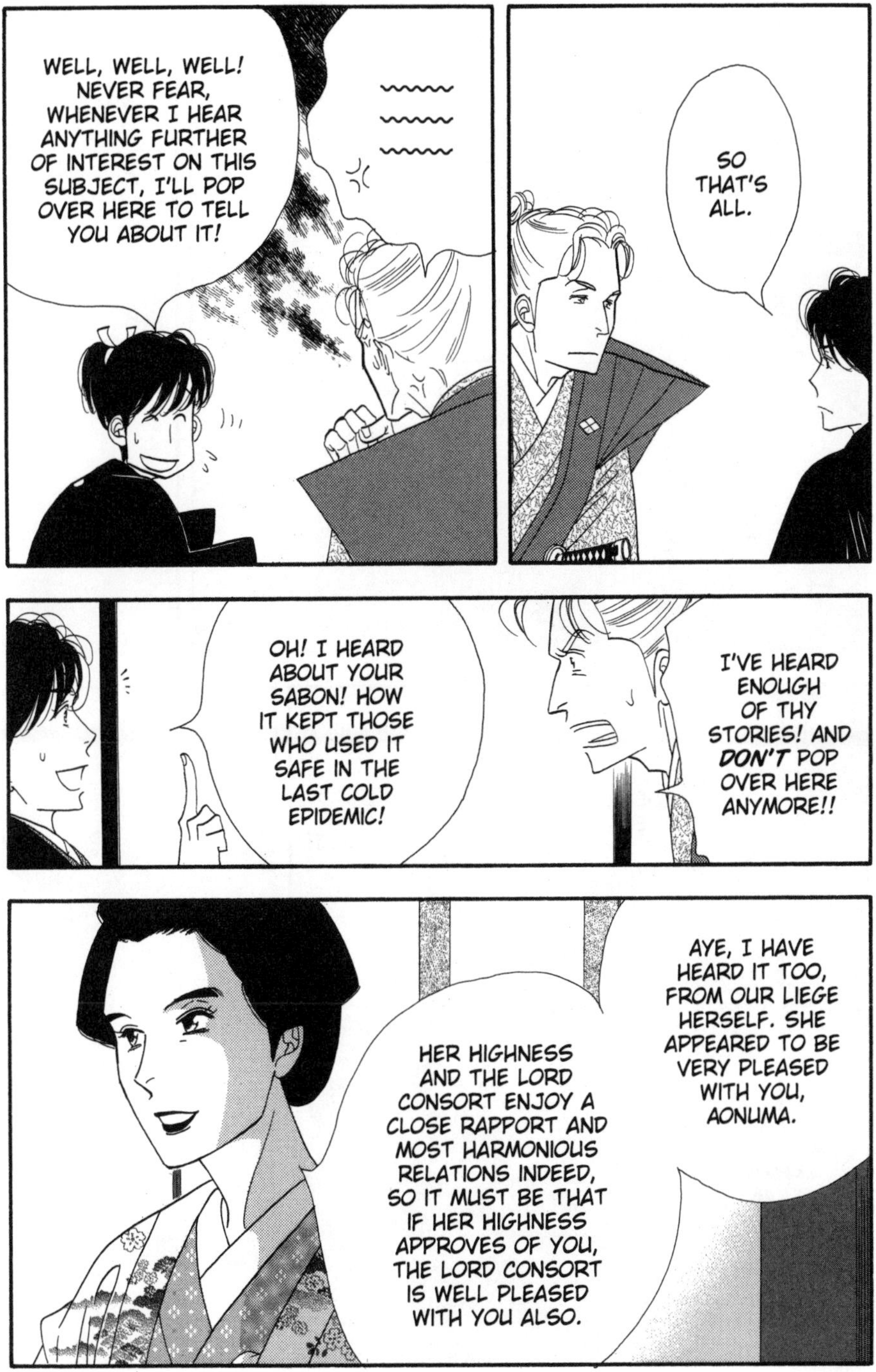
SO THAT'S ALL.
WELL, WELL, WELL! NEVER FEAR, WHENEVER I HEAR ANYTHING FURTHER OF INTEREST ON THIS SUBJECT, I'LL POP OVER HERE TO TELL YOU ABOUT IT!
I'VE HEARD ENOUGH OF THY STORIES! AND ***DON'T*** POP OVER HERE ANYMORE!!
OH! I HEARD ABOUT YOUR SABON! HOW IT KEPT THOSE WHO USED IT SAFE IN THE LAST COLD EPIDEMIC!
AYE, I HAVE HEARD IT TOO, FROM OUR LIEGE HERSELF. SHE APPEARED TO BE VERY PLEASED WITH YOU, AONUMA.
HER HIGHNESS AND THE LORD CONSORT ENJOY A CLOSE RAPPORT AND MOST HARMONIOUS RELATIONS INDEED, SO IT MUST BE THAT IF HER HIGHNESS APPROVES OF YOU, THE LORD CONSORT IS WELL PLEASED WITH YOU ALSO.

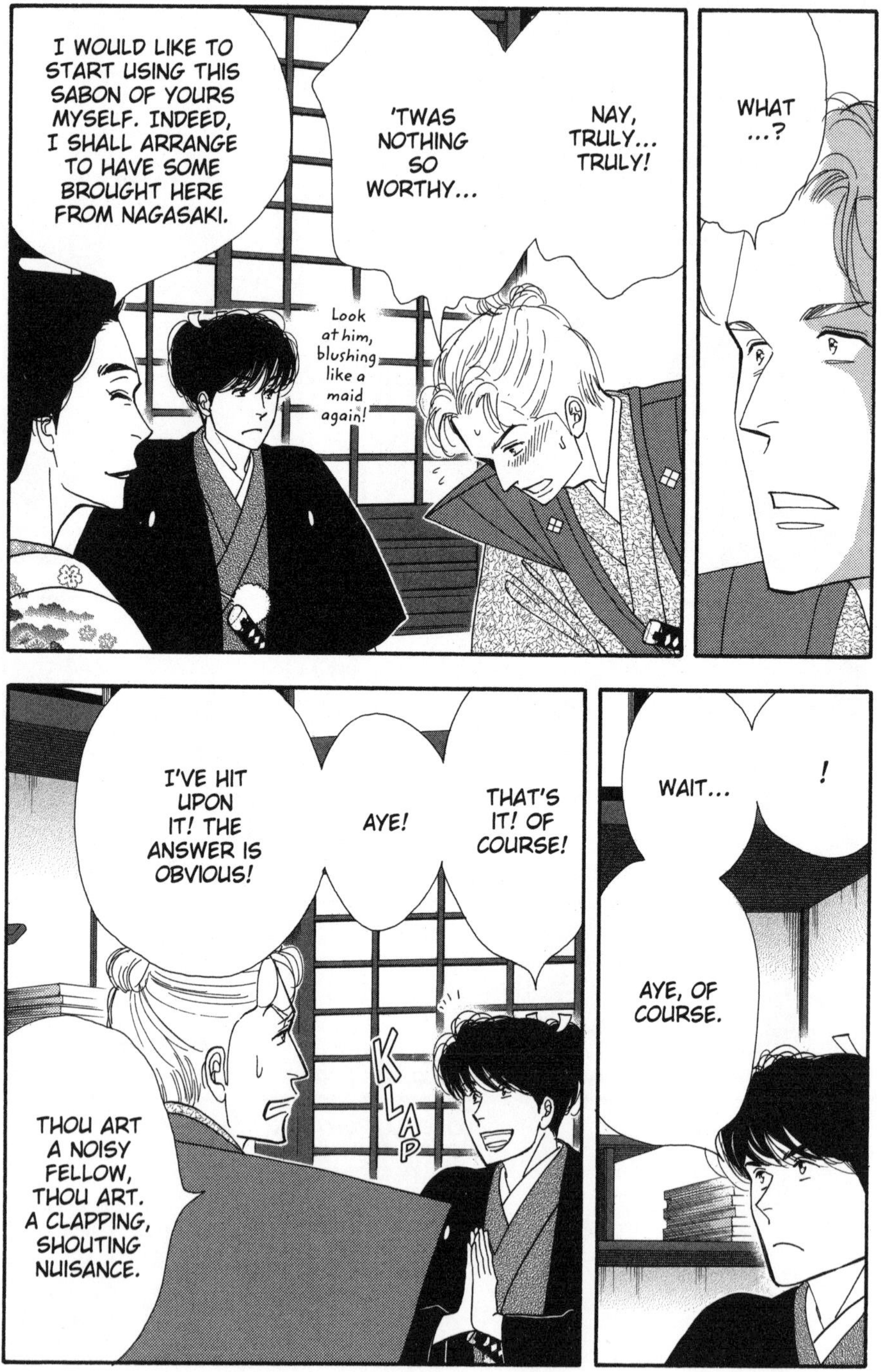

WHAT ...?
NAY, TRULY... TRULY!
'TWAS NOTHING SO WORTHY...
I WOULD LIKE TO START USING THIS SABON OF YOURS MYSELF. INDEED, I SHALL ARRANGE TO HAVE SOME BROUGHT HERE FROM NAGASAKI.
Look at him, blushing like a maid again!
!
WAIT...
AYE, OF COURSE.
THAT'S IT! OF COURSE!
AYE!
I'VE HIT UPON IT! THE ANSWER IS OBVIOUS!
KLAP
THOU ART A NOISY FELLOW, THOU ART. A CLAPPING, SHOUTING NUISANCE.

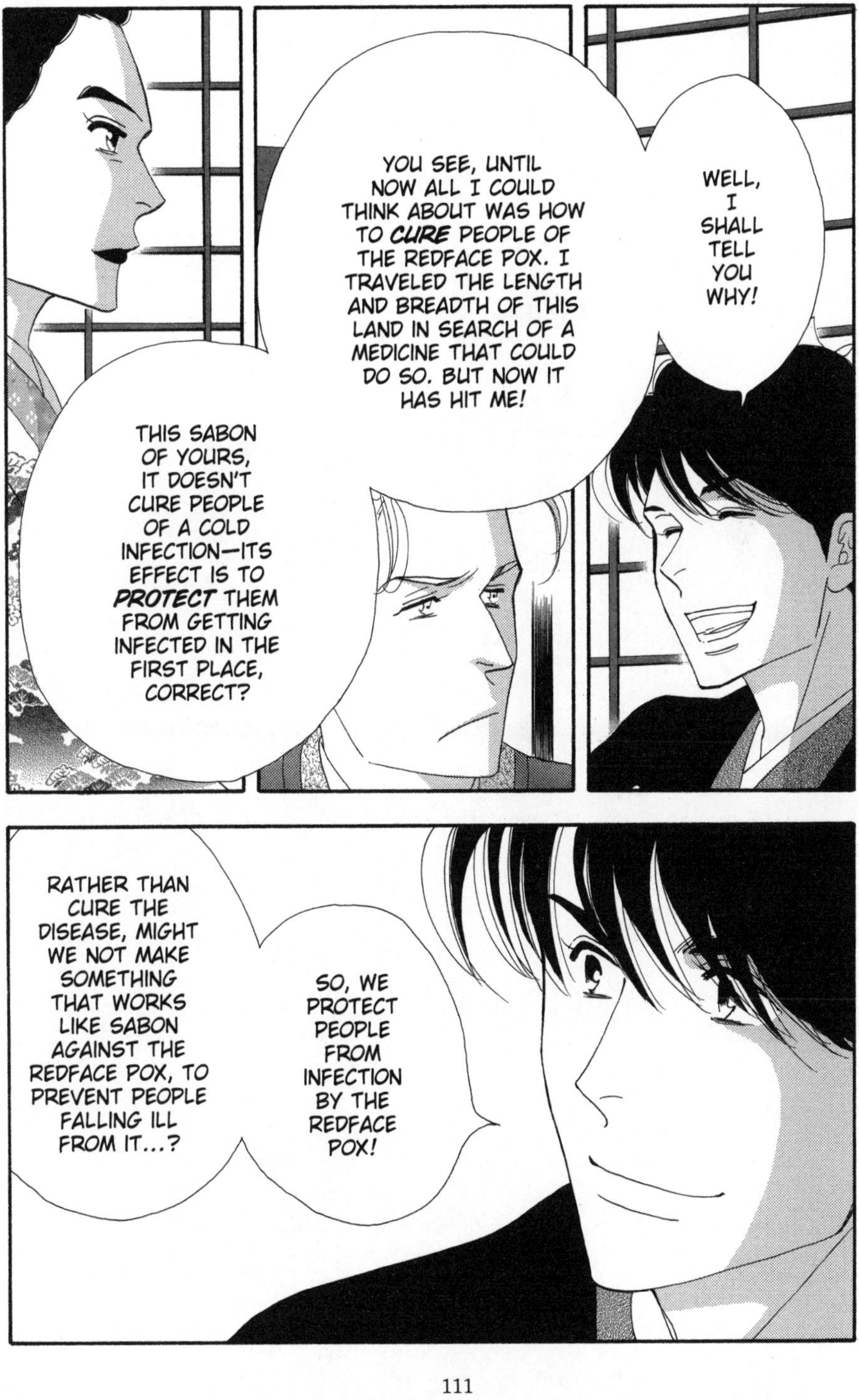
WELL, I SHALL TELL YOU WHY!
YOU SEE, UNTIL NOW ALL I COULD THINK ABOUT WAS HOW TO ***CURE*** PEOPLE OF THE REDFACE POX. I TRAVELED THE LENGTH AND BREADTH OF THIS LAND IN SEARCH OF A MEDICINE THAT COULD DO SO. BUT NOW IT HAS HIT ME!
THIS SABON OF YOURS, IT DOESN'T CURE PEOPLE OF A COLD INFECTION—ITS EFFECT IS TO ***PROTECT*** THEM FROM GETTING INFECTED IN THE FIRST PLACE, CORRECT?
RATHER THAN CURE THE DISEASE, MIGHT WE NOT MAKE SOMETHING THAT WORKS LIKE SABON AGAINST THE REDFACE POX, TO PREVENT PEOPLE FALLING ILL FROM IT...?
SO, WE PROTECT PEOPLE FROM INFECTION BY THE REDFACE POX!

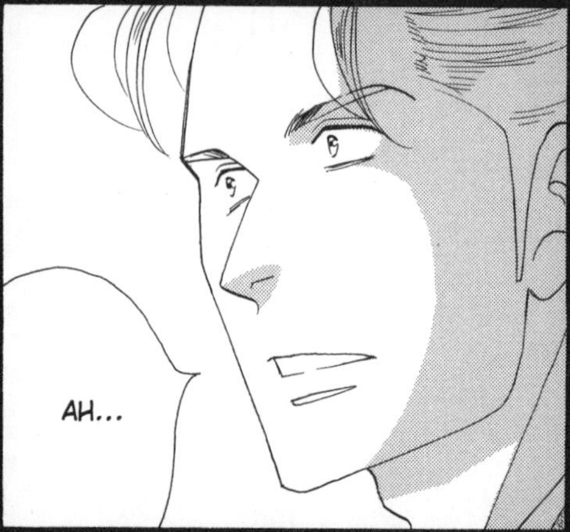
AH...

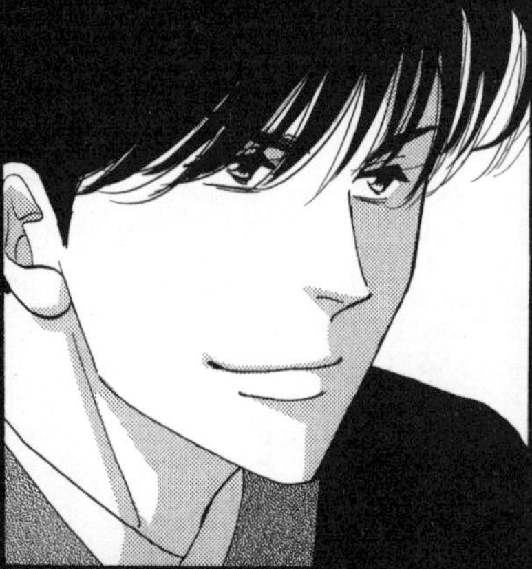

"Humanity hath
not as yet discovered
a way to prevent
disease entirely..."

Ōoku

THE INNER CHAMBERS

Ōoku

THE INNER CHAMBERS

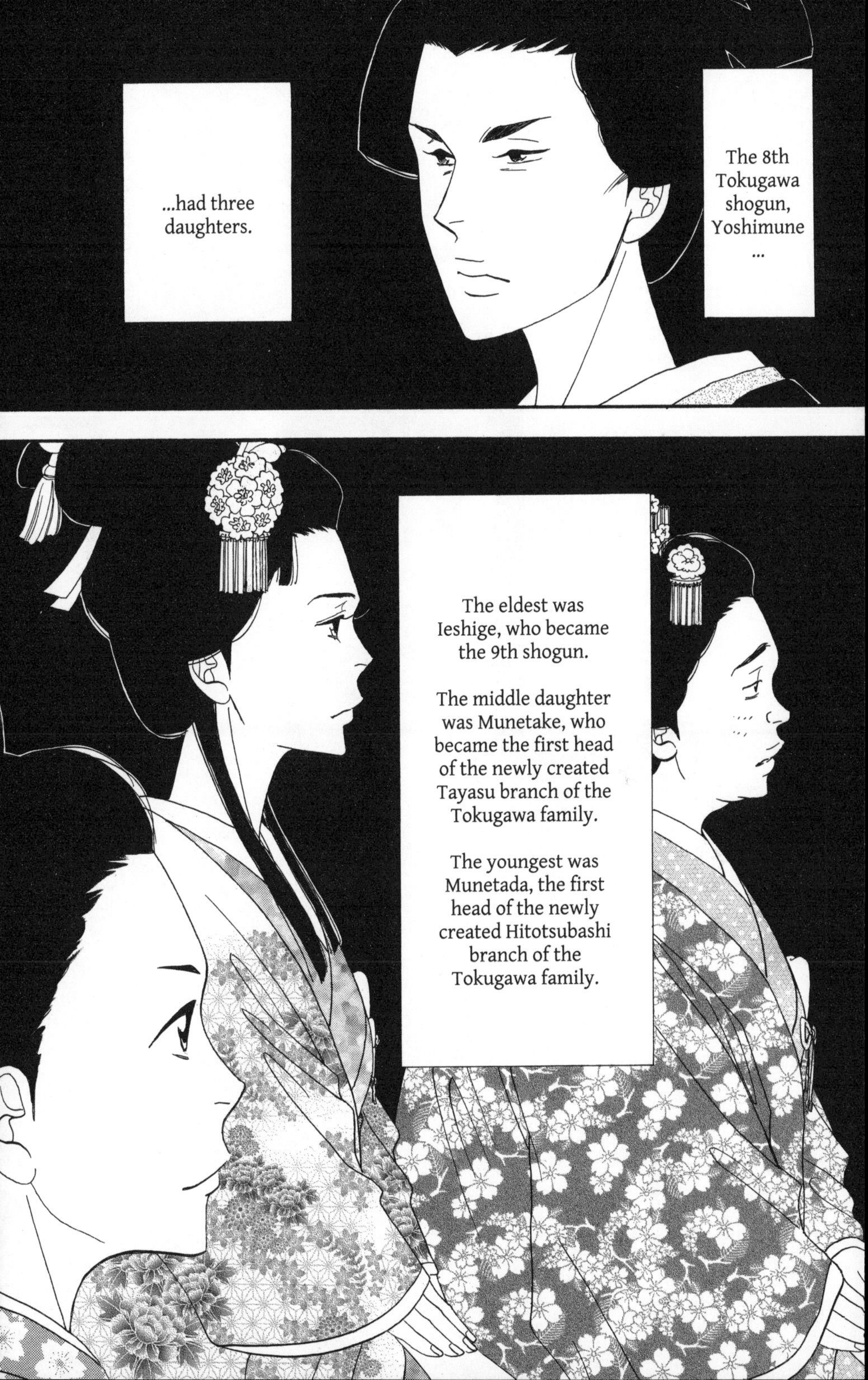
The 8th Tokugawa shogun, Yoshimune ...
...had three daughters.
The eldest was Ieshige, who became the 9th shogun.
The middle daughter was Munetake, who became the first head of the newly created Tayasu branch of the Tokugawa family.
The youngest was Munetada, the first head of the newly created Hitotsubashi branch of the Tokugawa family.

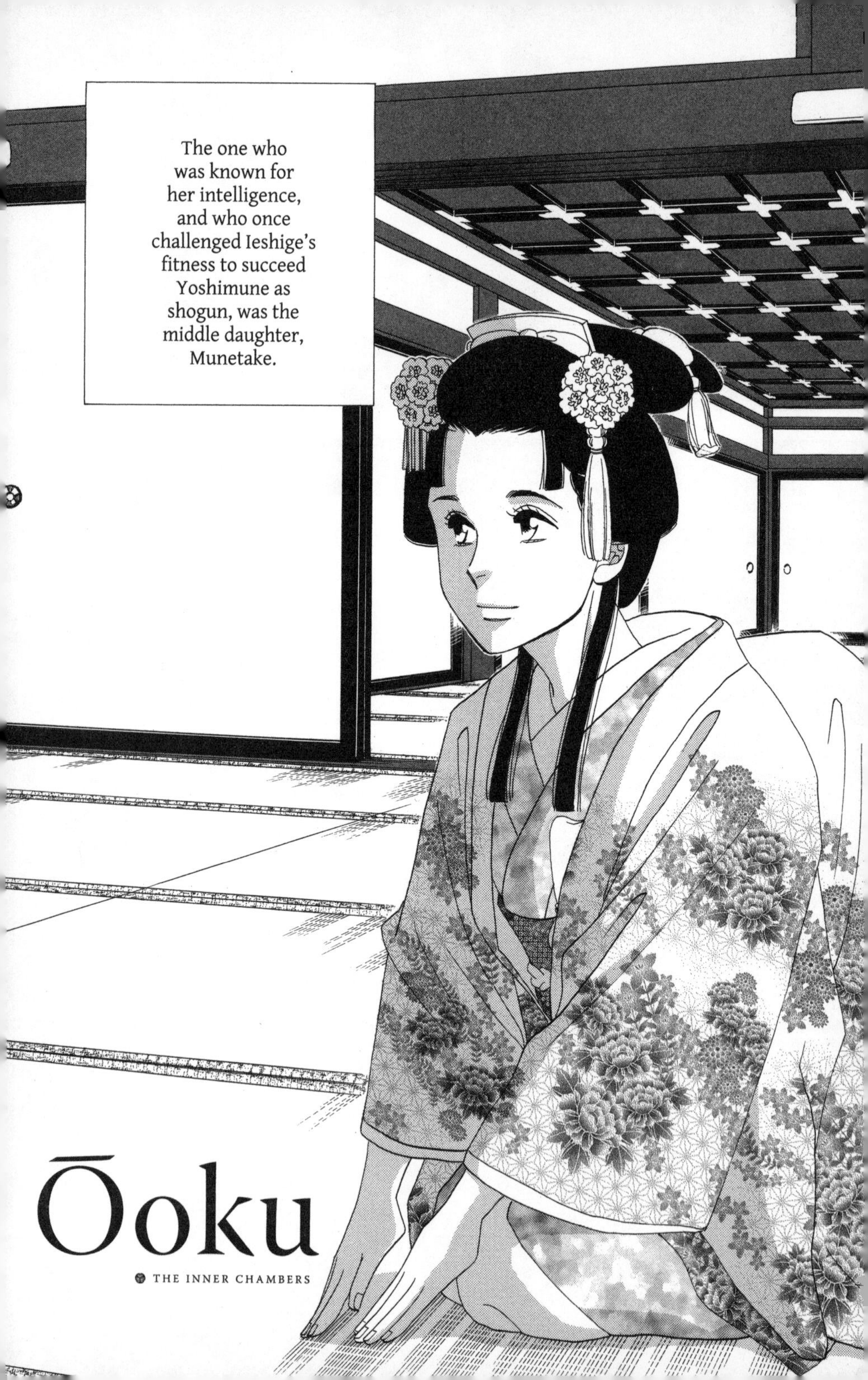
The one who was known for her intelligence, and who once challenged Ieshige's fitness to succeed Yoshimune as shogun, was the middle daughter, Munetake.
Ōoku
THE INNER CHAMBERS

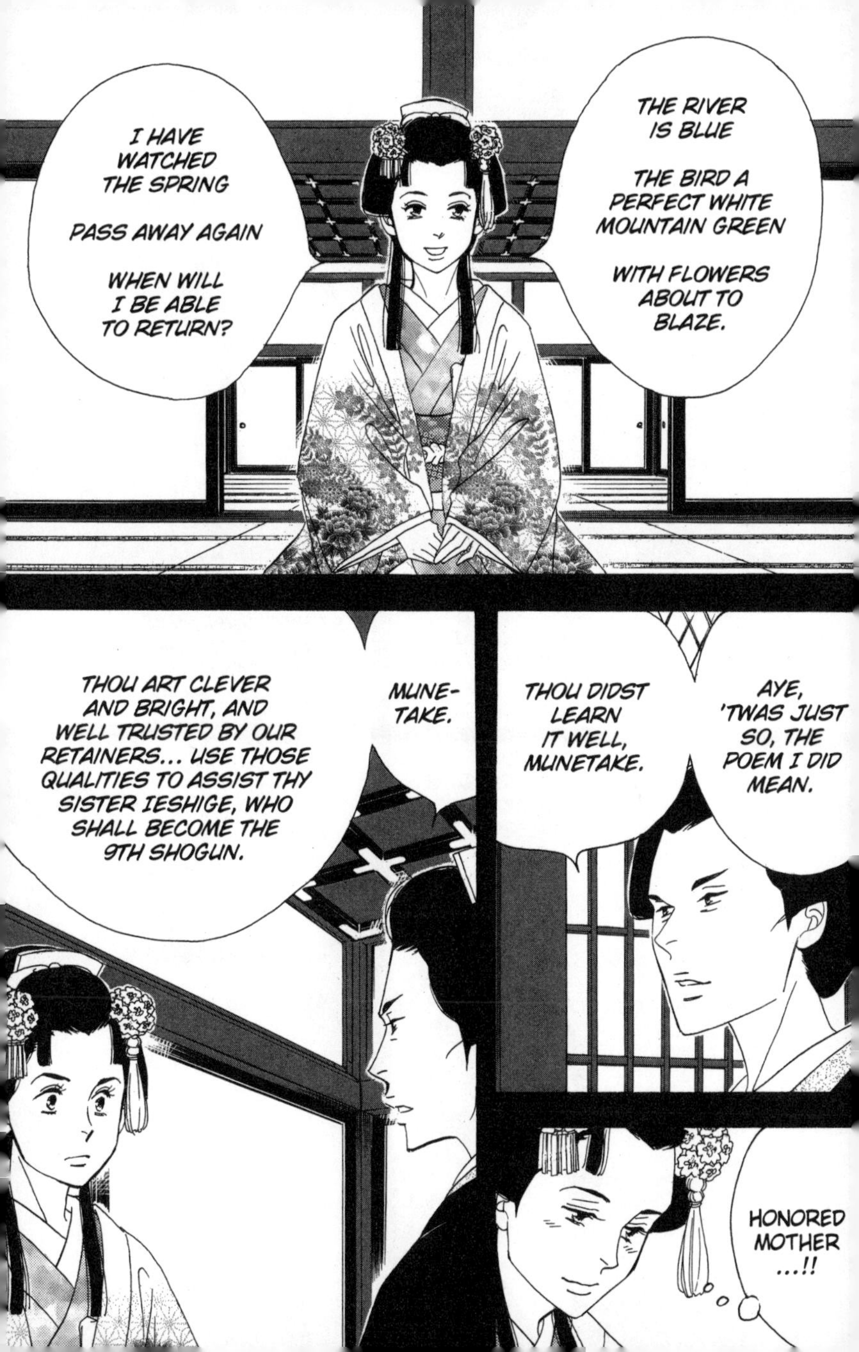
THE RIVER IS BLUE THE BIRD A PERFECT WHITE MOUNTAIN GREEN WITH FLOWERS ABOUT TO BLAZE.
I HAVE WATCHED THE SPRING PASS AWAY AGAIN WHEN WILL I BE ABLE TO RETURN?
AYE, 'TWAS JUST SO, THE POEM I DID MEAN.
THOU DIDST LEARN IT WELL, MUNETAKE.
HONORED MOTHER ...!!
MUNE-TAKE.
THOU ART CLEVER AND BRIGHT, AND WELL TRUSTED BY OUR RETAINERS... USE THOSE QUALITIES TO ASSIST THY SISTER IESHIGE, WHO SHALL BECOME THE 9TH SHOGUN.

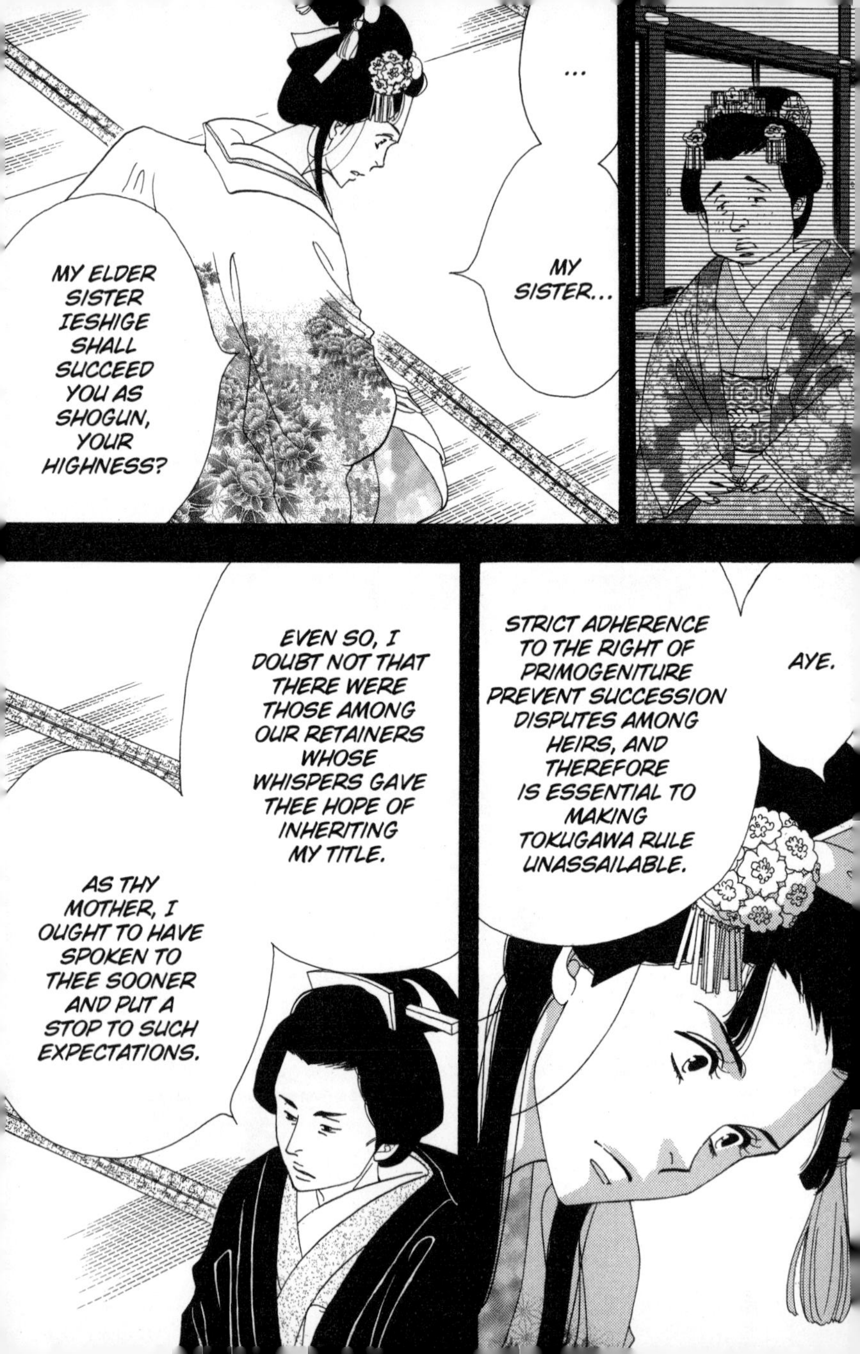
...
MY SISTER...
MY ELDER SISTER IESHIGE SHALL SUCCEED YOU AS SHOGUN, YOUR HIGHNESS?
AYE.
STRICT ADHERENCE TO THE RIGHT OF PRIMOGENITURE PREVENT SUCCESSION DISPUTES AMONG HEIRS, AND THEREFORE IS ESSENTIAL TO MAKING TOKUGAWA RULE UNASSAILABLE.
EVEN SO, I DOUBT NOT THAT THERE WERE THOSE AMONG OUR RETAINERS WHOSE WHISPERS GAVE THEE HOPE OF INHERITING MY TITLE.
AS THY MOTHER, I OUGHT TO HAVE SPOKEN TO THEE SOONER AND PUT A STOP TO SUCH EXPECTATIONS.

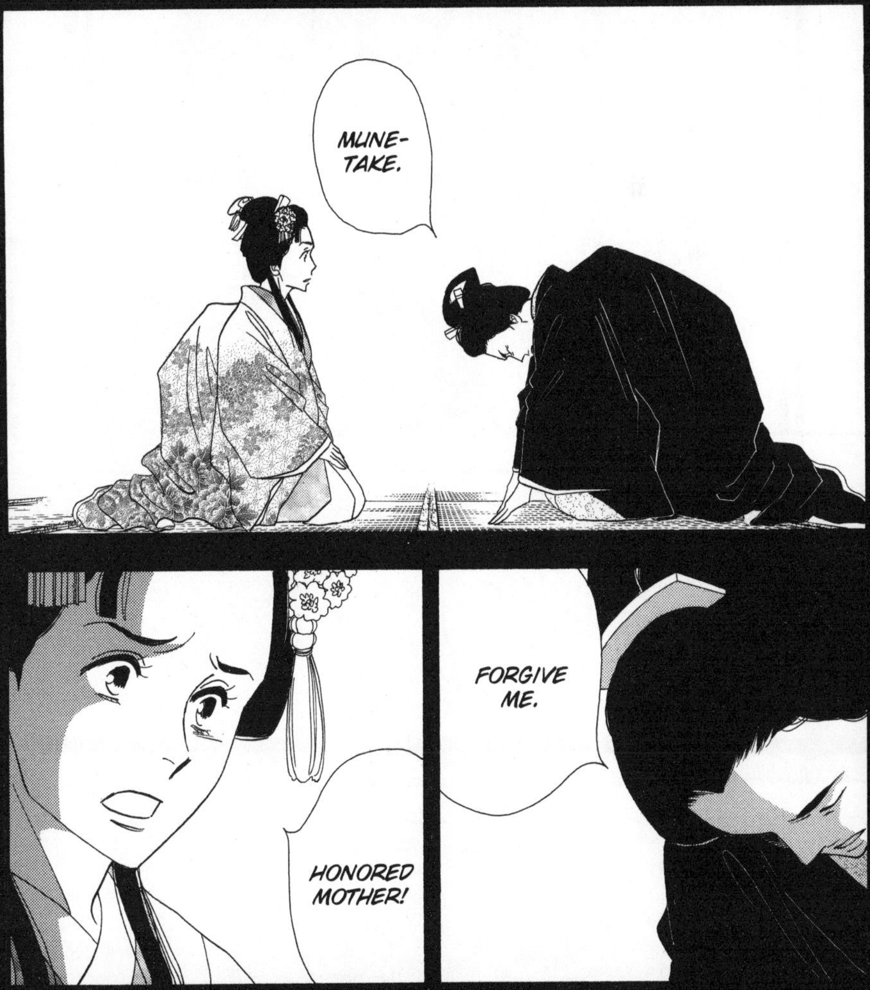
MUNE-TAKE.
FORGIVE ME.
HONORED MOTHER!

IF...

IF THERE WERE NO RULE DEMANDING THAT YOUR FIRSTBORN CHILD BE YOUR HEIR, YOU WOULD HAVE CHOSEN ME, NOT MY SISTER IESHIGE, BUT ME, MUNETAKE, TO SUCCEED YOU. RIGHT, HONORED MOTHER?

AFTER ALL... EVERYBODY ALWAYS SAID I WAS THE ONE, OF YOUR THREE DAUGHTERS, WHO MOST CLOSELY RESEMBLED YOU. EVERYBODY SAID SO!

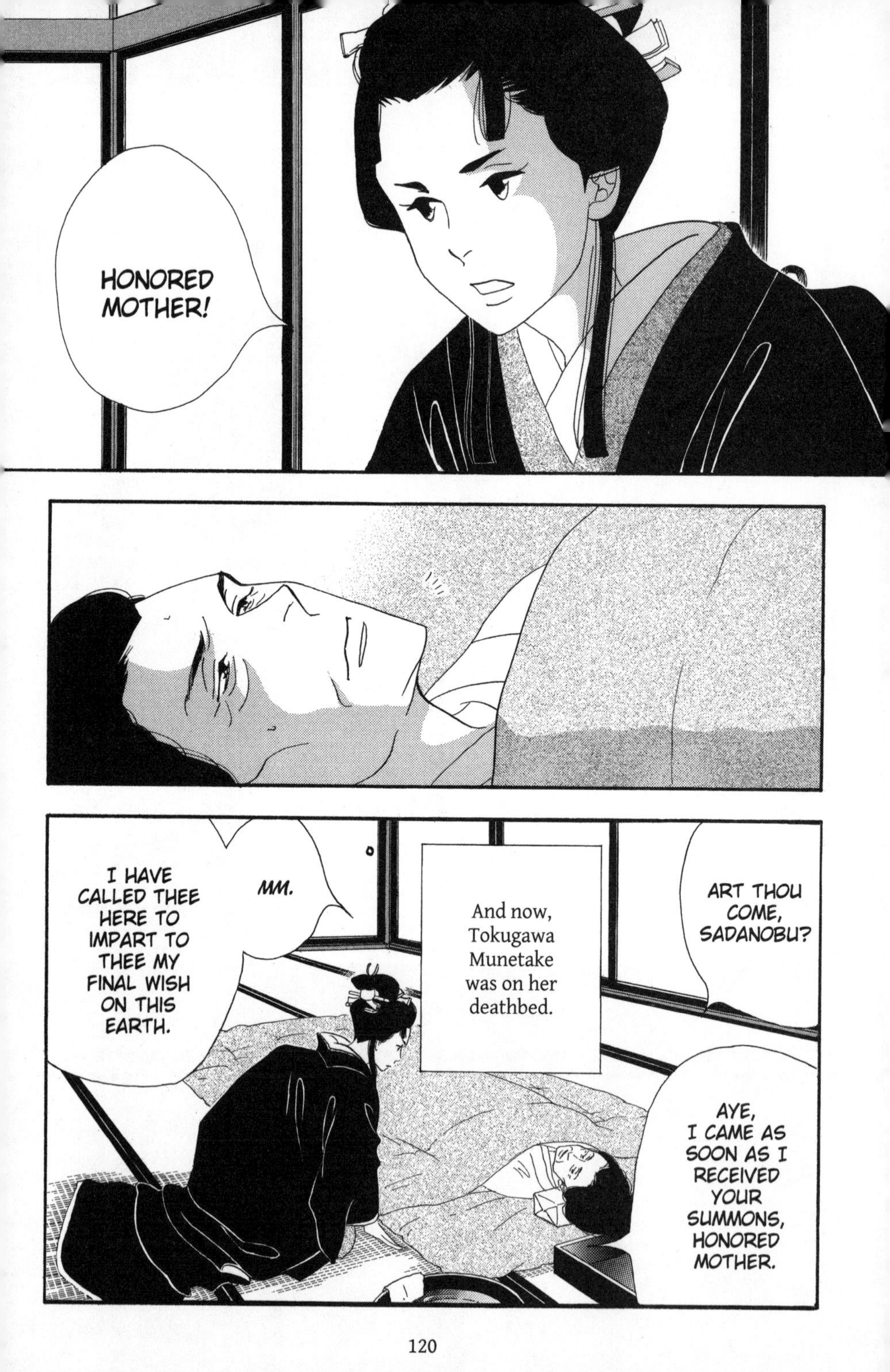
HONORED MOTHER!
ART THOU COME, SADANOBU?
And now, Tokugawa Munetake was on her deathbed.
AYE, I CAME AS SOON AS I RECEIVED YOUR SUMMONS, HONORED MOTHER.
MM.
I HAVE CALLED THEE HERE TO IMPART TO THEE MY FINAL WISH ON THIS EARTH.

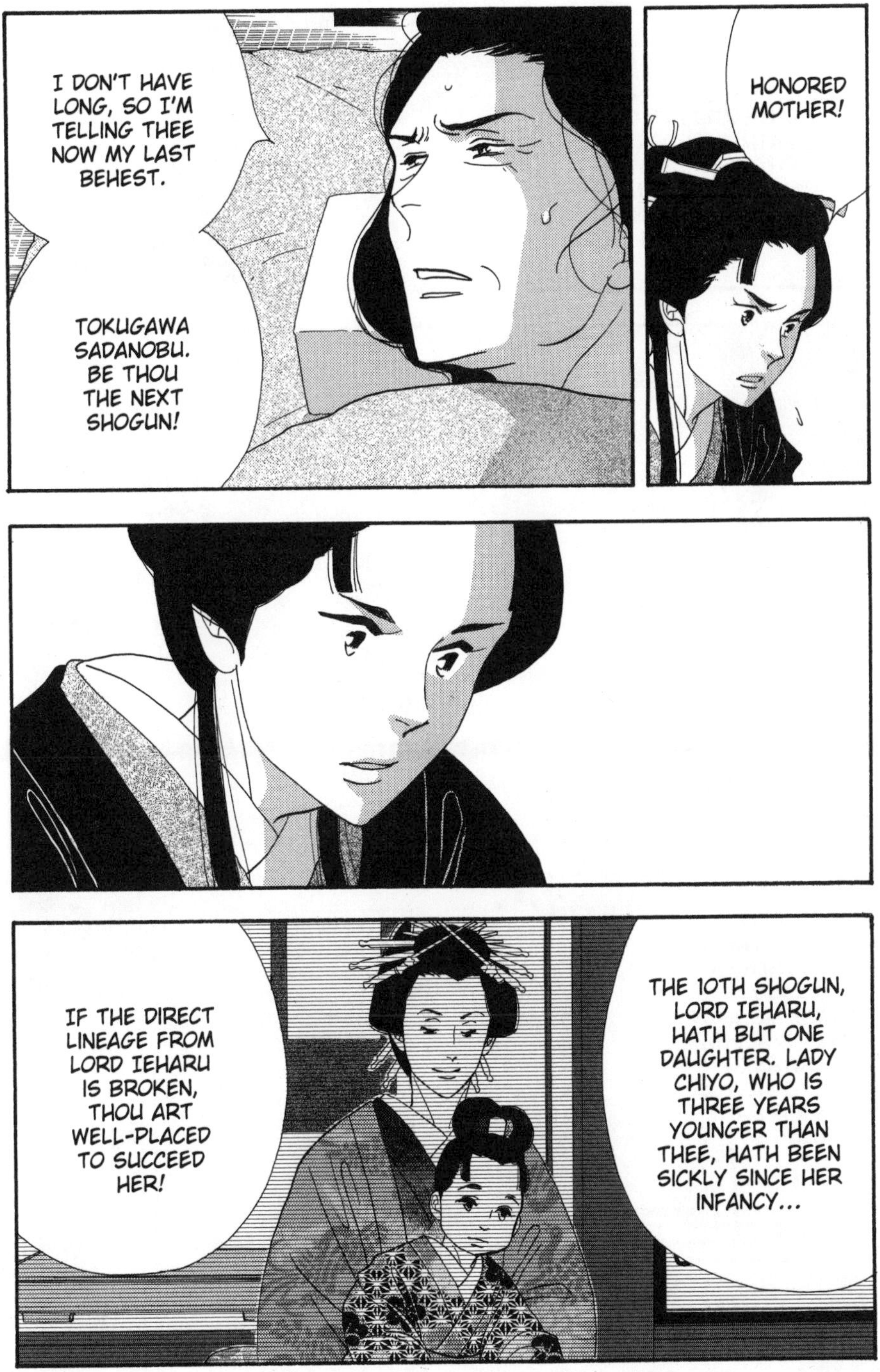
HONORED MOTHER!
I DON'T HAVE LONG, SO I'M TELLING THEE NOW MY LAST BEHEST.
TOKUGAWA SADANOBU. BE THOU THE NEXT SHOGUN!
THE 10TH SHOGUN, LORD IEHARU, HATH BUT ONE DAUGHTER. LADY CHIYO, WHO IS THREE YEARS YOUNGER THAN THEE, HATH BEEN SICKLY SINCE HER INFANCY...
IF THE DIRECT LINEAGE FROM LORD IEHARU IS BROKEN, THOU ART WELL-PLACED TO SUCCEED HER!

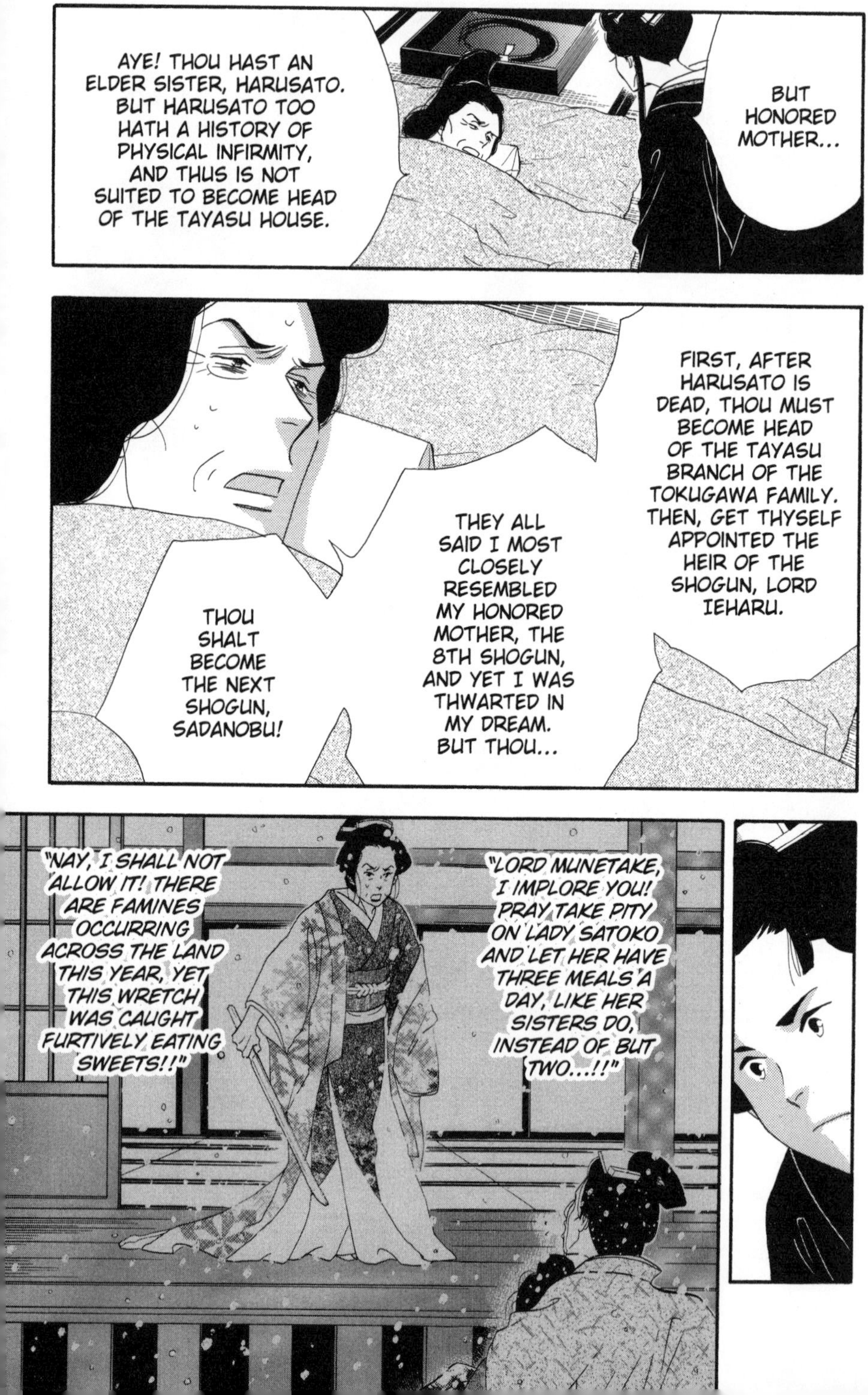
BUT HONORED MOTHER...
AYE! THOU HAST AN ELDER SISTER, HARUSATO. BUT HARUSATO TOO HATH A HISTORY OF PHYSICAL INFIRMITY, AND THUS IS NOT SUITED TO BECOME HEAD OF THE TAYASU HOUSE.
FIRST, AFTER HARUSATO IS DEAD, THOU MUST BECOME HEAD OF THE TAYASU BRANCH OF THE TOKUGAWA FAMILY. THEN, GET THYSELF APPOINTED THE HEIR OF THE SHOGUN, LORD IEHARU.
THEY ALL SAID I MOST CLOSELY RESEMBLED MY HONORED MOTHER, THE 8TH SHOGUN, AND YET I WAS THWARTED IN MY DREAM. BUT THOU...
THOU SHALT BECOME THE NEXT SHOGUN, SADANOBU!
"LORD MUNETAKE, I IMPLORE YOU! PRAY TAKE PITY ON LADY SATOKO AND LET HER HAVE THREE MEALS A DAY, LIKE HER SISTERS DO, INSTEAD OF BUT TWO...!!"
"NAY, I SHALL NOT ALLOW IT! THERE ARE FAMINES OCCURRING ACROSS THE LAND THIS YEAR, YET THIS WRETCH WAS CAUGHT FURTIVELY EATING SWEETS!!"

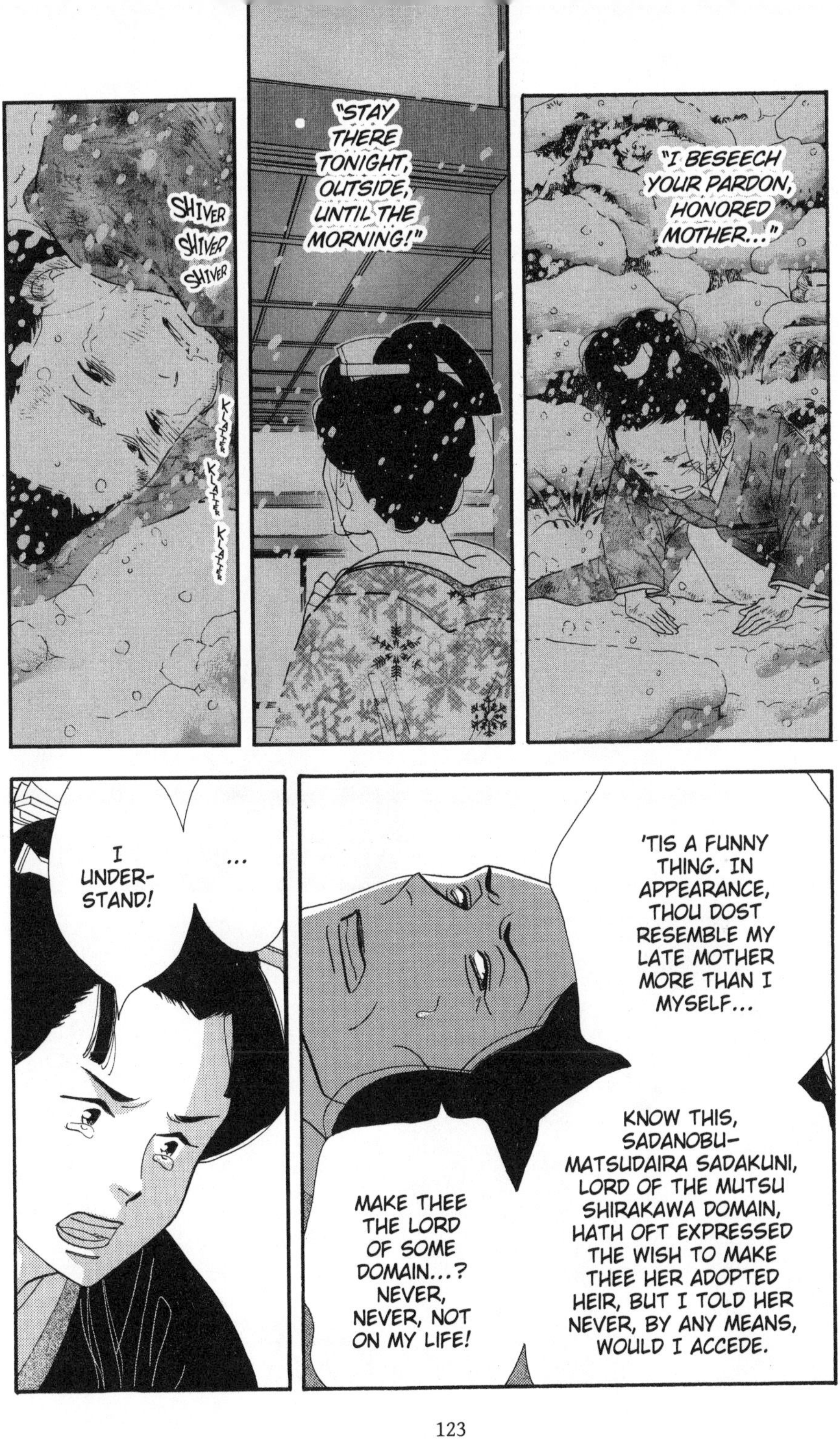
"I BESEECH YOUR PARDON, HONORED MOTHER..."
"STAY THERE TONIGHT, OUTSIDE, UNTIL THE MORNING!"
SHIVER SHIVER SHIVER
KLATTER KLATTER KLATTER
'TIS A FUNNY THING. IN APPEARANCE, THOU DOST RESEMBLE MY LATE MOTHER MORE THAN I MYSELF...
KNOW THIS, SADANOBU– MATSUDAIRA SADAKUNI, LORD OF THE MUTSU SHIRAKAWA DOMAIN, HATH OFT EXPRESSED THE WISH TO MAKE THEE HER ADOPTED HEIR, BUT I TOLD HER NEVER, BY ANY MEANS, WOULD I ACCEDE.
MAKE THEE THE LORD OF SOME DOMAIN...? NEVER, NEVER, NOT ON MY LIFE!
...
I UNDERSTAND!

THOU DOST UNDERSTAND NOW ALSO WHY THY MOTHER DID TREAT THEE SO HARSHLY THUS FAR?

AYE...!!

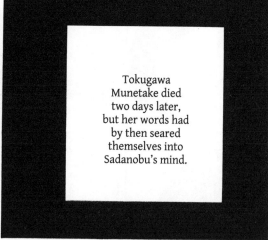

Tokugawa Munetake died two days later, but her words had by then seared themselves into Sadanobu's mind.

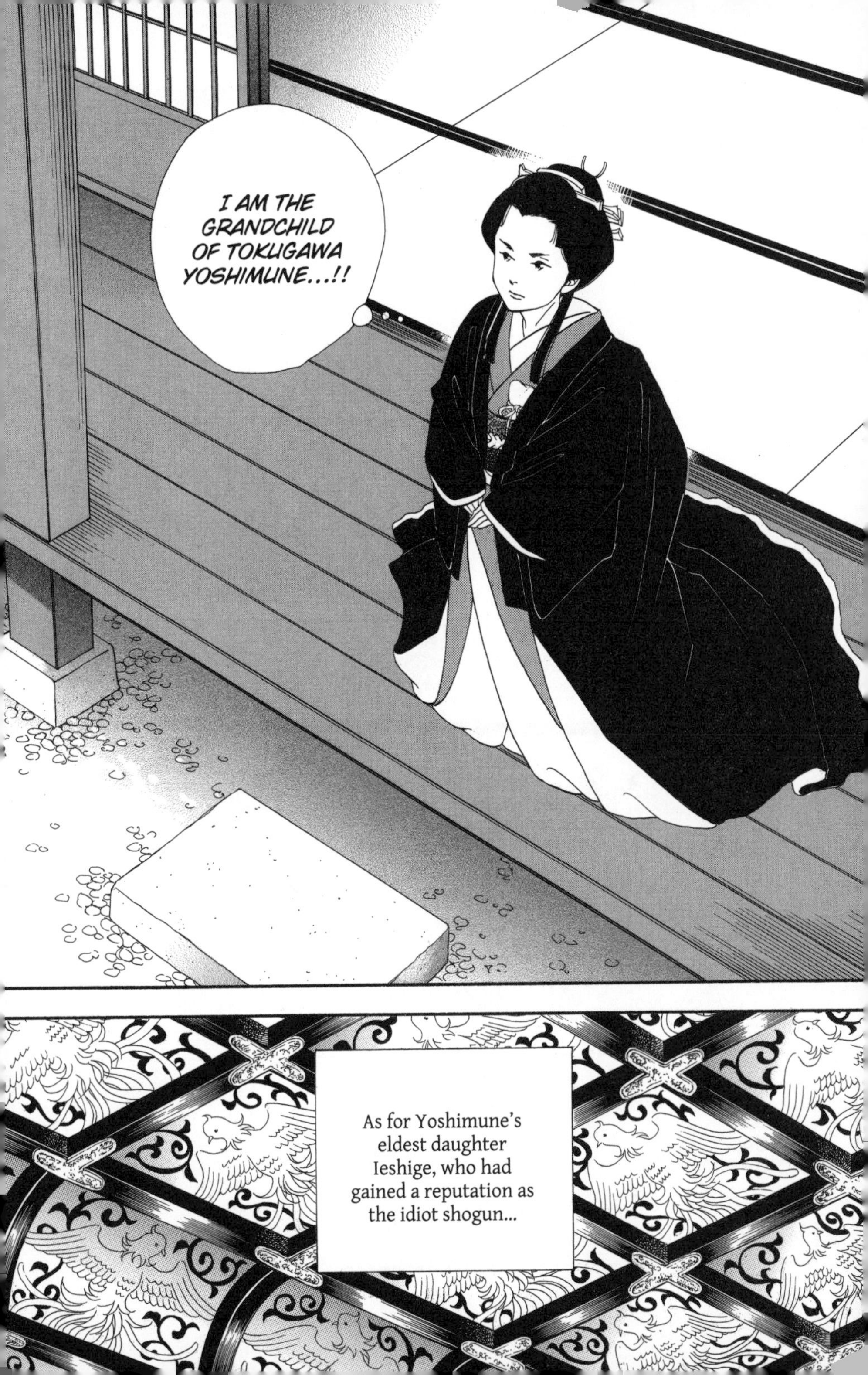
I AM THE GRANDCHILD OF TOKUGAWA YOSHIMUNE...!!
As for Yoshimune's eldest daughter Ieshige, who had gained a reputation as the idiot shogun...

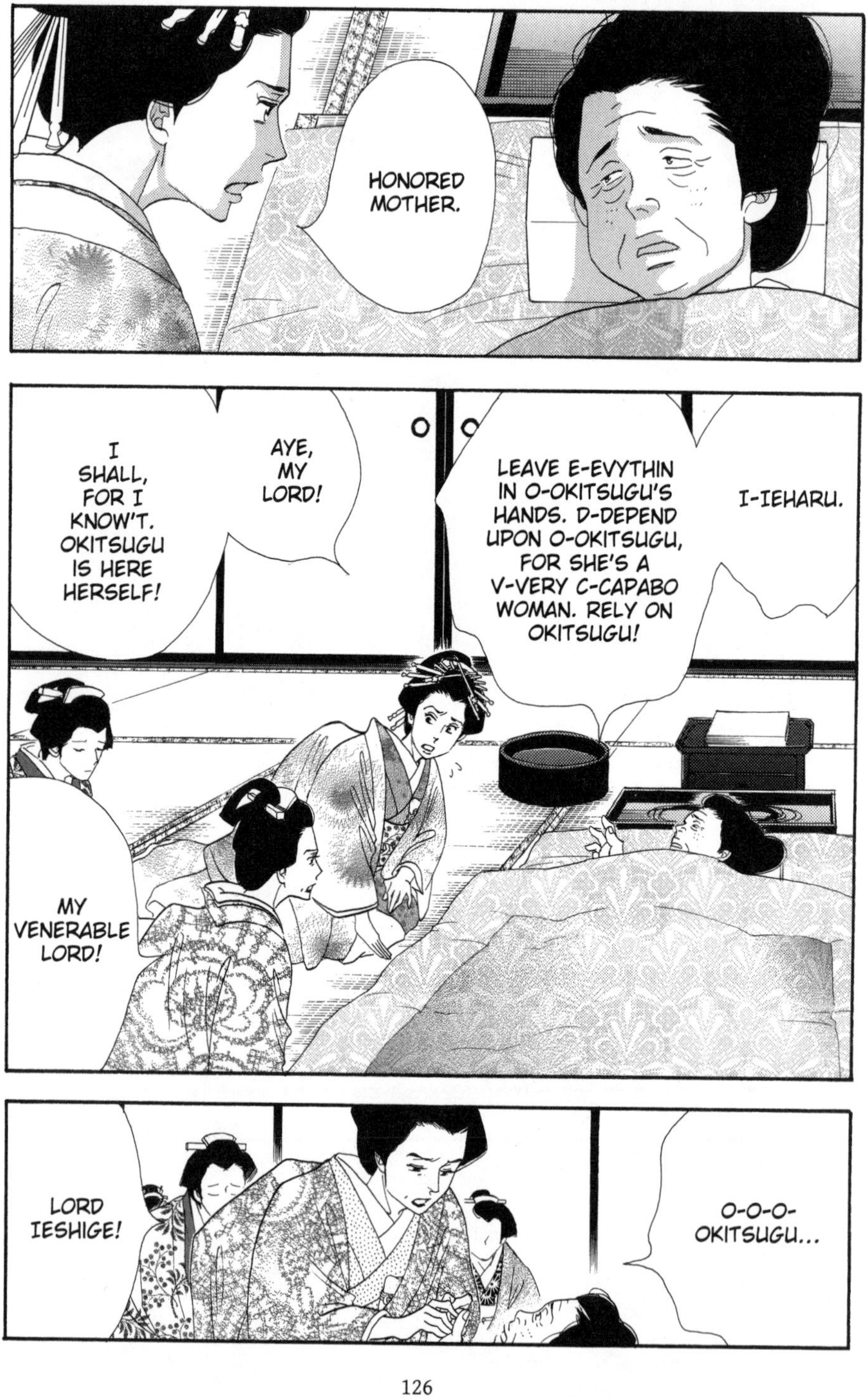
HONORED MOTHER.
I-IEHARU.
LEAVE E-EVYTHIN IN O-OKITSUGU'S HANDS. D-DEPEND UPON O-OKITSUGU, FOR SHE'S A V-VERY C-CAPABO WOMAN. RELY ON OKITSUGU!
AYE, MY LORD!
I SHALL, FOR I KNOW'T. OKITSUGU IS HERE HERSELF!
MY VENERABLE LORD!
O-O-O-OKITSUGU...
LORD IESHIGE!

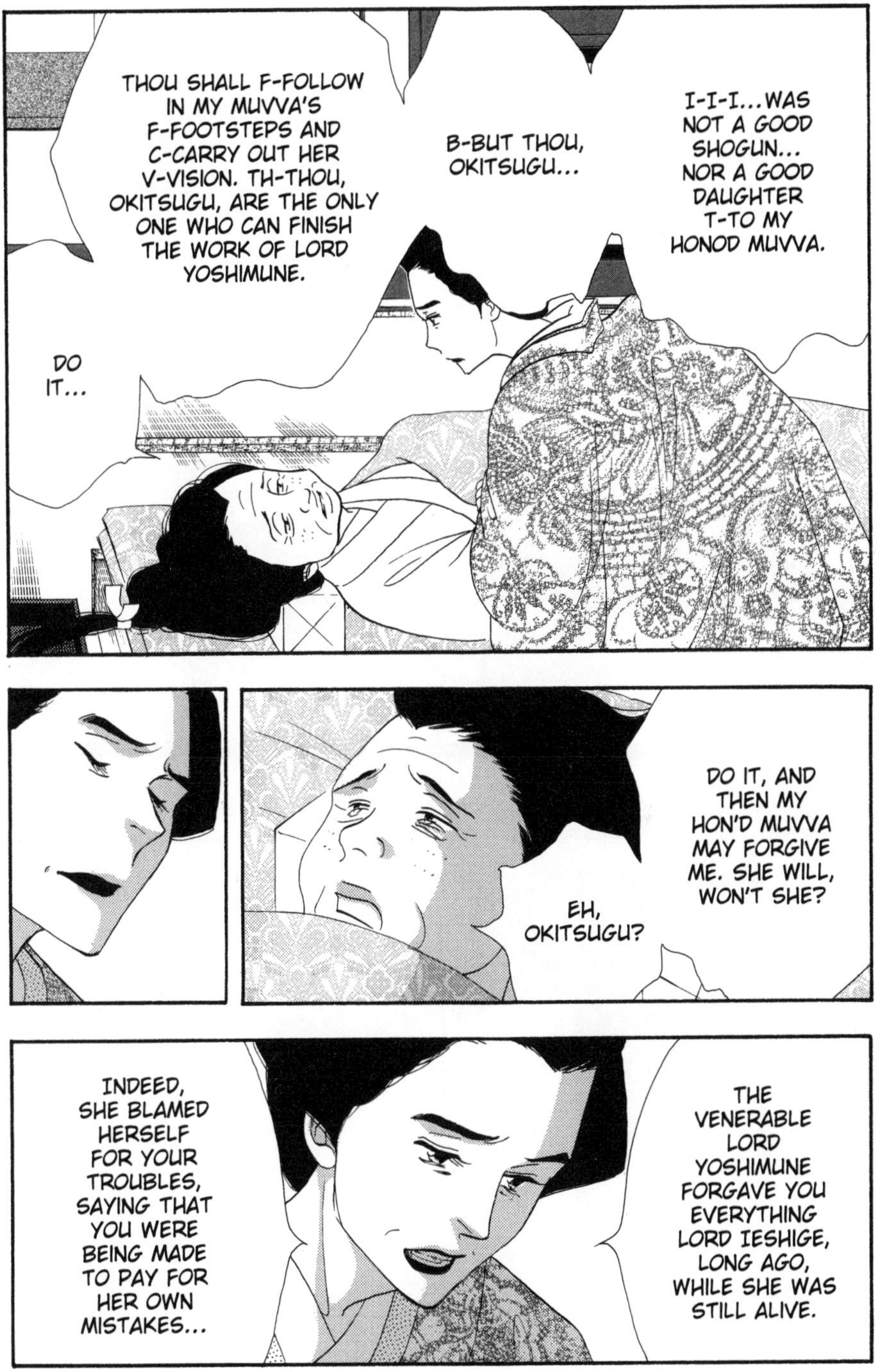
I-I-I...WAS NOT A GOOD SHOGUN... NOR A GOOD DAUGHTER T-TO MY HONOD MUVVA.
B-BUT THOU, OKITSUGU...
THOU SHALL F-FOLLOW IN MY MUVVA'S F-FOOTSTEPS AND C-CARRY OUT HER V-VISION. TH-THOU, OKITSUGU, ARE THE ONLY ONE WHO CAN FINISH THE WORK OF LORD YOSHIMUNE.
DO IT...
DO IT, AND THEN MY HON'D MUVVA MAY FORGIVE ME. SHE WILL, WON'T SHE?
EH, OKITSUGU?
THE VENERABLE LORD YOSHIMUNE FORGAVE YOU EVERYTHING LORD IESHIGE, LONG AGO, WHILE SHE WAS STILL ALIVE.
INDEED, SHE BLAMED HERSELF FOR YOUR TROUBLES, SAYING THAT YOU WERE BEING MADE TO PAY FOR HER OWN MISTAKES...

I PRAY YOU, MY LORD, TO ENJOY YOUR TIME IN PARADISE WITH YOUR HONORED MOTHER, THE VENERABLE YOSHIMUNE. MAY YOU DELIGHT IN EACH OTHER'S COMPANY.

NGH...!!

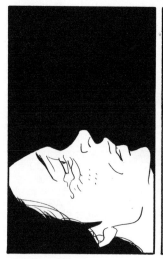

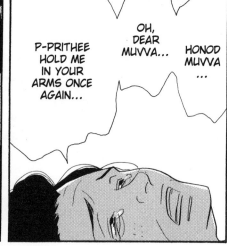

P-PRITHEE HOLD ME IN YOUR ARMS ONCE AGAIN...

OH, DEAR MUVVA...

HONOD MUVVA ...

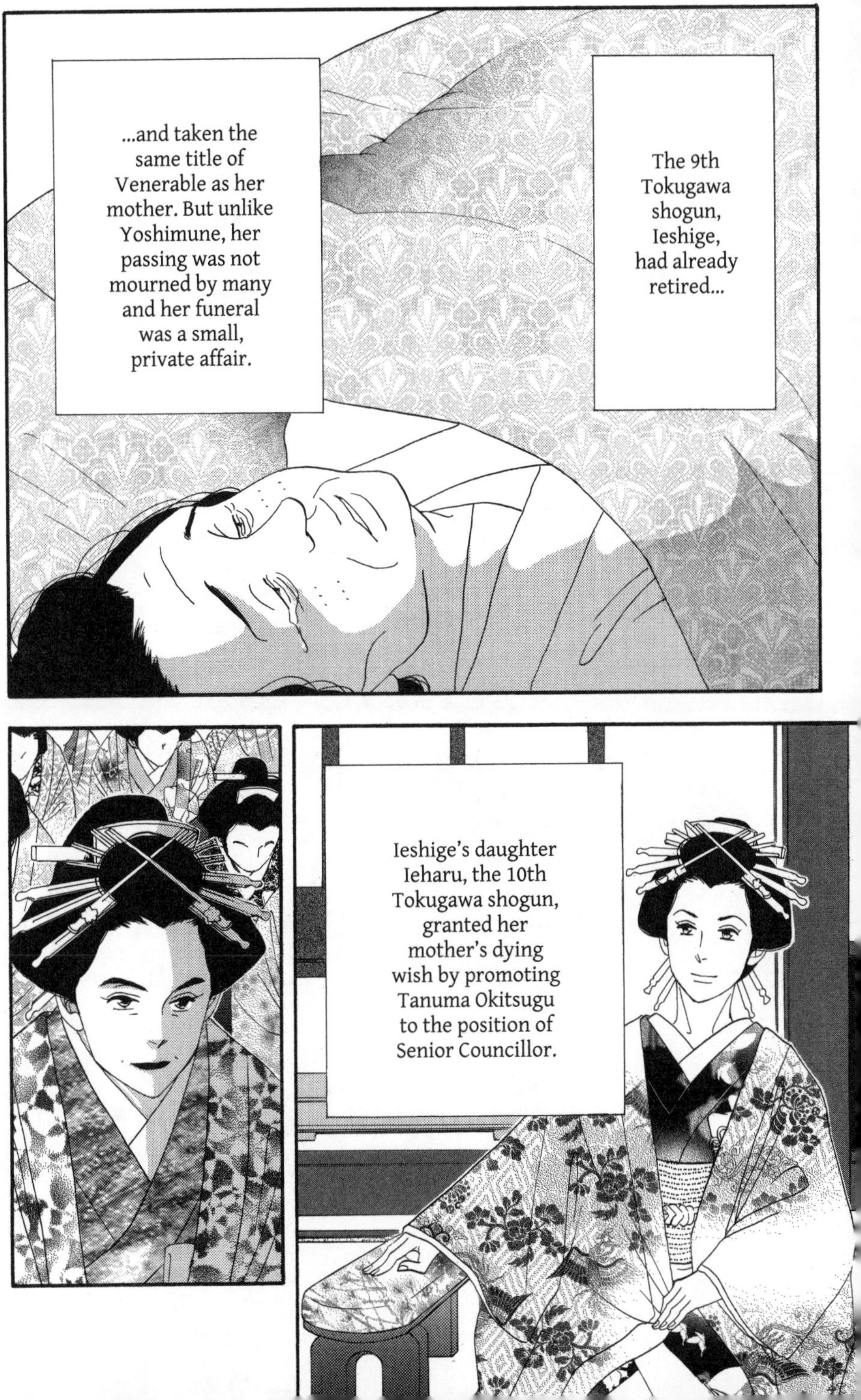
The 9th Tokugawa shogun, Ieshige, had already retired...
...and taken the same title of Venerable as her mother. But unlike Yoshimune, her passing was not mourned by many and her funeral was a small, private affair.
Ieshige's daughter Ieharu, the 10th Tokugawa shogun, granted her mother's dying wish by promoting Tanuma Okitsugu to the position of Senior Councillor.

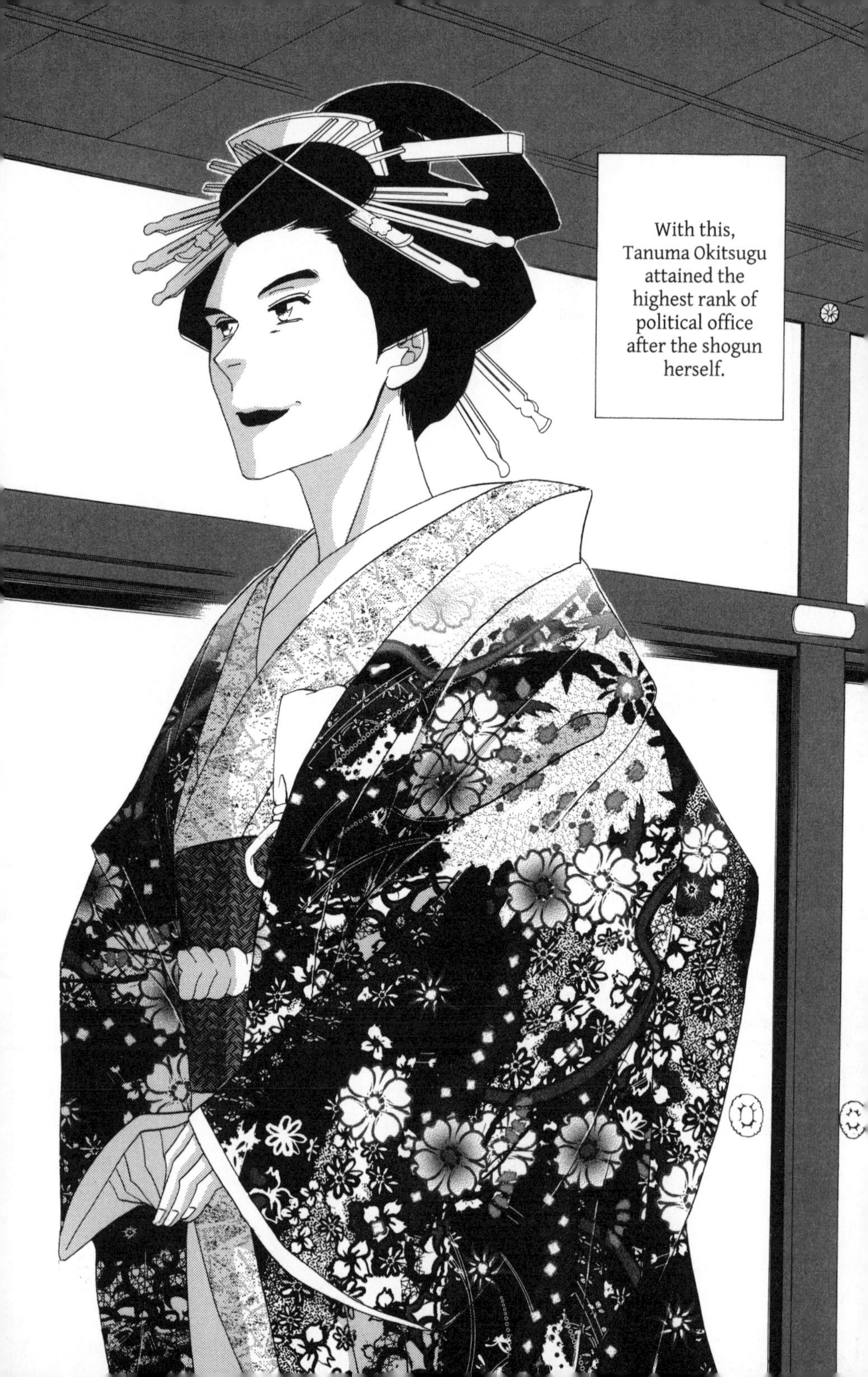
With this, Tanuma Okitsugu attained the highest rank of political office after the shogun herself.

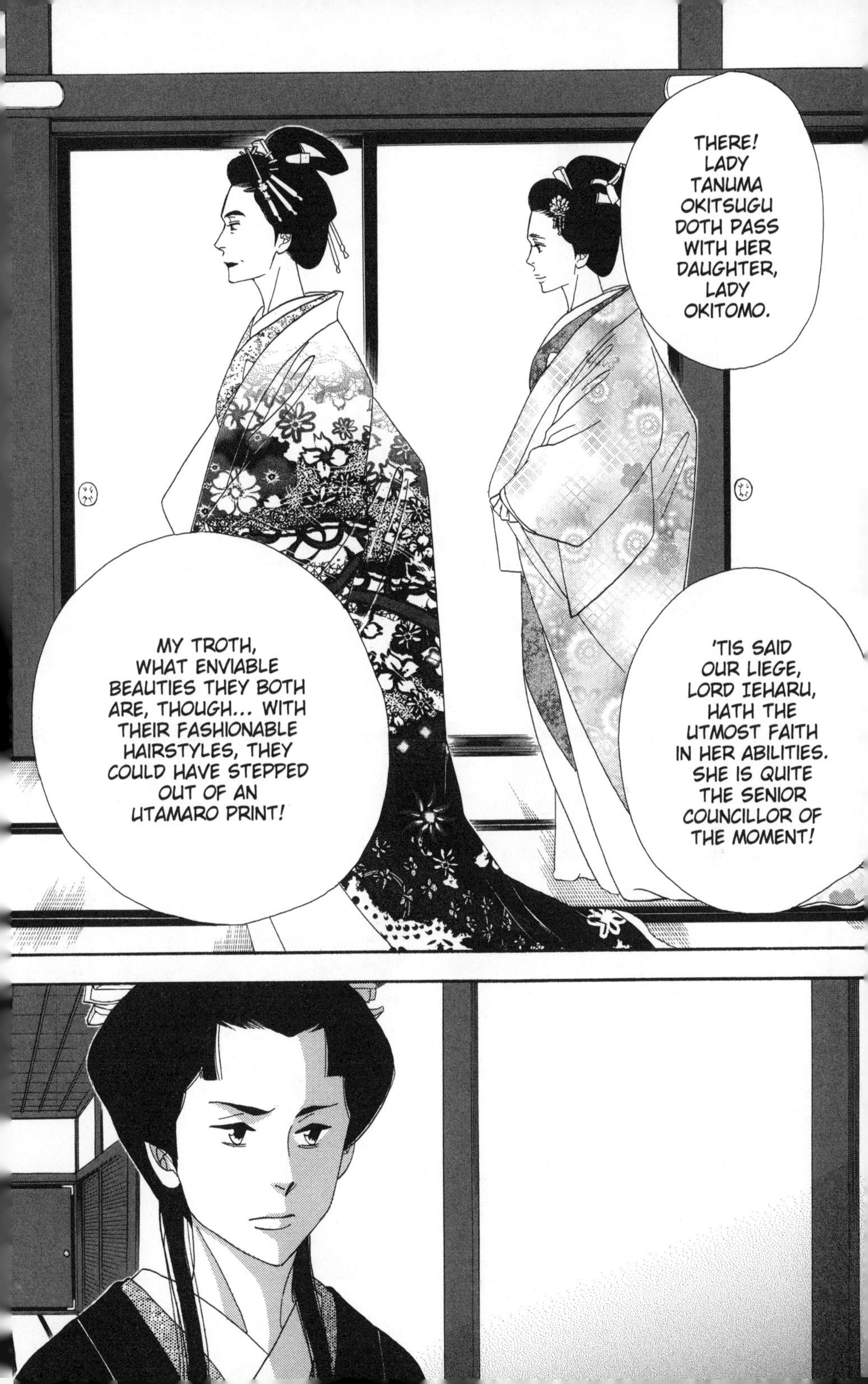
THERE! LADY TANUMA OKITSUGU DOTH PASS WITH HER DAUGHTER, LADY OKITOMO.
'TIS SAID OUR LIEGE, LORD IEHARU, HATH THE UTMOST FAITH IN HER ABILITIES. SHE IS QUITE THE SENIOR COUNCILLOR OF THE MOMENT!
MY TROTH, WHAT ENVIABLE BEAUTIES THEY BOTH ARE, THOUGH... WITH THEIR FASHIONABLE HAIRSTYLES, THEY COULD HAVE STEPPED OUT OF AN UTAMARO PRINT!

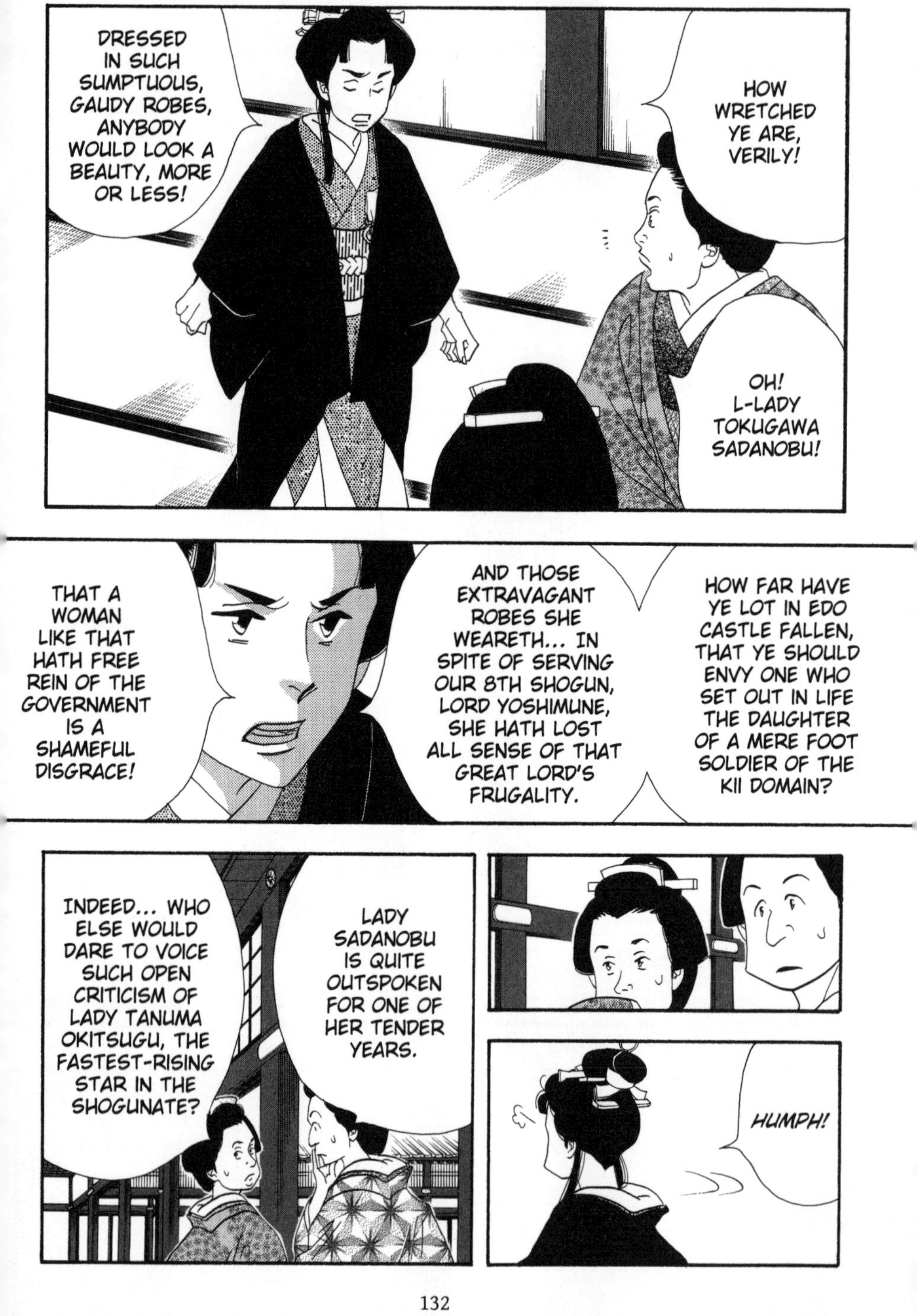
HOW WRETCHED YE ARE, VERILY!
DRESSED IN SUCH SUMPTUOUS, GAUDY ROBES, ANYBODY WOULD LOOK A BEAUTY, MORE OR LESS!
OH! L-LADY TOKUGAWA SADANOBU!
HOW FAR HAVE YE LOT IN EDO CASTLE FALLEN, THAT YE SHOULD ENVY ONE WHO SET OUT IN LIFE THE DAUGHTER OF A MERE FOOT SOLDIER OF THE KII DOMAIN?
AND THOSE EXTRAVAGANT ROBES SHE WEARETH... IN SPITE OF SERVING OUR 8TH SHOGUN, LORD YOSHIMUNE, SHE HATH LOST ALL SENSE OF THAT GREAT LORD'S FRUGALITY.
THAT A WOMAN LIKE THAT HATH FREE REIN OF THE GOVERNMENT IS A SHAMEFUL DISGRACE!
HUMPH!
LADY SADANOBU IS QUITE OUTSPOKEN FOR ONE OF HER TENDER YEARS.
INDEED... WHO ELSE WOULD DARE TO VOICE SUCH OPEN CRITICISM OF LADY TANUMA OKITSUGU, THE FASTEST-RISING STAR IN THE SHOGUNATE?

SURE, FOR ONE WHO IS LORD YOSHIMUNE'S OWN GRANDCHILD, AS LADY SADANOBU IS, LADY TANUMA MAY APPEAR TO BE A SHOCKING UPSTART.
YOU DID NOTE LADY SADANOBU'S ARDENT ADMIRATION OF LORD YOSHIMUNE... FOR INSTANCE, THAT BLACK SWEPT-UP GOWN SHE WEARETH IS A COPY OF HER GRANDAM'S.
AYE, BUT DIRECT DESCENDANT OF A SHOGUN THOUGH SHE BE, I CANNOT HELP BUT FEEL THAT RECKLESS WORDS AND ACTIONS COULD BRING HER HARM, OR AT LEAST SERVE HER ILL...
LADY TANUMA. ALLOW ME TO CONGRATULATE YOU ON YOUR APPOINTMENT AS A SENIOR COUNCILLOR.
BARON OF SUO. I AM MOST GRATEFUL FOR YOUR KIND WORDS.

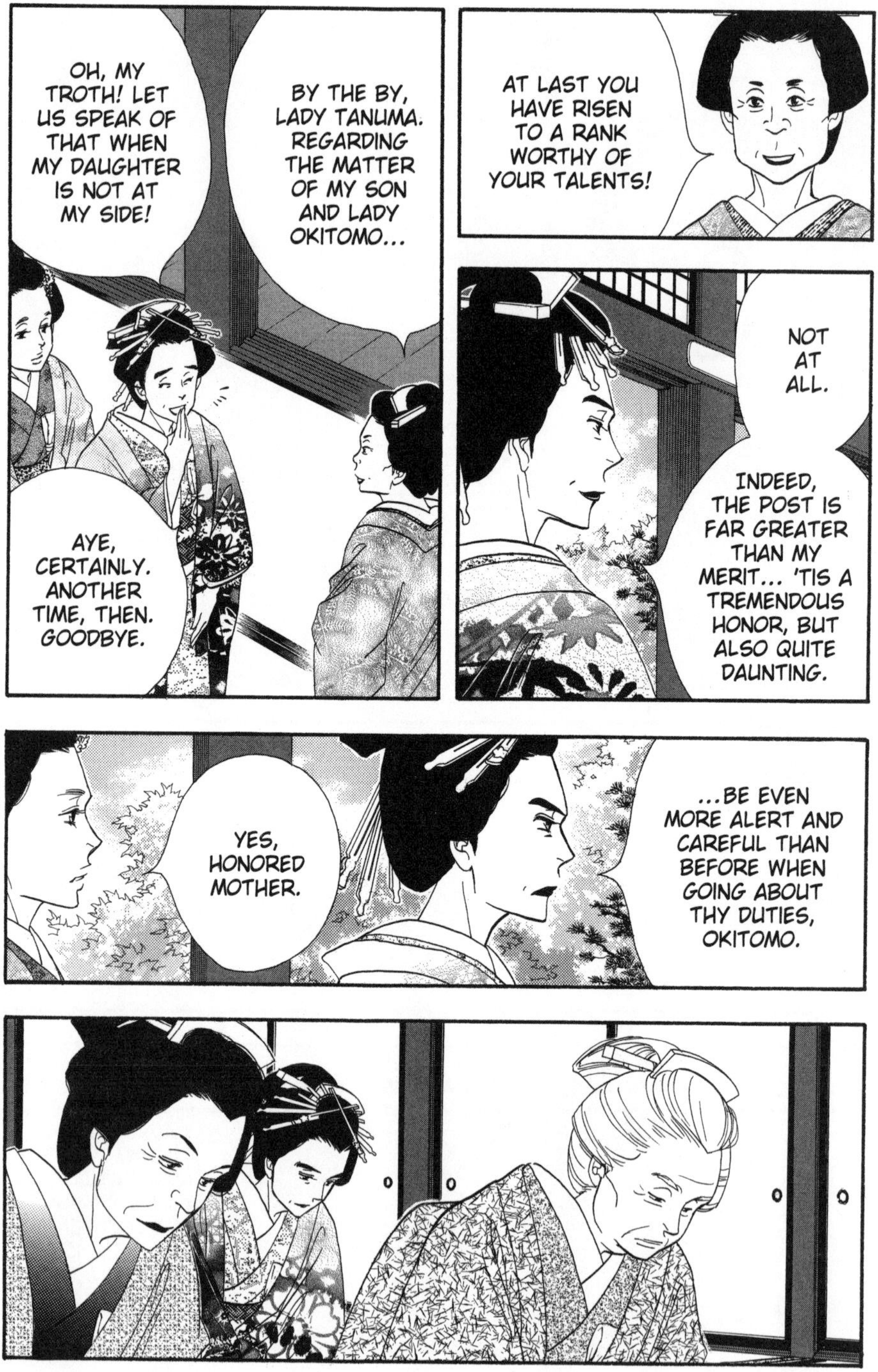
AT LAST YOU HAVE RISEN TO A RANK WORTHY OF YOUR TALENTS!
NOT AT ALL.
INDEED, THE POST IS FAR GREATER THAN MY MERIT... 'TIS A TREMENDOUS HONOR, BUT ALSO QUITE DAUNTING.
BY THE BY, LADY TANUMA. REGARDING THE MATTER OF MY SON AND LADY OKITOMO...
OH, MY TROTH! LET US SPEAK OF THAT WHEN MY DAUGHTER IS NOT AT MY SIDE!
AYE, CERTAINLY. ANOTHER TIME, THEN. GOODBYE.
...BE EVEN MORE ALERT AND CAREFUL THAN BEFORE WHEN GOING ABOUT THY DUTIES, OKITOMO.
YES, HONORED MOTHER.

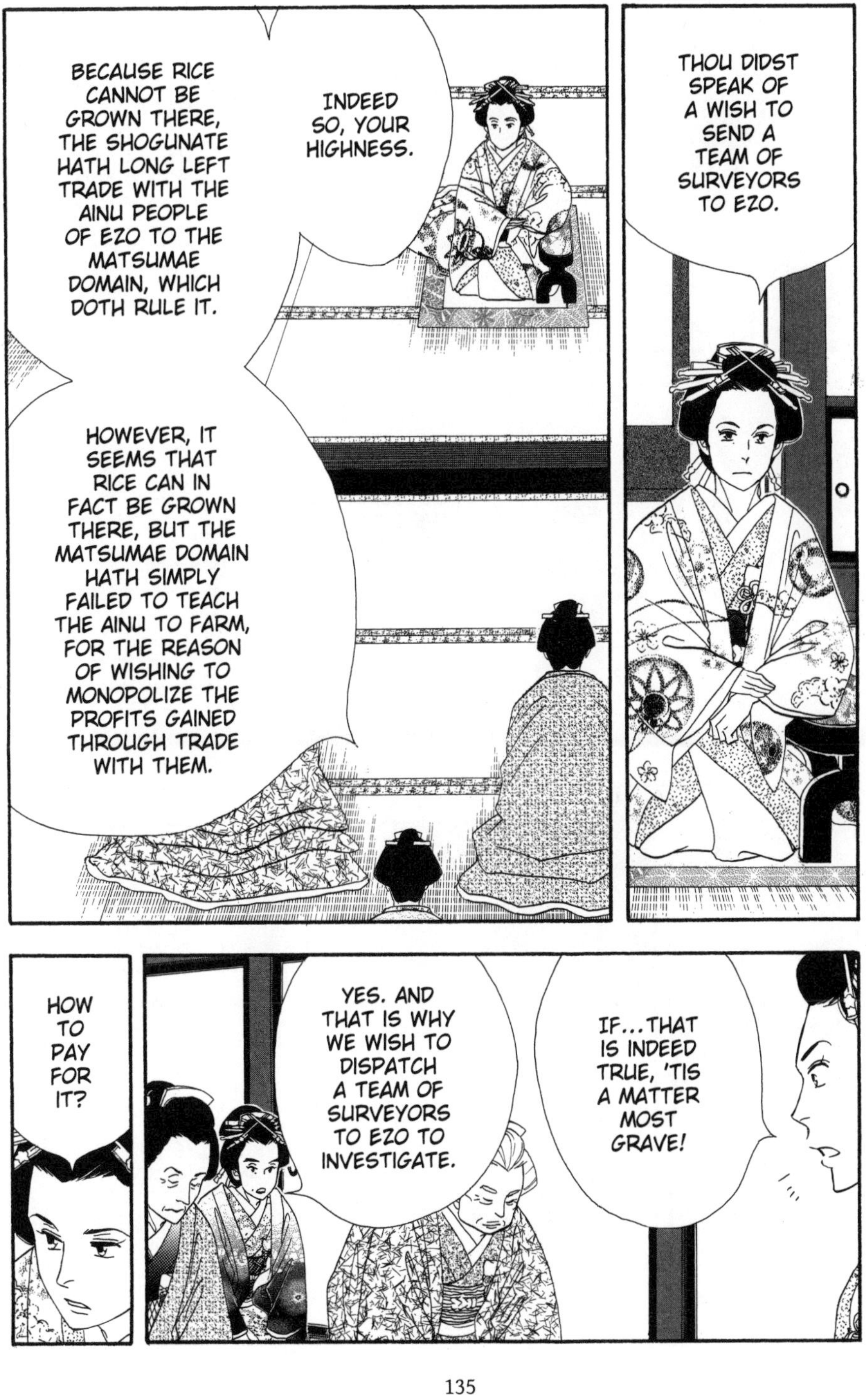
THOU DIDST SPEAK OF A WISH TO SEND A TEAM OF SURVEYORS TO EZO.
INDEED SO, YOUR HIGHNESS.
BECAUSE RICE CANNOT BE GROWN THERE, THE SHOGUNATE HATH LONG LEFT TRADE WITH THE AINU PEOPLE OF EZO TO THE MATSUMAE DOMAIN, WHICH DOTH RULE IT.
HOWEVER, IT SEEMS THAT RICE CAN IN FACT BE GROWN THERE, BUT THE MATSUMAE DOMAIN HATH SIMPLY FAILED TO TEACH THE AINU TO FARM, FOR THE REASON OF WISHING TO MONOPOLIZE THE PROFITS GAINED THROUGH TRADE WITH THEM.
IF...THAT IS INDEED TRUE, 'TIS A MATTER MOST GRAVE!
YES. AND THAT IS WHY WE WISH TO DISPATCH A TEAM OF SURVEYORS TO EZO TO INVESTIGATE.
HOW TO PAY FOR IT?

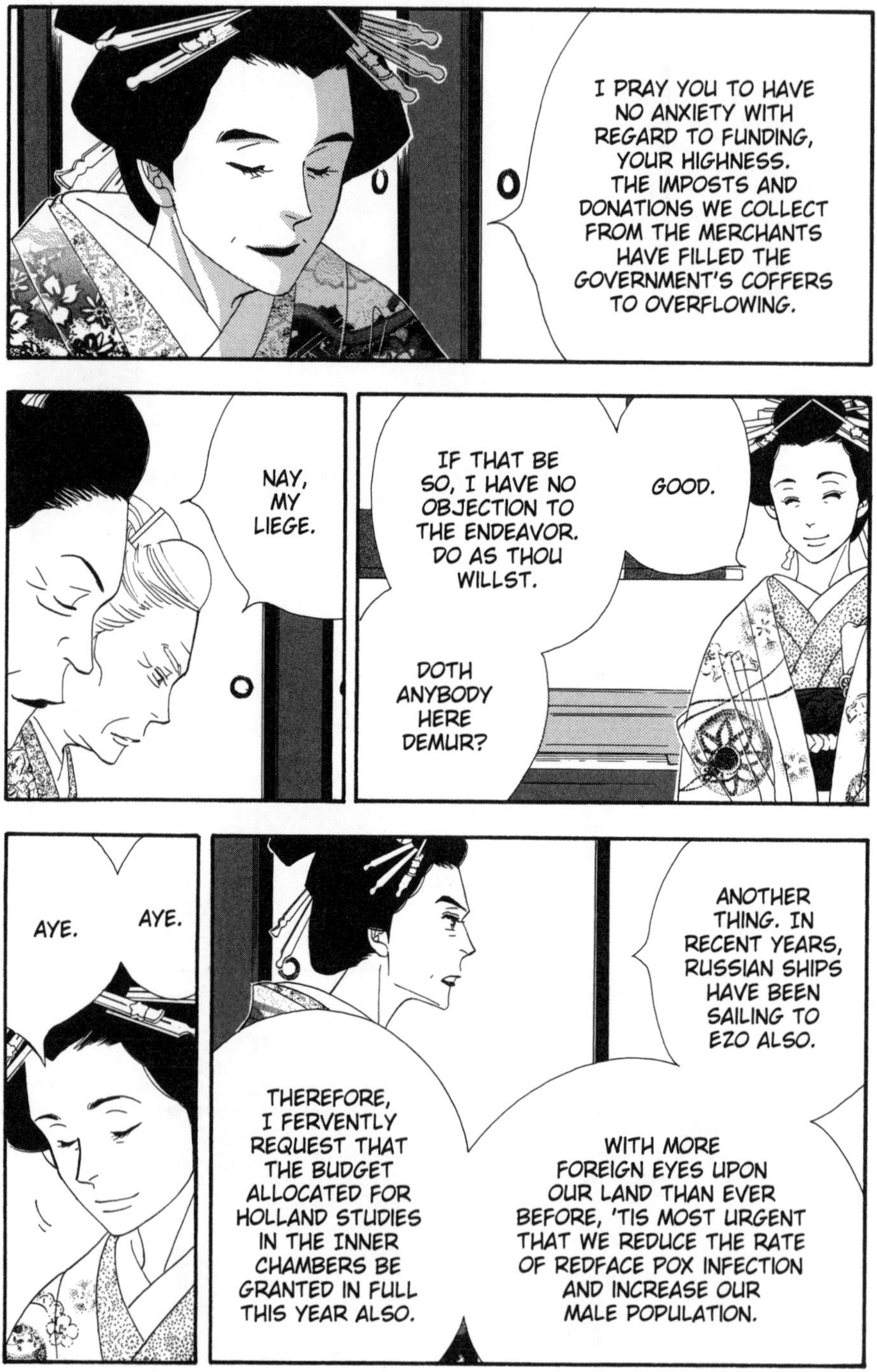
I PRAY YOU TO HAVE NO ANXIETY WITH REGARD TO FUNDING, YOUR HIGHNESS. THE IMPOSTS AND DONATIONS WE COLLECT FROM THE MERCHANTS HAVE FILLED THE GOVERNMENT'S COFFERS TO OVERFLOWING.
GOOD.
IF THAT BE SO, I HAVE NO OBJECTION TO THE ENDEAVOR. DO AS THOU WILLST.
DOTH ANYBODY HERE DEMUR?
NAY, MY LIEGE.
ANOTHER THING. IN RECENT YEARS, RUSSIAN SHIPS HAVE BEEN SAILING TO EZO ALSO.
WITH MORE FOREIGN EYES UPON OUR LAND THAN EVER BEFORE, 'TIS MOST URGENT THAT WE REDUCE THE RATE OF REDFACE POX INFECTION AND INCREASE OUR MALE POPULATION.
THEREFORE, I FERVENTLY REQUEST THAT THE BUDGET ALLOCATED FOR HOLLAND STUDIES IN THE INNER CHAMBERS BE GRANTED IN FULL THIS YEAR ALSO.
AYE.
AYE.

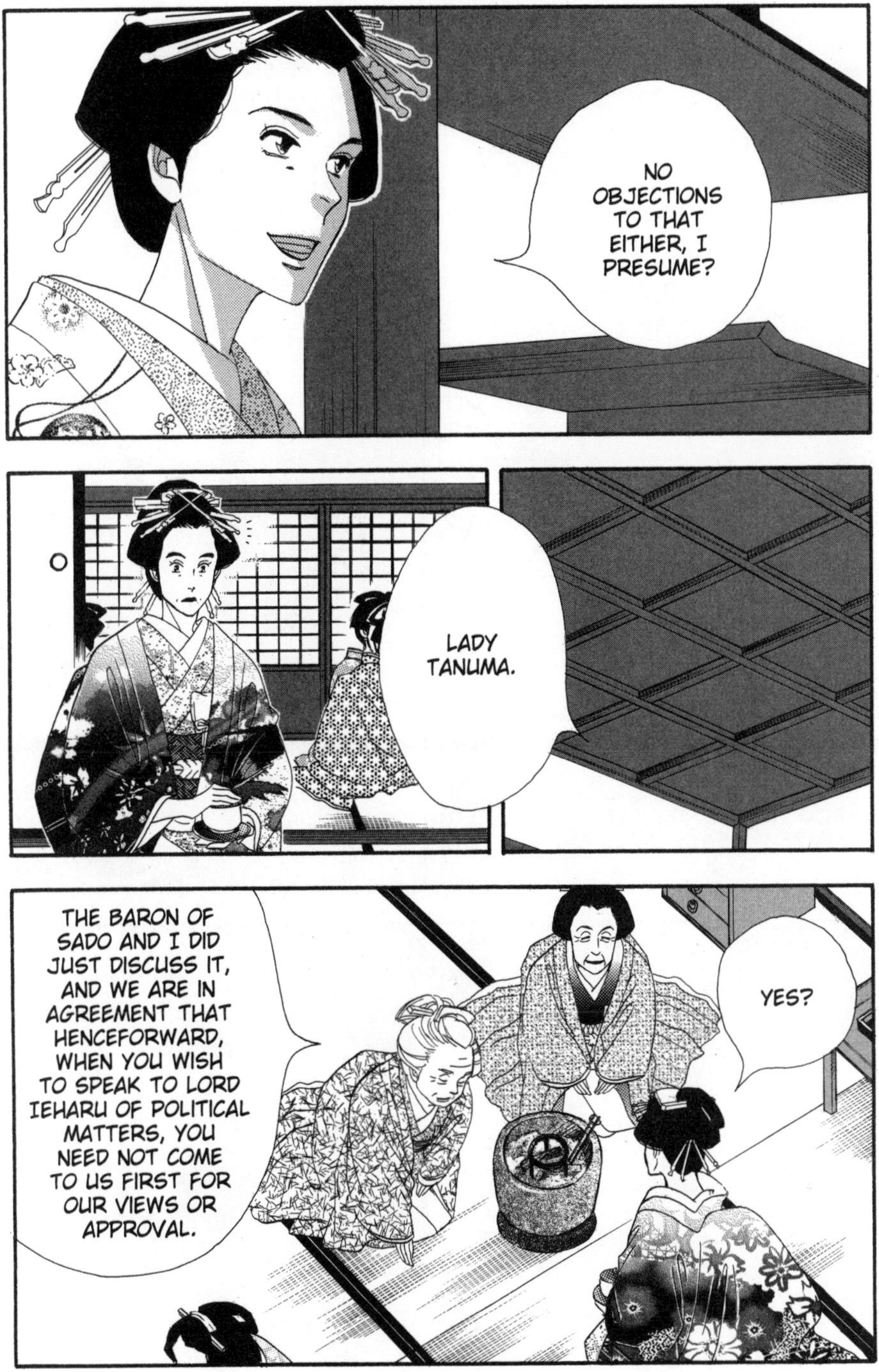
NO OBJECTIONS TO THAT EITHER, I PRESUME?
LADY TANUMA.
YES?
THE BARON OF SADO AND I DID JUST DISCUSS IT, AND WE ARE IN AGREEMENT THAT HENCEFORWARD, WHEN YOU WISH TO SPEAK TO LORD IEHARU OF POLITICAL MATTERS, YOU NEED NOT COME TO US FIRST FOR OUR VIEWS OR APPROVAL.

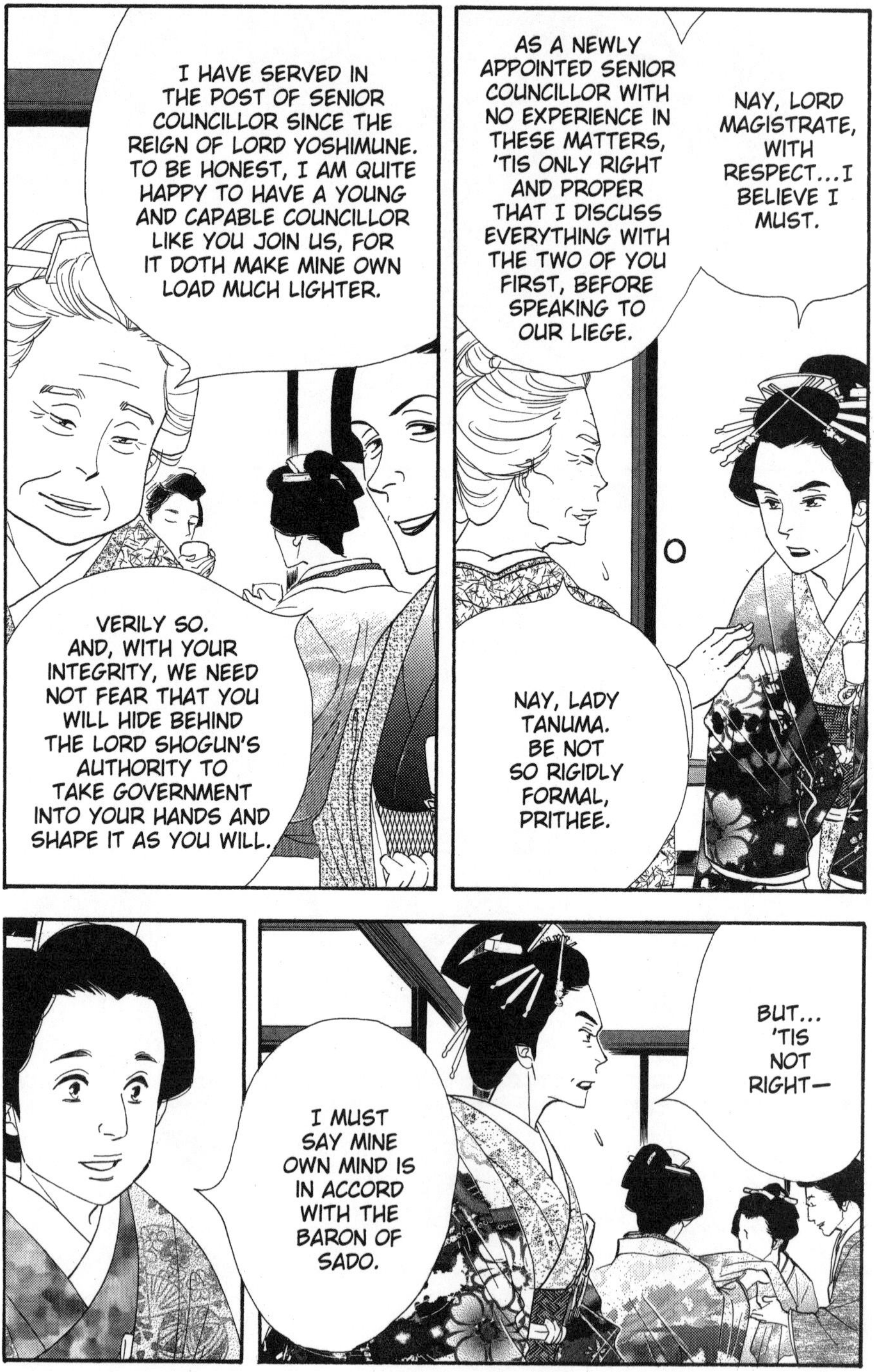
NAY, LORD MAGISTRATE, WITH RESPECT...I BELIEVE I MUST.
AS A NEWLY APPOINTED SENIOR COUNCILLOR WITH NO EXPERIENCE IN THESE MATTERS, 'TIS ONLY RIGHT AND PROPER THAT I DISCUSS EVERYTHING WITH THE TWO OF YOU FIRST, BEFORE SPEAKING TO OUR LIEGE.
NAY, LADY TANUMA. BE NOT SO RIGIDLY FORMAL, PRITHEE.
I HAVE SERVED IN THE POST OF SENIOR COUNCILLOR SINCE THE REIGN OF LORD YOSHIMUNE. TO BE HONEST, I AM QUITE HAPPY TO HAVE A YOUNG AND CAPABLE COUNCILLOR LIKE YOU JOIN US, FOR IT DOTH MAKE MINE OWN LOAD MUCH LIGHTER.
VERILY SO. AND, WITH YOUR INTEGRITY, WE NEED NOT FEAR THAT YOU WILL HIDE BEHIND THE LORD SHOGUN'S AUTHORITY TO TAKE GOVERNMENT INTO YOUR HANDS AND SHAPE IT AS YOU WILL.
BUT... 'TIS NOT RIGHT—
I MUST SAY MINE OWN MIND IS IN ACCORD WITH THE BARON OF SADO.

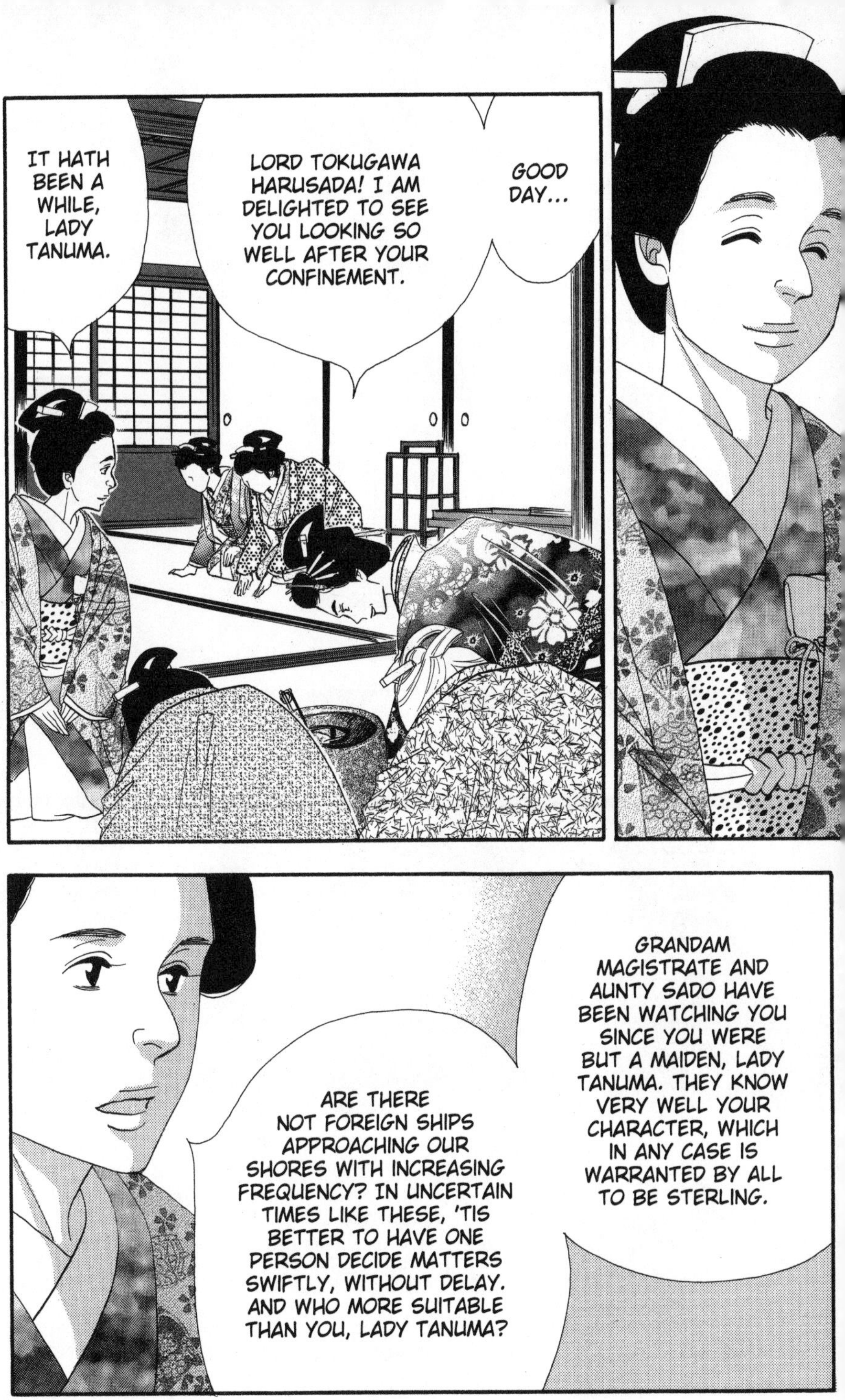
GOOD DAY...
LORD TOKUGAWA HARUSADA! I AM DELIGHTED TO SEE YOU LOOKING SO WELL AFTER YOUR CONFINEMENT.
IT HATH BEEN A WHILE, LADY TANUMA.
GRANDAM MAGISTRATE AND AUNTY SADO HAVE BEEN WATCHING YOU SINCE YOU WERE BUT A MAIDEN, LADY TANUMA. THEY KNOW VERY WELL YOUR CHARACTER, WHICH IN ANY CASE IS WARRANTED BY ALL TO BE STERLING.
ARE THERE NOT FOREIGN SHIPS APPROACHING OUR SHORES WITH INCREASING FREQUENCY? IN UNCERTAIN TIMES LIKE THESE, 'TIS BETTER TO HAVE ONE PERSON DECIDE MATTERS SWIFTLY, WITHOUT DELAY. AND WHO MORE SUITABLE THAN YOU, LADY TANUMA?

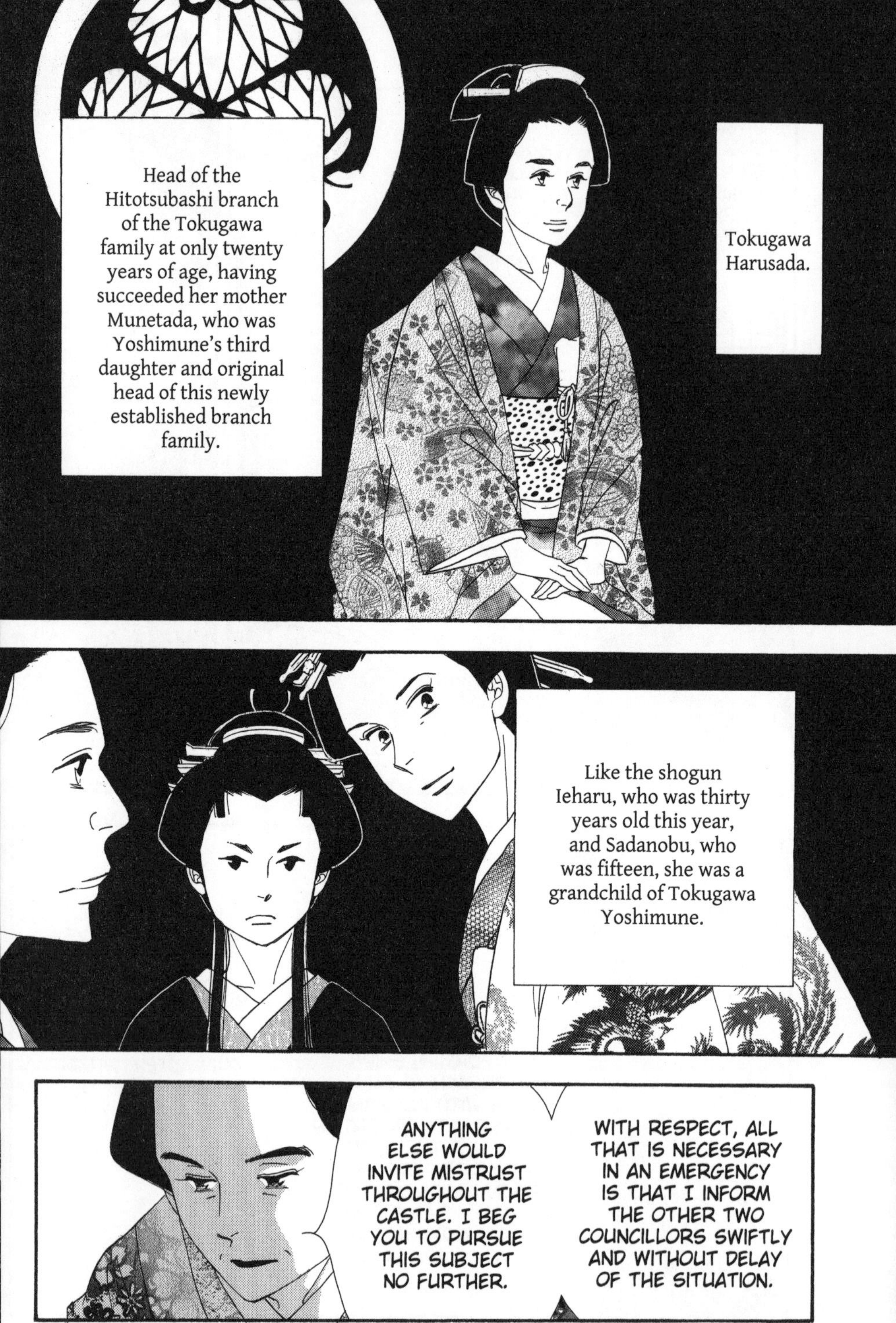
Tokugawa Harusada.
Head of the Hitotsubashi branch of the Tokugawa family at only twenty years of age, having succeeded her mother Munetada, who was Yoshimune's third daughter and original head of this newly established branch family.
Like the shogun Ieharu, who was thirty years old this year, and Sadanobu, who was fifteen, she was a grandchild of Tokugawa Yoshimune.
WITH RESPECT, ALL THAT IS NECESSARY IN AN EMERGENCY IS THAT I INFORM THE OTHER TWO COUNCILLORS SWIFTLY AND WITHOUT DELAY OF THE SITUATION.
ANYTHING ELSE WOULD INVITE MISTRUST THROUGHOUT THE CASTLE. I BEG YOU TO PURSUE THIS SUBJECT NO FURTHER.

...OH, YES. THE MATTER OF LORD MATSUDAIRA SADAKUNI OF THE SHIROKAWA DOMAIN IN MUTSU PROVINCE, WHO HATH PETITIONED THE SHOGUNATE FOR PERMISSION TO ADOPT AN HEIR...

IS NOT TOKUGAWA SADANOBU OF THE TAYASU BRANCH THE MOST FITTING PERSON?

HMMM... BUT LORD SADANOBU'S MOTHER, LORD MUNETAKE, DID OPPOSE IT SO VIGOROUSLY...

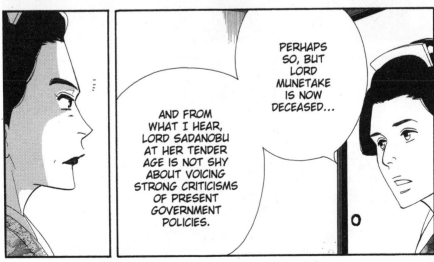

PERHAPS SO, BUT LORD MUNETAKE IS NOW DECEASED...

AND FROM WHAT I HEAR, LORD SADANOBU AT HER TENDER AGE IS NOT SHY ABOUT VOICING STRONG CRITICISMS OF PRESENT GOVERNMENT POLICIES.

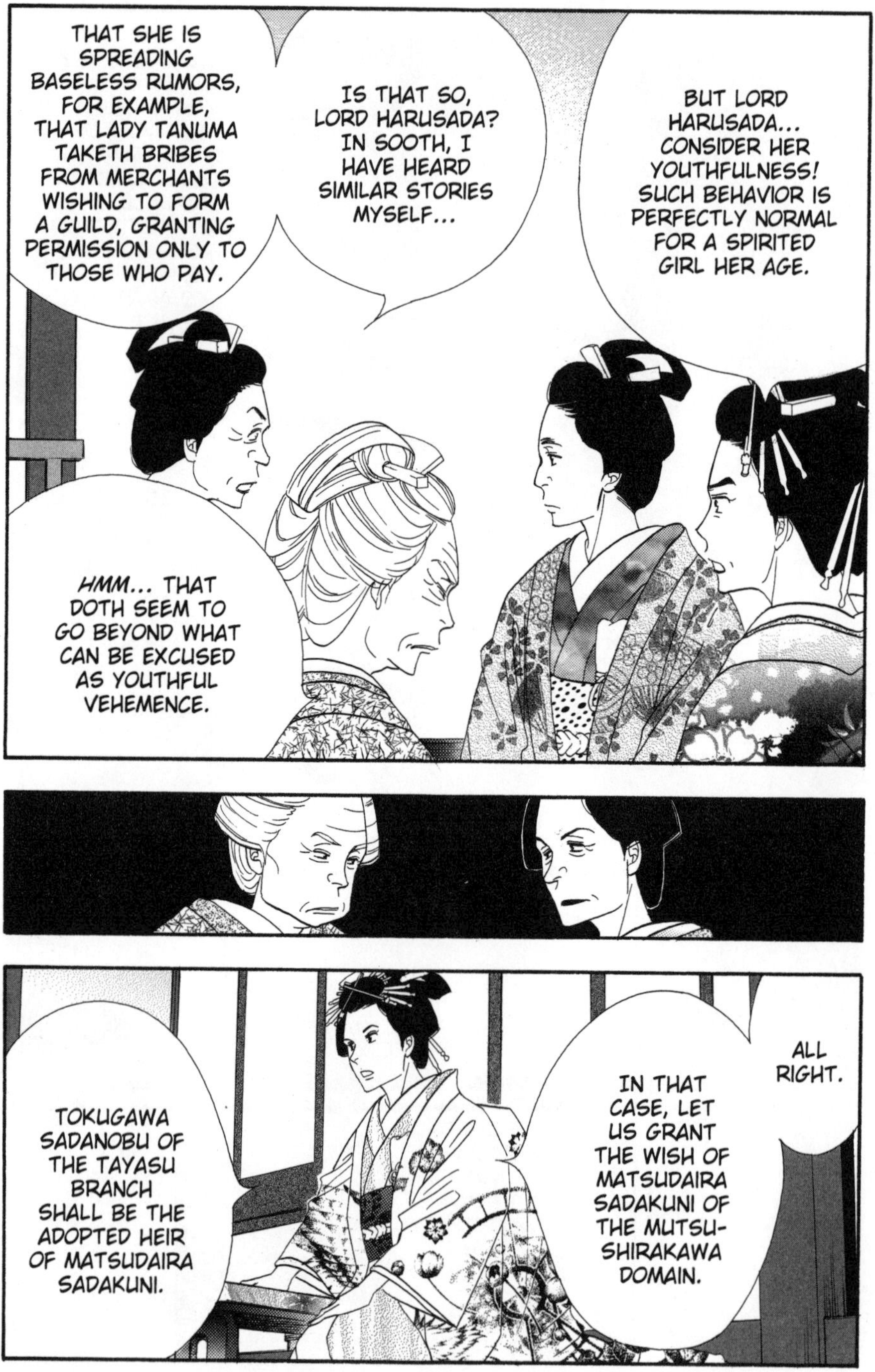
BUT LORD HARUSADA... CONSIDER HER YOUTHFULNESS! SUCH BEHAVIOR IS PERFECTLY NORMAL FOR A SPIRITED GIRL HER AGE.
IS THAT SO, LORD HARUSADA? IN SOOTH, I HAVE HEARD SIMILAR STORIES MYSELF...
THAT SHE IS SPREADING BASELESS RUMORS, FOR EXAMPLE, THAT LADY TANUMA TAKETH BRIBES FROM MERCHANTS WISHING TO FORM A GUILD, GRANTING PERMISSION ONLY TO THOSE WHO PAY.
HMM... THAT DOTH SEEM TO GO BEYOND WHAT CAN BE EXCUSED AS YOUTHFUL VEHEMENCE.
ALL RIGHT.
IN THAT CASE, LET US GRANT THE WISH OF MATSUDAIRA SADAKUNI OF THE MUTSU-SHIRAKAWA DOMAIN.
TOKUGAWA SADANOBU OF THE TAYASU BRANCH SHALL BE THE ADOPTED HEIR OF MATSUDAIRA SADAKUNI.

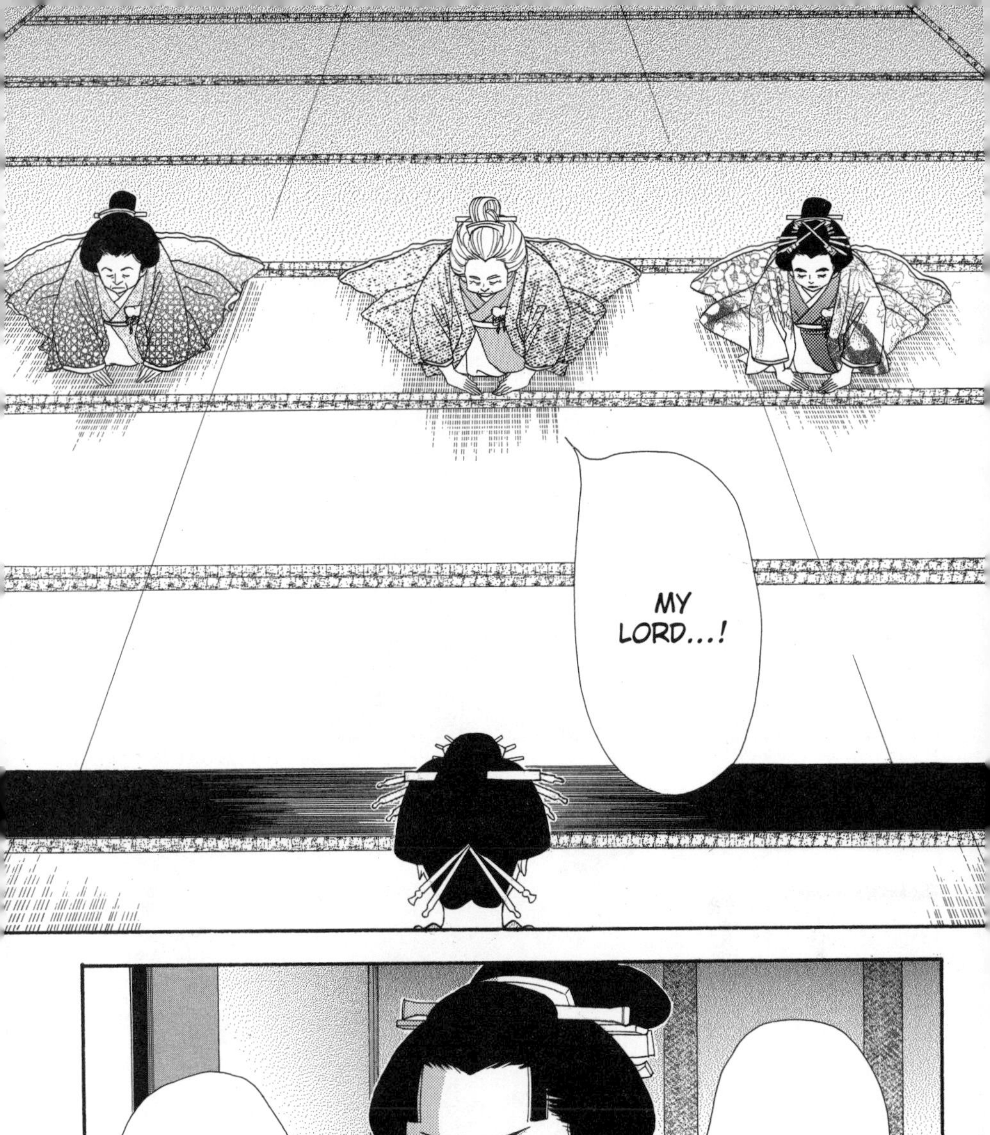
MY LORD...!

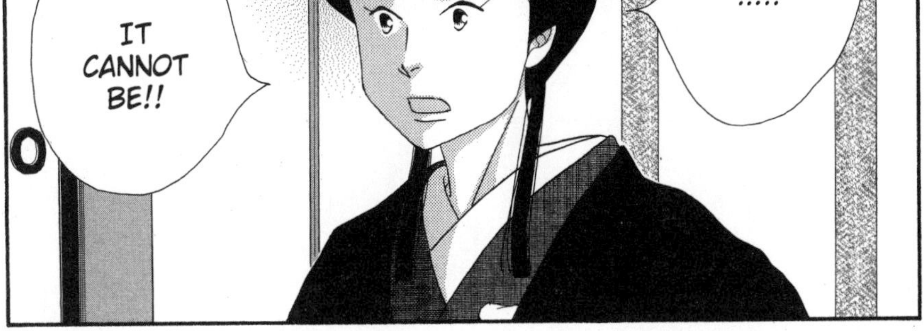
...!!
IT CANNOT BE!!

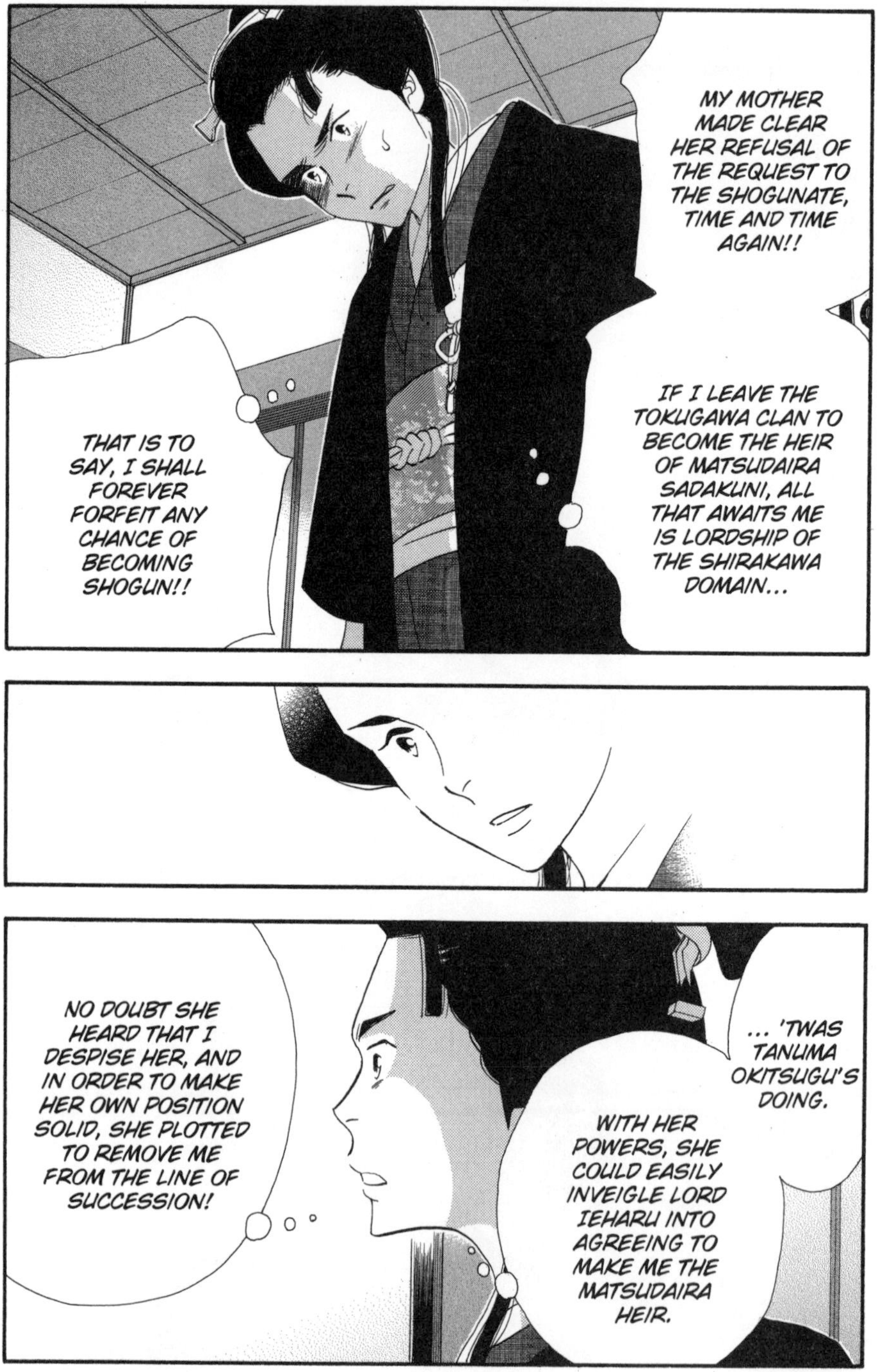
MY MOTHER MADE CLEAR HER REFUSAL OF THE REQUEST TO THE SHOGUNATE, TIME AND TIME AGAIN!!
IF I LEAVE THE TOKUGAWA CLAN TO BECOME THE HEIR OF MATSUDAIRA SADAKUNI, ALL THAT AWAITS ME IS LORDSHIP OF THE SHIRAKAWA DOMAIN...
THAT IS TO SAY, I SHALL FOREVER FORFEIT ANY CHANCE OF BECOMING SHOGUN!!
... 'TWAS TANUMA OKITSUGU'S DOING.
WITH HER POWERS, SHE COULD EASILY INVEIGLE LORD IEHARU INTO AGREEING TO MAKE ME THE MATSUDAIRA HEIR.
NO DOUBT SHE HEARD THAT I DESPISE HER, AND IN ORDER TO MAKE HER OWN POSITION SOLID, SHE PLOTTED TO REMOVE ME FROM THE LINE OF SUCCESSION!

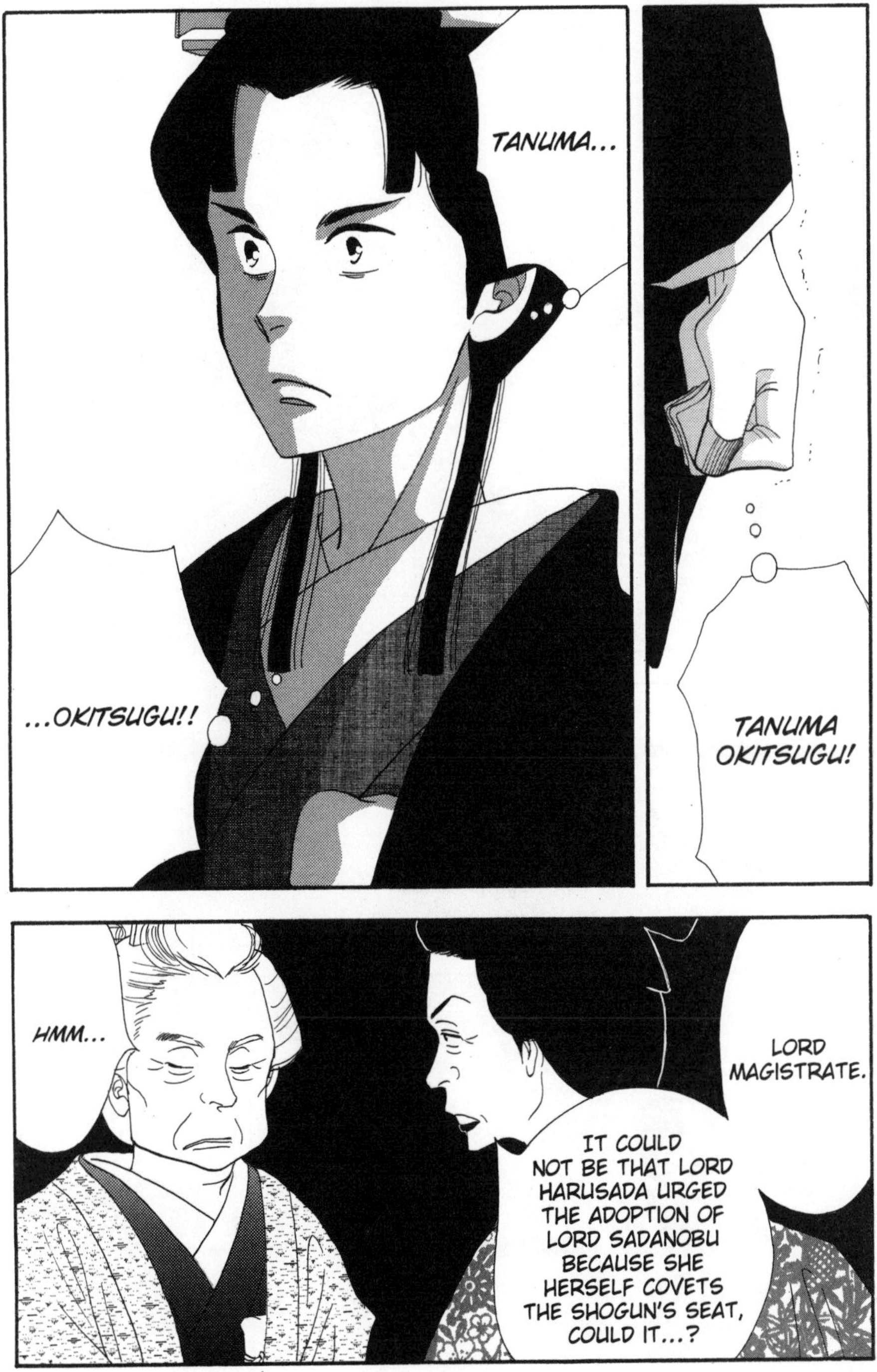
TANUMA OKITSUGU!
TANUMA...
...OKITSUGU!!
LORD MAGISTRATE.
IT COULD NOT BE THAT LORD HARUSADA URGED THE ADOPTION OF LORD SADANOBU BECAUSE SHE HERSELF COVETS THE SHOGUN'S SEAT, COULD IT...?
HMM...

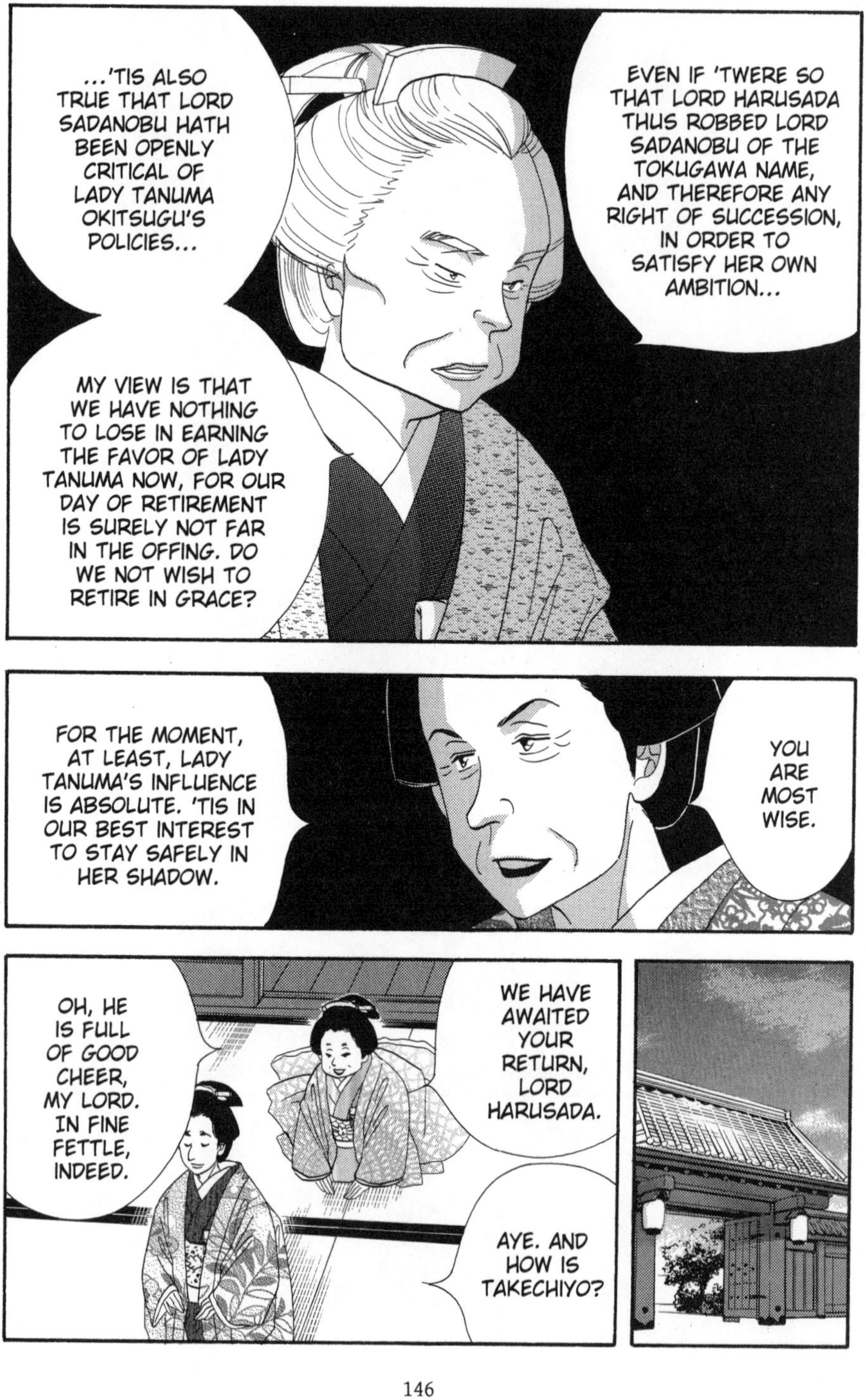

EVEN IF 'TWERE SO THAT LORD HARUSADA THUS ROBBED LORD SADANOBU OF THE TOKUGAWA NAME, AND THEREFORE ANY RIGHT OF SUCCESSION, IN ORDER TO SATISFY HER OWN AMBITION...
...'TIS ALSO TRUE THAT LORD SADANOBU HATH BEEN OPENLY CRITICAL OF LADY TANUMA OKITSUGU'S POLICIES...
MY VIEW IS THAT WE HAVE NOTHING TO LOSE IN EARNING THE FAVOR OF LADY TANUMA NOW, FOR OUR DAY OF RETIREMENT IS SURELY NOT FAR IN THE OFFING. DO WE NOT WISH TO RETIRE IN GRACE?
YOU ARE MOST WISE.
FOR THE MOMENT, AT LEAST, LADY TANUMA'S INFLUENCE IS ABSOLUTE. 'TIS IN OUR BEST INTEREST TO STAY SAFELY IN HER SHADOW.
WE HAVE AWAITED YOUR RETURN, LORD HARUSADA.
AYE. AND HOW IS TAKECHIYO?
OH, HE IS FULL OF GOOD CHEER, MY LORD. IN FINE FETTLE, INDEED.

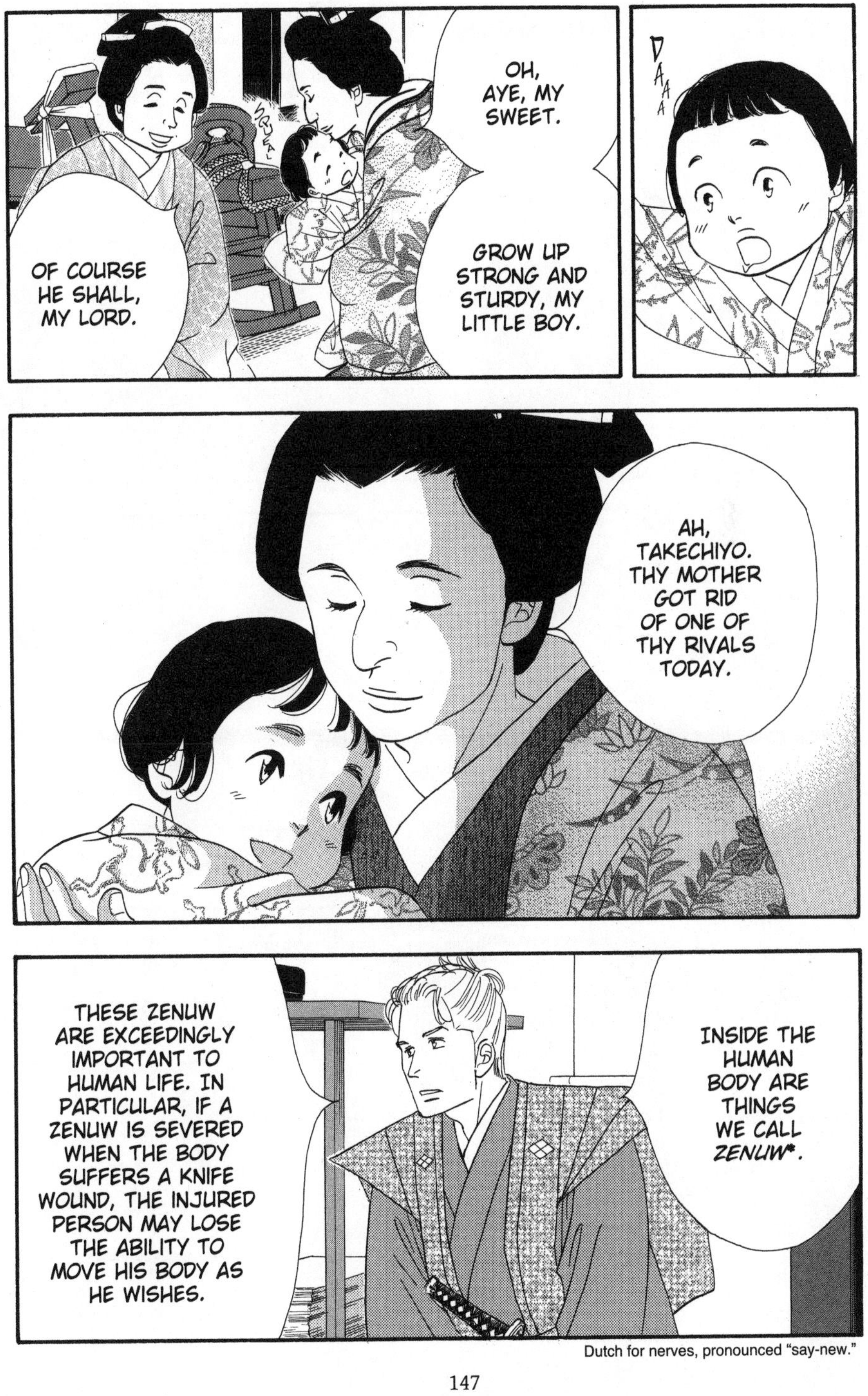
DAAA
OH, AYE, MY SWEET.
GROW UP STRONG AND STURDY, MY LITTLE BOY.
SQUEAL
OF COURSE HE SHALL, MY LORD.
AH, TAKECHIYO. THY MOTHER GOT RID OF ONE OF THY RIVALS TODAY.
INSIDE THE HUMAN BODY ARE THINGS WE CALL *ZENUW**.
THESE ZENUW ARE EXCEEDINGLY IMPORTANT TO HUMAN LIFE. IN PARTICULAR, IF A ZENUW IS SEVERED WHEN THE BODY SUFFERS A KNIFE WOUND, THE INJURED PERSON MAY LOSE THE ABILITY TO MOVE HIS BODY AS HE WISHES.

Dutch for nerves, pronounced "say-new."

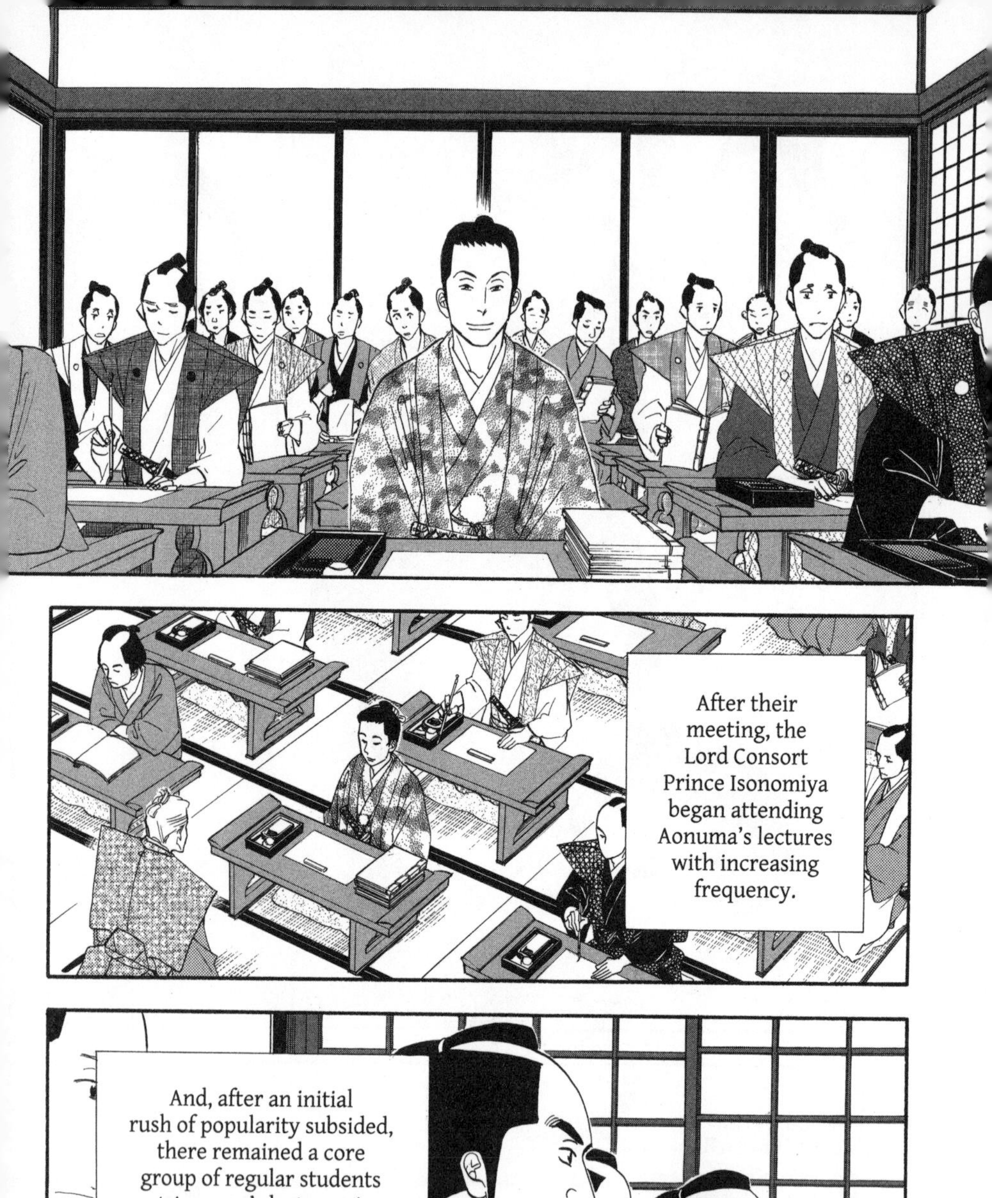
After their meeting, the Lord Consort Prince Isonomiya began attending Aonuma's lectures with increasing frequency.
And, after an initial rush of popularity subsided, there remained a core group of regular students at Aonuma's lectures, in addition to Kisuke (now permitted to attend in the daytime), Kuroki and Ihei, all of them young men with a genuine interest in Western science and medicine.

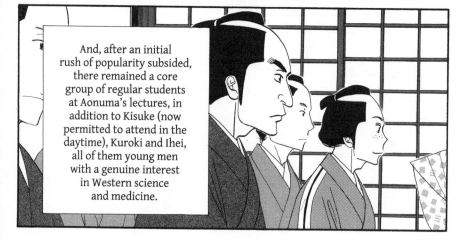

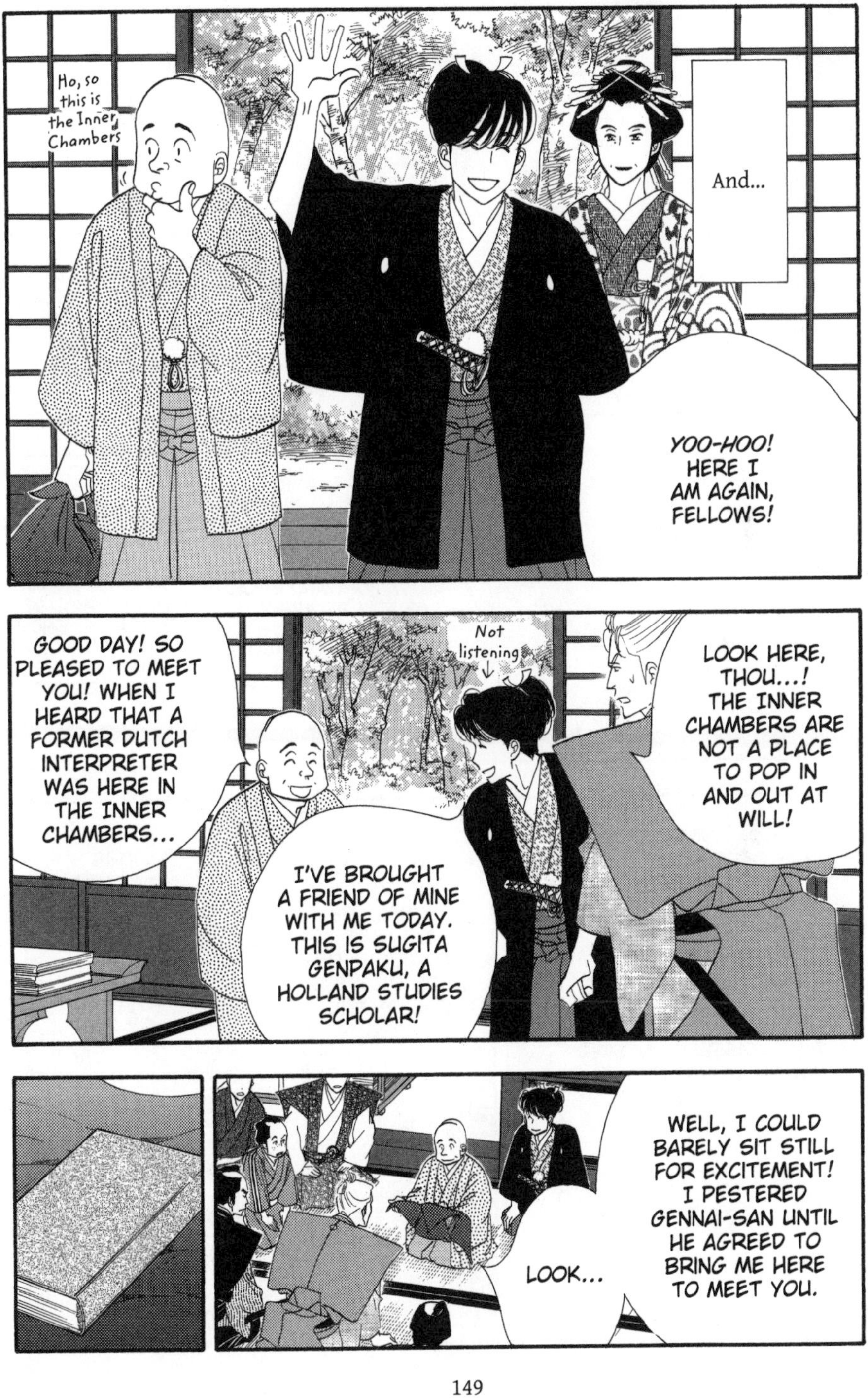
And...
YOO-HOO! HERE I AM AGAIN, FELLOWS!
Ho, so this is the Inner Chambers
LOOK HERE, THOU...! THE INNER CHAMBERS ARE NOT A PLACE TO POP IN AND OUT AT WILL!
Not listening
I'VE BROUGHT A FRIEND OF MINE WITH ME TODAY. THIS IS SUGITA GENPAKU, A HOLLAND STUDIES SCHOLAR!
GOOD DAY! SO PLEASED TO MEET YOU! WHEN I HEARD THAT A FORMER DUTCH INTERPRETER WAS HERE IN THE INNER CHAMBERS...
WELL, I COULD BARELY SIT STILL FOR EXCITEMENT! I PESTERED GENNAI-SAN UNTIL HE AGREED TO BRING ME HERE TO MEET YOU.
LOOK...

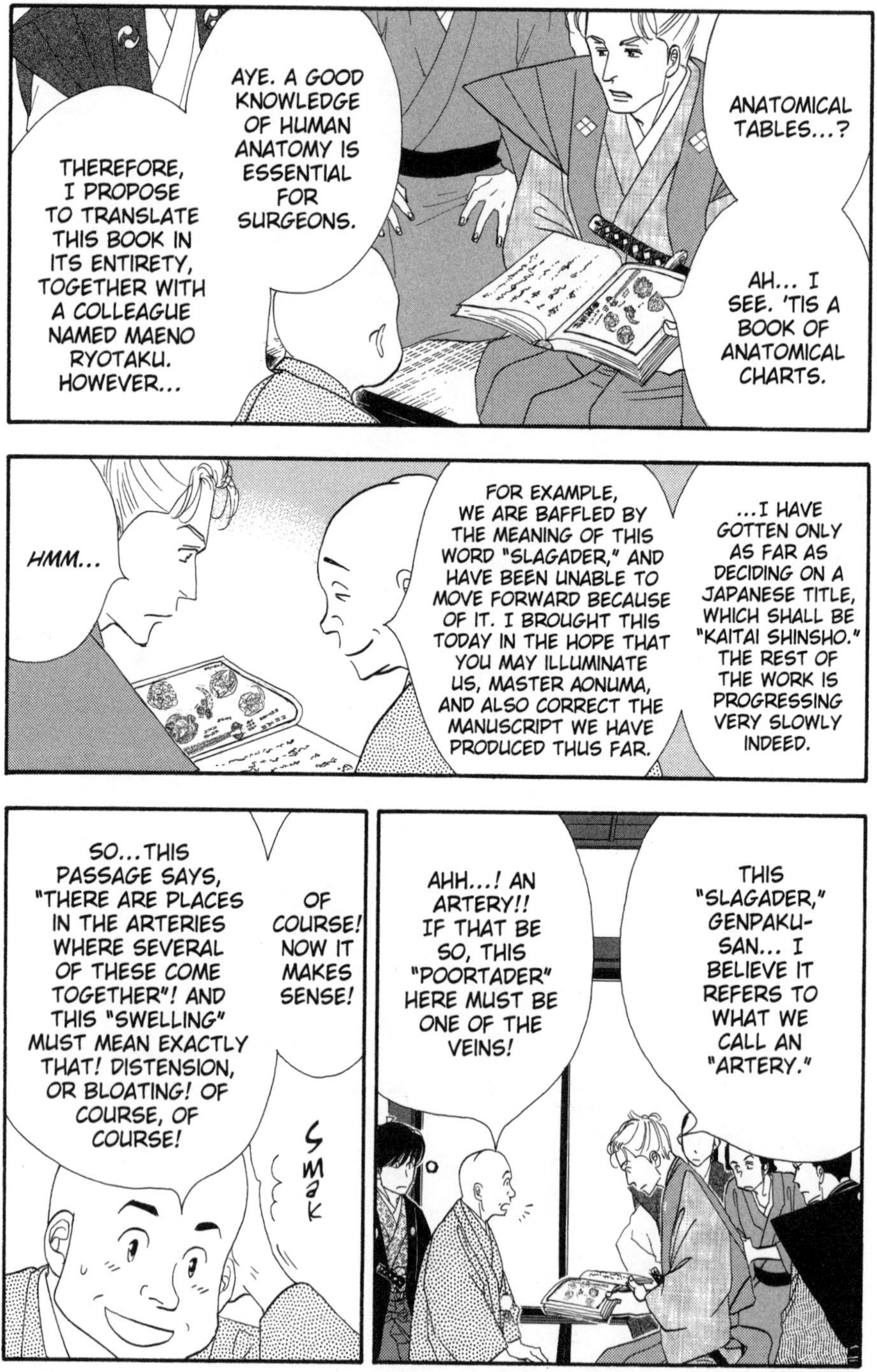
ANATOMICAL TABLES...?
AH... I SEE. 'TIS A BOOK OF ANATOMICAL CHARTS.
AYE. A GOOD KNOWLEDGE OF HUMAN ANATOMY IS ESSENTIAL FOR SURGEONS.
THEREFORE, I PROPOSE TO TRANSLATE THIS BOOK IN ITS ENTIRETY, TOGETHER WITH A COLLEAGUE NAMED MAENO RYOTAKU. HOWEVER...
...I HAVE GOTTEN ONLY AS FAR AS DECIDING ON A JAPANESE TITLE, WHICH SHALL BE "KAITAI SHINSHO." THE REST OF THE WORK IS PROGRESSING VERY SLOWLY INDEED.
FOR EXAMPLE, WE ARE BAFFLED BY THE MEANING OF THIS WORD "SLAGADER," AND HAVE BEEN UNABLE TO MOVE FORWARD BECAUSE OF IT. I BROUGHT THIS TODAY IN THE HOPE THAT YOU MAY ILLUMINATE US, MASTER AONUMA, AND ALSO CORRECT THE MANUSCRIPT WE HAVE PRODUCED THUS FAR.
HMM...
THIS "SLAGADER," GENPAKU-SAN... I BELIEVE IT REFERS TO WHAT WE CALL AN "ARTERY."
AHH...! AN ARTERY!! IF THAT BE SO, THIS "POORTADER" HERE MUST BE ONE OF THE VEINS!
OF COURSE! NOW IT MAKES SENSE!
SO...THIS PASSAGE SAYS, "THERE ARE PLACES IN THE ARTERIES WHERE SEVERAL OF THESE COME TOGETHER"! AND THIS "SWELLING" MUST MEAN EXACTLY THAT! DISTENSION, OR BLOATING! OF COURSE, OF COURSE!
SMAK

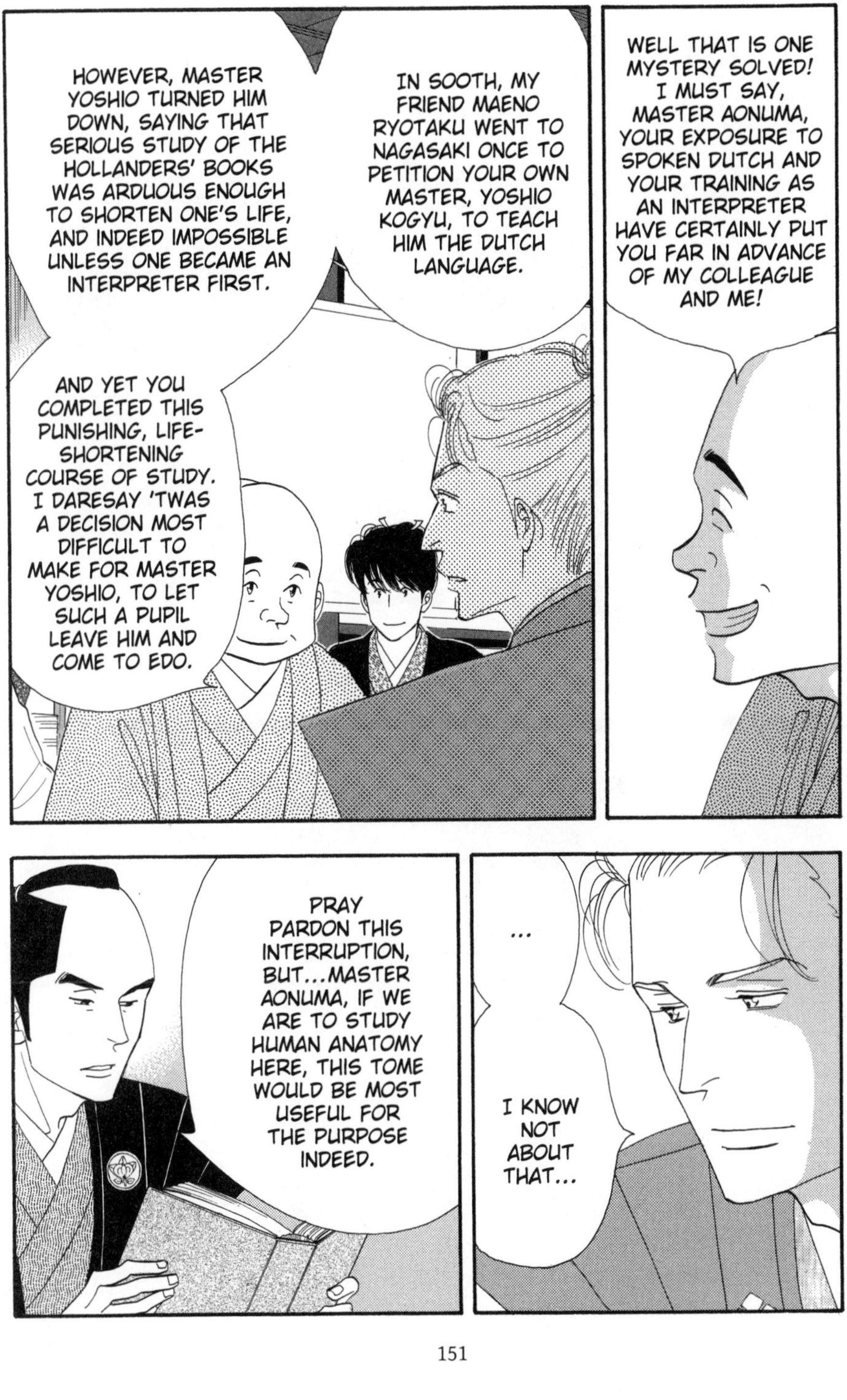
WELL THAT IS ONE MYSTERY SOLVED! I MUST SAY, MASTER AONUMA, YOUR EXPOSURE TO SPOKEN DUTCH AND YOUR TRAINING AS AN INTERPRETER HAVE CERTAINLY PUT YOU FAR IN ADVANCE OF MY COLLEAGUE AND ME!
IN SOOTH, MY FRIEND MAENO RYOTAKU WENT TO NAGASAKI ONCE TO PETITION YOUR OWN MASTER, YOSHIO KOGYU, TO TEACH HIM THE DUTCH LANGUAGE.
HOWEVER, MASTER YOSHIO TURNED HIM DOWN, SAYING THAT SERIOUS STUDY OF THE HOLLANDERS' BOOKS WAS ARDUOUS ENOUGH TO SHORTEN ONE'S LIFE, AND INDEED IMPOSSIBLE UNLESS ONE BECAME AN INTERPRETER FIRST.
AND YET YOU COMPLETED THIS PUNISHING, LIFE-SHORTENING COURSE OF STUDY. I DARESAY 'TWAS A DECISION MOST DIFFICULT TO MAKE FOR MASTER YOSHIO, TO LET SUCH A PUPIL LEAVE HIM AND COME TO EDO.
...
I KNOW NOT ABOUT THAT...
PRAY PARDON THIS INTERRUPTION, BUT...MASTER AONUMA, IF WE ARE TO STUDY HUMAN ANATOMY HERE, THIS TOME WOULD BE MOST USEFUL FOR THE PURPOSE INDEED.

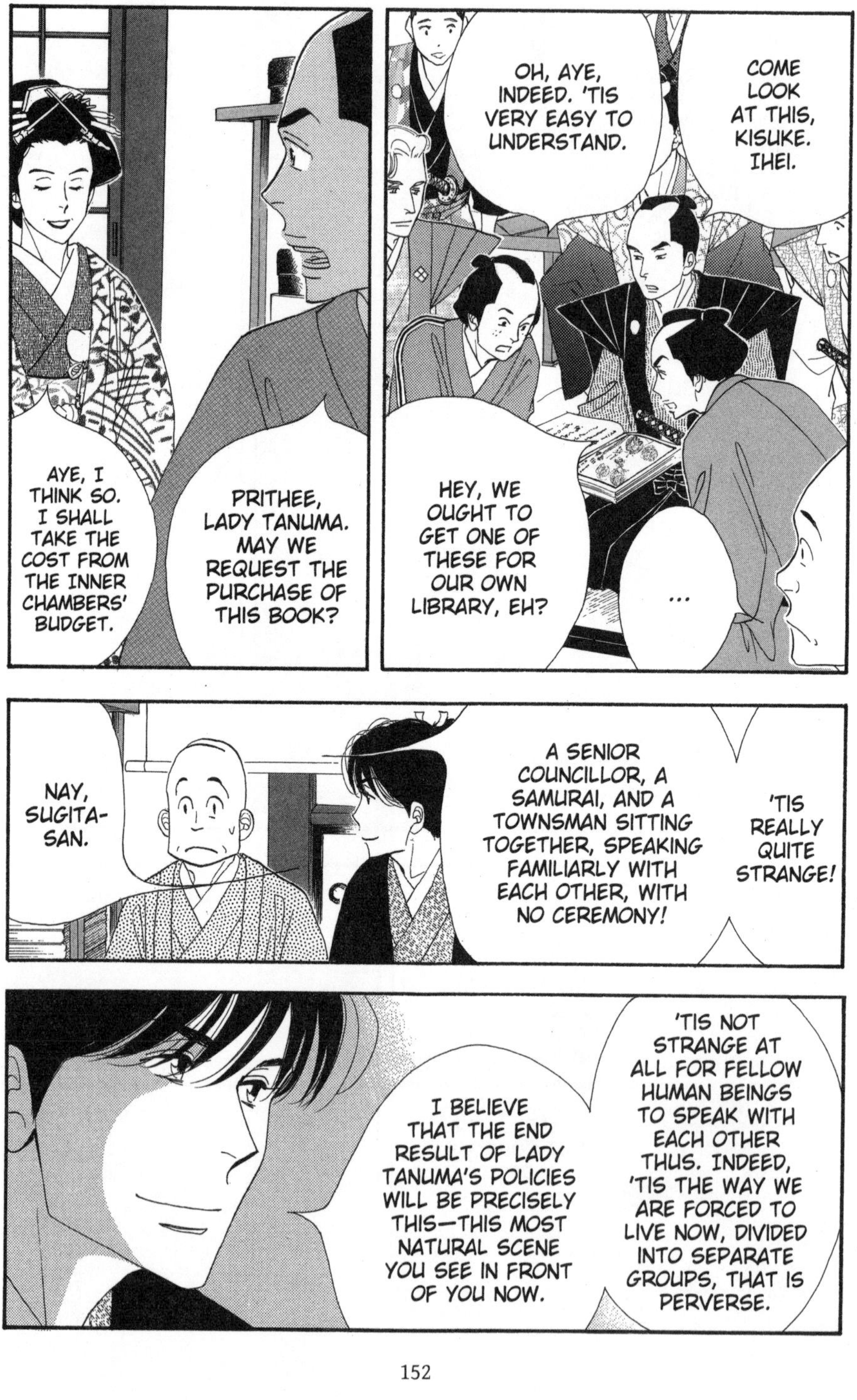
COME LOOK AT THIS, KISUKE. IHEI.
OH, AYE, INDEED. 'TIS VERY EASY TO UNDERSTAND.
HEY, WE OUGHT TO GET ONE OF THESE FOR OUR OWN LIBRARY, EH?
...
PRITHEE, LADY TANUMA. MAY WE REQUEST THE PURCHASE OF THIS BOOK?
AYE, I THINK SO. I SHALL TAKE THE COST FROM THE INNER CHAMBERS' BUDGET.
'TIS REALLY QUITE STRANGE!
A SENIOR COUNCILLOR, A SAMURAI, AND A TOWNSMAN SITTING TOGETHER, SPEAKING FAMILIARLY WITH EACH OTHER, WITH NO CEREMONY!
NAY, SUGITA-SAN.
'TIS NOT STRANGE AT ALL FOR FELLOW HUMAN BEINGS TO SPEAK WITH EACH OTHER THUS. INDEED, 'TIS THE WAY WE ARE FORCED TO LIVE NOW, DIVIDED INTO SEPARATE GROUPS, THAT IS PERVERSE.
I BELIEVE THAT THE END RESULT OF LADY TANUMA'S POLICIES WILL BE PRECISELY THIS—THIS MOST NATURAL SCENE YOU SEE IN FRONT OF YOU NOW.

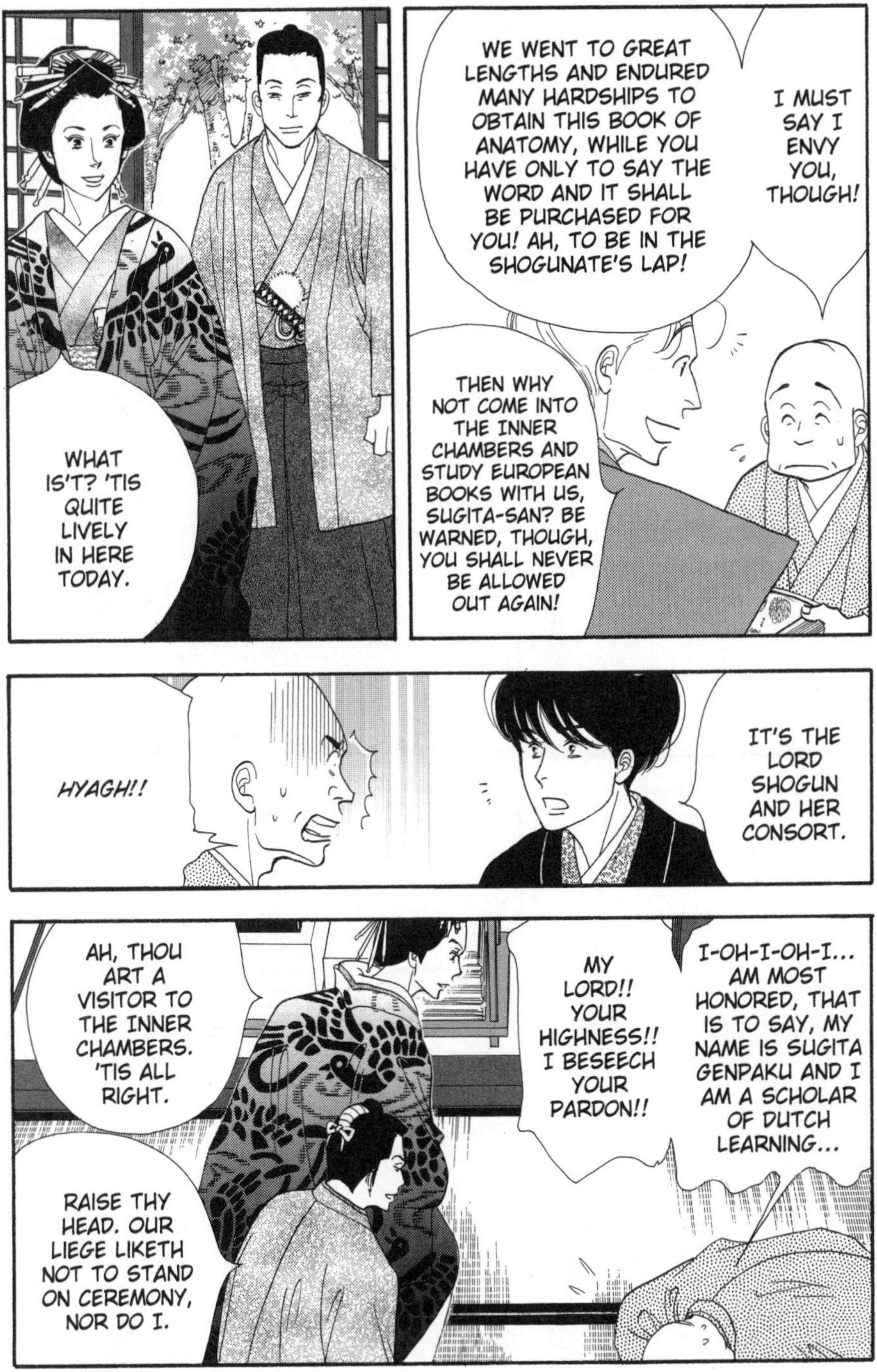
I MUST SAY I ENVY YOU, THOUGH!
WE WENT TO GREAT LENGTHS AND ENDURED MANY HARDSHIPS TO OBTAIN THIS BOOK OF ANATOMY, WHILE YOU HAVE ONLY TO SAY THE WORD AND IT SHALL BE PURCHASED FOR YOU! AH, TO BE IN THE SHOGUNATE'S LAP!
THEN WHY NOT COME INTO THE INNER CHAMBERS AND STUDY EUROPEAN BOOKS WITH US, SUGITA-SAN? BE WARNED, THOUGH, YOU SHALL NEVER BE ALLOWED OUT AGAIN!
WHAT IS'T? 'TIS QUITE LIVELY IN HERE TODAY.
IT'S THE LORD SHOGUN AND HER CONSORT.
HYAGH!!
I-OH-I-OH-I... AM MOST HONORED, THAT IS TO SAY, MY NAME IS SUGITA GENPAKU AND I AM A SCHOLAR OF DUTCH LEARNING...
MY LORD!! YOUR HIGHNESS!! I BESEECH YOUR PARDON!!
AH, THOU ART A VISITOR TO THE INNER CHAMBERS. 'TIS ALL RIGHT.
RAISE THY HEAD. OUR LIEGE LIKETH NOT TO STAND ON CEREMONY, NOR DO I.

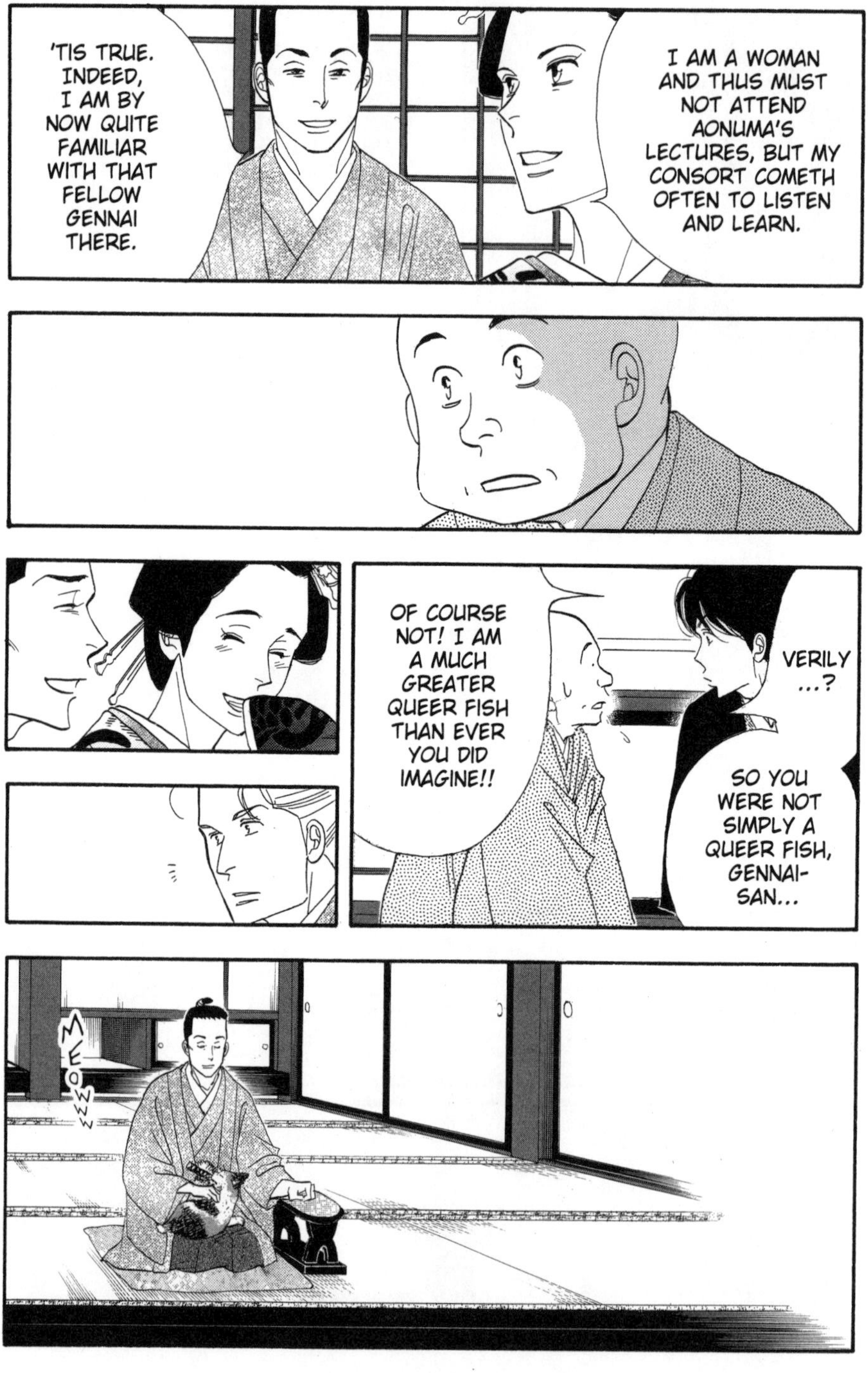
I AM A WOMAN AND THUS MUST NOT ATTEND AONUMA'S LECTURES, BUT MY CONSORT COMETH OFTEN TO LISTEN AND LEARN.
'TIS TRUE. INDEED, I AM BY NOW QUITE FAMILIAR WITH THAT FELLOW GENNAI THERE.
VERILY ...?
SO YOU WERE NOT SIMPLY A QUEER FISH, GENNAI-SAN...
OF COURSE NOT! I AM A MUCH GREATER QUEER FISH THAN EVER YOU DID IMAGINE!!
MEOWWW

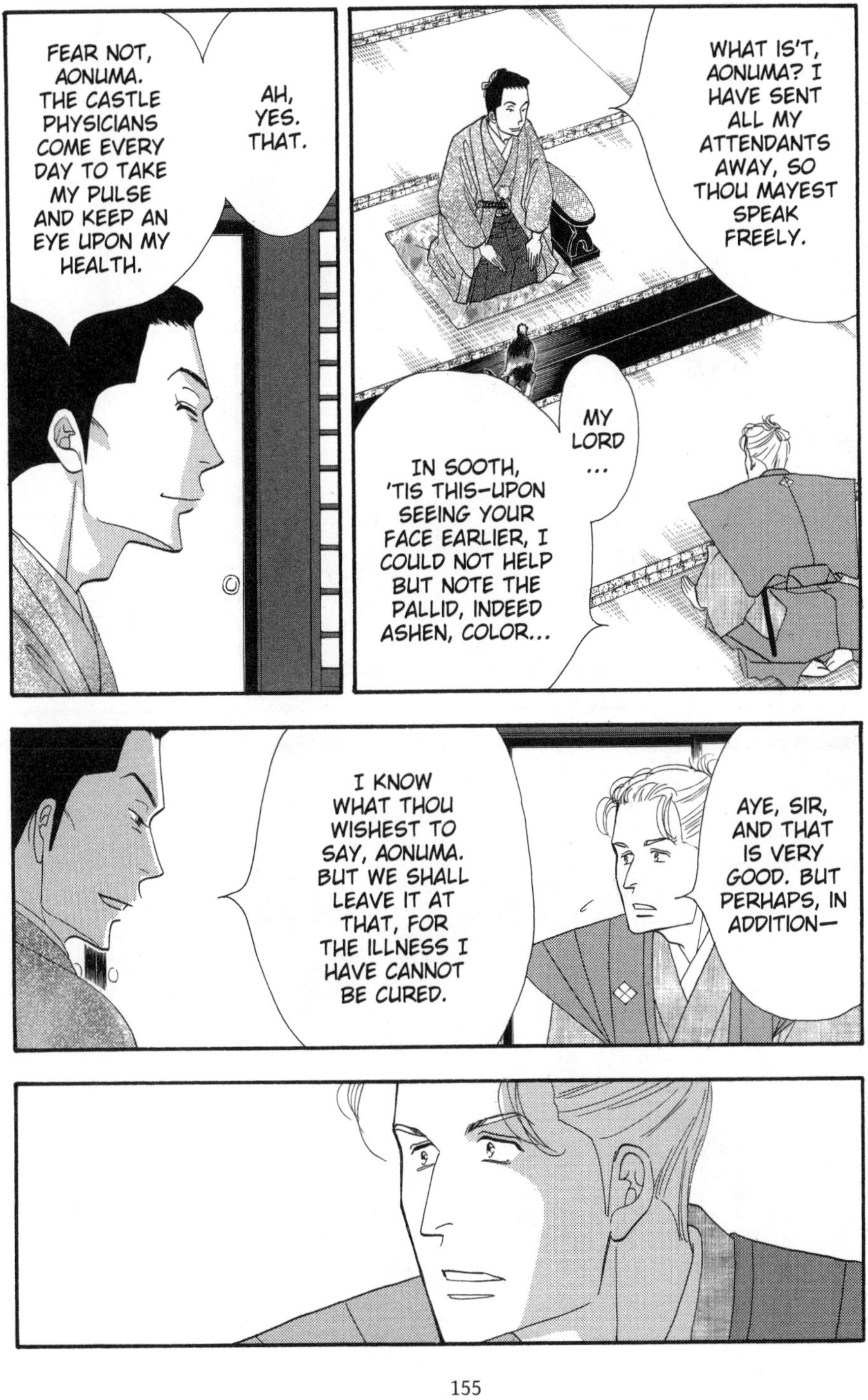
WHAT IS'T, AONUMA? I HAVE SENT ALL MY ATTENDANTS AWAY, SO THOU MAYEST SPEAK FREELY.
MY LORD...
IN SOOTH, 'TIS THIS—UPON SEEING YOUR FACE EARLIER, I COULD NOT HELP BUT NOTE THE PALLID, INDEED ASHEN, COLOR...
AH, YES. THAT.
FEAR NOT, AONUMA. THE CASTLE PHYSICIANS COME EVERY DAY TO TAKE MY PULSE AND KEEP AN EYE UPON MY HEALTH.
AYE, SIR, AND THAT IS VERY GOOD. BUT PERHAPS, IN ADDITION—
I KNOW WHAT THOU WISHEST TO SAY, AONUMA. BUT WE SHALL LEAVE IT AT THAT, FOR THE ILLNESS I HAVE CANNOT BE CURED.

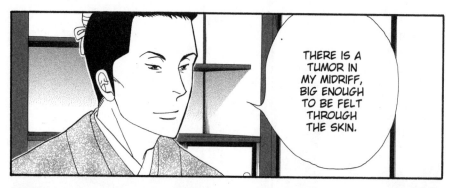

THERE IS A TUMOR IN MY MIDRIFF, BIG ENOUGH TO BE FELT THROUGH THE SKIN.
...
AYE?
'TIS BETTER LEFT TO THE CASTLE PHYSICIANS. IF THOU DOTH TREAT ME FOR SOMETHING INCURABLE, LATER THEY WILL SAY 'TWAS THE FAULT OF HOLLANDER MEDICINE THAT I AM DEAD.
I WISH NOT TO SEE THEE BANISHED FROM THE INNER CHAMBERS.
THAT IS MY FINAL DESIRE—THAT THY LECTURES CONTINUE.

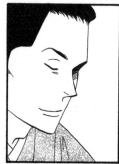

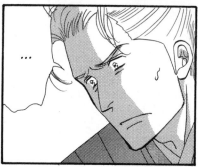

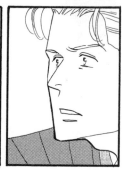

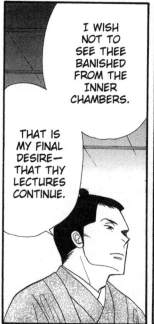

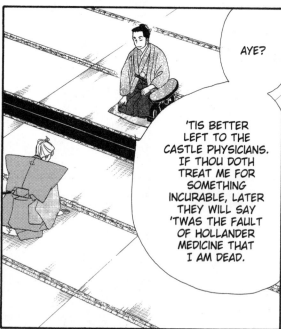

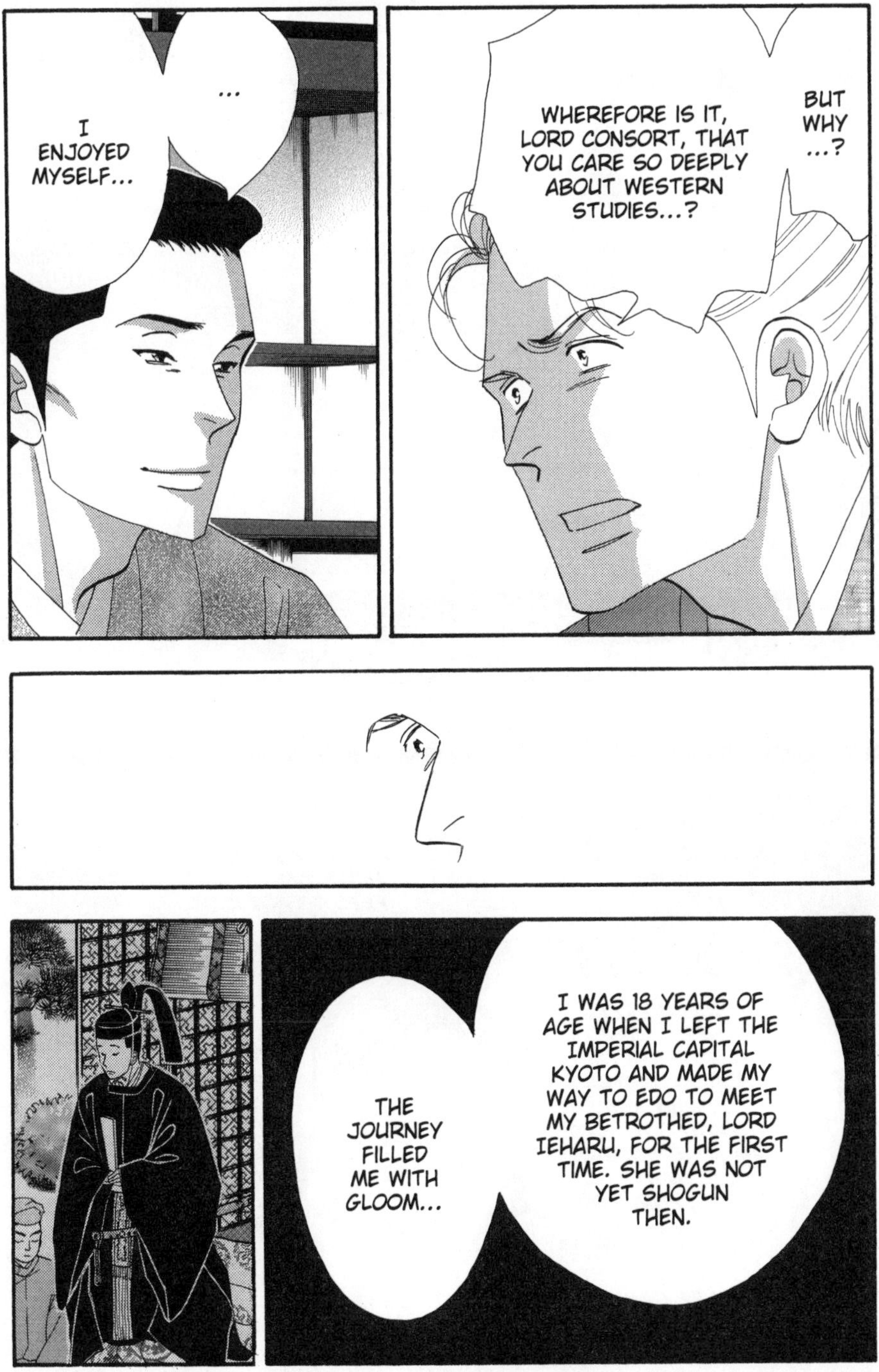
BUT WHY ...?
WHEREFORE IS IT, LORD CONSORT, THAT YOU CARE SO DEEPLY ABOUT WESTERN STUDIES...?
...
I ENJOYED MYSELF...
I WAS 18 YEARS OF AGE WHEN I LEFT THE IMPERIAL CAPITAL KYOTO AND MADE MY WAY TO EDO TO MEET MY BETROTHED, LORD IEHARU, FOR THE FIRST TIME. SHE WAS NOT YET SHOGUN THEN.
THE JOURNEY FILLED ME WITH GLOOM...

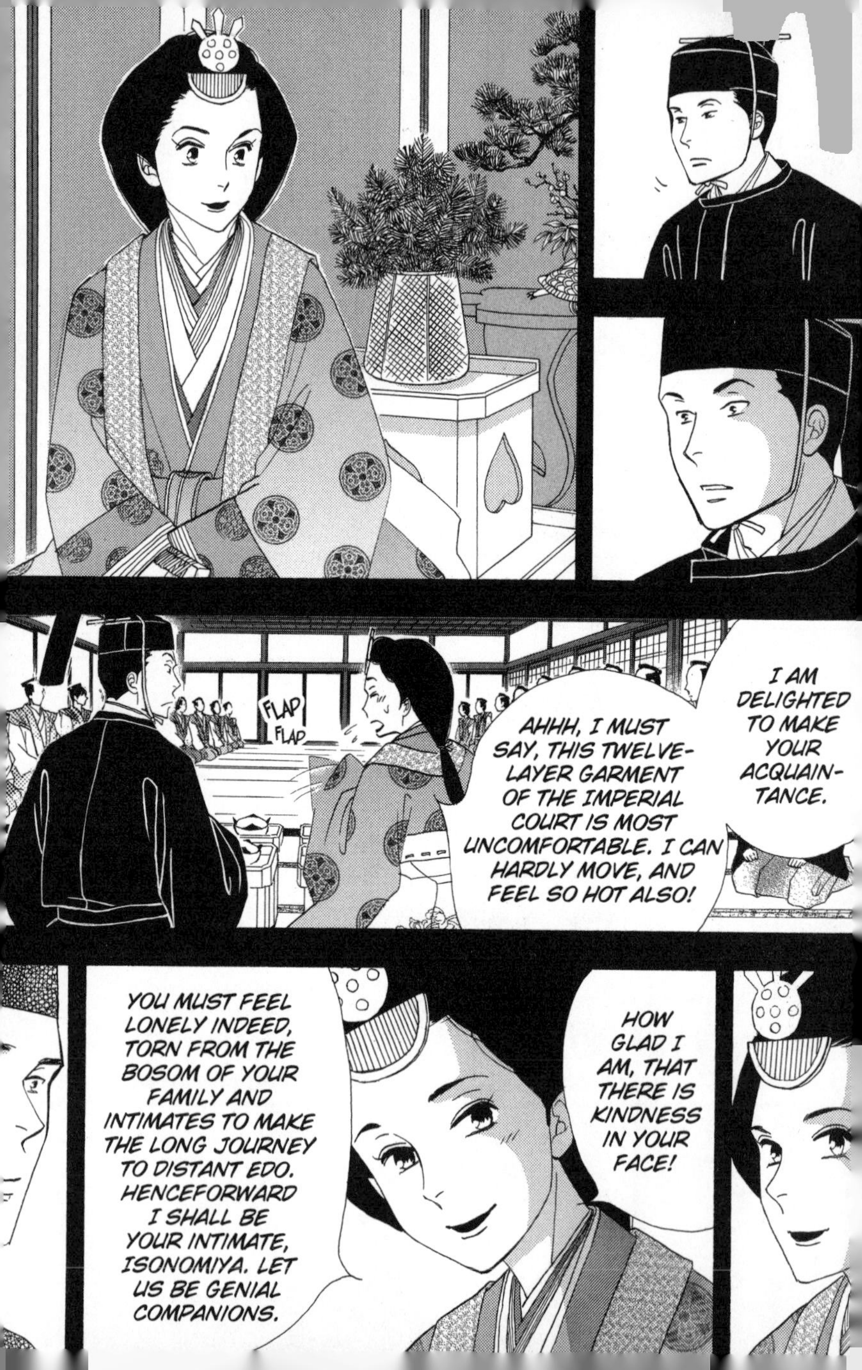
I AM DELIGHTED TO MAKE YOUR ACQUAINTANCE.
AHHH, I MUST SAY, THIS TWELVE-LAYER GARMENT OF THE IMPERIAL COURT IS MOST UNCOMFORTABLE. I CAN HARDLY MOVE, AND FEEL SO HOT ALSO!
FLAP
FLAP
HOW GLAD I AM, THAT THERE IS KINDNESS IN YOUR FACE!
YOU MUST FEEL LONELY INDEED, TORN FROM THE BOSOM OF YOUR FAMILY AND INTIMATES TO MAKE THE LONG JOURNEY TO DISTANT EDO. HENCEFORWARD I SHALL BE YOUR INTIMATE, ISONOMIYA. LET US BE GENIAL COMPANIONS.

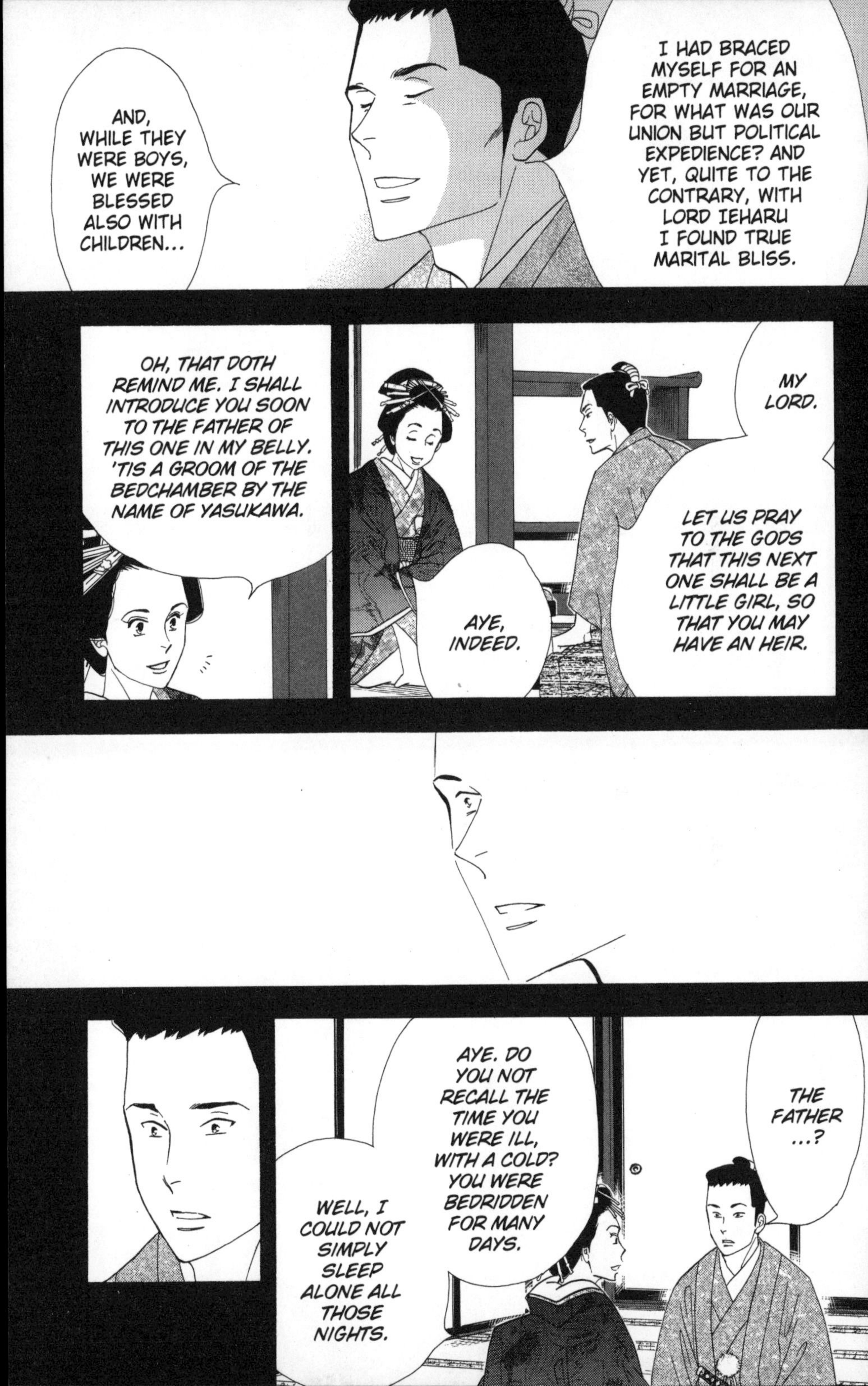
I HAD BRACED MYSELF FOR AN EMPTY MARRIAGE, FOR WHAT WAS OUR UNION BUT POLITICAL EXPEDIENCE? AND YET, QUITE TO THE CONTRARY, WITH LORD IEHARU I FOUND TRUE MARITAL BLISS.
AND, WHILE THEY WERE BOYS, WE WERE BLESSED ALSO WITH CHILDREN...
MY LORD.
LET US PRAY TO THE GODS THAT THIS NEXT ONE SHALL BE A LITTLE GIRL, SO THAT YOU MAY HAVE AN HEIR.
AYE, INDEED.
OH, THAT DOTH REMIND ME. I SHALL INTRODUCE YOU SOON TO THE FATHER OF THIS ONE IN MY BELLY. 'TIS A GROOM OF THE BEDCHAMBER BY THE NAME OF YASUKAWA.
THE FATHER ...?
AYE. DO YOU NOT RECALL THE TIME YOU WERE ILL, WITH A COLD? YOU WERE BEDRIDDEN FOR MANY DAYS.
WELL, I COULD NOT SIMPLY SLEEP ALONE ALL THOSE NIGHTS.

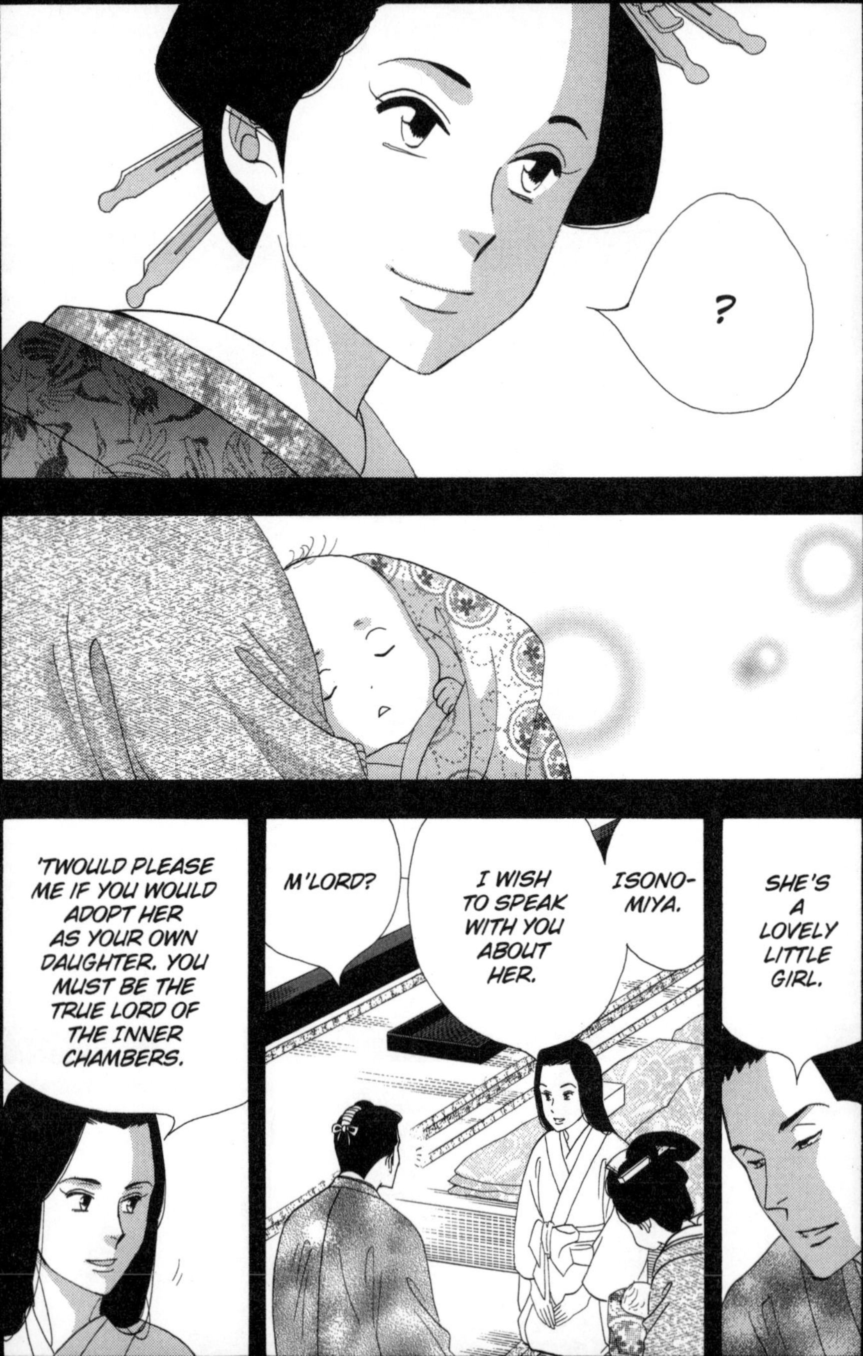
?
SHE'S A LOVELY LITTLE GIRL.
ISONO-MIYA.
I WISH TO SPEAK WITH YOU ABOUT HER.
M'LORD?
'TWOULD PLEASE ME IF YOU WOULD ADOPT HER AS YOUR OWN DAUGHTER. YOU MUST BE THE TRUE LORD OF THE INNER CHAMBERS.

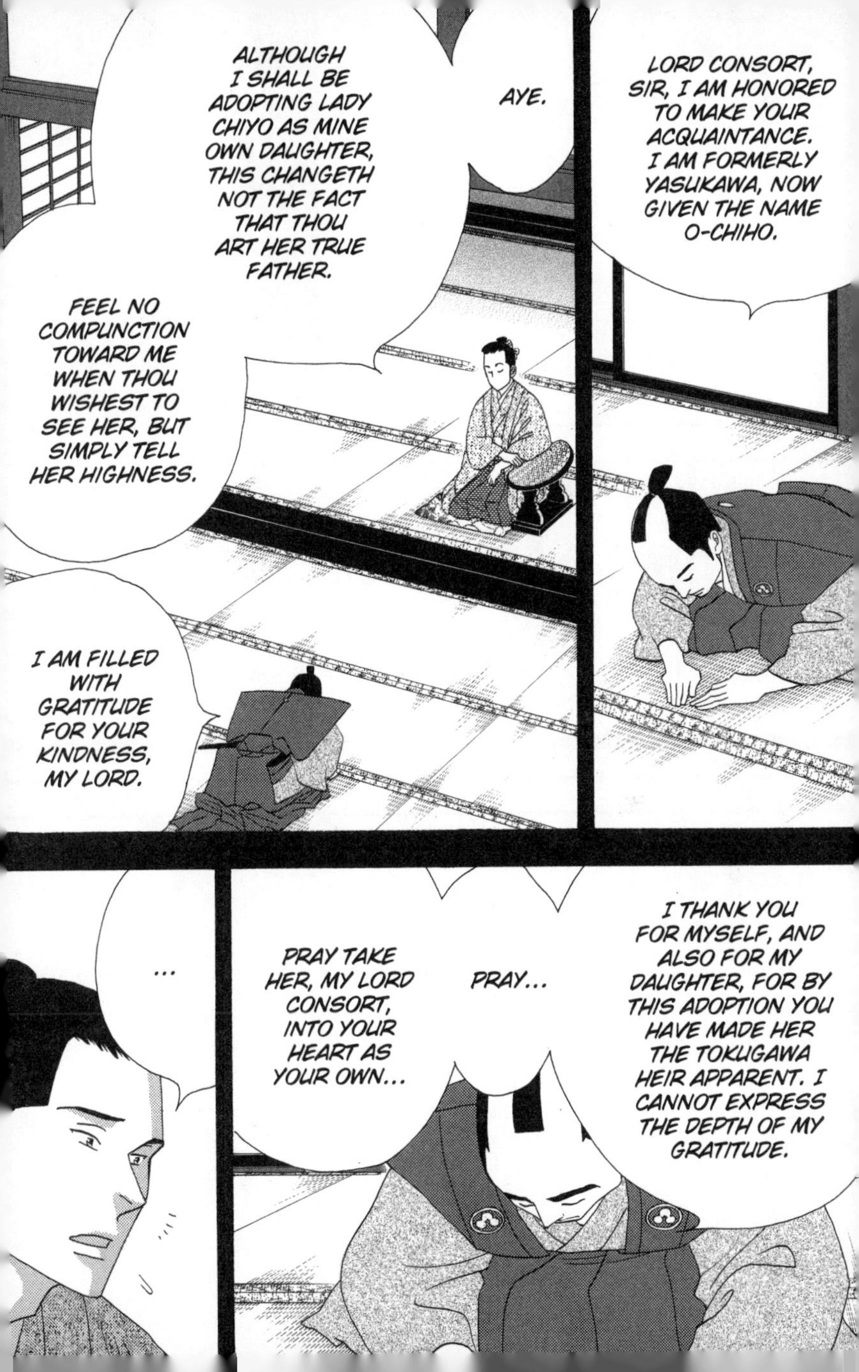
LORD CONSORT, SIR, I AM HONORED TO MAKE YOUR ACQUAINTANCE. I AM FORMERLY YASUKAWA, NOW GIVEN THE NAME O-CHIHO.
AYE.
ALTHOUGH I SHALL BE ADOPTING LADY CHIYO AS MINE OWN DAUGHTER, THIS CHANGETH NOT THE FACT THAT THOU ART HER TRUE FATHER.
FEEL NO COMPUNCTION TOWARD ME WHEN THOU WISHEST TO SEE HER, BUT SIMPLY TELL HER HIGHNESS.
I AM FILLED WITH GRATITUDE FOR YOUR KINDNESS, MY LORD.
I THANK YOU FOR MYSELF, AND ALSO FOR MY DAUGHTER, FOR BY THIS ADOPTION YOU HAVE MADE HER THE TOKUGAWA HEIR APPARENT. I CANNOT EXPRESS THE DEPTH OF MY GRATITUDE.
PRAY...
PRAY TAKE HER, MY LORD CONSORT, INTO YOUR HEART AS YOUR OWN...
...

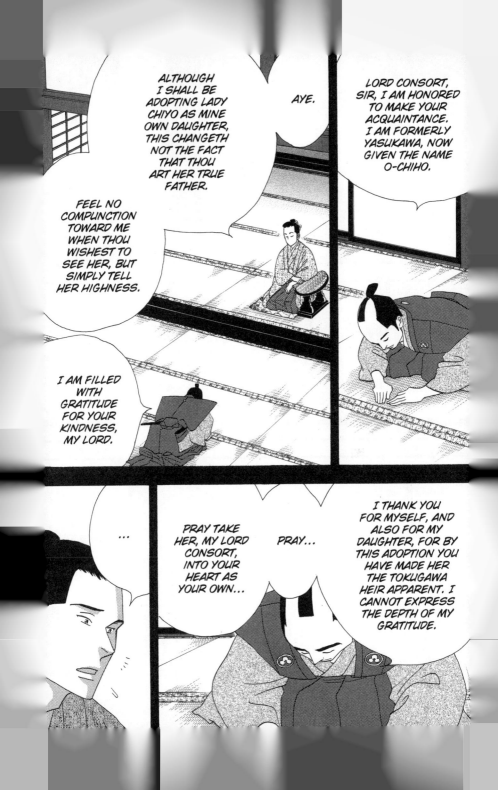

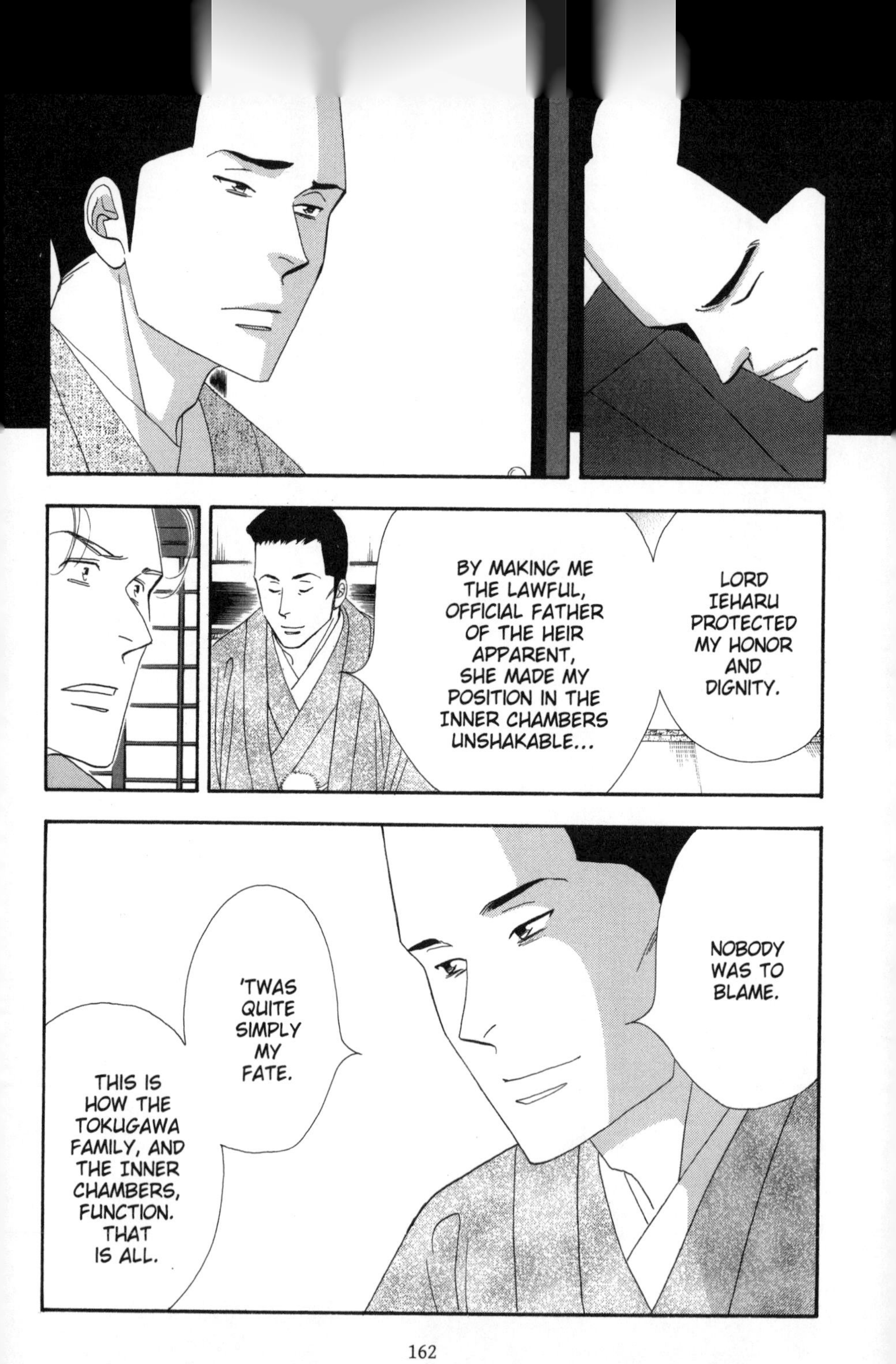
LORD IEHARU PROTECTED MY HONOR AND DIGNITY.
BY MAKING ME THE LAWFUL, OFFICIAL FATHER OF THE HEIR APPARENT, SHE MADE MY POSITION IN THE INNER CHAMBERS UNSHAKABLE...
NOBODY WAS TO BLAME.
'TWAS QUITE SIMPLY MY FATE.
THIS IS HOW THE TOKUGAWA FAMILY, AND THE INNER CHAMBERS, FUNCTION. THAT IS ALL.

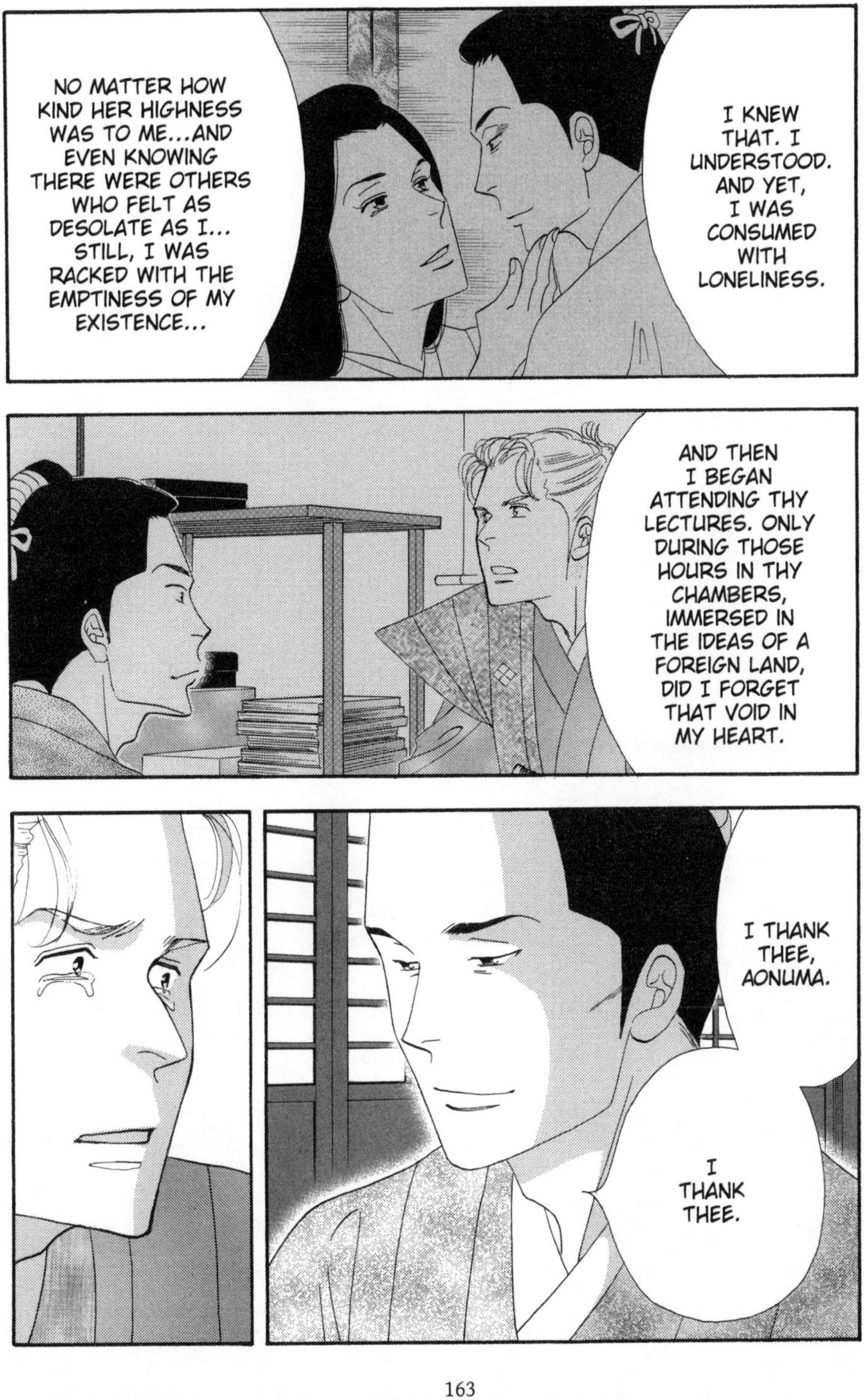
NO MATTER HOW KIND HER HIGHNESS WAS TO ME...AND EVEN KNOWING THERE WERE OTHERS WHO FELT AS DESOLATE AS I... STILL, I WAS RACKED WITH THE EMPTINESS OF MY EXISTENCE...
I KNEW THAT. I UNDERSTOOD. AND YET, I WAS CONSUMED WITH LONELINESS.
AND THEN I BEGAN ATTENDING THY LECTURES. ONLY DURING THOSE HOURS IN THY CHAMBERS, IMMERSED IN THE IDEAS OF A FOREIGN LAND, DID I FORGET THAT VOID IN MY HEART.
I THANK THEE, AONUMA.
I THANK THEE.

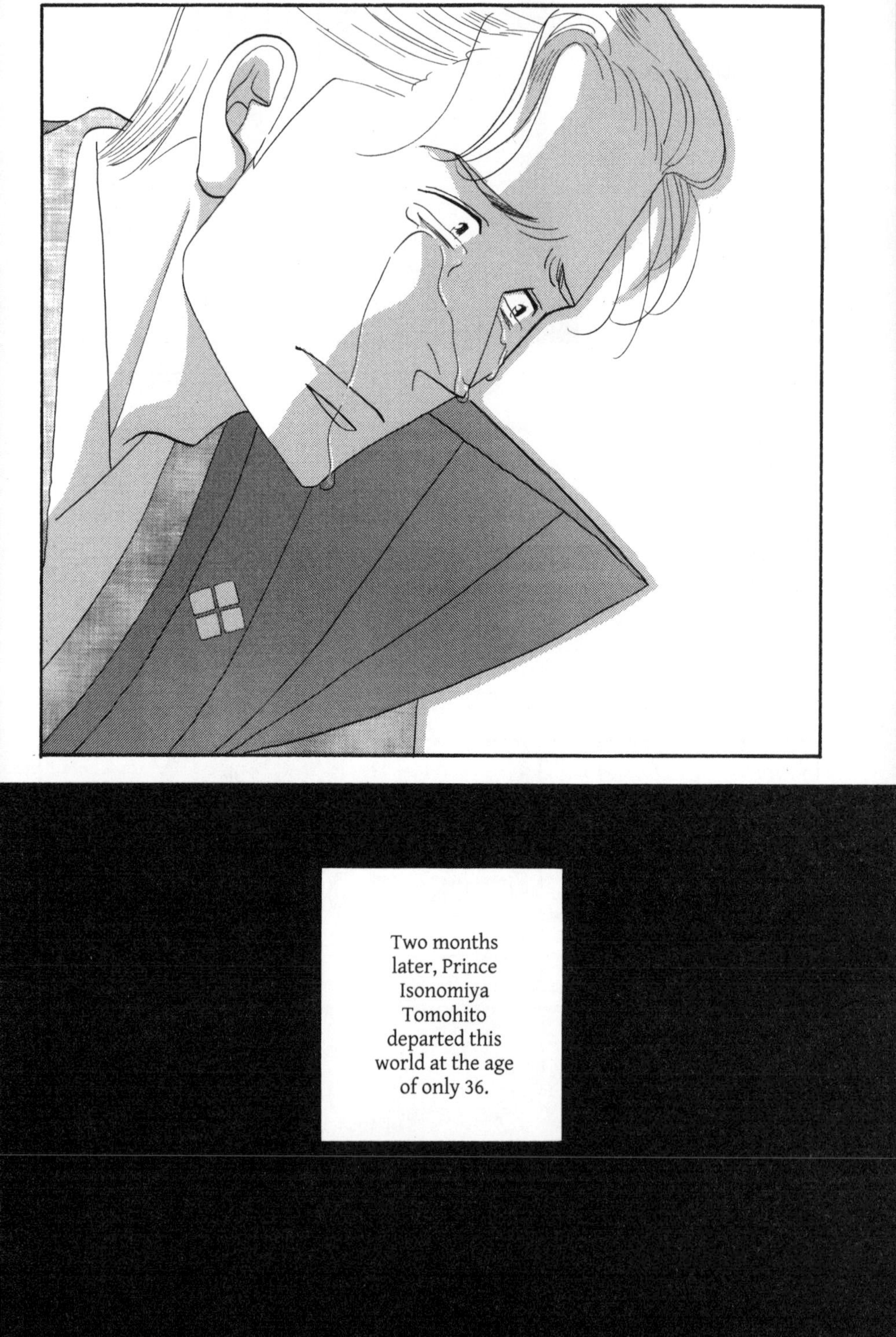
Two months later, Prince Isonomiya Tomohito departed this world at the age of only 36.

Ōoku
THE INNER CHAMBERS

Ōoku

THE INNER CHAMBERS

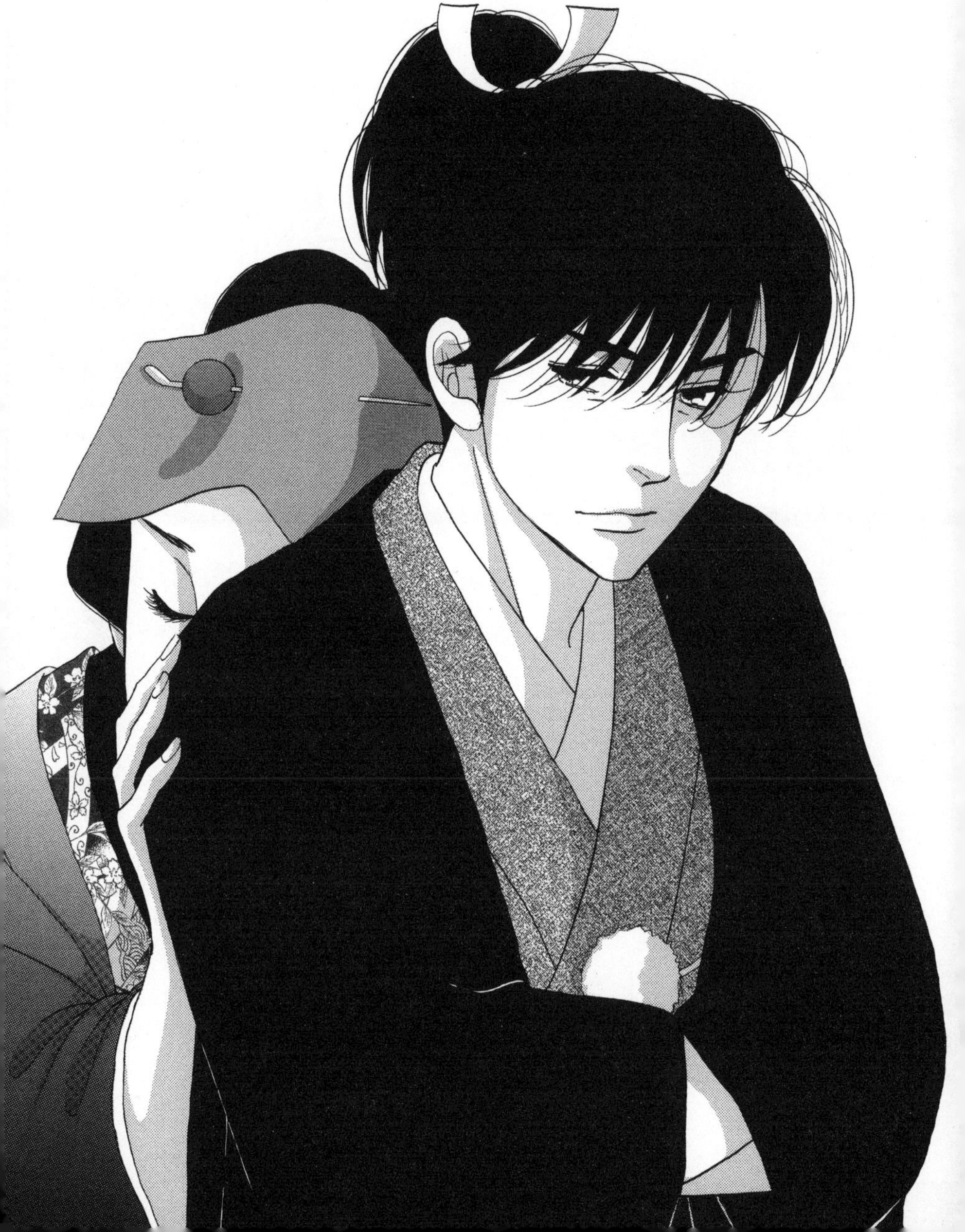

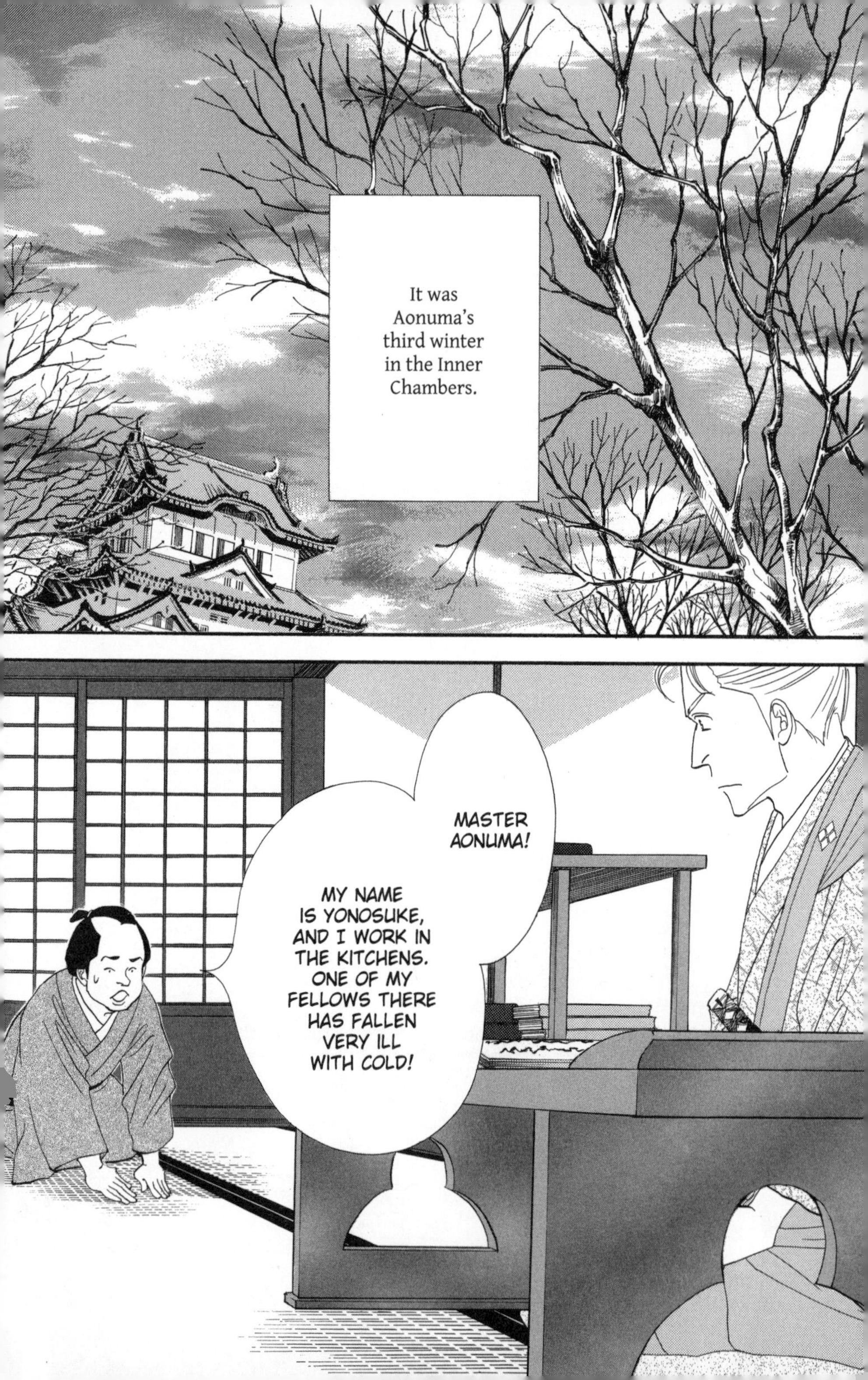
It was Aonuma's third winter in the Inner Chambers.
MASTER AONUMA!
MY NAME IS YONOSUKE, AND I WORK IN THE KITCHENS. ONE OF MY FELLOWS THERE HAS FALLEN VERY ILL WITH COLD!

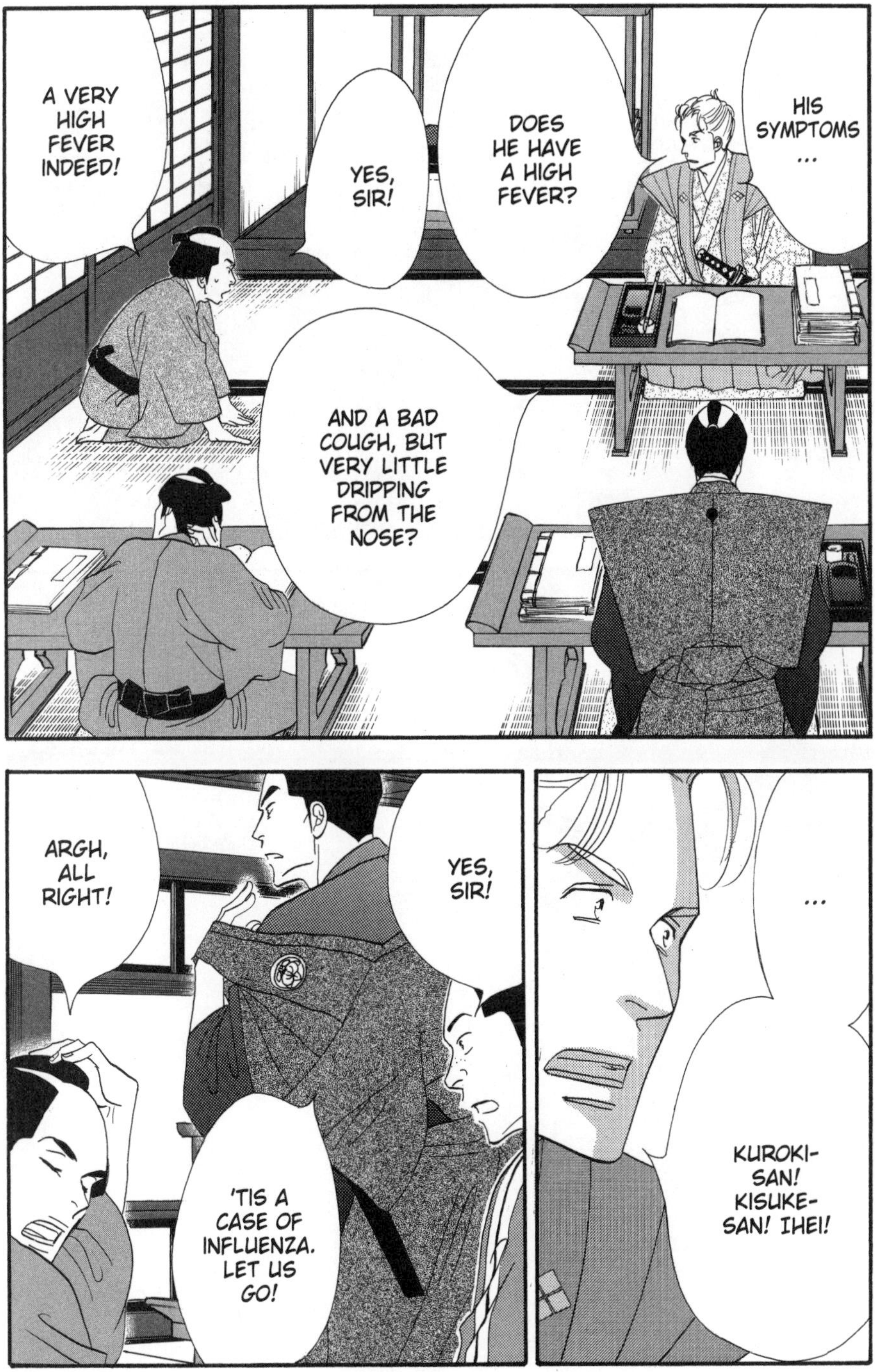
HIS SYMPTOMS ...
DOES HE HAVE A HIGH FEVER?
YES, SIR!
A VERY HIGH FEVER INDEED!
AND A BAD COUGH, BUT VERY LITTLE DRIPPING FROM THE NOSE?
...
KUROKI-SAN! KISUKE-SAN! IHEI!
YES, SIR!
ARGH, ALL RIGHT!
'TIS A CASE OF INFLUENZA. LET US GO!

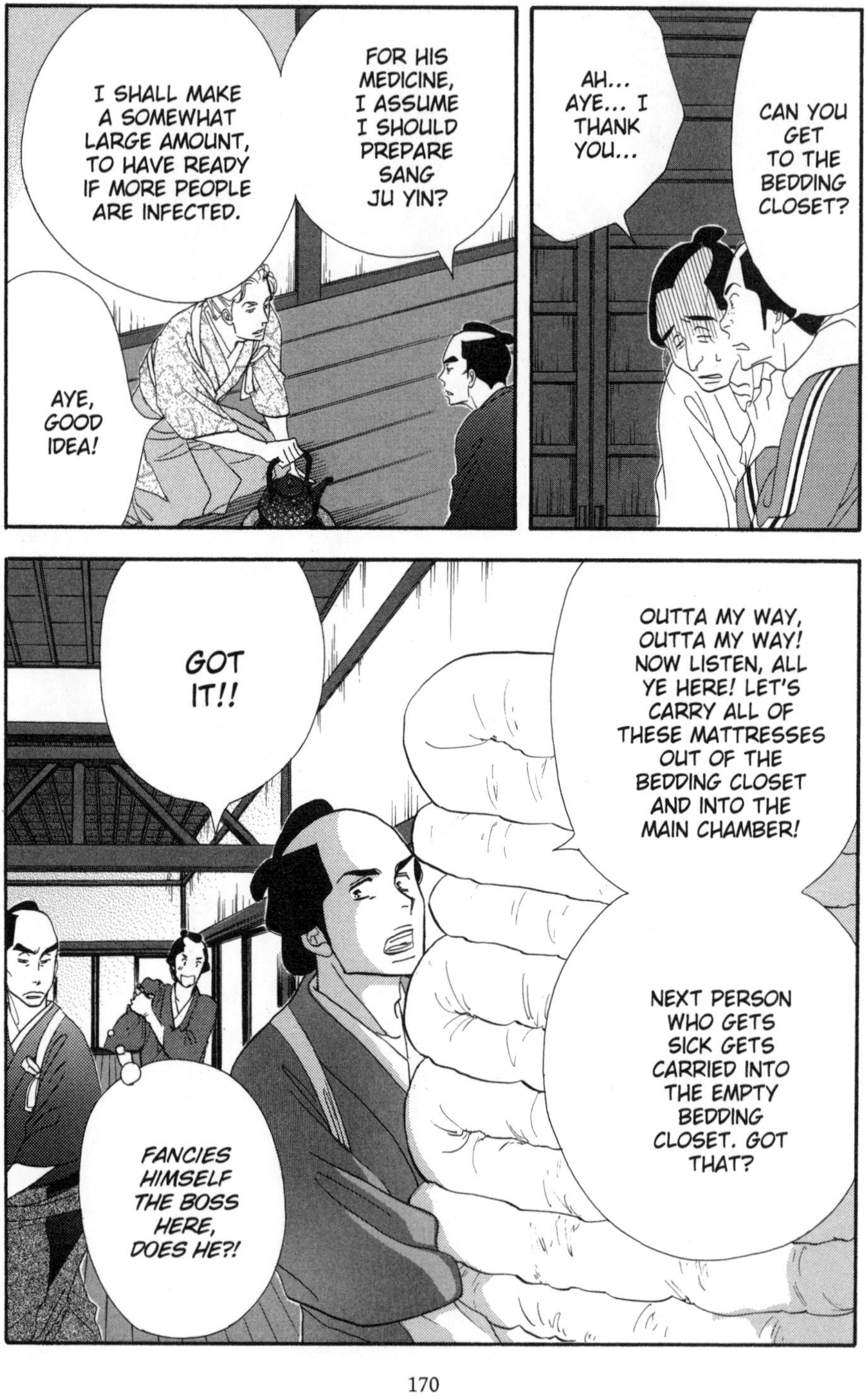
CAN YOU GET TO THE BEDDING CLOSET?
AH... AYE... I THANK YOU...
FOR HIS MEDICINE, I ASSUME I SHOULD PREPARE SANG JU YIN?
I SHALL MAKE A SOMEWHAT LARGE AMOUNT, TO HAVE READY IF MORE PEOPLE ARE INFECTED.
AYE, GOOD IDEA!
GOT IT!!
OUTTA MY WAY, OUTTA MY WAY! NOW LISTEN, ALL YE HERE! LET'S CARRY ALL OF THESE MATTRESSES OUT OF THE BEDDING CLOSET AND INTO THE MAIN CHAMBER!
NEXT PERSON WHO GETS SICK GETS CARRIED INTO THE EMPTY BEDDING CLOSET. GOT THAT?
FANCIES HIMSELF THE BOSS HERE, DOES HE?!

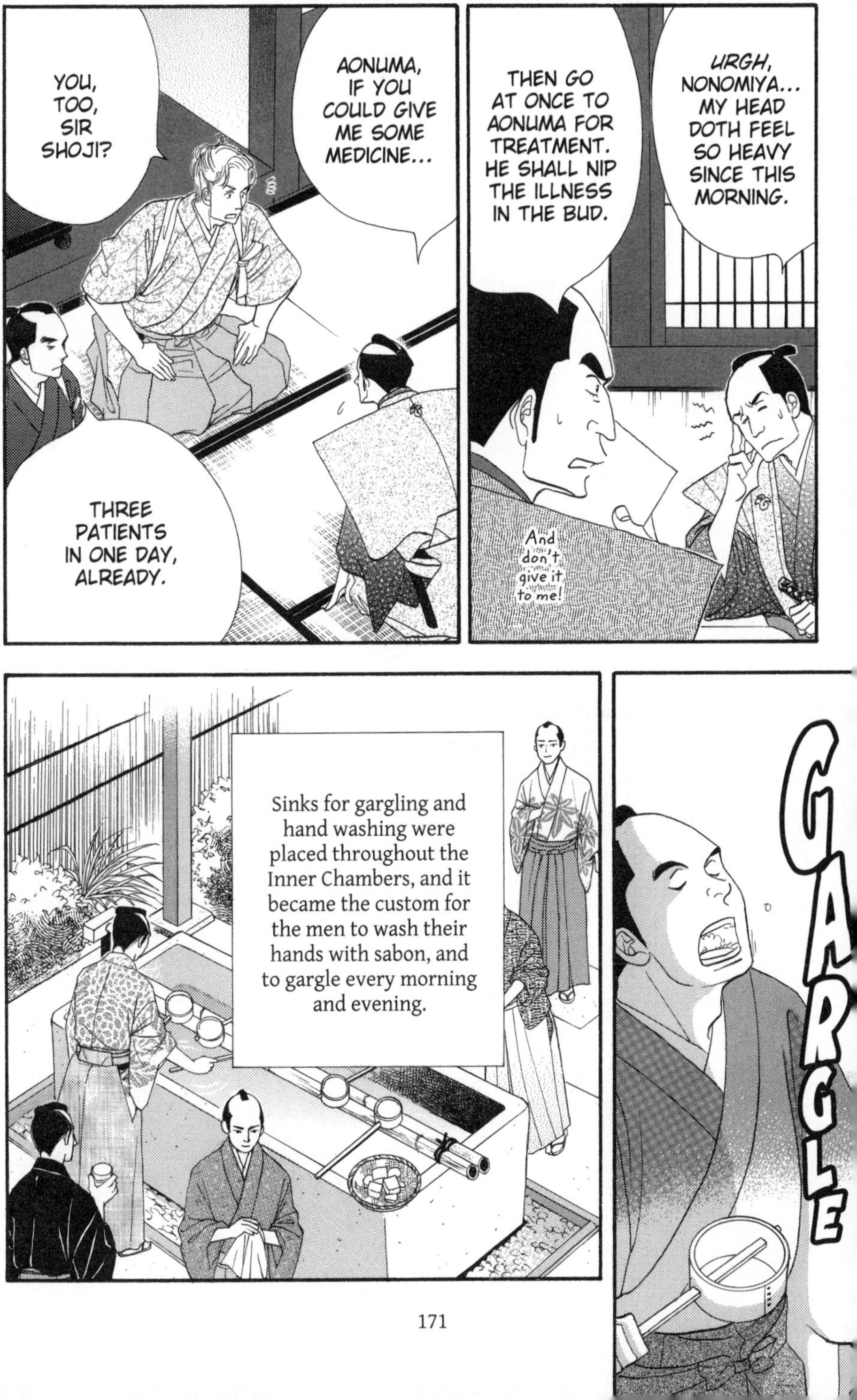
URGH, NONOMIYA... MY HEAD DOTH FEEL SO HEAVY SINCE THIS MORNING.
THEN GO AT ONCE TO AONUMA FOR TREATMENT. HE SHALL NIP THE ILLNESS IN THE BUD.
And don't give it to me!
AONUMA, IF YOU COULD GIVE ME SOME MEDICINE...
YOU, TOO, SIR SHOJI?
THREE PATIENTS IN ONE DAY, ALREADY.
GARGLE
Sinks for gargling and hand washing were placed throughout the Inner Chambers, and it became the custom for the men to wash their hands with sabon, and to gargle every morning and evening.

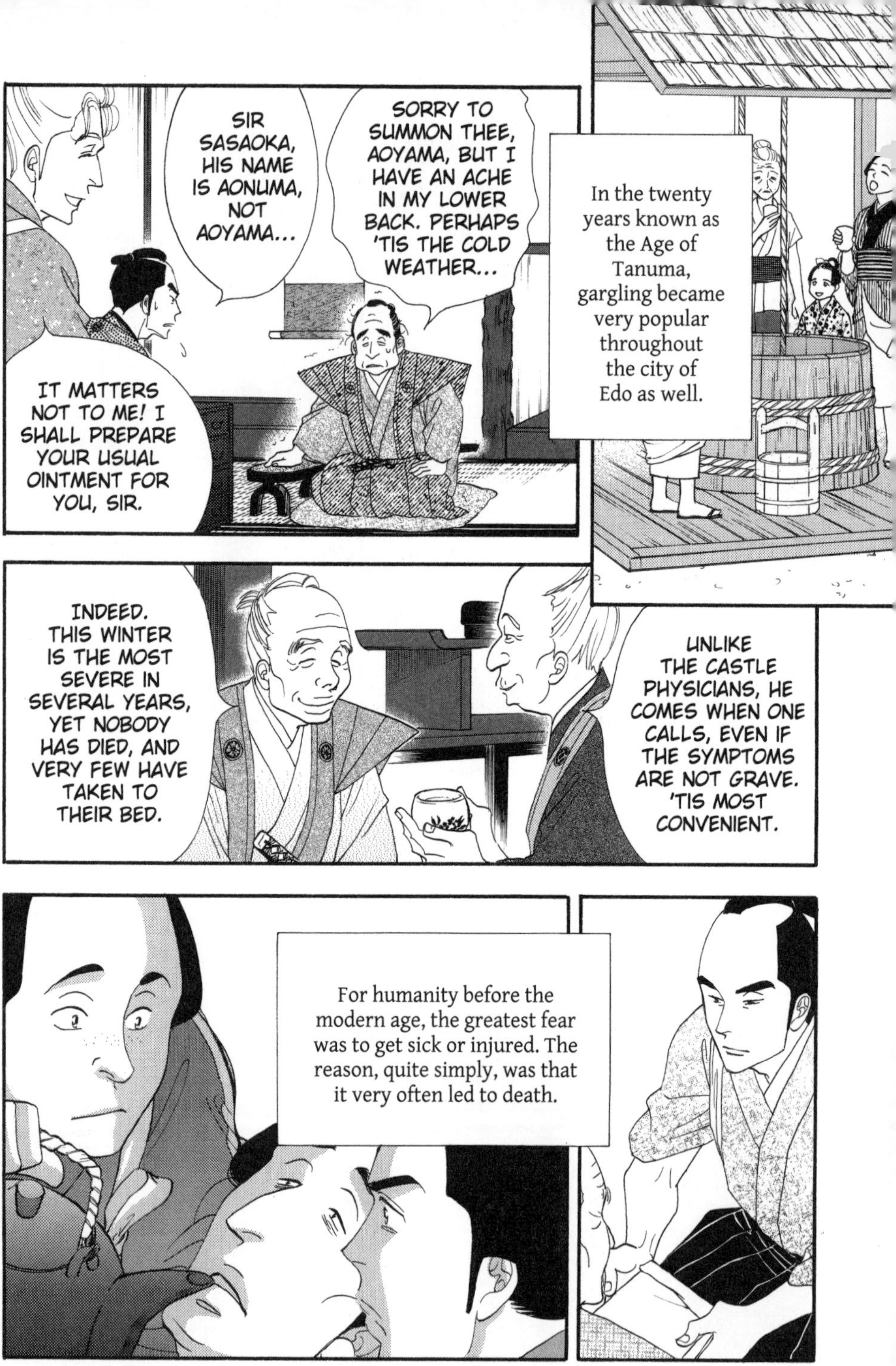
In the twenty years known as the Age of Tanuma, gargling became very popular throughout the city of Edo as well.
SORRY TO SUMMON THEE, AOYAMA, BUT I HAVE AN ACHE IN MY LOWER BACK. PERHAPS 'TIS THE COLD WEATHER...
SIR SASAOKA, HIS NAME IS AONUMA, NOT AOYAMA...
IT MATTERS NOT TO ME! I SHALL PREPARE YOUR USUAL OINTMENT FOR YOU, SIR.
UNLIKE THE CASTLE PHYSICIANS, HE COMES WHEN ONE CALLS, EVEN IF THE SYMPTOMS ARE NOT GRAVE. 'TIS MOST CONVENIENT.
INDEED. THIS WINTER IS THE MOST SEVERE IN SEVERAL YEARS, YET NOBODY HAS DIED, AND VERY FEW HAVE TAKEN TO THEIR BED.
For humanity before the modern age, the greatest fear was to get sick or injured. The reason, quite simply, was that it very often led to death.

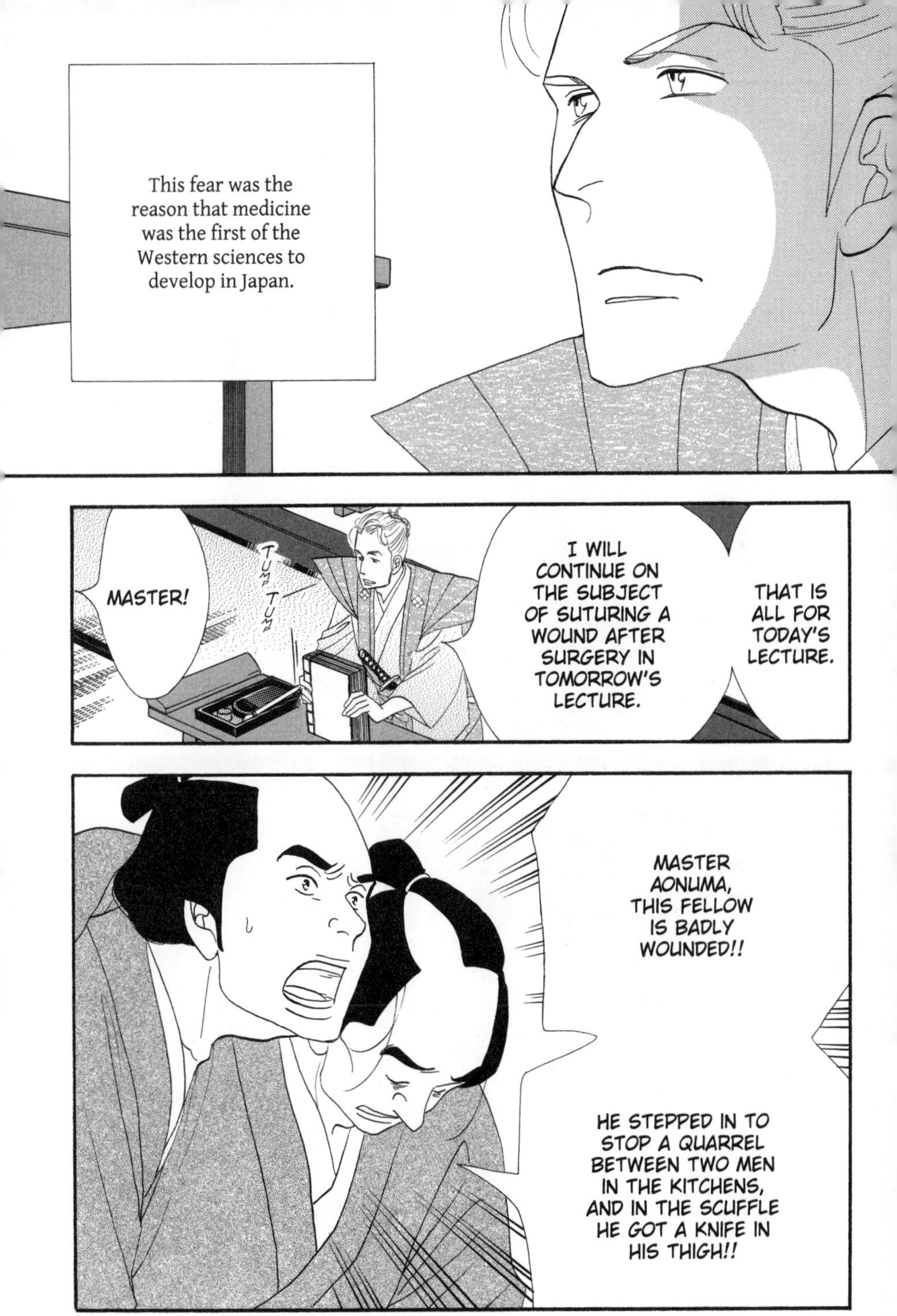
This fear was the reason that medicine was the first of the Western sciences to develop in Japan.
THAT IS ALL FOR TODAY'S LECTURE.
I WILL CONTINUE ON THE SUBJECT OF SUTURING A WOUND AFTER SURGERY IN TOMORROW'S LECTURE.
TUMP TUMP
MASTER!
MASTER AONUMA, THIS FELLOW IS BADLY WOUNDED!!
HE STEPPED IN TO STOP A QUARREL BETWEEN TWO MEN IN THE KITCHENS, AND IN THE SCUFFLE HE GOT A KNIFE IN HIS THIGH!!

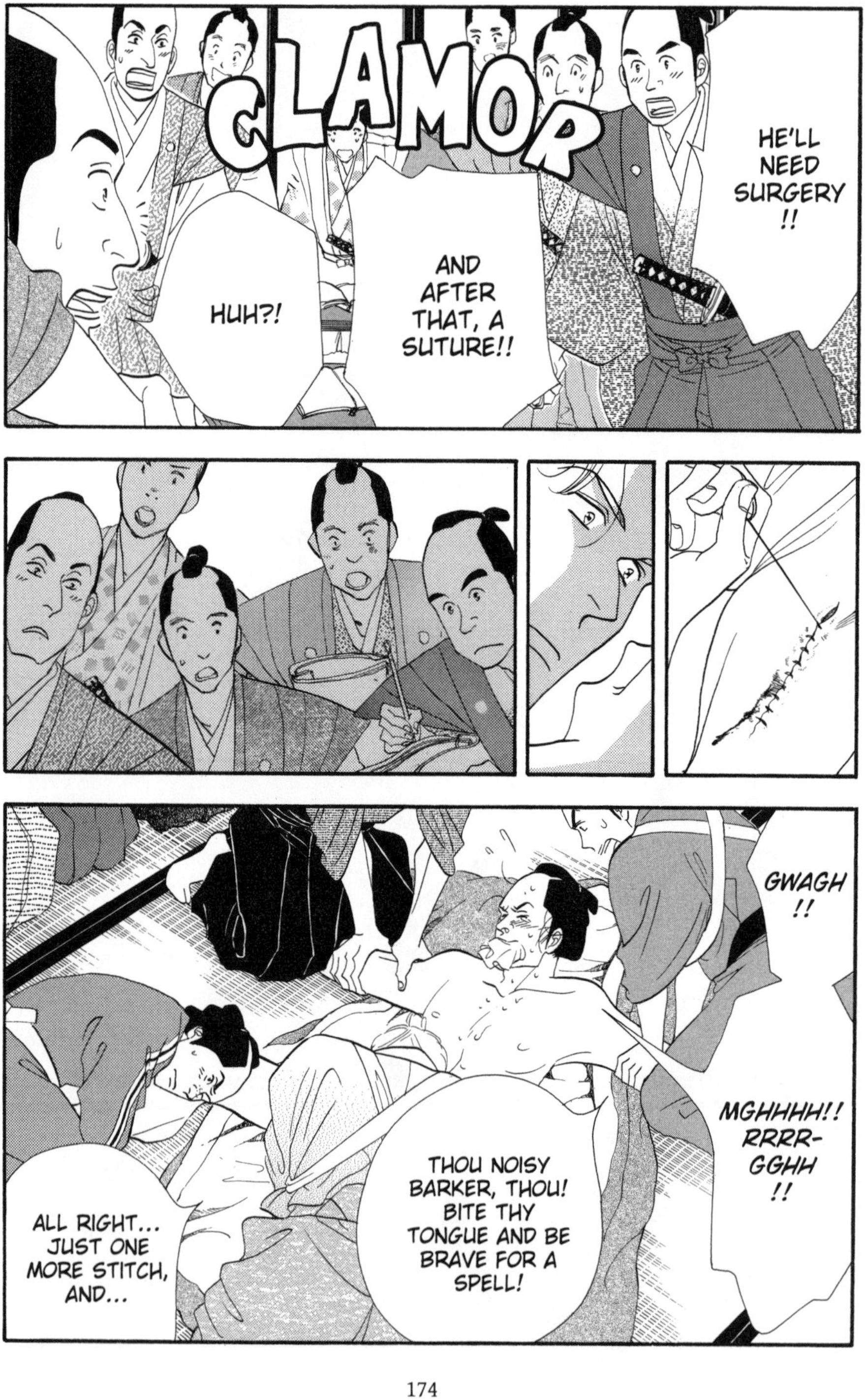
HE'LL NEED SURGERY !!
CLAMOR
AND AFTER THAT, A SUTURE!!
HUH?!
GWAGH !!
MGHHHH!! RRRR-GGHH !!
THOU NOISY BARKER, THOU! BITE THY TONGUE AND BE BRAVE FOR A SPELL!
ALL RIGHT... JUST ONE MORE STITCH, AND...

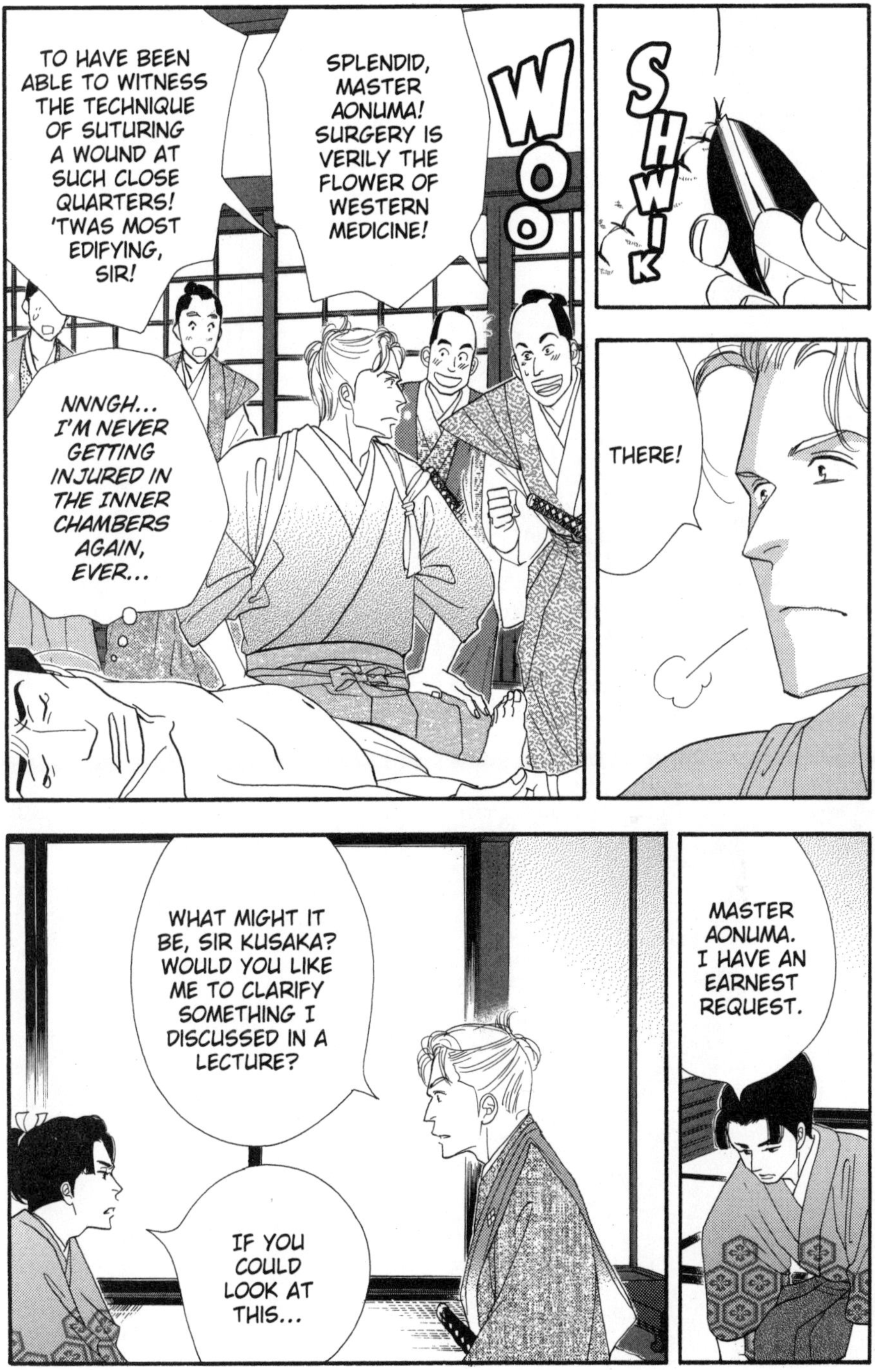
SHWIK
THERE!
WOOO
SPLENDID, MASTER AONUMA! SURGERY IS VERILY THE FLOWER OF WESTERN MEDICINE!
TO HAVE BEEN ABLE TO WITNESS THE TECHNIQUE OF SUTURING A WOUND AT SUCH CLOSE QUARTERS! 'TWAS MOST EDIFYING, SIR!
NNNGH... I'M NEVER GETTING INJURED IN THE INNER CHAMBERS AGAIN, EVER...
MASTER AONUMA. I HAVE AN EARNEST REQUEST.
WHAT MIGHT IT BE, SIR KUSAKA? WOULD YOU LIKE ME TO CLARIFY SOMETHING I DISCUSSED IN A LECTURE?
IF YOU COULD LOOK AT THIS...

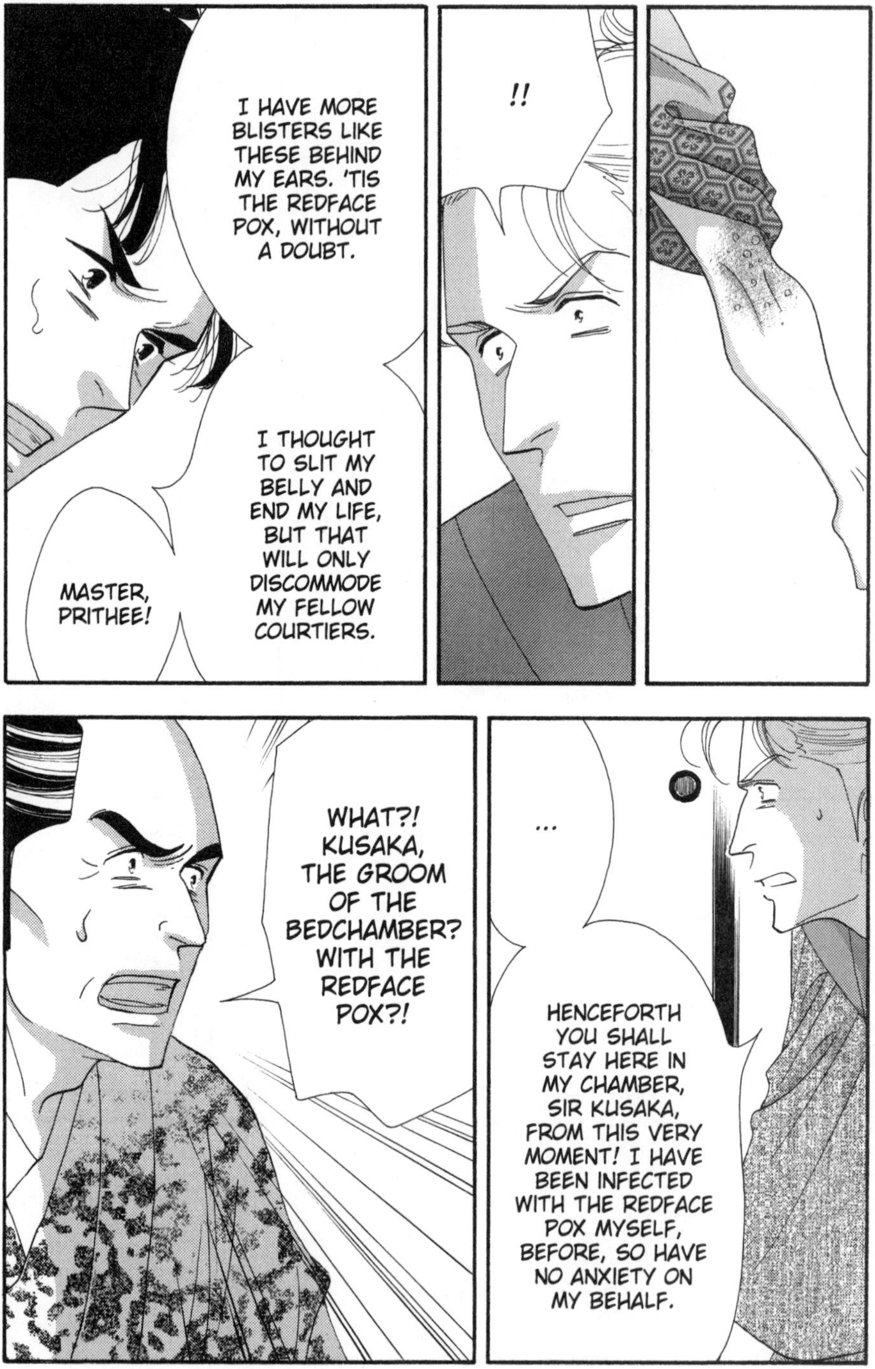
!!
I HAVE MORE BLISTERS LIKE THESE BEHIND MY EARS. 'TIS THE REDFACE POX, WITHOUT A DOUBT.
I THOUGHT TO SLIT MY BELLY AND END MY LIFE, BUT THAT WILL ONLY DISCOMMODE MY FELLOW COURTIERS.
MASTER, PRITHEE!
...
HENCEFORTH YOU SHALL STAY HERE IN MY CHAMBER, SIR KUSAKA, FROM THIS VERY MOMENT! I HAVE BEEN INFECTED WITH THE REDFACE POX MYSELF, BEFORE, SO HAVE NO ANXIETY ON MY BEHALF.
WHAT?! KUSAKA, THE GROOM OF THE BEDCHAMBER? WITH THE REDFACE POX?!

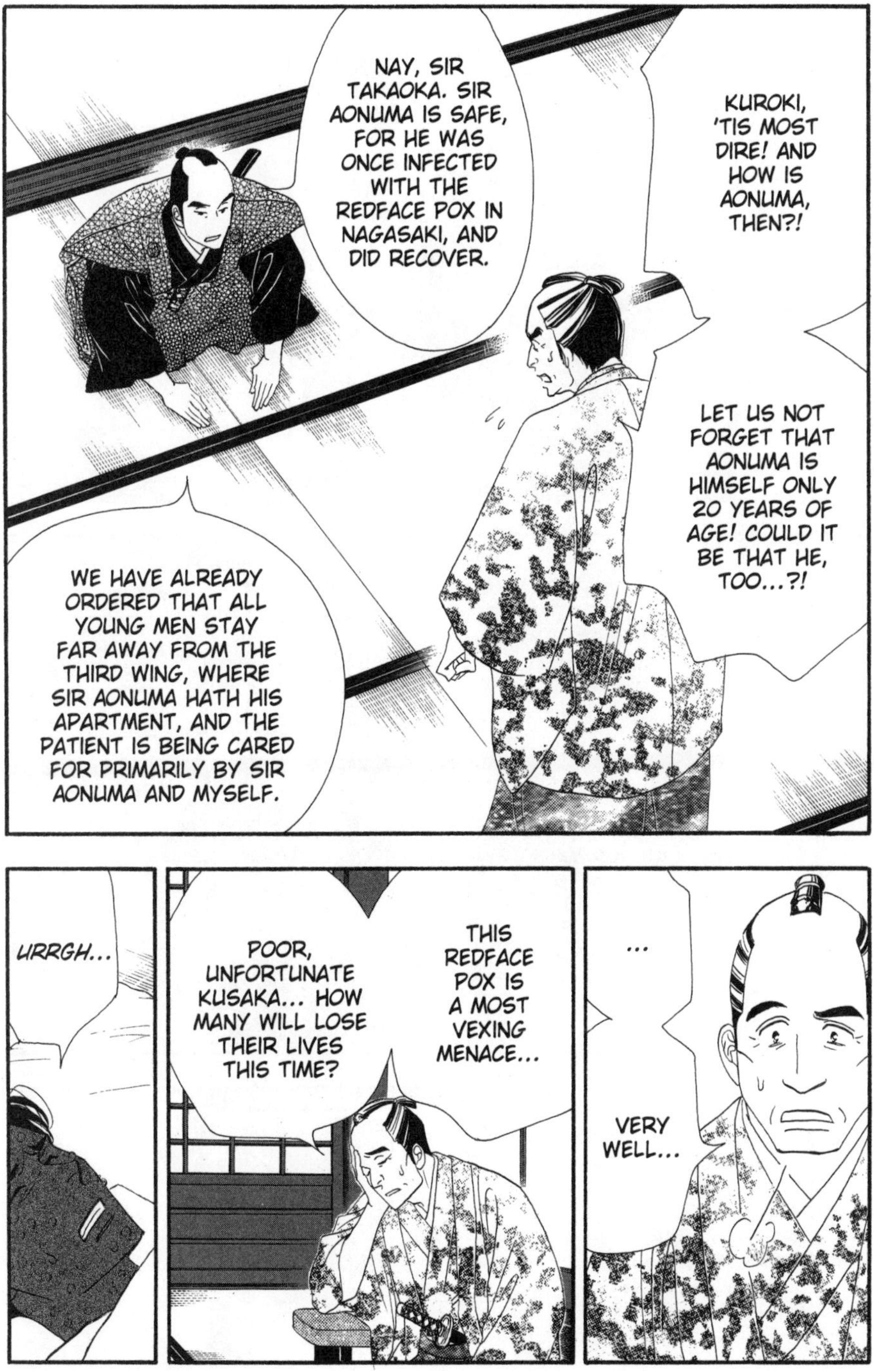
KUROKI, 'TIS MOST DIRE! AND HOW IS AONUMA, THEN?!
LET US NOT FORGET THAT AONUMA IS HIMSELF ONLY 20 YEARS OF AGE! COULD IT BE THAT HE, TOO...?!
NAY, SIR TAKAOKA. SIR AONUMA IS SAFE, FOR HE WAS ONCE INFECTED WITH THE REDFACE POX IN NAGASAKI, AND DID RECOVER.
WE HAVE ALREADY ORDERED THAT ALL YOUNG MEN STAY FAR AWAY FROM THE THIRD WING, WHERE SIR AONUMA HATH HIS APARTMENT, AND THE PATIENT IS BEING CARED FOR PRIMARILY BY SIR AONUMA AND MYSELF.
...
VERY WELL...
THIS REDFACE POX IS A MOST VEXING MENACE...
POOR, UNFORTUNATE KUSAKA... HOW MANY WILL LOSE THEIR LIVES THIS TIME?
URRGH...

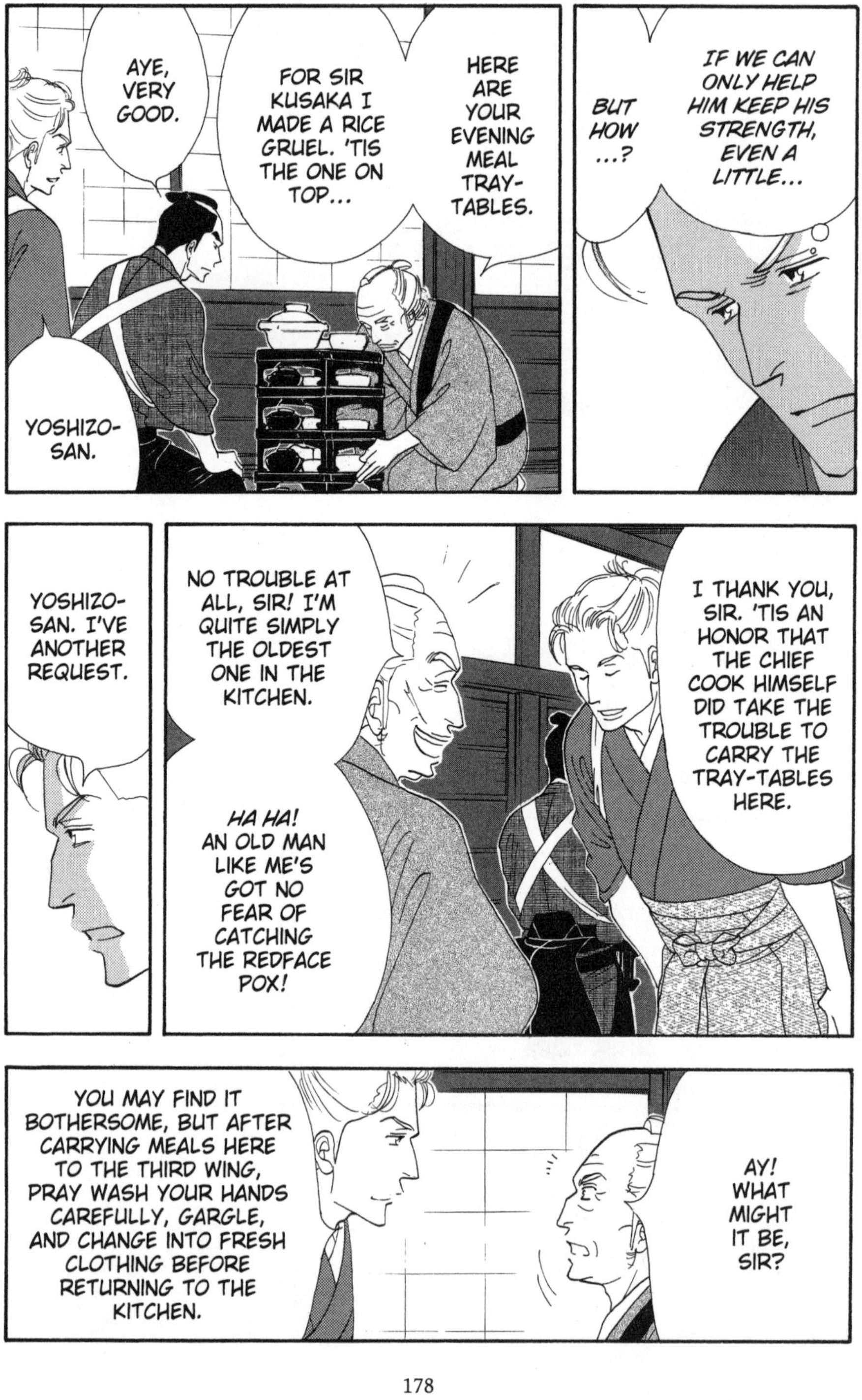
IF WE CAN ONLY HELP HIM KEEP HIS STRENGTH, EVEN A LITTLE...
BUT HOW ...?
HERE ARE YOUR EVENING MEAL TRAY-TABLES.
FOR SIR KUSAKA I MADE A RICE GRUEL. 'TIS THE ONE ON TOP...
AYE, VERY GOOD.
YOSHIZO-SAN.
I THANK YOU, SIR. 'TIS AN HONOR THAT THE CHIEF COOK HIMSELF DID TAKE THE TROUBLE TO CARRY THE TRAY-TABLES HERE.
NO TROUBLE AT ALL, SIR! I'M QUITE SIMPLY THE OLDEST ONE IN THE KITCHEN.
HA HA! AN OLD MAN LIKE ME'S GOT NO FEAR OF CATCHING THE REDFACE POX!
YOSHIZO-SAN. I'VE ANOTHER REQUEST.
AY! WHAT MIGHT IT BE, SIR?
YOU MAY FIND IT BOTHERSOME, BUT AFTER CARRYING MEALS HERE TO THE THIRD WING, PRAY WASH YOUR HANDS CAREFULLY, GARGLE, AND CHANGE INTO FRESH CLOTHING BEFORE RETURNING TO THE KITCHEN.

SMILE

I PRAY YOU!

AND, WHEN WASHING THE DISHES AFTERWARDS, PRAY WASH THEM YOURSELF, YOSHIZO-SAN, SEPARATELY FROM THE OTHER DISHES. AND WHEN YOU ARE FINISHED, ONCE AGAIN WASH YOUR HANDS AND GARGLE.

VERY WELL, SIR!

YOUR ADVICE IS A HUNDRED TIMES MORE HELPFUL THAN ANY AMULET I COULD BUY TO WARD OFF THE REDFACE POX, MASTER AONUMA. I'LL WASH MY HANDS AND GARGLE WITH CARE, JUST AS YOU SAY.

KUROKI-SAN! GET ME SOME GUIZHI TANG...NAY, HUO XIANG ZHENG QI SAN!

KUROKI-SAN!!

HANH HANH HANH HANH

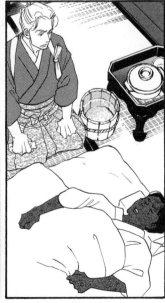

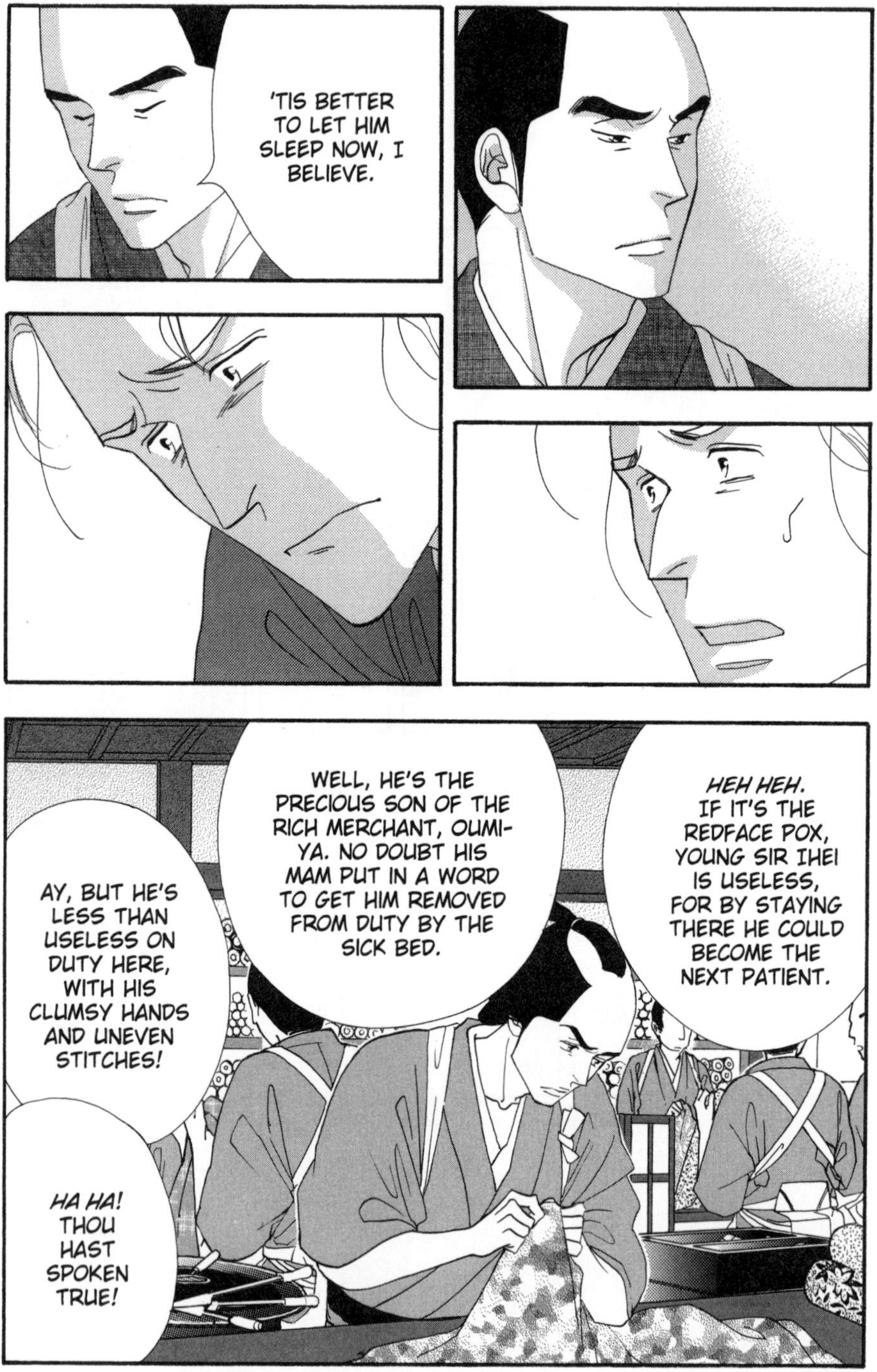
'TIS BETTER TO LET HIM SLEEP NOW, I BELIEVE.
HEH HEH. IF IT'S THE REDFACE POX, YOUNG SIR IHEI IS USELESS, FOR BY STAYING THERE HE COULD BECOME THE NEXT PATIENT.
WELL, HE'S THE PRECIOUS SON OF THE RICH MERCHANT, OUMI-YA. NO DOUBT HIS MAM PUT IN A WORD TO GET HIM REMOVED FROM DUTY BY THE SICK BED.
AY, BUT HE'S LESS THAN USELESS ON DUTY HERE, WITH HIS CLUMSY HANDS AND UNEVEN STITCHES!
HA HA! THOU HAST SPOKEN TRUE!

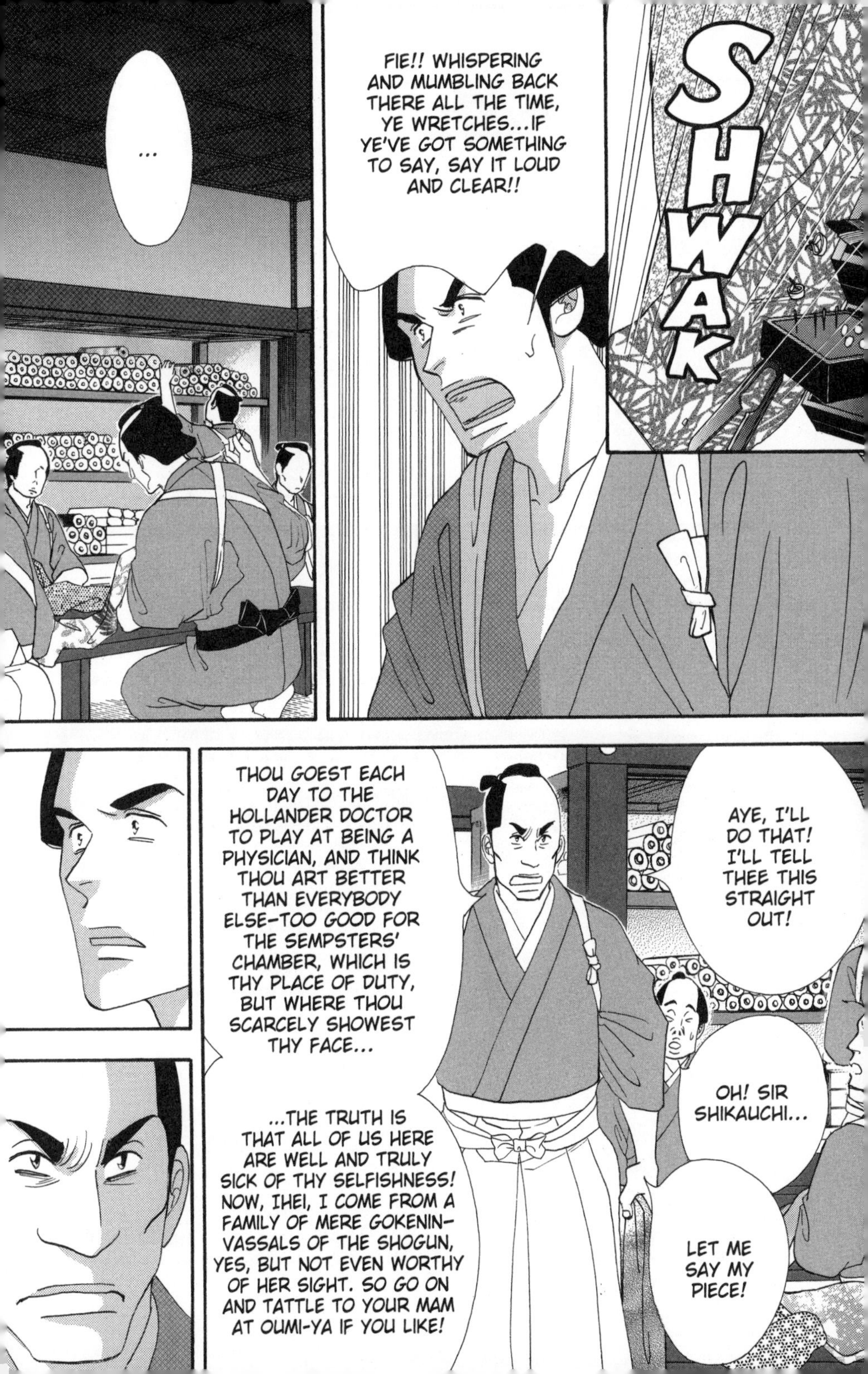
SHWAK
FIE!! WHISPERING AND MUMBLING BACK THERE ALL THE TIME, YE WRETCHES...IF YE'VE GOT SOMETHING TO SAY, SAY IT LOUD AND CLEAR!!
...
AYE, I'LL DO THAT! I'LL TELL THEE THIS STRAIGHT OUT!
THOU GOEST EACH DAY TO THE HOLLANDER DOCTOR TO PLAY AT BEING A PHYSICIAN, AND THINK THOU ART BETTER THAN EVERYBODY ELSE–TOO GOOD FOR THE SEMPSTERS' CHAMBER, WHICH IS THY PLACE OF DUTY, BUT WHERE THOU SCARCELY SHOWEST THY FACE...
OH! SIR SHIKAUCHI...
...THE TRUTH IS THAT ALL OF US HERE ARE WELL AND TRULY SICK OF THY SELFISHNESS! NOW, IHEI, I COME FROM A FAMILY OF MERE GOKENIN–VASSALS OF THE SHOGUN, YES, BUT NOT EVEN WORTHY OF HER SIGHT. SO GO ON AND TATTLE TO YOUR MAM AT OUMI-YA IF YOU LIKE!
LET ME SAY MY PIECE!

NOT ME!!
I AIN'T A
TATTLER!!

...

HMPH!

...NOT
ME.

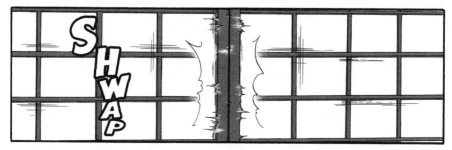

SHWAP

Aye, perhaps,
but he left
without
doing a jot of
needlework,
after all!!

...

HMMM...

HAS THAT
FELLOW
CHANGED?

A bit.

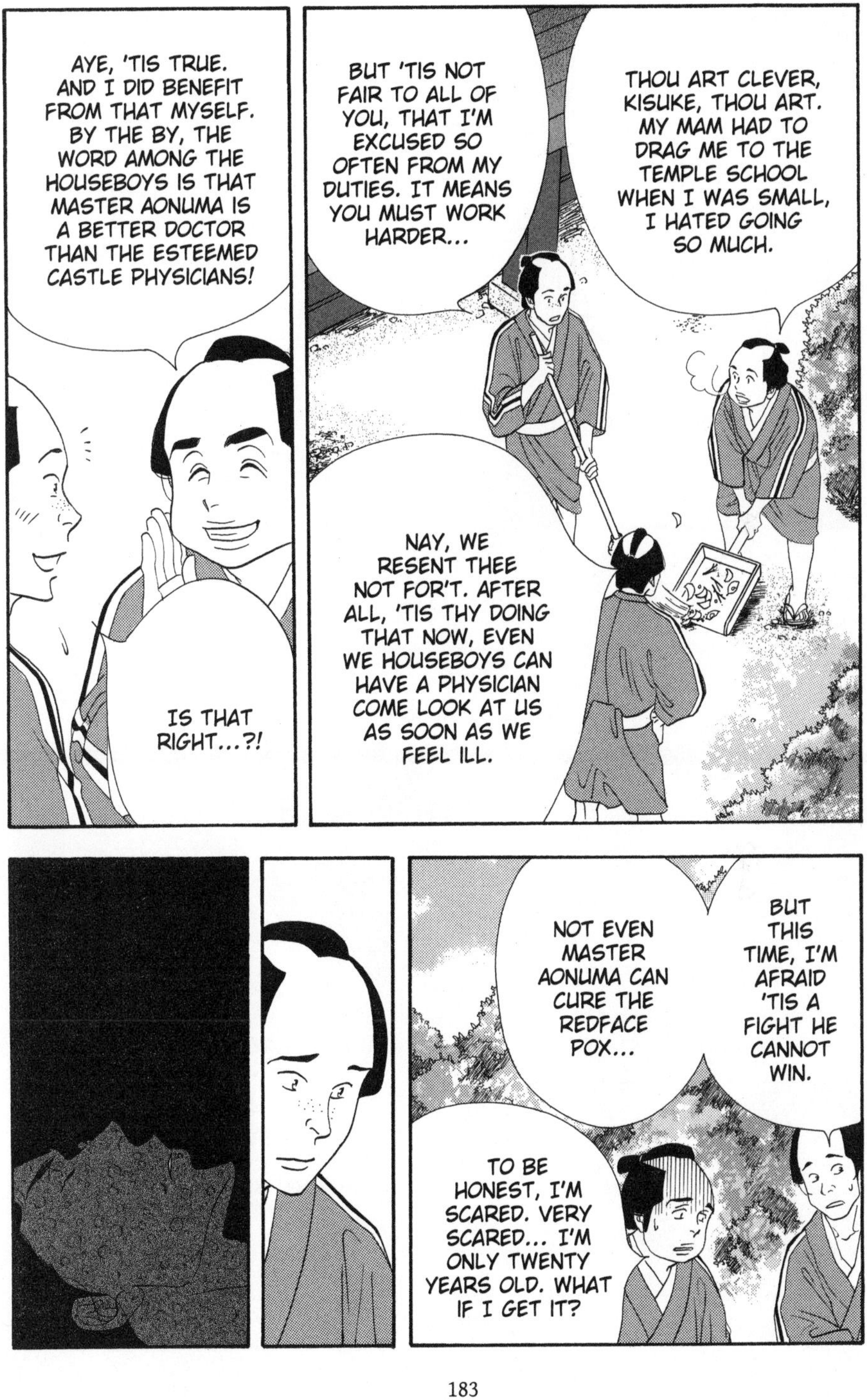
THOU ART CLEVER, KISUKE, THOU ART. MY MAM HAD TO DRAG ME TO THE TEMPLE SCHOOL WHEN I WAS SMALL, I HATED GOING SO MUCH.
BUT 'TIS NOT FAIR TO ALL OF YOU, THAT I'M EXCUSED SO OFTEN FROM MY DUTIES. IT MEANS YOU MUST WORK HARDER...
NAY, WE RESENT THEE NOT FOR'T. AFTER ALL, 'TIS THY DOING THAT NOW, EVEN WE HOUSEBOYS CAN HAVE A PHYSICIAN COME LOOK AT US AS SOON AS WE FEEL ILL.
AYE, 'TIS TRUE. AND I DID BENEFIT FROM THAT MYSELF. BY THE BY, THE WORD AMONG THE HOUSEBOYS IS THAT MASTER AONUMA IS A BETTER DOCTOR THAN THE ESTEEMED CASTLE PHYSICIANS!
IS THAT RIGHT...?!
BUT THIS TIME, I'M AFRAID 'TIS A FIGHT HE CANNOT WIN.
NOT EVEN MASTER AONUMA CAN CURE THE REDFACE POX...
TO BE HONEST, I'M SCARED. VERY SCARED... I'M ONLY TWENTY YEARS OLD. WHAT IF I GET IT?

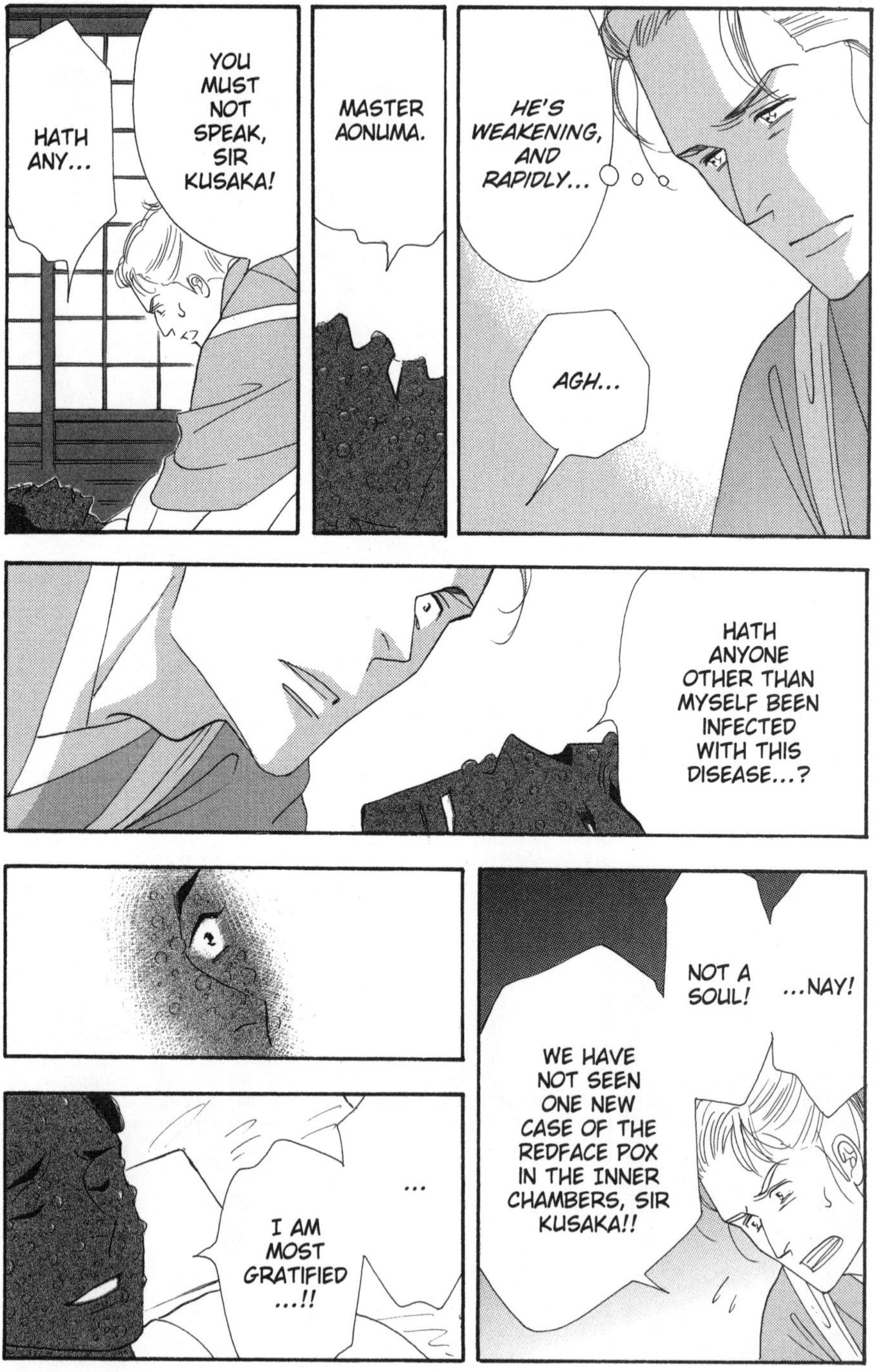
HE'S WEAKENING, AND RAPIDLY...
AGH...
MASTER AONUMA.
YOU MUST NOT SPEAK, SIR KUSAKA!
HATH ANY...
HATH ANYONE OTHER THAN MYSELF BEEN INFECTED WITH THIS DISEASE...?
...NAY!
NOT A SOUL!
WE HAVE NOT SEEN ONE NEW CASE OF THE REDFACE POX IN THE INNER CHAMBERS, SIR KUSAKA!!
...
I AM MOST GRATIFIED ...!!

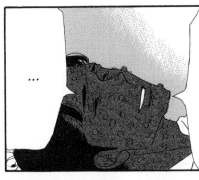

ALL OF MY PEERS ARE GROOMS OF THE BEDCHAMBER, WHO SERVE OUR LIEGE DIRECTLY. AHH...HOW TRULY GRATIFYING, THAT I WAS THE ONLY ONE TO FALL ILL!

'TWAS THANKS TO YOU, MASTER AONUMA. I AM MOST GRATEFUL... MOST GRATEFUL INDEED!

...

SIR KUSAKA!

DAMN IT...!!

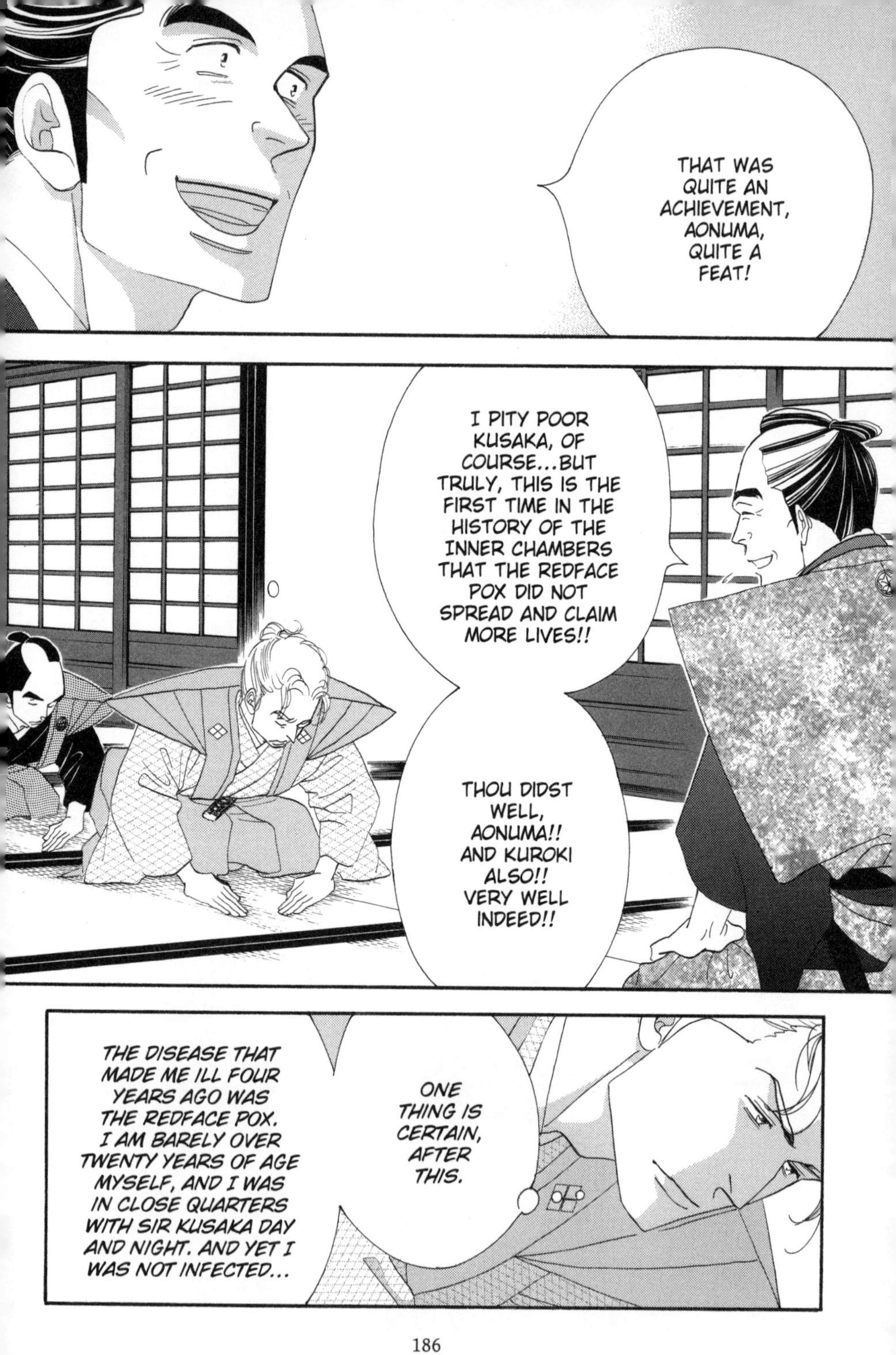
THAT WAS QUITE AN ACHIEVEMENT, AONUMA, QUITE A FEAT!
I PITY POOR KUSAKA, OF COURSE...BUT TRULY, THIS IS THE FIRST TIME IN THE HISTORY OF THE INNER CHAMBERS THAT THE REDFACE POX DID NOT SPREAD AND CLAIM MORE LIVES!!
THOU DIDST WELL, AONUMA!! AND KUROKI ALSO!! VERY WELL INDEED!!
ONE THING IS CERTAIN, AFTER THIS.
THE DISEASE THAT MADE ME ILL FOUR YEARS AGO WAS THE REDFACE POX. I AM BARELY OVER TWENTY YEARS OF AGE MYSELF, AND I WAS IN CLOSE QUARTERS WITH SIR KUSAKA DAY AND NIGHT. AND YET I WAS NOT INFECTED...

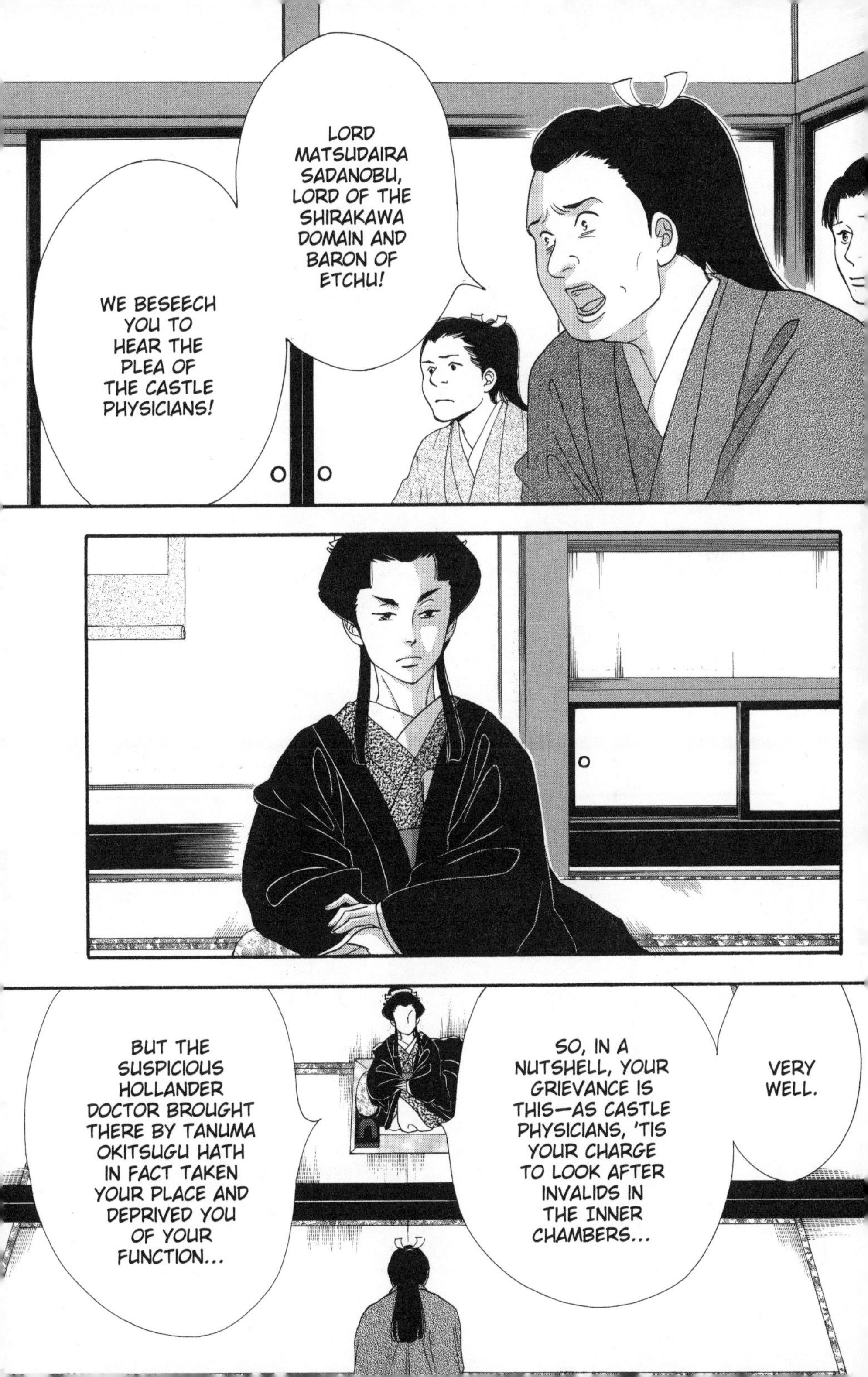
LORD MATSUDAIRA SADANOBU, LORD OF THE SHIRAKAWA DOMAIN AND BARON OF ETCHU!
WE BESEECH YOU TO HEAR THE PLEA OF THE CASTLE PHYSICIANS!
VERY WELL.
SO, IN A NUTSHELL, YOUR GRIEVANCE IS THIS—AS CASTLE PHYSICIANS, 'TIS YOUR CHARGE TO LOOK AFTER INVALIDS IN THE INNER CHAMBERS...
BUT THE SUSPICIOUS HOLLANDER DOCTOR BROUGHT THERE BY TANUMA OKITSUGU HATH IN FACT TAKEN YOUR PLACE AND DEPRIVED YOU OF YOUR FUNCTION...

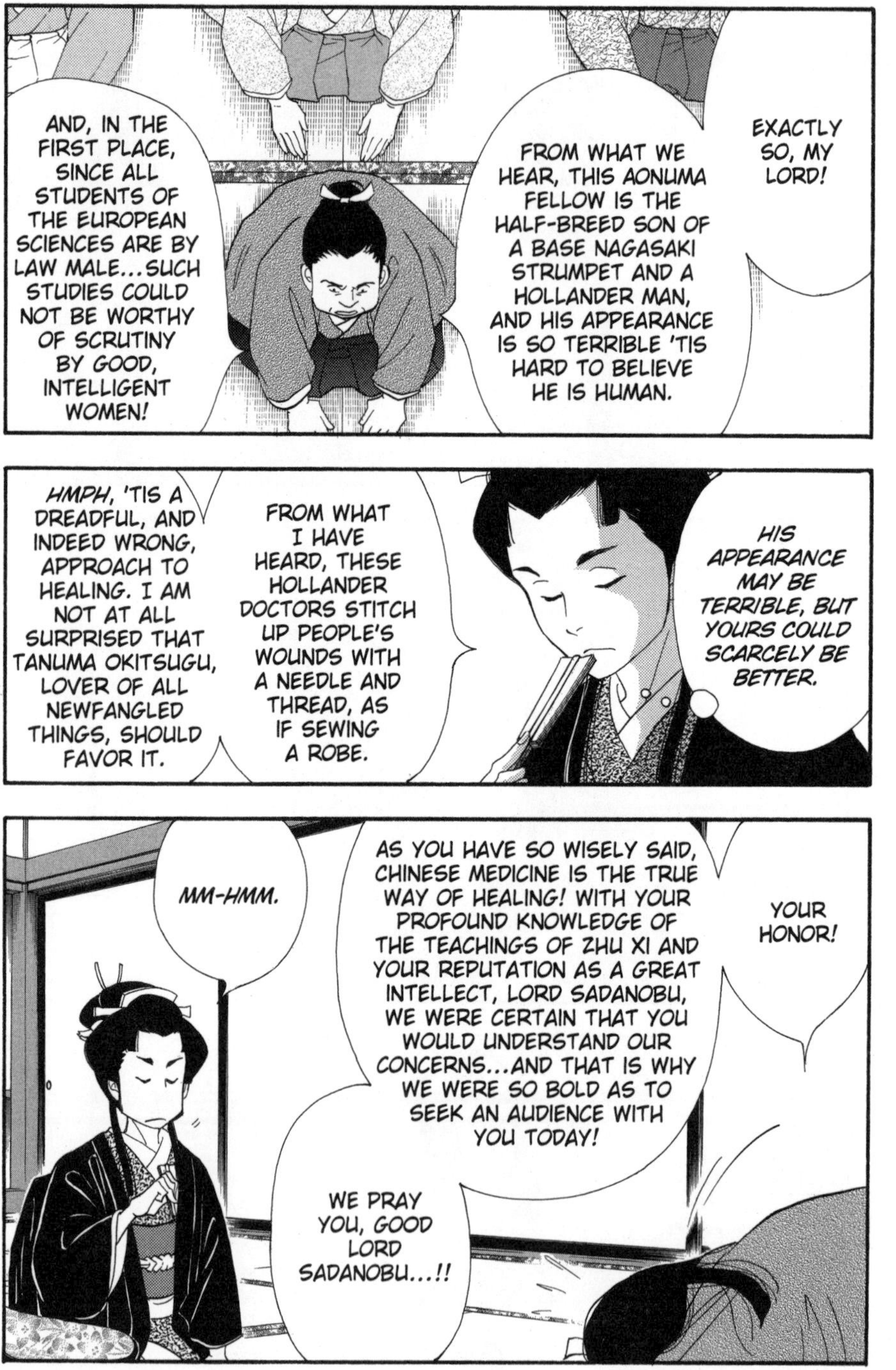
EXACTLY SO, MY LORD!
FROM WHAT WE HEAR, THIS AONUMA FELLOW IS THE HALF-BREED SON OF A BASE NAGASAKI STRUMPET AND A HOLLANDER MAN, AND HIS APPEARANCE IS SO TERRIBLE 'TIS HARD TO BELIEVE HE IS HUMAN.
AND, IN THE FIRST PLACE, SINCE ALL STUDENTS OF THE EUROPEAN SCIENCES ARE BY LAW MALE...SUCH STUDIES COULD NOT BE WORTHY OF SCRUTINY BY GOOD, INTELLIGENT WOMEN!
HIS APPEARANCE MAY BE TERRIBLE, BUT YOURS COULD SCARCELY BE BETTER.
FROM WHAT I HAVE HEARD, THESE HOLLANDER DOCTORS STITCH UP PEOPLE'S WOUNDS WITH A NEEDLE AND THREAD, AS IF SEWING A ROBE.
HMPH, 'TIS A DREADFUL, AND INDEED WRONG, APPROACH TO HEALING. I AM NOT AT ALL SURPRISED THAT TANUMA OKITSUGU, LOVER OF ALL NEWFANGLED THINGS, SHOULD FAVOR IT.
YOUR HONOR!
AS YOU HAVE SO WISELY SAID, CHINESE MEDICINE IS THE TRUE WAY OF HEALING! WITH YOUR PROFOUND KNOWLEDGE OF THE TEACHINGS OF ZHU XI AND YOUR REPUTATION AS A GREAT INTELLECT, LORD SADANOBU, WE WERE CERTAIN THAT YOU WOULD UNDERSTAND OUR CONCERNS...AND THAT IS WHY WE WERE SO BOLD AS TO SEEK AN AUDIENCE WITH YOU TODAY!
MM-HMM.
WE PRAY YOU, GOOD LORD SADANOBU...!!

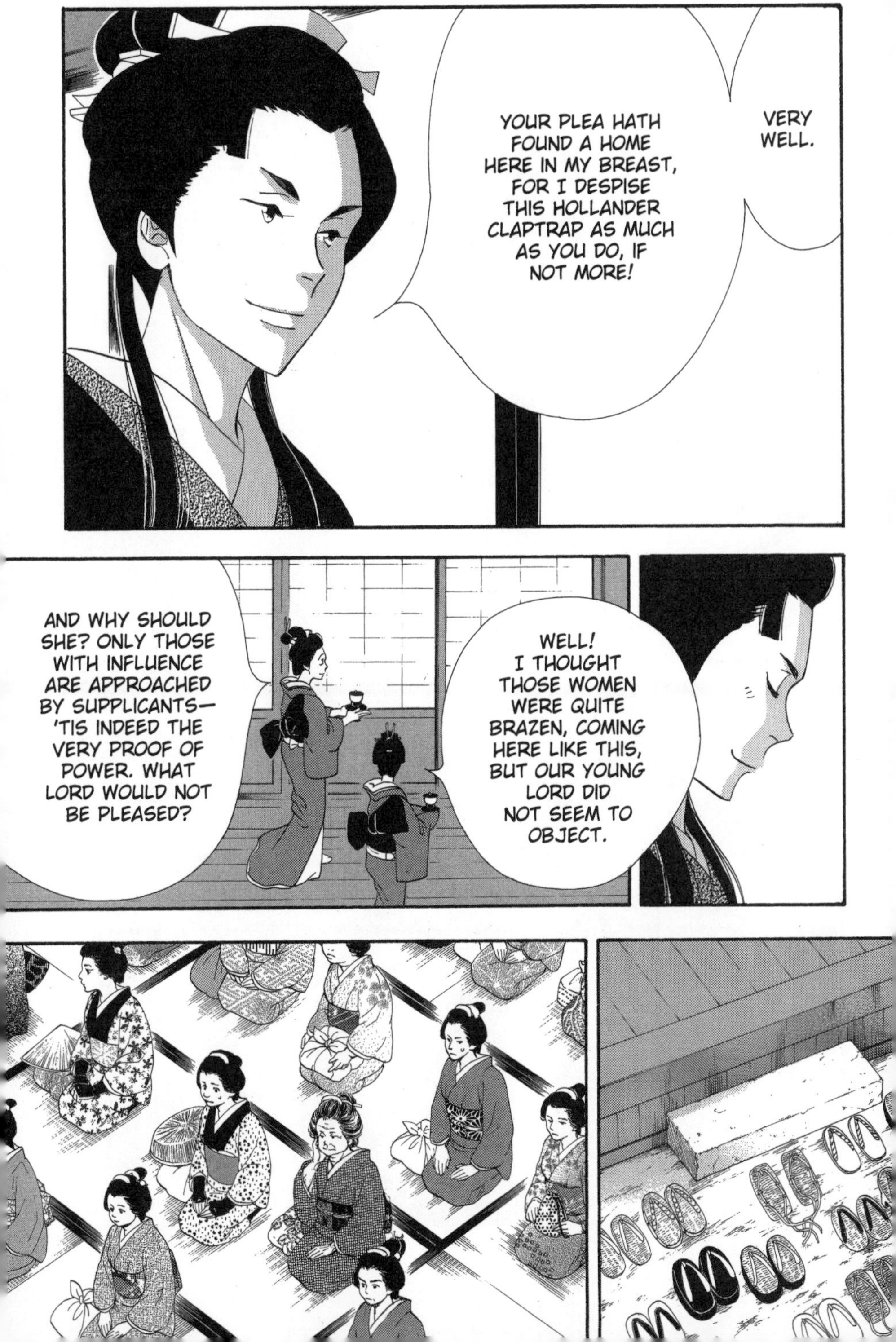
VERY WELL.
YOUR PLEA HATH FOUND A HOME HERE IN MY BREAST, FOR I DESPISE THIS HOLLANDER CLAPTRAP AS MUCH AS YOU DO, IF NOT MORE!
WELL! I THOUGHT THOSE WOMEN WERE QUITE BRAZEN, COMING HERE LIKE THIS, BUT OUR YOUNG LORD DID NOT SEEM TO OBJECT.
AND WHY SHOULD SHE? ONLY THOSE WITH INFLUENCE ARE APPROACHED BY SUPPLICANTS—'TIS INDEED THE VERY PROOF OF POWER. WHAT LORD WOULD NOT BE PLEASED?

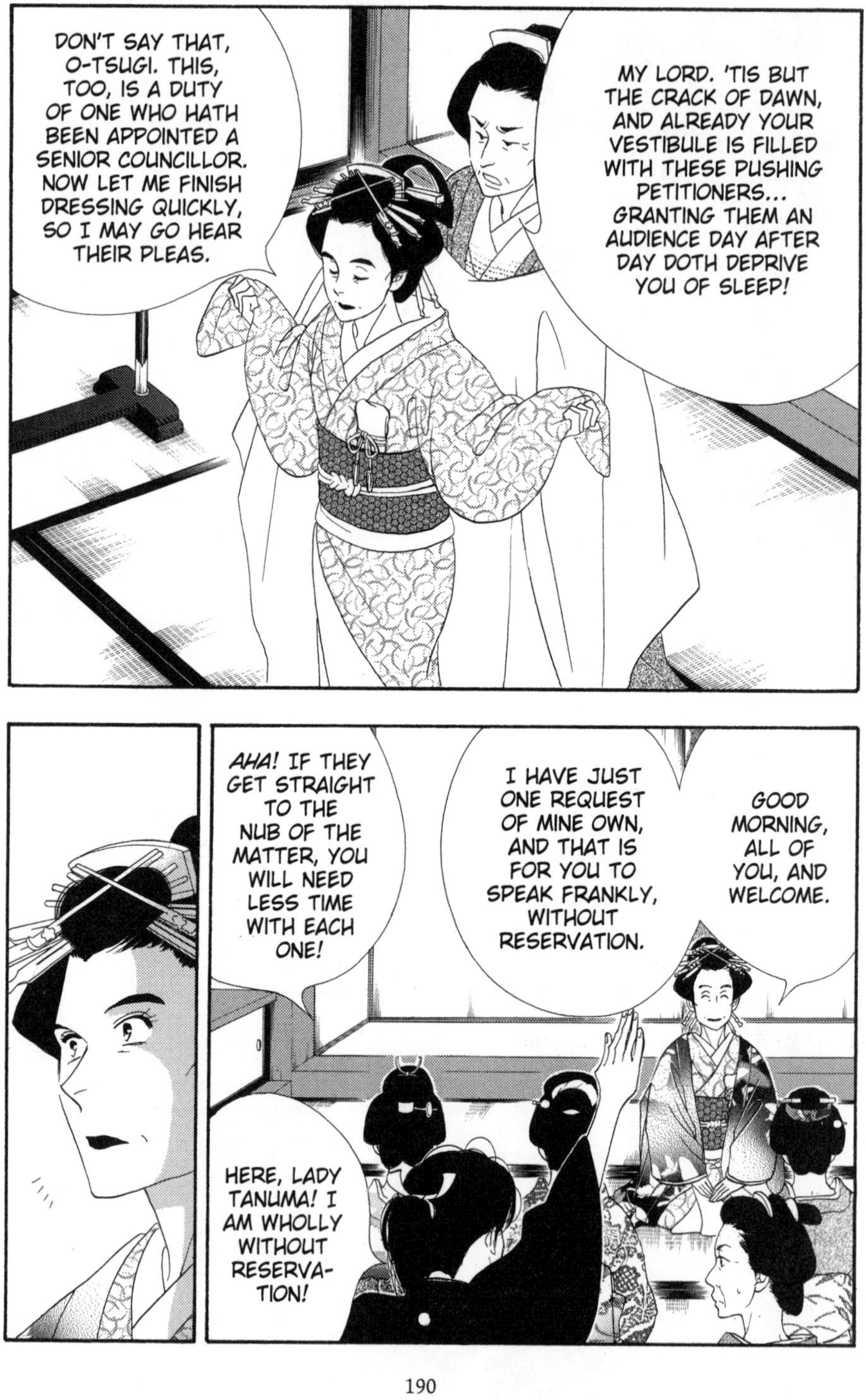
MY LORD. 'TIS BUT THE CRACK OF DAWN, AND ALREADY YOUR VESTIBULE IS FILLED WITH THESE PUSHING PETITIONERS... GRANTING THEM AN AUDIENCE DAY AFTER DAY DOTH DEPRIVE YOU OF SLEEP!
DON'T SAY THAT, O-TSUGI. THIS, TOO, IS A DUTY OF ONE WHO HATH BEEN APPOINTED A SENIOR COUNCILLOR. NOW LET ME FINISH DRESSING QUICKLY, SO I MAY GO HEAR THEIR PLEAS.
GOOD MORNING, ALL OF YOU, AND WELCOME.
I HAVE JUST ONE REQUEST OF MINE OWN, AND THAT IS FOR YOU TO SPEAK FRANKLY, WITHOUT RESERVATION.
AHA! IF THEY GET STRAIGHT TO THE NUB OF THE MATTER, YOU WILL NEED LESS TIME WITH EACH ONE!
HERE, LADY TANUMA! I AM WHOLLY WITHOUT RESERVATION!

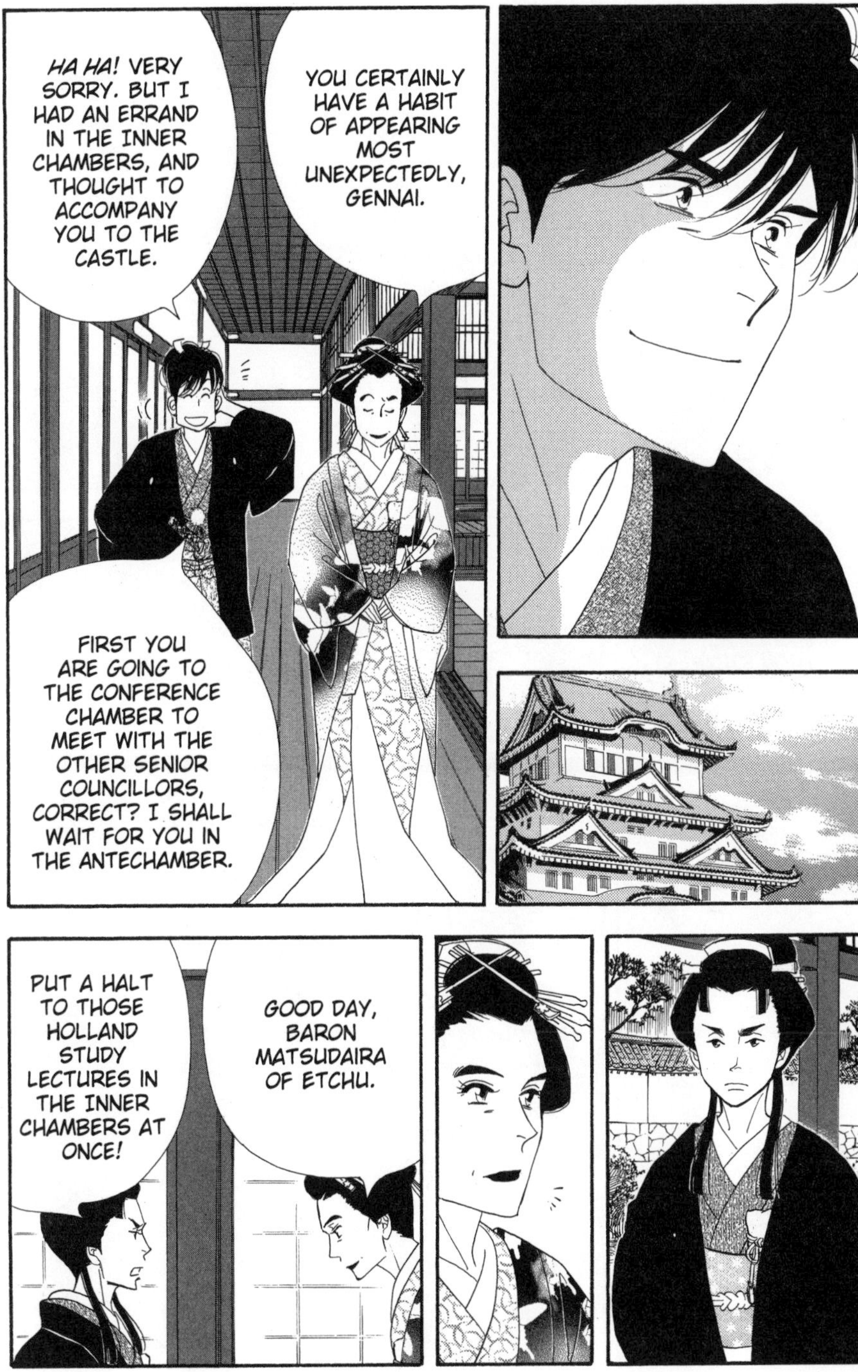
YOU CERTAINLY HAVE A HABIT OF APPEARING MOST UNEXPECTEDLY, GENNAI.
HA HA! VERY SORRY. BUT I HAD AN ERRAND IN THE INNER CHAMBERS, AND THOUGHT TO ACCOMPANY YOU TO THE CASTLE.
FIRST YOU ARE GOING TO THE CONFERENCE CHAMBER TO MEET WITH THE OTHER SENIOR COUNCILLORS, CORRECT? I SHALL WAIT FOR YOU IN THE ANTECHAMBER.
GOOD DAY, BARON MATSUDAIRA OF ETCHU.
PUT A HALT TO THOSE HOLLAND STUDY LECTURES IN THE INNER CHAMBERS AT ONCE!

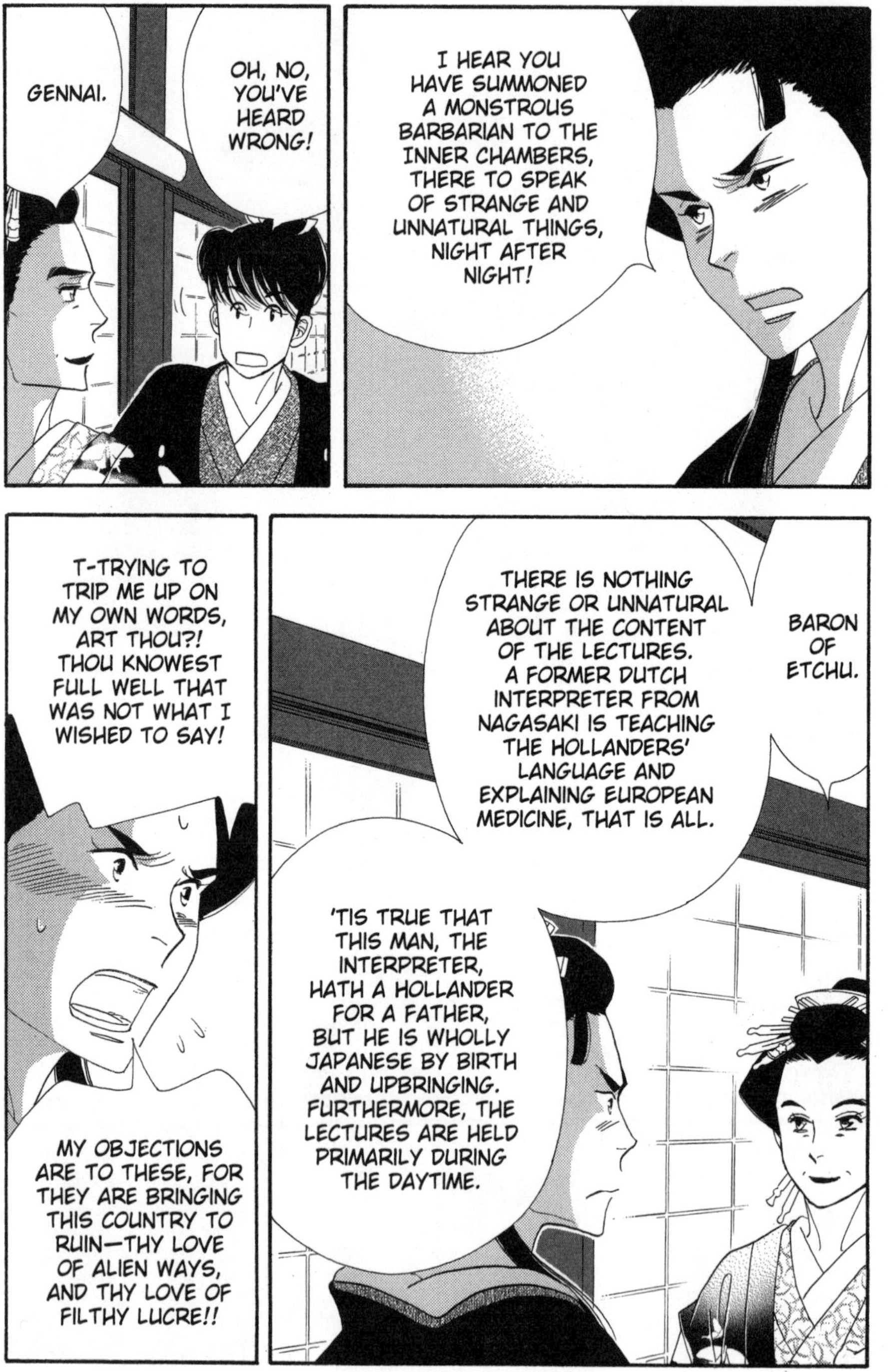
I HEAR YOU HAVE SUMMONED A MONSTROUS BARBARIAN TO THE INNER CHAMBERS, THERE TO SPEAK OF STRANGE AND UNNATURAL THINGS, NIGHT AFTER NIGHT!
OH, NO, YOU'VE HEARD WRONG!
GENNAI.
BARON OF ETCHU.
THERE IS NOTHING STRANGE OR UNNATURAL ABOUT THE CONTENT OF THE LECTURES. A FORMER DUTCH INTERPRETER FROM NAGASAKI IS TEACHING THE HOLLANDERS' LANGUAGE AND EXPLAINING EUROPEAN MEDICINE, THAT IS ALL.
'TIS TRUE THAT THIS MAN, THE INTERPRETER, HATH A HOLLANDER FOR A FATHER, BUT HE IS WHOLLY JAPANESE BY BIRTH AND UPBRINGING. FURTHERMORE, THE LECTURES ARE HELD PRIMARILY DURING THE DAYTIME.
T-TRYING TO TRIP ME UP ON MY OWN WORDS, ART THOU?! THOU KNOWEST FULL WELL THAT WAS NOT WHAT I WISHED TO SAY!
MY OBJECTIONS ARE TO THESE, FOR THEY ARE BRINGING THIS COUNTRY TO RUIN—THY LOVE OF ALIEN WAYS, AND THY LOVE OF FILTHY LUCRE!!

'TIS SAID THE FAVORITE PHRASE OF THE MOMENT AMONG THE TOWNSPEOPLE OF EDO IS PRECISELY THIS—"WITH ENOUGH MONEY, EVEN HELL CAN BE MADE A PARADISE!"
MOREOVER, I HEAR THOU HAST DESIGNS TO CONTRAVENE THE POLICY OF NATIONAL SECLUSION AND COMMENCE TRADING WITH RUSSIA IN THE NORTH. DOST THOU DENY IT?!
Oh! Perhaps ...
Yes, let us turn back.
NAY, I DO NOT.
'TIS DESPICABLE...!! A MEMBER OF THE PROUD WARRIOR CLASS, WILLING TO BREACH A HALLOWED AND AGE-OLD BAN IN ORDER TO MAKE MONEY LIKE A VULGAR MERCHANT!
MY GRANDAM, THE 8TH SHOGUN LORD YOSHIMUNE, IS SURELY TURNING IN HER GRAVE AT THIS WORLD OF LAVISH LUXURY, IN WHICH ALL THE SHOGUN'S COUNCILLORS GAD ABOUT IN SUMPTUOUS OVERGARMENTS!!
I'M NOT SO CERTAIN ABOUT THAT, ACTUALLY. IN FACT, I BELIEVE LORD YOSHIMUNE WOULD BE GLAD TO SEE THE WORLD AS IT IS TODAY—LADY TANUMA'S RISE TO THE POST OF SENIOR COUNCILLOR INCLUDED.

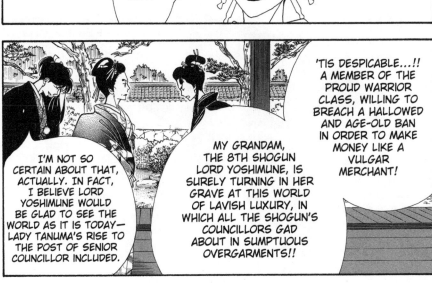

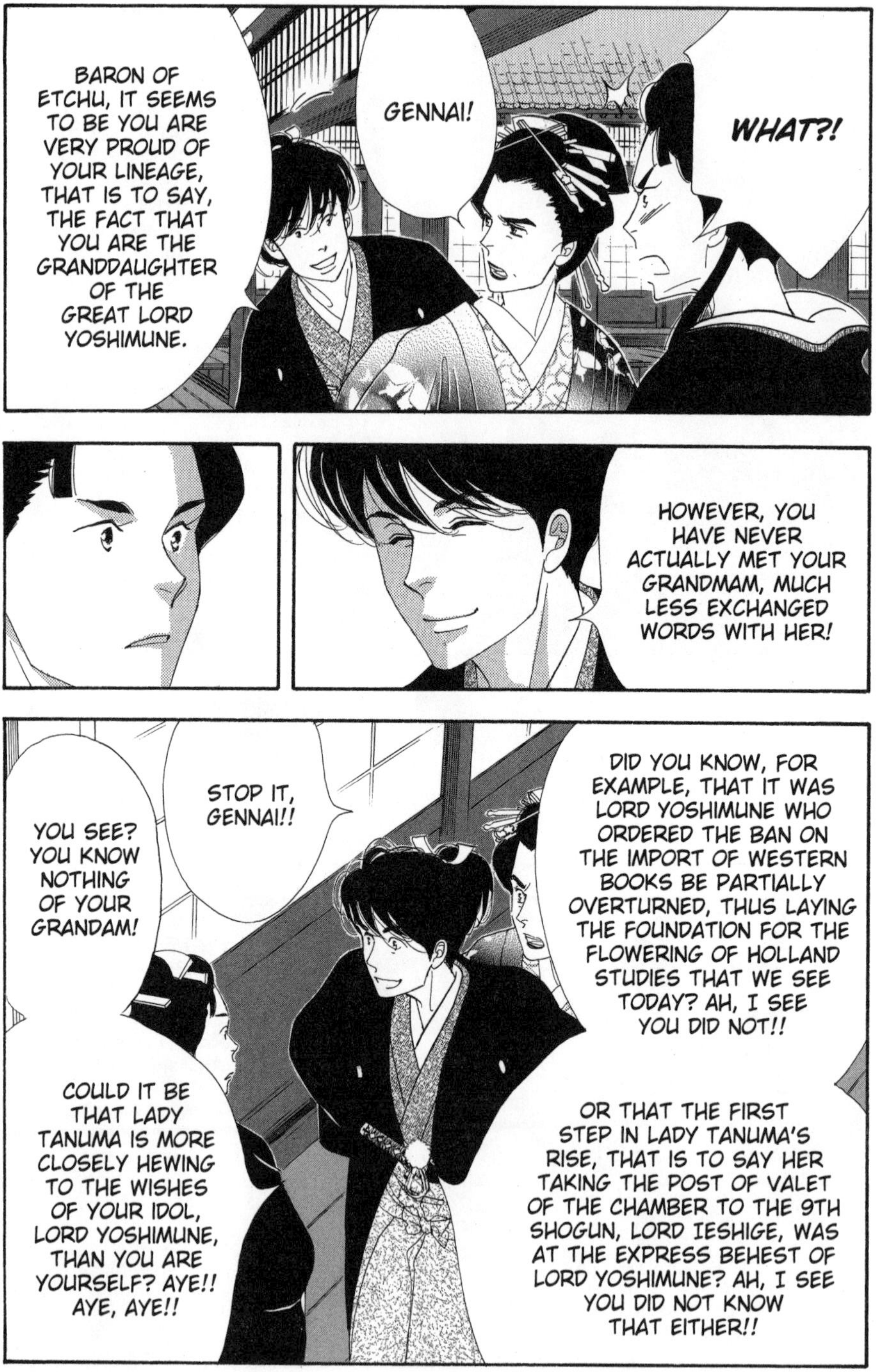
WHAT?!
GENNAI!
BARON OF ETCHU, IT SEEMS TO BE YOU ARE VERY PROUD OF YOUR LINEAGE, THAT IS TO SAY, THE FACT THAT YOU ARE THE GRANDDAUGHTER OF THE GREAT LORD YOSHIMUNE.
HOWEVER, YOU HAVE NEVER ACTUALLY MET YOUR GRANDMAM, MUCH LESS EXCHANGED WORDS WITH HER!
DID YOU KNOW, FOR EXAMPLE, THAT IT WAS LORD YOSHIMUNE WHO ORDERED THE BAN ON THE IMPORT OF WESTERN BOOKS BE PARTIALLY OVERTURNED, THUS LAYING THE FOUNDATION FOR THE FLOWERING OF HOLLAND STUDIES THAT WE SEE TODAY? AH, I SEE YOU DID NOT!!
OR THAT THE FIRST STEP IN LADY TANUMA'S RISE, THAT IS TO SAY HER TAKING THE POST OF VALET OF THE CHAMBER TO THE 9TH SHOGUN, LORD IESHIGE, WAS AT THE EXPRESS BEHEST OF LORD YOSHIMUNE? AH, I SEE YOU DID NOT KNOW THAT EITHER!!
STOP IT, GENNAI!!
YOU SEE? YOU KNOW NOTHING OF YOUR GRANDAM!
COULD IT BE THAT LADY TANUMA IS MORE CLOSELY HEWING TO THE WISHES OF YOUR IDOL, LORD YOSHIMUNE, THAN YOU ARE YOURSELF? AYE!! AYE, AYE!!

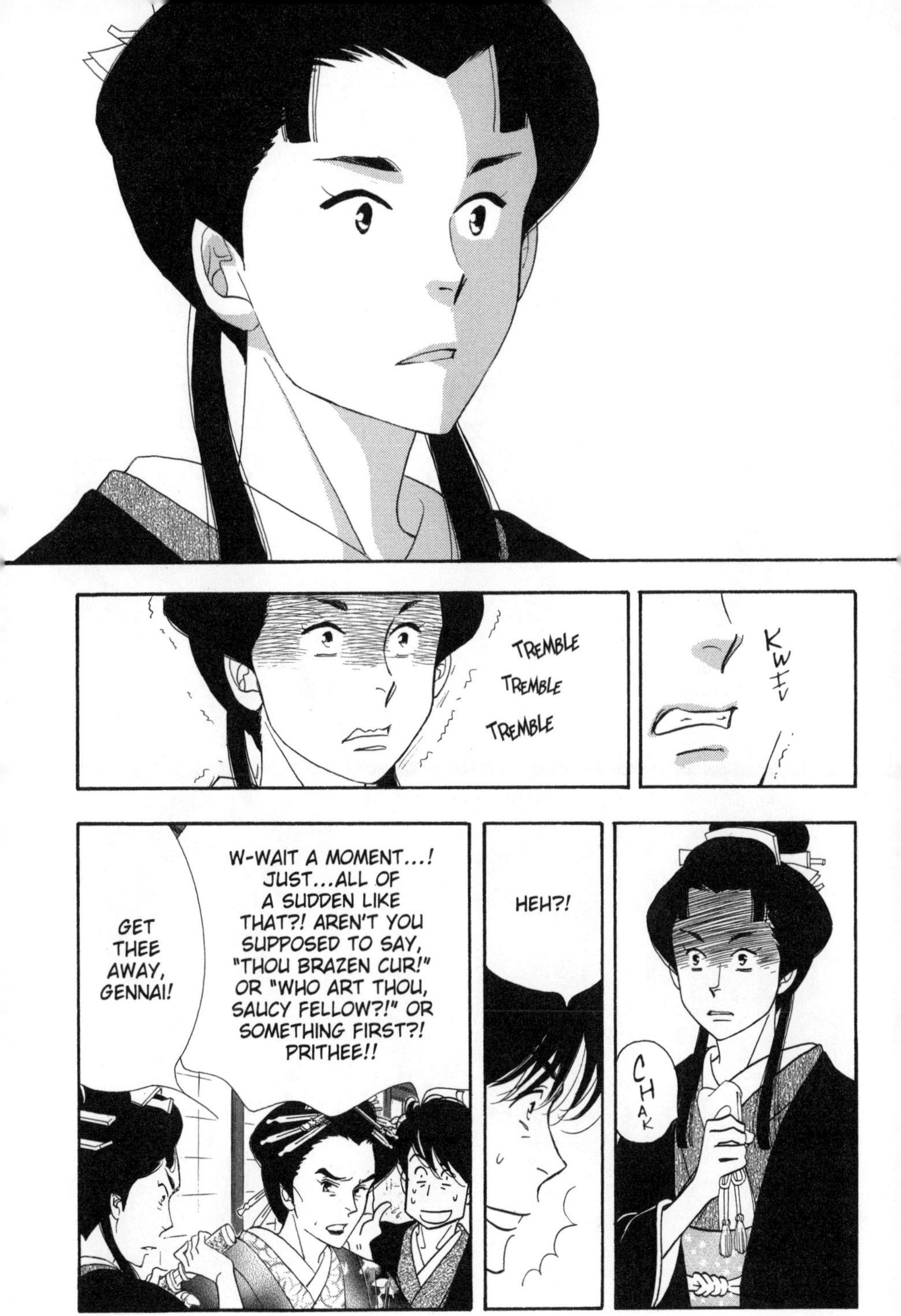
KWIV
TREMBLE TREMBLE TREMBLE
CHAK
HEH?!
W-WAIT A MOMENT...! JUST...ALL OF A SUDDEN LIKE THAT?! AREN'T YOU SUPPOSED TO SAY, "THOU BRAZEN CUR!" OR "WHO ART THOU, SAUCY FELLOW?!" OR SOMETHING FIRST?! PRITHEE!!
GET THEE AWAY, GENNAI!

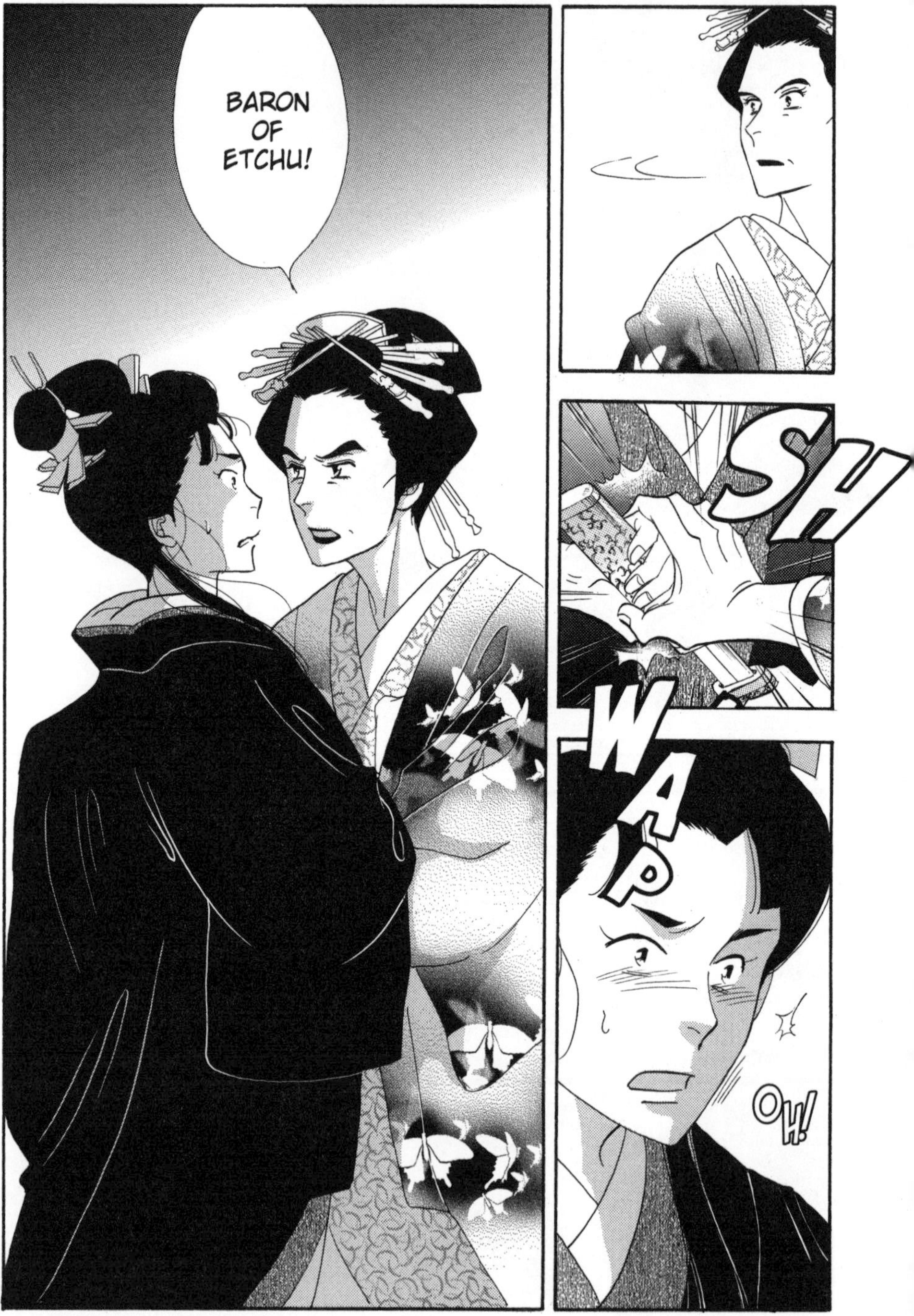

SH-WAP
OH!
BARON OF ETCHU!

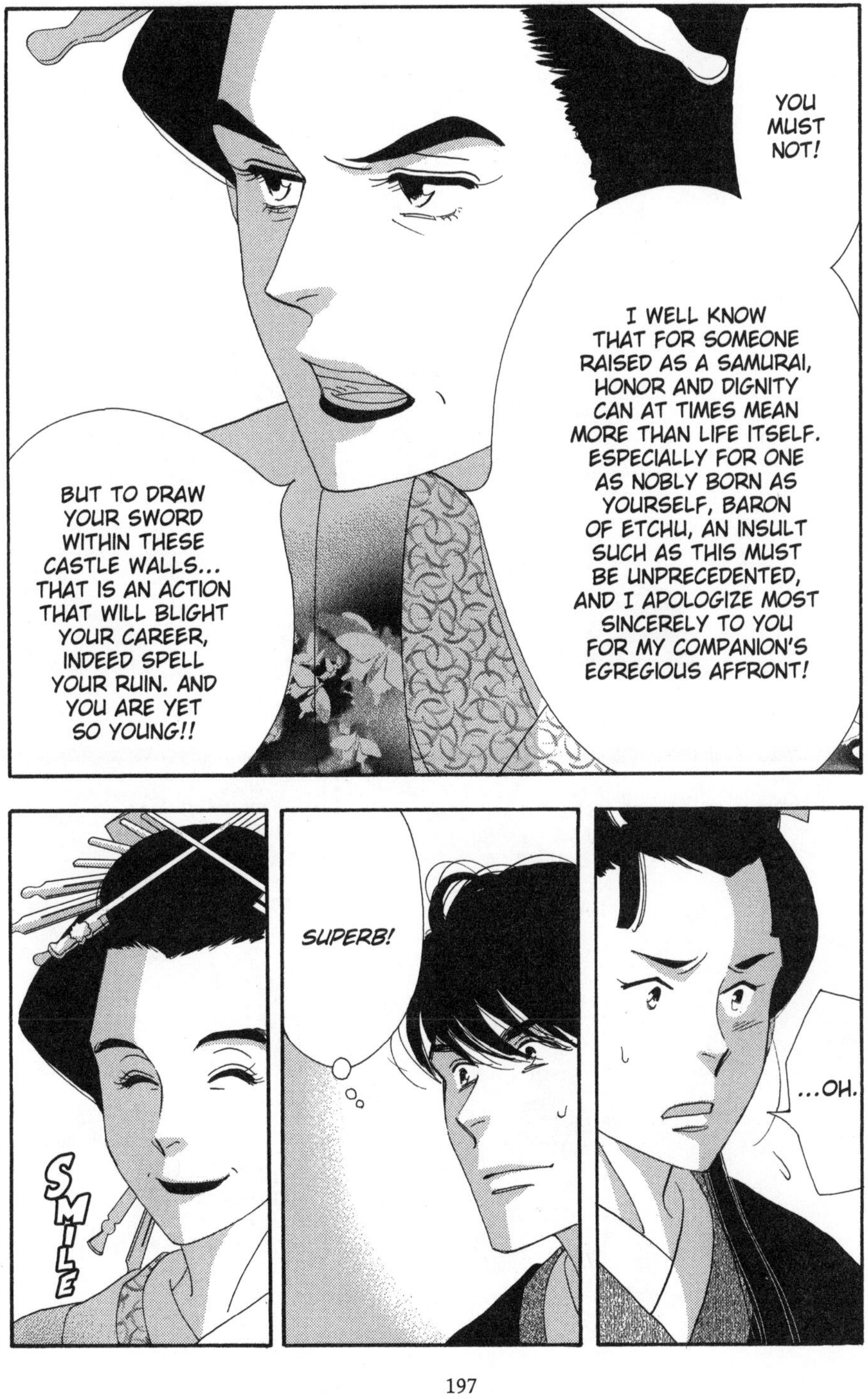
YOU MUST NOT!
I WELL KNOW THAT FOR SOMEONE RAISED AS A SAMURAI, HONOR AND DIGNITY CAN AT TIMES MEAN MORE THAN LIFE ITSELF. ESPECIALLY FOR ONE AS NOBLY BORN AS YOURSELF, BARON OF ETCHU, AN INSULT SUCH AS THIS MUST BE UNPRECEDENTED, AND I APOLOGIZE MOST SINCERELY TO YOU FOR MY COMPANION'S EGREGIOUS AFFRONT!
BUT TO DRAW YOUR SWORD WITHIN THESE CASTLE WALLS... THAT IS AN ACTION THAT WILL BLIGHT YOUR CAREER, INDEED SPELL YOUR RUIN. AND YOU ARE YET SO YOUNG!!
...OH.
SUPERB!
SMILE

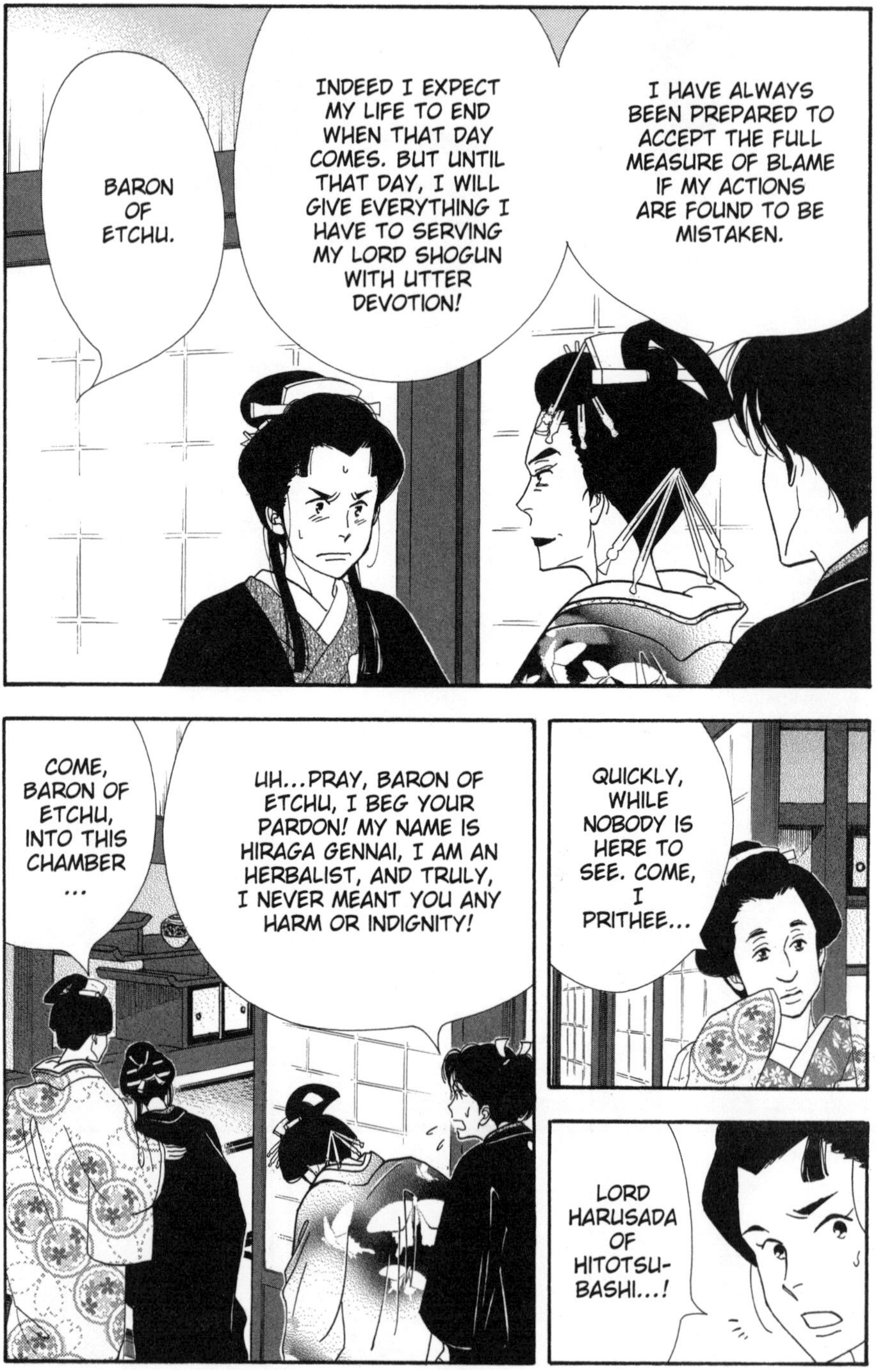
I HAVE ALWAYS BEEN PREPARED TO ACCEPT THE FULL MEASURE OF BLAME IF MY ACTIONS ARE FOUND TO BE MISTAKEN.
INDEED I EXPECT MY LIFE TO END WHEN THAT DAY COMES. BUT UNTIL THAT DAY, I WILL GIVE EVERYTHING I HAVE TO SERVING MY LORD SHOGUN WITH UTTER DEVOTION!
BARON OF ETCHU.
QUICKLY, WHILE NOBODY IS HERE TO SEE. COME, I PRITHEE...
LORD HARUSADA OF HITOTSU-BASHI...!
UH...PRAY, BARON OF ETCHU, I BEG YOUR PARDON! MY NAME IS HIRAGA GENNAI, I AM AN HERBALIST, AND TRULY, I NEVER MEANT YOU ANY HARM OR INDIGNITY!
COME, BARON OF ETCHU, INTO THIS CHAMBER ...

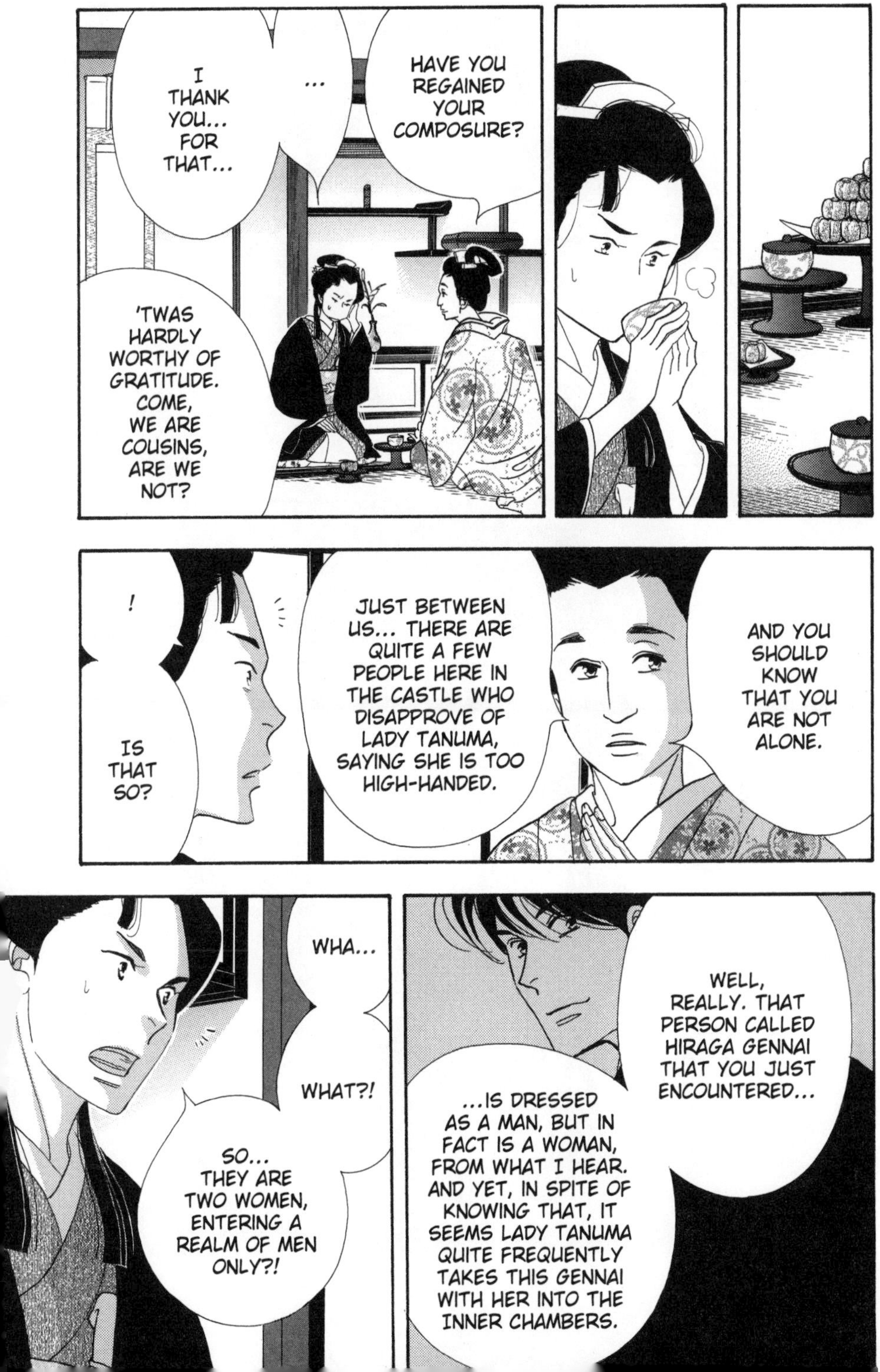
HAVE YOU REGAINED YOUR COMPOSURE?
...
I THANK YOU... FOR THAT...
'TWAS HARDLY WORTHY OF GRATITUDE. COME, WE ARE COUSINS, ARE WE NOT?
AND YOU SHOULD KNOW THAT YOU ARE NOT ALONE.
JUST BETWEEN US... THERE ARE QUITE A FEW PEOPLE HERE IN THE CASTLE WHO DISAPPROVE OF LADY TANUMA, SAYING SHE IS TOO HIGH-HANDED.
!
IS THAT SO?
WELL, REALLY. THAT PERSON CALLED HIRAGA GENNAI THAT YOU JUST ENCOUNTERED...
...IS DRESSED AS A MAN, BUT IN FACT IS A WOMAN, FROM WHAT I HEAR. AND YET, IN SPITE OF KNOWING THAT, IT SEEMS LADY TANUMA QUITE FREQUENTLY TAKES THIS GENNAI WITH HER INTO THE INNER CHAMBERS.
WHA...
WHAT?!
SO... THEY ARE TWO WOMEN, ENTERING A REALM OF MEN ONLY?!

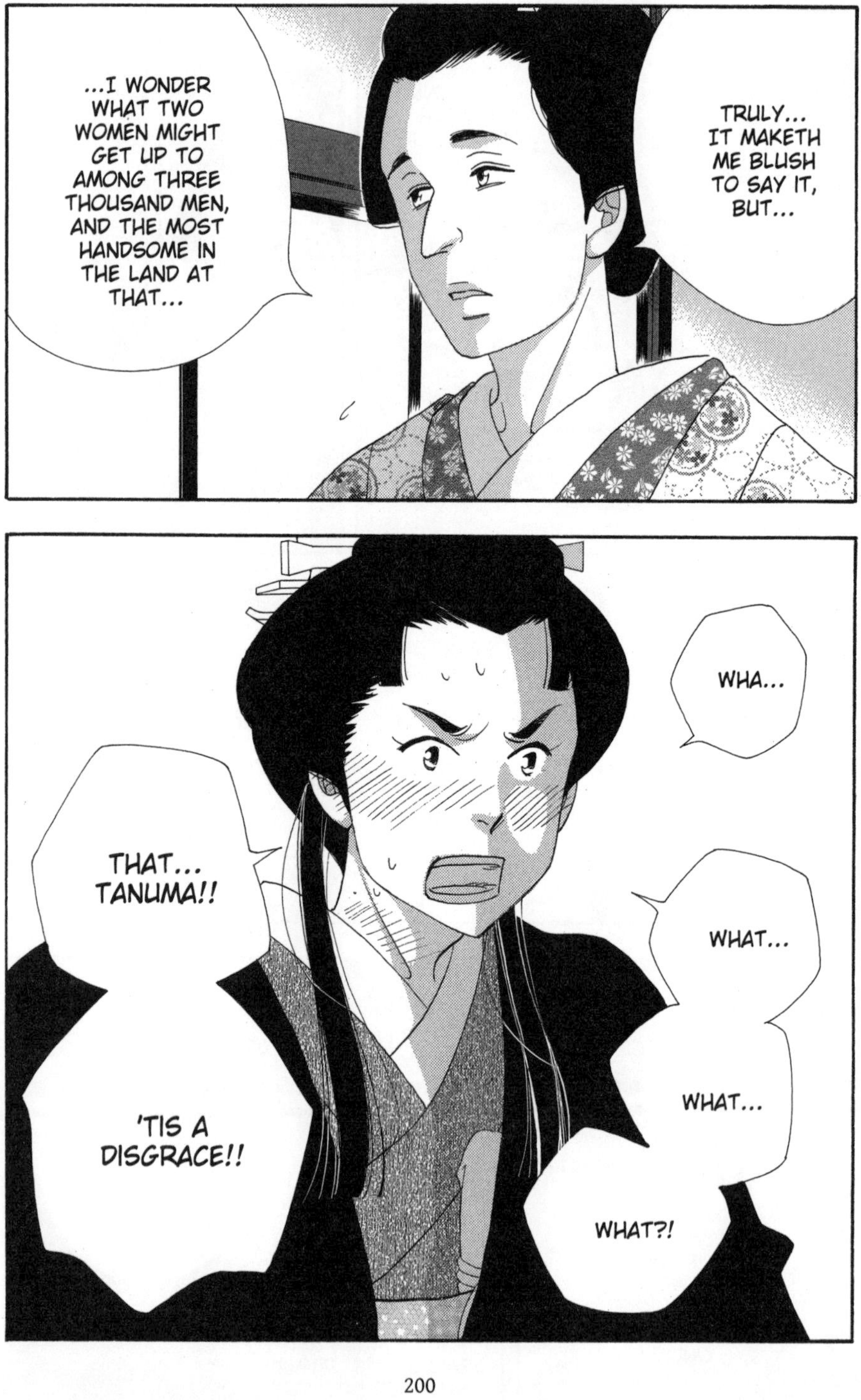
TRULY... IT MAKETH ME BLUSH TO SAY IT, BUT...
...I WONDER WHAT TWO WOMEN MIGHT GET UP TO AMONG THREE THOUSAND MEN, AND THE MOST HANDSOME IN THE LAND AT THAT...
WHA...
WHAT...
WHAT...
WHAT?!
THAT... TANUMA!!
'TIS A DISGRACE!!

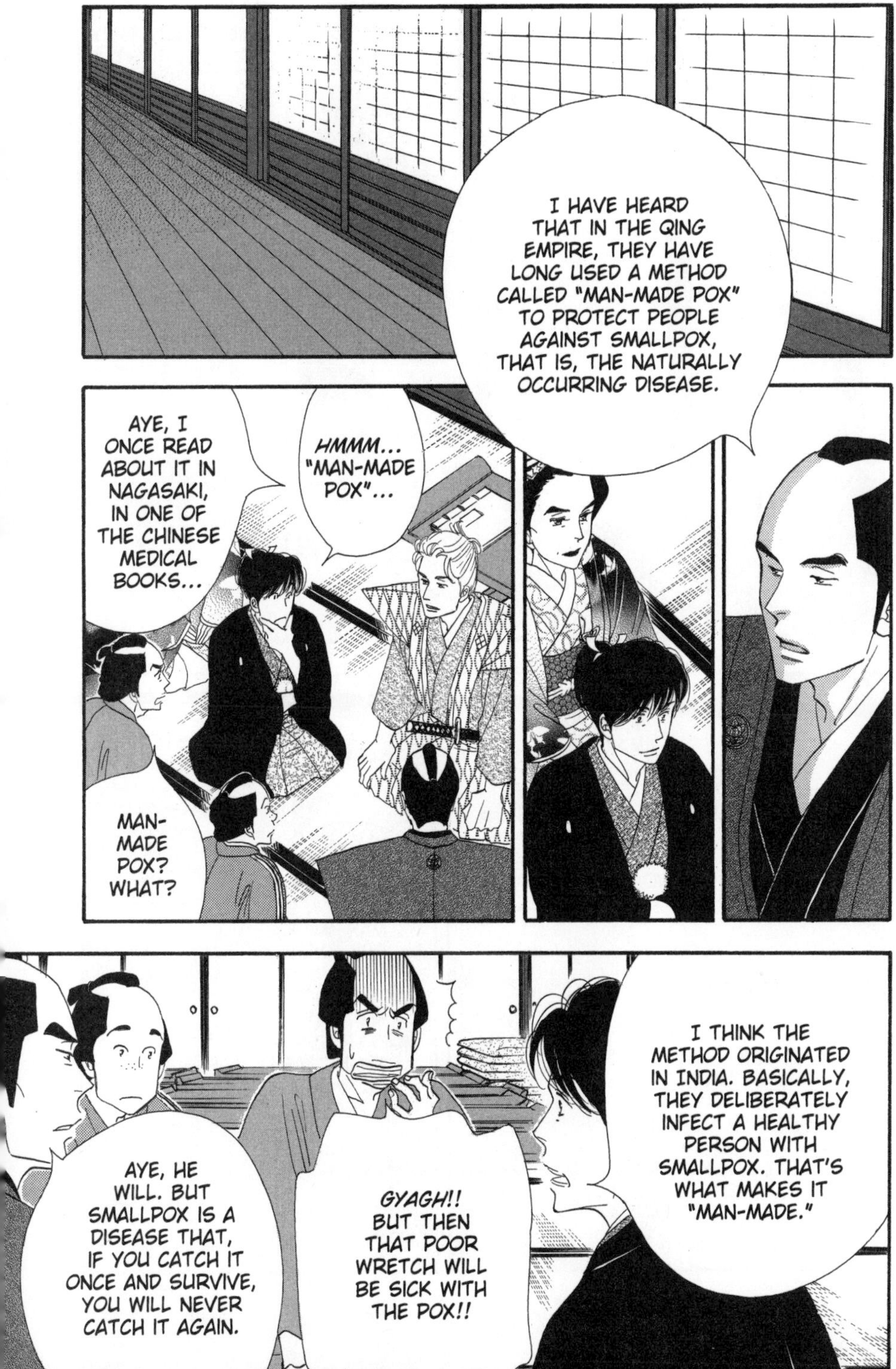
I HAVE HEARD THAT IN THE QING EMPIRE, THEY HAVE LONG USED A METHOD CALLED "MAN-MADE POX" TO PROTECT PEOPLE AGAINST SMALLPOX, THAT IS, THE NATURALLY OCCURRING DISEASE.
HMMM... "MAN-MADE POX"...
AYE, I ONCE READ ABOUT IT IN NAGASAKI, IN ONE OF THE CHINESE MEDICAL BOOKS...
MAN-MADE POX? WHAT?
I THINK THE METHOD ORIGINATED IN INDIA. BASICALLY, THEY DELIBERATELY INFECT A HEALTHY PERSON WITH SMALLPOX. THAT'S WHAT MAKES IT "MAN-MADE."
GYAGH!! BUT THEN THAT POOR WRETCH WILL BE SICK WITH THE POX!!
AYE, HE WILL. BUT SMALLPOX IS A DISEASE THAT, IF YOU CATCH IT ONCE AND SURVIVE, YOU WILL NEVER CATCH IT AGAIN.

THIS IS HOW THEY DO IT... FIRST, THEY REMOVE A SCAB FROM A DRIED PUSTULE ON THE SKIN OF SOMEONE SICK WITH NATURALLY OCCURRING SMALLPOX, AND GRIND THAT SCAB INTO A POWDER.
THEY PUT THIS POWDER TO THE NOSE OF A HEALTHY PERSON AND MAKE THEM INHALE IT INTO THEIR LUNGS.
BUT THEN THE HEALTHY PERSON WILL GET SICK AND DIE!!
NAY, FOR SOME REASON, WHEN THE INFECTION IS DELIBERATELY DONE LIKE THAT, THE SYMPTOMS ARE MUCH MILDER THAN WHEN THE DISEASE IS NATURALLY CONTRACTED.
MASTER! I FOUND IT HERE, IN THIS BOOK—*YIZONG JINJIAN*, "THE GOLDEN MIRROR OF MEDICINE"!
IT SAYS THAT WITH INFECTION BY MAN-MADE POX, ONLY THREE OUT OF A HUNDRED PATIENTS SUFFER SEVERE SYMPTOMS LEADING TO DEATH.
WOW, THAT'S AMAZING! IN A NATURAL SMALLPOX OUTBREAK, THE DEATH RATE IS ONE IN THREE, AIN'T IT? AND THAT'S A DISEASE THAT WOMEN GET, TOO, NOT JUST MEN!
EGADS, THREE OUT OF A HUNDRED COMPARED TO ONE IN THREE—THAT'S JUST ONE-TENTH THE MORTALITY RATE! WE OUGHT TO USE THIS MAN-MADE METHOD IN JAPAN, TOO! WHY DON'T WE, MASTER? EH?!

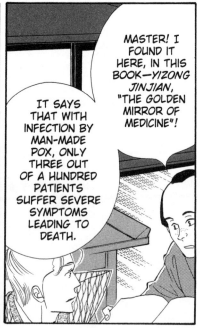

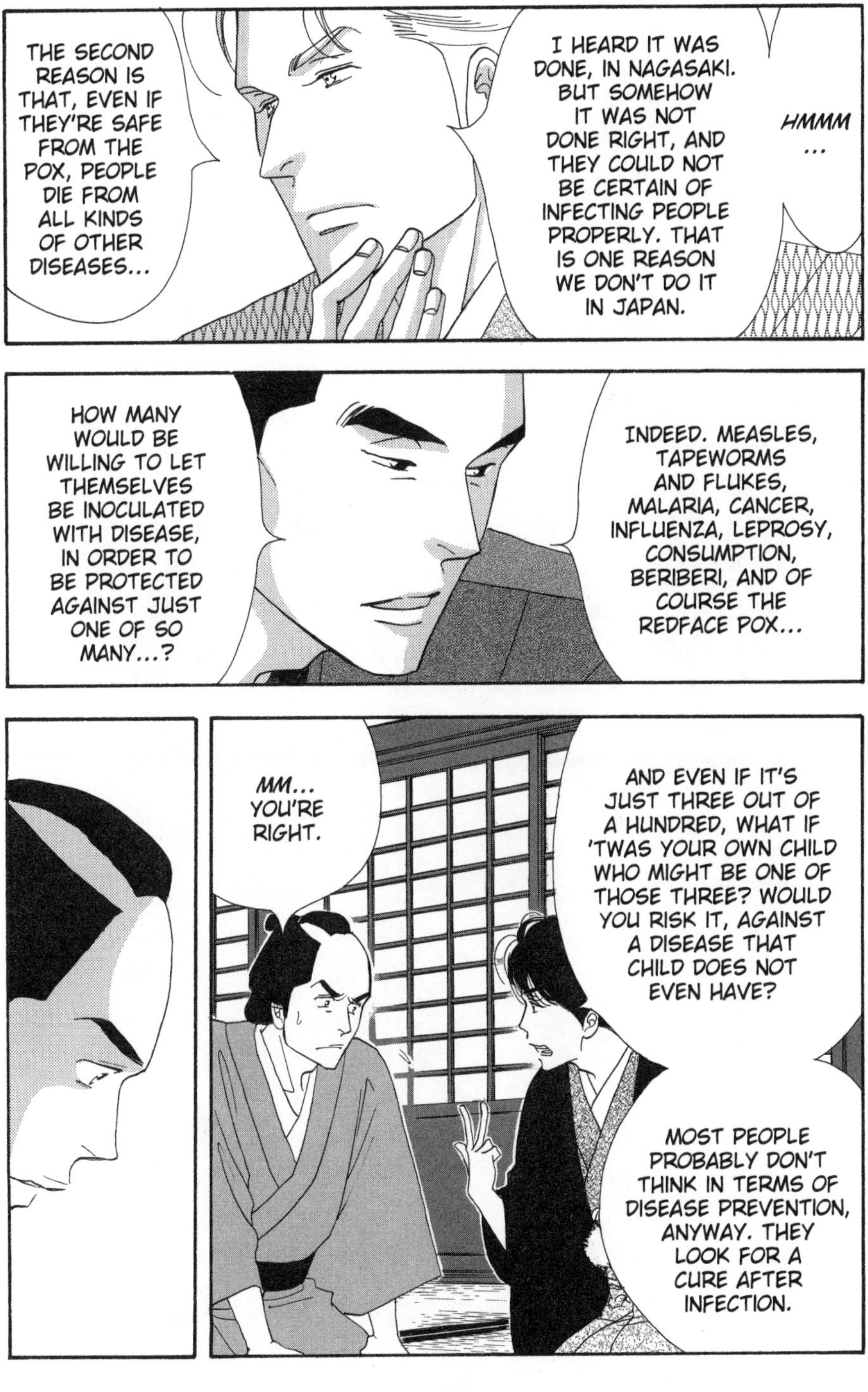
HMMM...
I HEARD IT WAS DONE, IN NAGASAKI. BUT SOMEHOW IT WAS NOT DONE RIGHT, AND THEY COULD NOT BE CERTAIN OF INFECTING PEOPLE PROPERLY. THAT IS ONE REASON WE DON'T DO IT IN JAPAN.
THE SECOND REASON IS THAT, EVEN IF THEY'RE SAFE FROM THE POX, PEOPLE DIE FROM ALL KINDS OF OTHER DISEASES...
INDEED. MEASLES, TAPEWORMS AND FLUKES, MALARIA, CANCER, INFLUENZA, LEPROSY, CONSUMPTION, BERIBERI, AND OF COURSE THE REDFACE POX...
HOW MANY WOULD BE WILLING TO LET THEMSELVES BE INOCULATED WITH DISEASE, IN ORDER TO BE PROTECTED AGAINST JUST ONE OF SO MANY...?
AND EVEN IF IT'S JUST THREE OUT OF A HUNDRED, WHAT IF 'TWAS YOUR OWN CHILD WHO MIGHT BE ONE OF THOSE THREE? WOULD YOU RISK IT, AGAINST A DISEASE THAT CHILD DOES NOT EVEN HAVE?
MM... YOU'RE RIGHT.
MOST PEOPLE PROBABLY DON'T THINK IN TERMS OF DISEASE PREVENTION, ANYWAY. THEY LOOK FOR A CURE AFTER INFECTION.

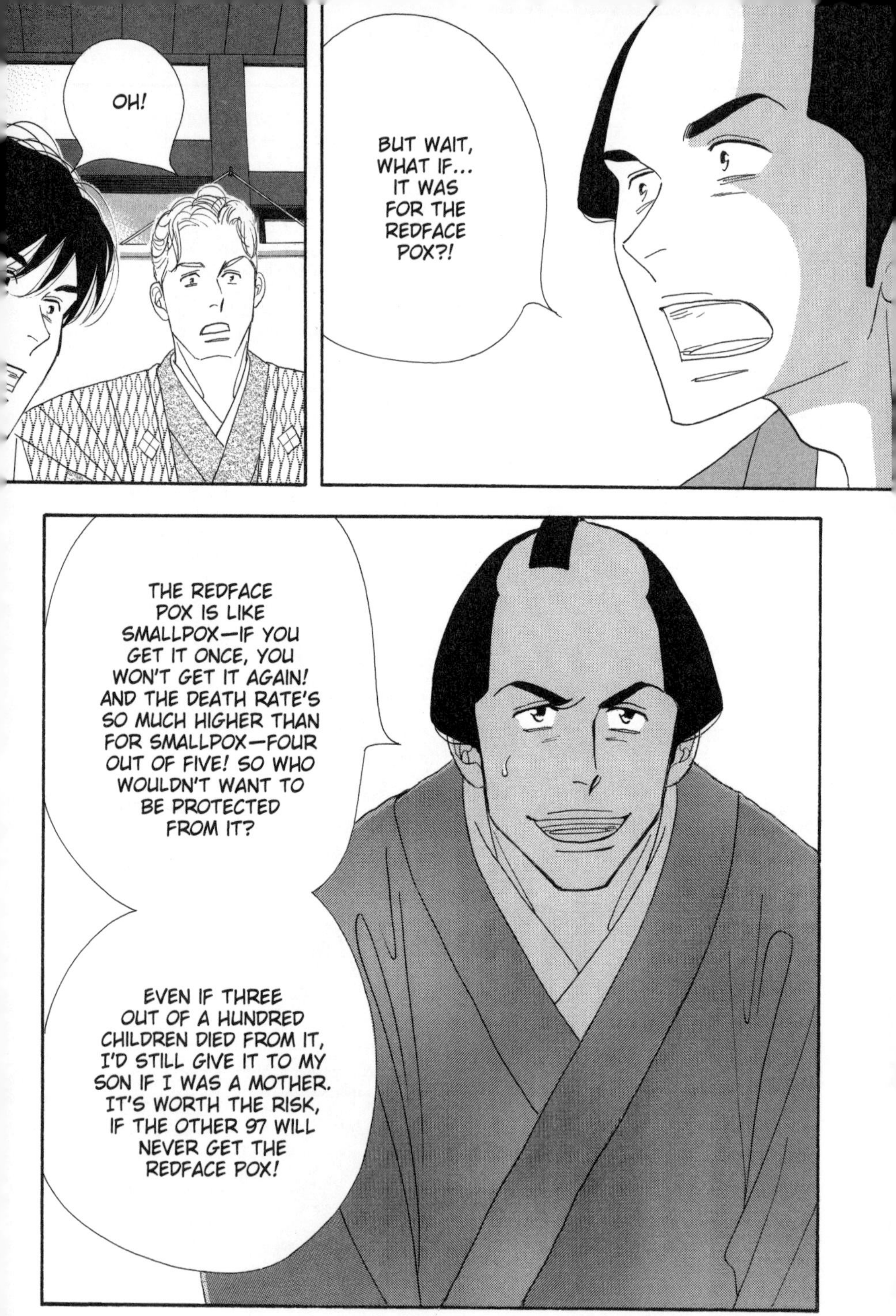
BUT WAIT, WHAT IF... IT WAS FOR THE REDFACE POX?!
OH!
THE REDFACE POX IS LIKE SMALLPOX—IF YOU GET IT ONCE, YOU WON'T GET IT AGAIN! AND THE DEATH RATE'S SO MUCH HIGHER THAN FOR SMALLPOX—FOUR OUT OF FIVE! SO WHO WOULDN'T WANT TO BE PROTECTED FROM IT?
EVEN IF THREE OUT OF A HUNDRED CHILDREN DIED FROM IT, I'D STILL GIVE IT TO MY SON IF I WAS A MOTHER. IT'S WORTH THE RISK, IF THE OTHER 97 WILL NEVER GET THE REDFACE POX!

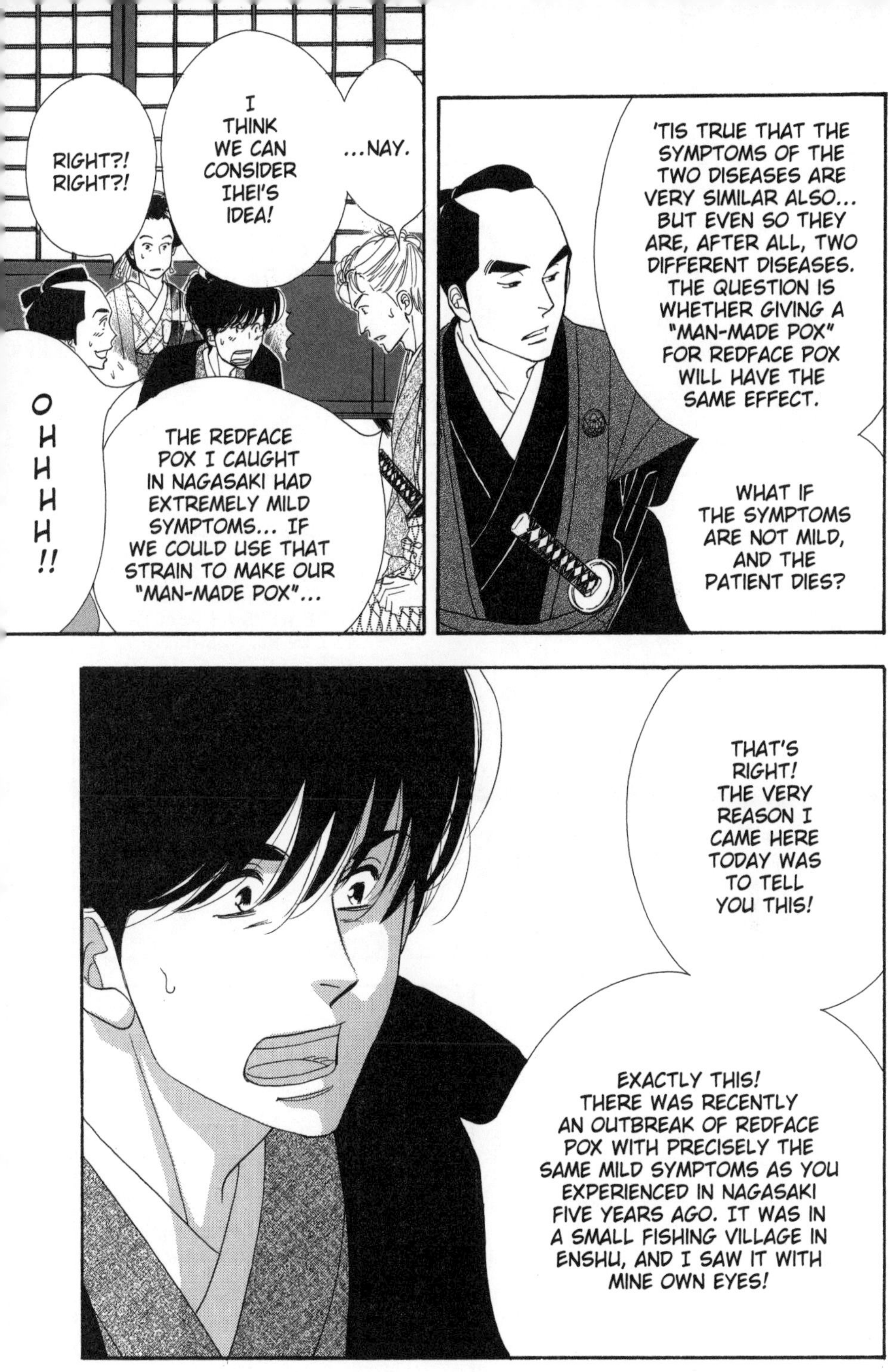
'TIS TRUE THAT THE SYMPTOMS OF THE TWO DISEASES ARE VERY SIMILAR ALSO... BUT EVEN SO THEY ARE, AFTER ALL, TWO DIFFERENT DISEASES. THE QUESTION IS WHETHER GIVING A "MAN-MADE POX" FOR REDFACE POX WILL HAVE THE SAME EFFECT.
WHAT IF THE SYMPTOMS ARE NOT MILD, AND THE PATIENT DIES?
...NAY.
I THINK WE CAN CONSIDER IHEI'S IDEA!
RIGHT?! RIGHT?!
THE REDFACE POX I CAUGHT IN NAGASAKI HAD EXTREMELY MILD SYMPTOMS... IF WE COULD USE THAT STRAIN TO MAKE OUR "MAN-MADE POX"...
OHHHH!!
THAT'S RIGHT! THE VERY REASON I CAME HERE TODAY WAS TO TELL YOU THIS!
EXACTLY THIS! THERE WAS RECENTLY AN OUTBREAK OF REDFACE POX WITH PRECISELY THE SAME MILD SYMPTOMS AS YOU EXPERIENCED IN NAGASAKI FIVE YEARS AGO. IT WAS IN A SMALL FISHING VILLAGE IN ENSHU, AND I SAW IT WITH MINE OWN EYES!

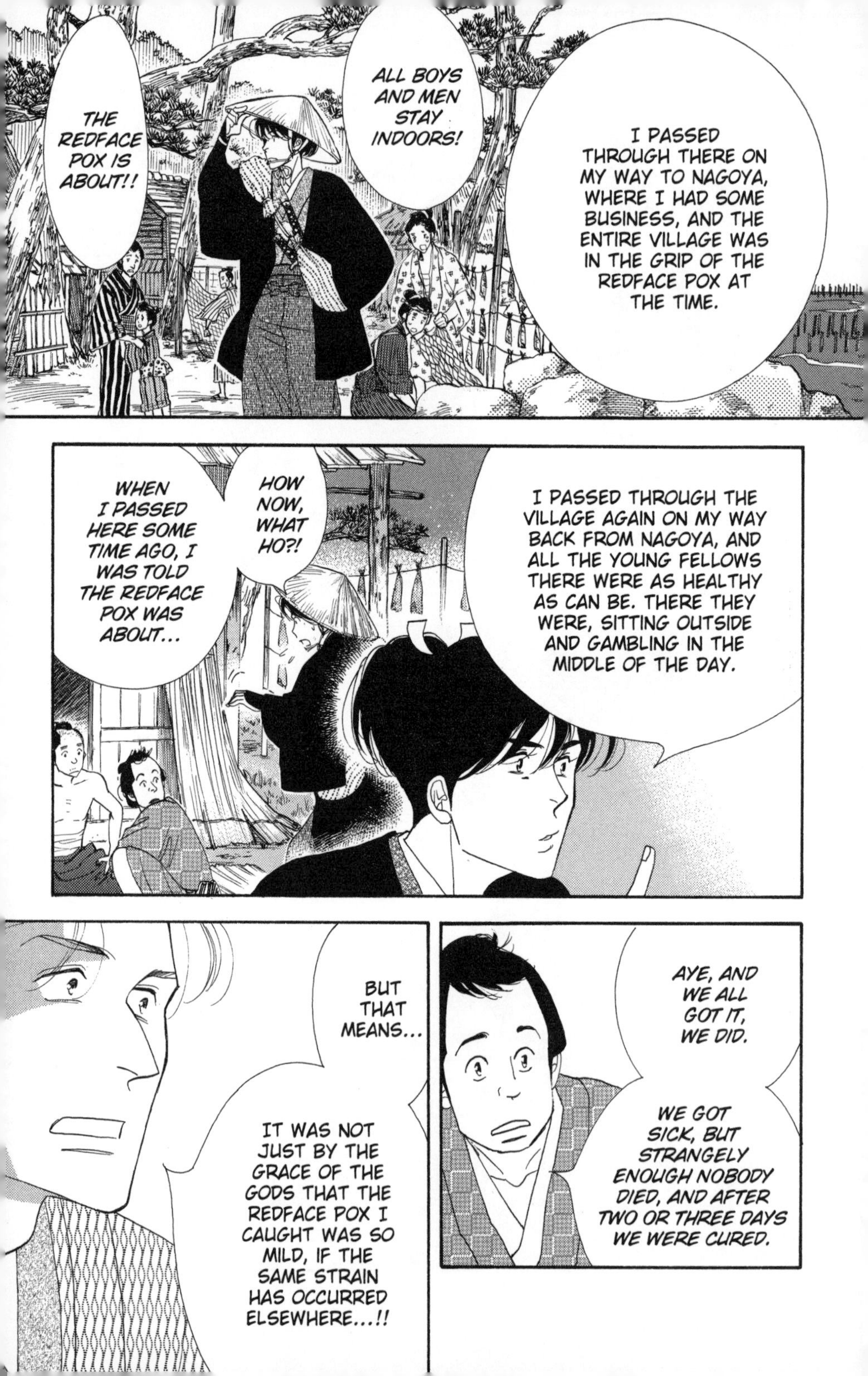
I PASSED THROUGH THERE ON MY WAY TO NAGOYA, WHERE I HAD SOME BUSINESS, AND THE ENTIRE VILLAGE WAS IN THE GRIP OF THE REDFACE POX AT THE TIME.
ALL BOYS AND MEN STAY INDOORS!
THE REDFACE POX IS ABOUT!!
I PASSED THROUGH THE VILLAGE AGAIN ON MY WAY BACK FROM NAGOYA, AND ALL THE YOUNG FELLOWS THERE WERE AS HEALTHY AS CAN BE. THERE THEY WERE, SITTING OUTSIDE AND GAMBLING IN THE MIDDLE OF THE DAY.
HOW NOW, WHAT HO?!
WHEN I PASSED HERE SOME TIME AGO, I WAS TOLD THE REDFACE POX WAS ABOUT...
AYE, AND WE ALL GOT IT, WE DID.
WE GOT SICK, BUT STRANGELY ENOUGH NOBODY DIED, AND AFTER TWO OR THREE DAYS WE WERE CURED.
BUT THAT MEANS...
IT WAS NOT JUST BY THE GRACE OF THE GODS THAT THE REDFACE POX I CAUGHT WAS SO MILD, IF THE SAME STRAIN HAS OCCURRED ELSEWHERE...!!

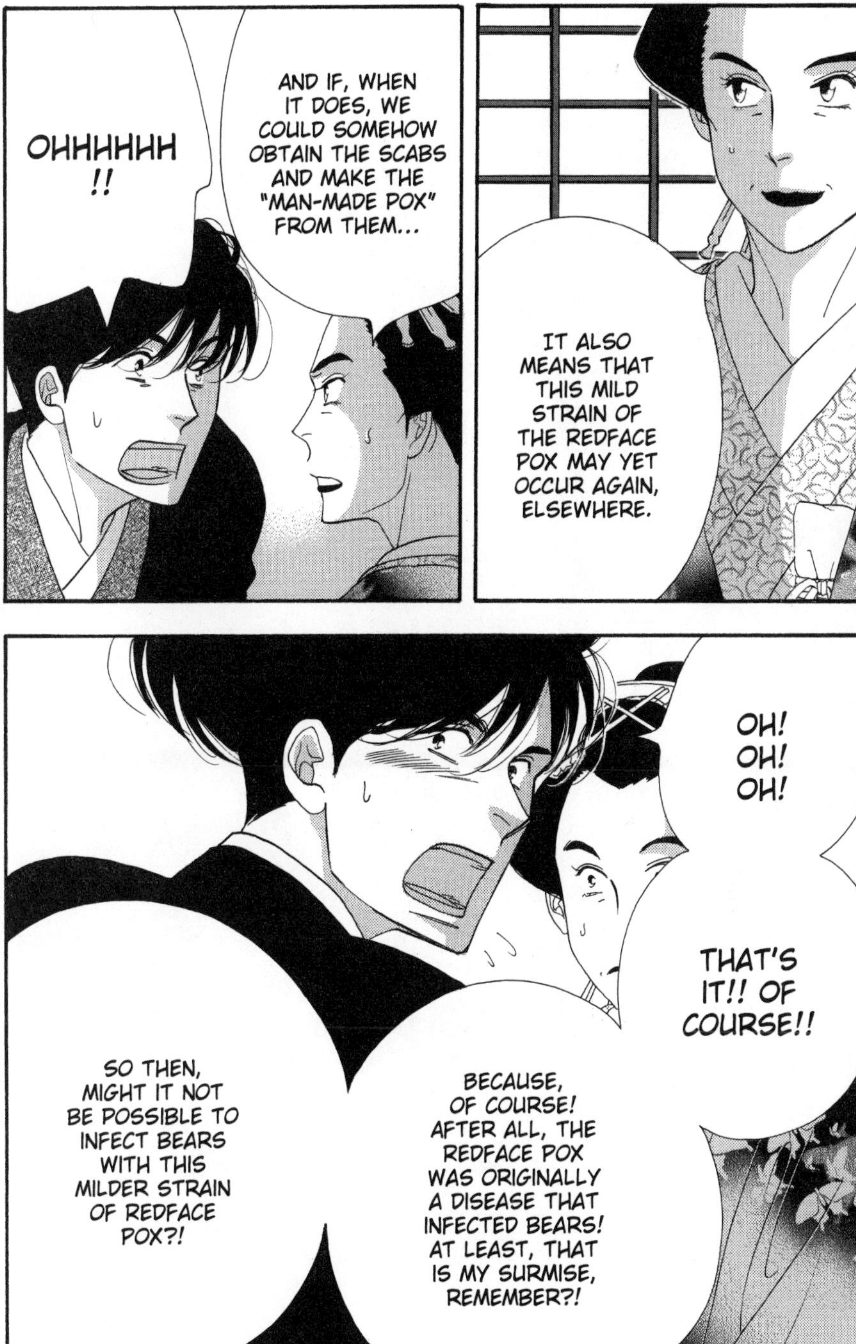
IT ALSO MEANS THAT THIS MILD STRAIN OF THE REDFACE POX MAY YET OCCUR AGAIN, ELSEWHERE.
AND IF, WHEN IT DOES, WE COULD SOMEHOW OBTAIN THE SCABS AND MAKE THE "MAN-MADE POX" FROM THEM...
OHHHHHH !!
OH! OH! OH!
THAT'S IT!! OF COURSE!!
BECAUSE, OF COURSE! AFTER ALL, THE REDFACE POX WAS ORIGINALLY A DISEASE THAT INFECTED BEARS! AT LEAST, THAT IS MY SURMISE, REMEMBER?!
SO THEN, MIGHT IT NOT BE POSSIBLE TO INFECT BEARS WITH THIS MILDER STRAIN OF REDFACE POX?!

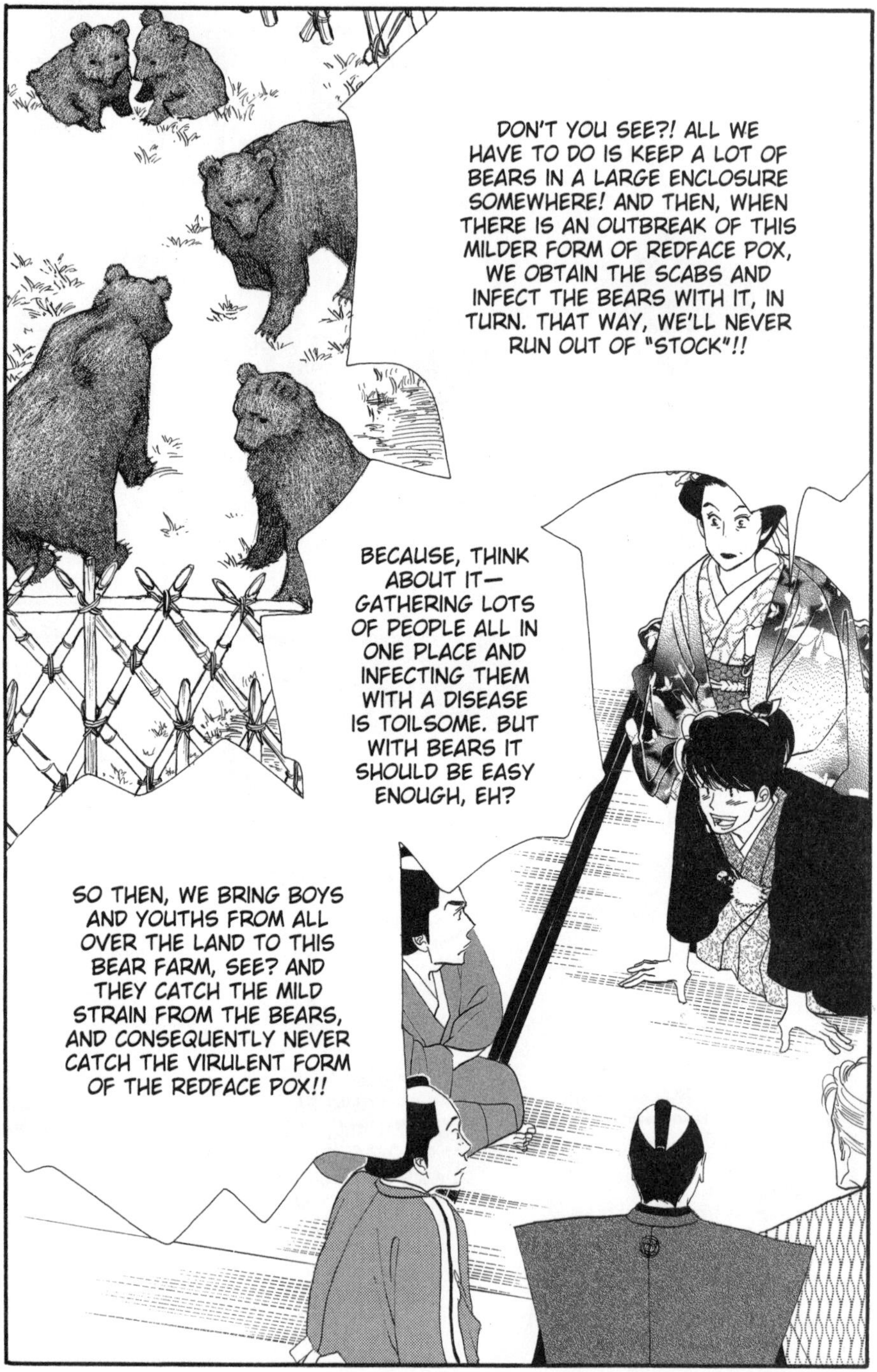
DON'T YOU SEE?! ALL WE HAVE TO DO IS KEEP A LOT OF BEARS IN A LARGE ENCLOSURE SOMEWHERE! AND THEN, WHEN THERE IS AN OUTBREAK OF THIS MILDER FORM OF REDFACE POX, WE OBTAIN THE SCABS AND INFECT THE BEARS WITH IT, IN TURN. THAT WAY, WE'LL NEVER RUN OUT OF "STOCK"!!
BECAUSE, THINK ABOUT IT—GATHERING LOTS OF PEOPLE ALL IN ONE PLACE AND INFECTING THEM WITH A DISEASE IS TOILSOME. BUT WITH BEARS IT SHOULD BE EASY ENOUGH, EH?
SO THEN, WE BRING BOYS AND YOUTHS FROM ALL OVER THE LAND TO THIS BEAR FARM, SEE? AND THEY CATCH THE MILD STRAIN FROM THE BEARS, AND CONSEQUENTLY NEVER CATCH THE VIRULENT FORM OF THE REDFACE POX!!

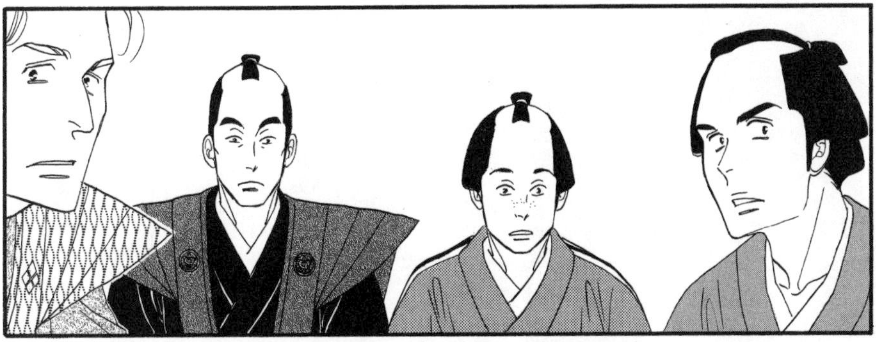

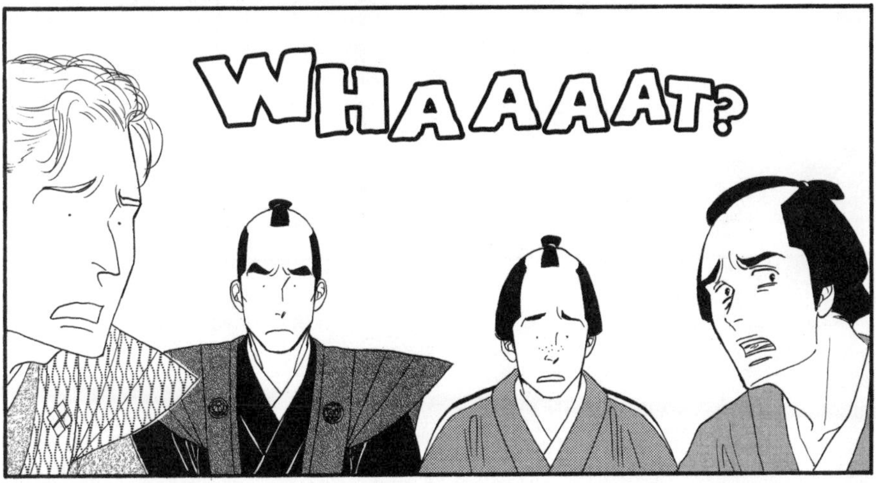
WHAAAAT?

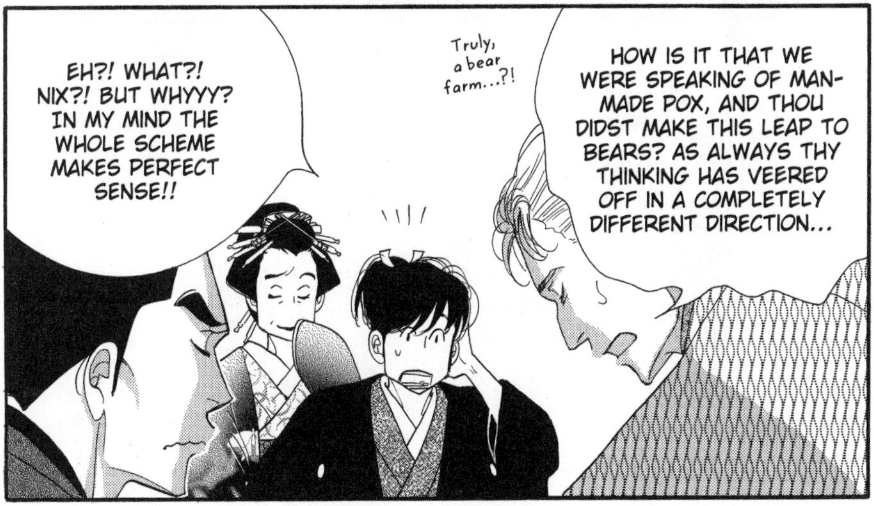
HOW IS IT THAT WE WERE SPEAKING OF MAN-MADE POX, AND THOU DIDST MAKE THIS LEAP TO BEARS? AS ALWAYS THY THINKING HAS VEERED OFF IN A COMPLETELY DIFFERENT DIRECTION...
Truly, a bear farm...?!
EH?! WHAT?! NIX?! BUT WHYYY? IN MY MIND THE WHOLE SCHEME MAKES PERFECT SENSE!!

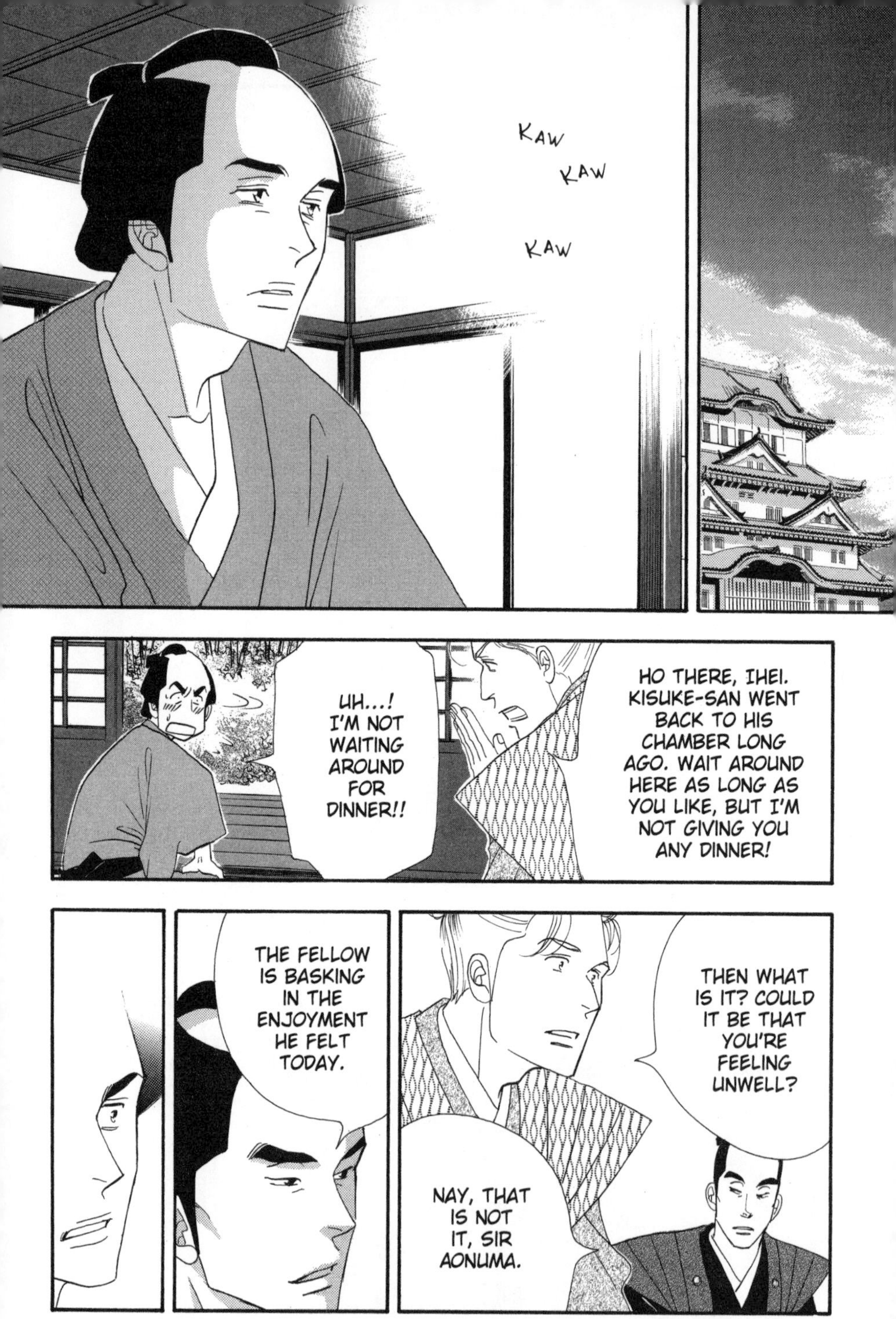
KAW
KAW
KAW
HO THERE, IHEI. KISUKE-SAN WENT BACK TO HIS CHAMBER LONG AGO. WAIT AROUND HERE AS LONG AS YOU LIKE, BUT I'M NOT GIVING YOU ANY DINNER!
UH...! I'M NOT WAITING AROUND FOR DINNER!!
THEN WHAT IS IT? COULD IT BE THAT YOU'RE FEELING UNWELL?
NAY, THAT IS NOT IT, SIR AONUMA.
THE FELLOW IS BASKING IN THE ENJOYMENT HE FELT TODAY.

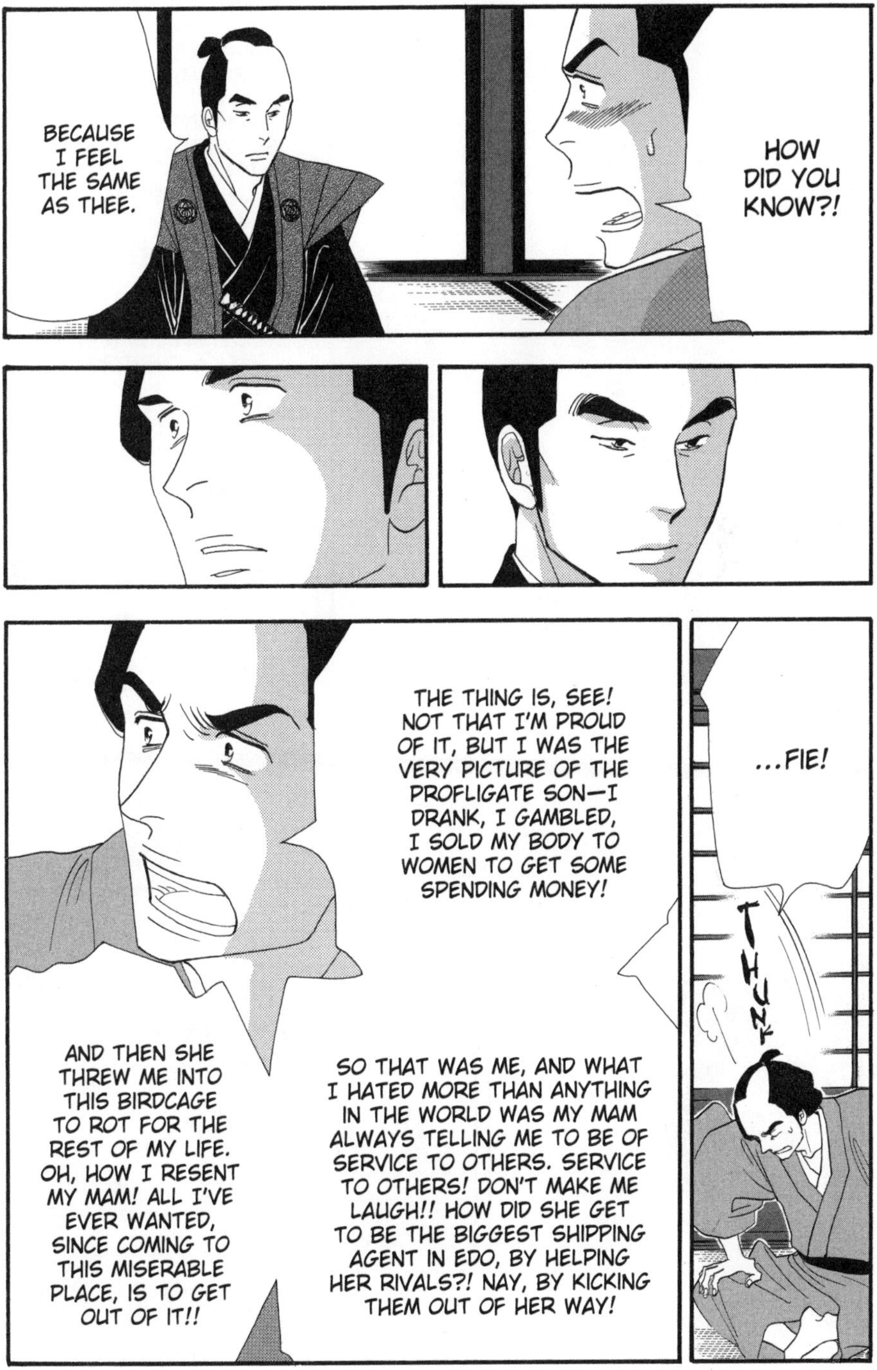
HOW DID YOU KNOW?!
BECAUSE I FEEL THE SAME AS THEE.
...FIE!
THUNK
THE THING IS, SEE! NOT THAT I'M PROUD OF IT, BUT I WAS THE VERY PICTURE OF THE PROFLIGATE SON—I DRANK, I GAMBLED, I SOLD MY BODY TO WOMEN TO GET SOME SPENDING MONEY!
SO THAT WAS ME, AND WHAT I HATED MORE THAN ANYTHING IN THE WORLD WAS MY MAM ALWAYS TELLING ME TO BE OF SERVICE TO OTHERS. SERVICE TO OTHERS! DON'T MAKE ME LAUGH!! HOW DID SHE GET TO BE THE BIGGEST SHIPPING AGENT IN EDO, BY HELPING HER RIVALS?! NAY, BY KICKING THEM OUT OF HER WAY!
AND THEN SHE THREW ME INTO THIS BIRDCAGE TO ROT FOR THE REST OF MY LIFE. OH, HOW I RESENT MY MAM! ALL I'VE EVER WANTED, SINCE COMING TO THIS MISERABLE PLACE, IS TO GET OUT OF IT!!

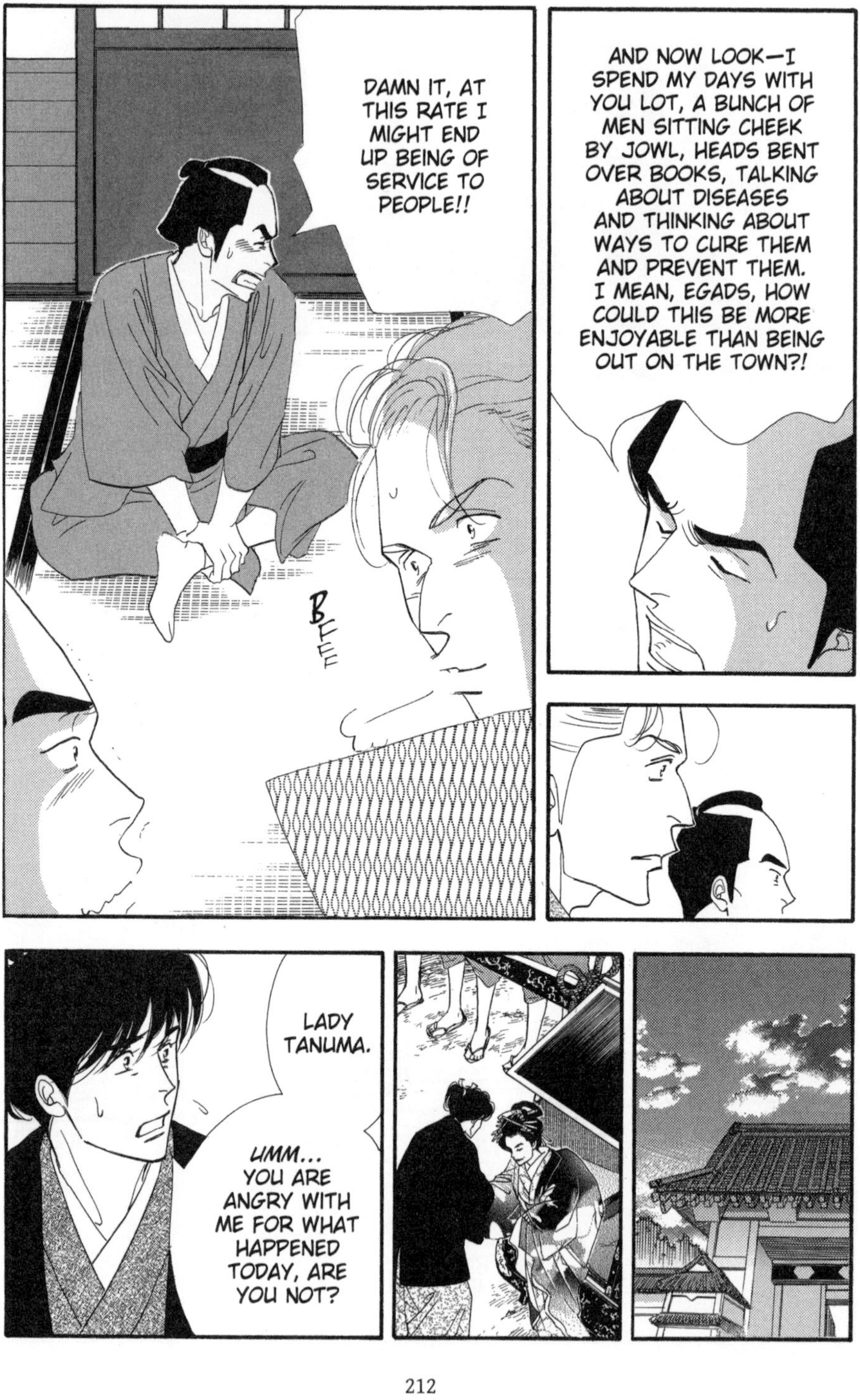
AND NOW LOOK—I SPEND MY DAYS WITH YOU LOT, A BUNCH OF MEN SITTING CHEEK BY JOWL, HEADS BENT OVER BOOKS, TALKING ABOUT DISEASES AND THINKING ABOUT WAYS TO CURE THEM AND PREVENT THEM. I MEAN, EGADS, HOW COULD THIS BE MORE ENJOYABLE THAN BEING OUT ON THE TOWN?!
DAMN IT, AT THIS RATE I MIGHT END UP BEING OF SERVICE TO PEOPLE!!
BFFF
LADY TANUMA.
UMM... YOU ARE ANGRY WITH ME FOR WHAT HAPPENED TODAY, ARE YOU NOT?

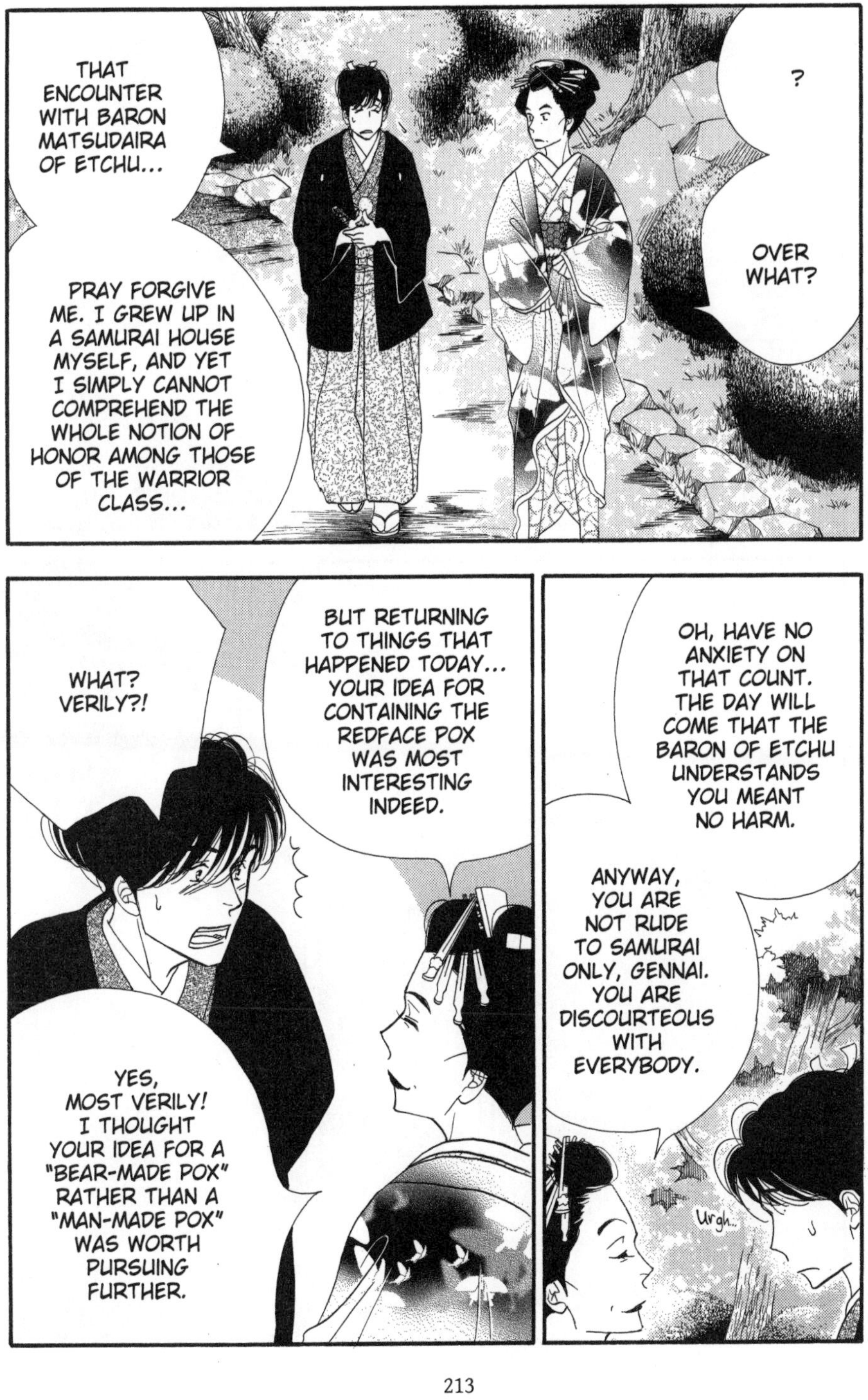
?
OVER WHAT?
THAT ENCOUNTER WITH BARON MATSUDAIRA OF ETCHU...
PRAY FORGIVE ME. I GREW UP IN A SAMURAI HOUSE MYSELF, AND YET I SIMPLY CANNOT COMPREHEND THE WHOLE NOTION OF HONOR AMONG THOSE OF THE WARRIOR CLASS...
OH, HAVE NO ANXIETY ON THAT COUNT. THE DAY WILL COME THAT THE BARON OF ETCHU UNDERSTANDS YOU MEANT NO HARM.
ANYWAY, YOU ARE NOT RUDE TO SAMURAI ONLY, GENNAI. YOU ARE DISCOURTEOUS WITH EVERYBODY.
Urgh..
BUT RETURNING TO THINGS THAT HAPPENED TODAY... YOUR IDEA FOR CONTAINING THE REDFACE POX WAS MOST INTERESTING INDEED.
WHAT? VERILY?!
YES, MOST VERILY! I THOUGHT YOUR IDEA FOR A "BEAR-MADE POX" RATHER THAN A "MAN-MADE POX" WAS WORTH PURSUING FURTHER.

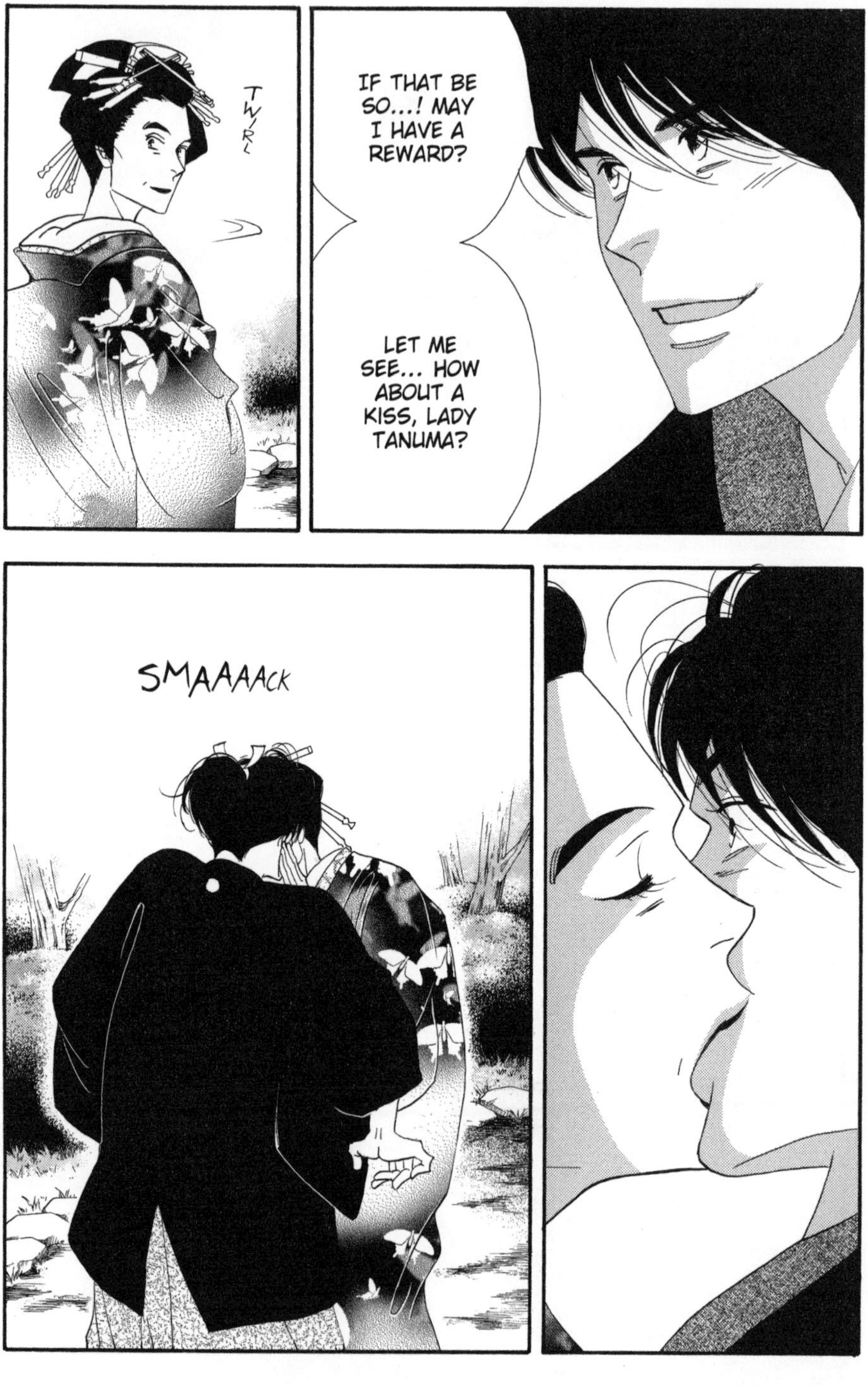
IF THAT BE SO...! MAY I HAVE A REWARD?
LET ME SEE... HOW ABOUT A KISS, LADY TANUMA?
TWIRL
SMAAAACK

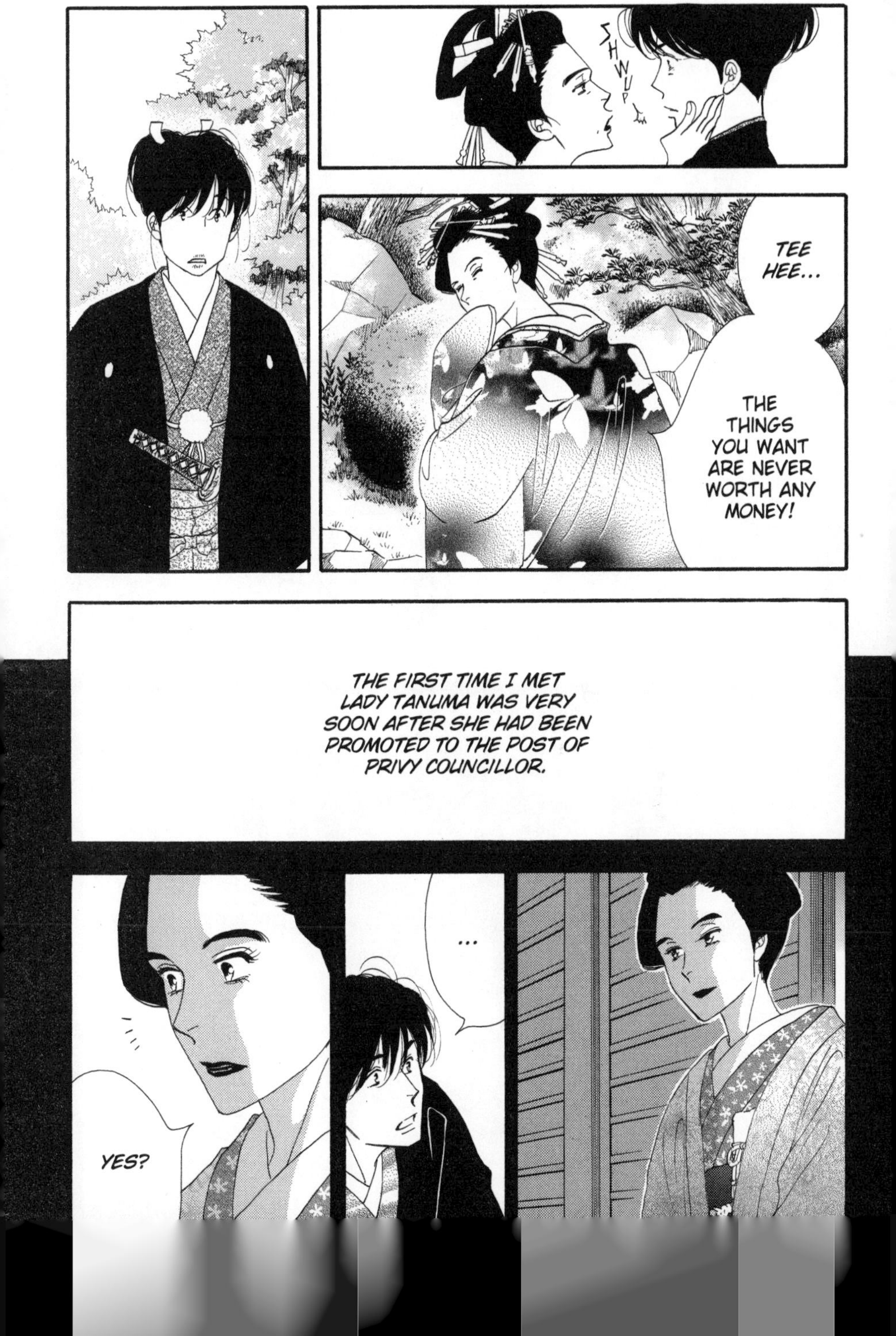
SHWUP
TEE HEE...
THE THINGS YOU WANT ARE NEVER WORTH ANY MONEY!
THE FIRST TIME I MET LADY TANUMA WAS VERY SOON AFTER SHE HAD BEEN PROMOTED TO THE POST OF PRIVY COUNCILLOR.
...
YES?

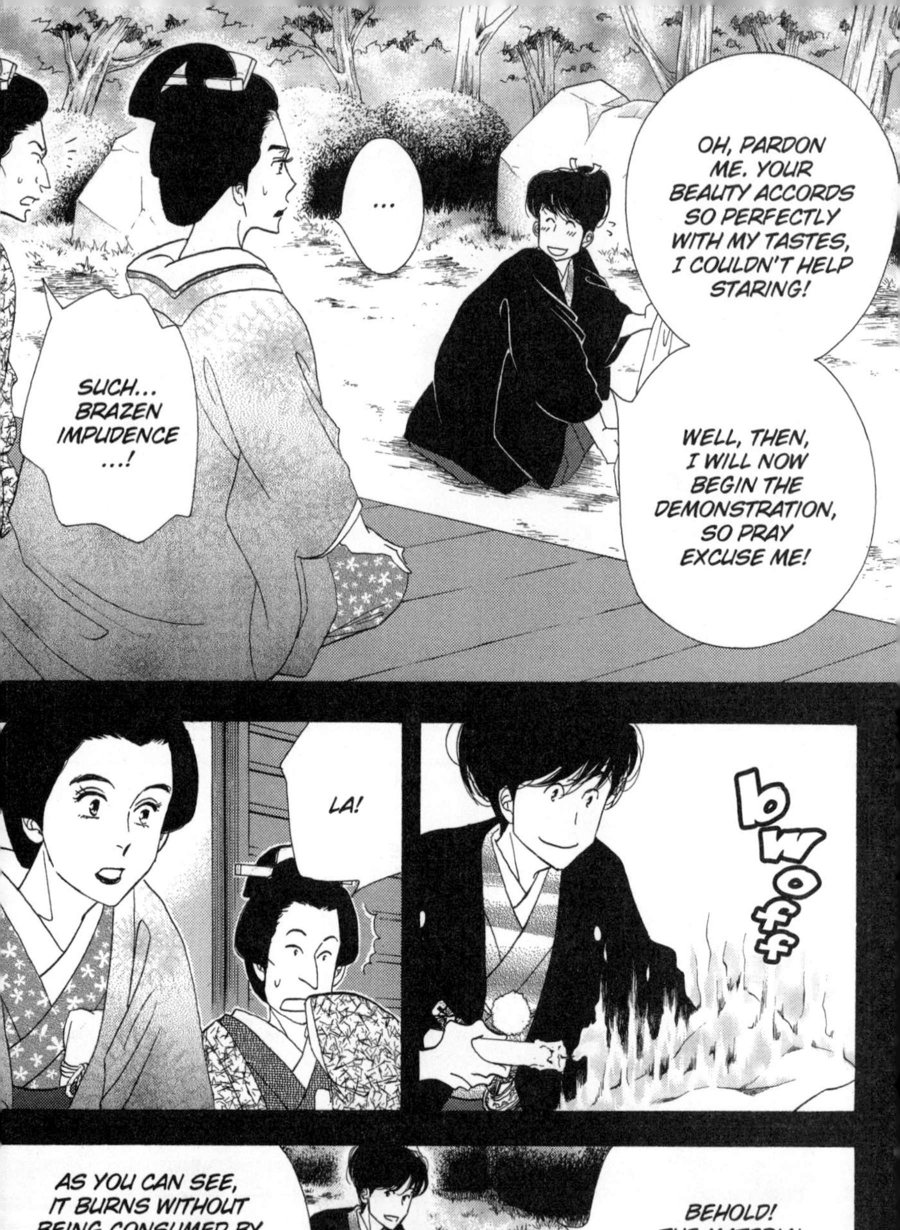
OH, PARDON ME. YOUR BEAUTY ACCORDS SO PERFECTLY WITH MY TASTES, I COULDN'T HELP STARING!
...
WELL, THEN, I WILL NOW BEGIN THE DEMONSTRATION, SO PRAY EXCUSE ME!
SUCH... BRAZEN IMPUDENCE ...!
bwoff
LA!
BEHOLD! THE MATERIAL USED TO WEAVE THIS TEXTILE IS A MINERAL CALLED "STONE COTTON."
AS YOU CAN SEE, IT BURNS WITHOUT BEING CONSUMED BY THE FIRE. AND FIRE SO OFTEN RAVAGES THE HOUSES OF EDO. IF VALUABLES WERE WRAPPED IN THIS CLOTH, PEOPLE WOULD NOT LOSE THEIR PRECIOUS POSSESSIONS!

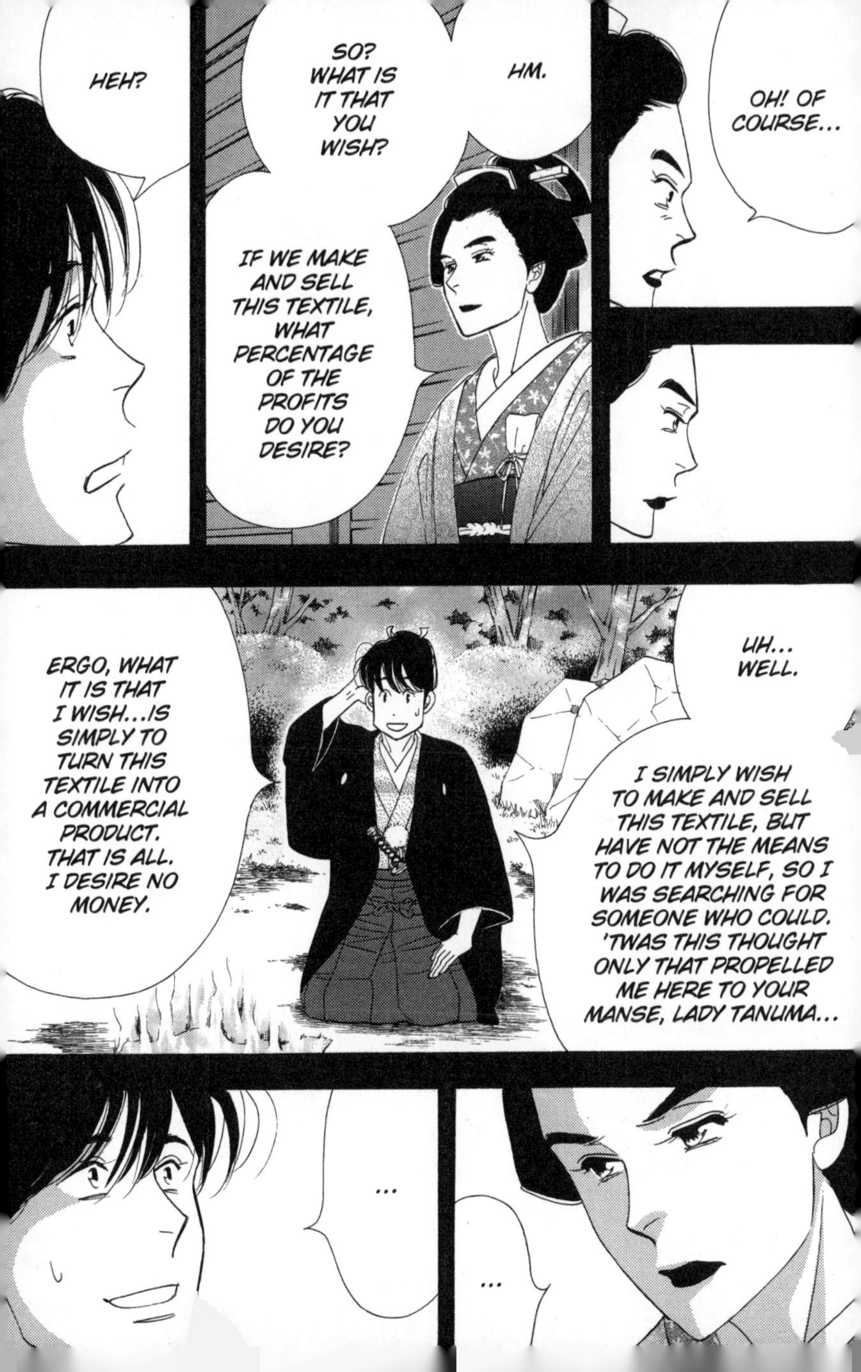
OH! OF COURSE...
HM.
SO? WHAT IS IT THAT YOU WISH?
IF WE MAKE AND SELL THIS TEXTILE, WHAT PERCENTAGE OF THE PROFITS DO YOU DESIRE?
HEH?
UH... WELL.
I SIMPLY WISH TO MAKE AND SELL THIS TEXTILE, BUT HAVE NOT THE MEANS TO DO IT MYSELF, SO I WAS SEARCHING FOR SOMEONE WHO COULD. 'TWAS THIS THOUGHT ONLY THAT PROPELLED ME HERE TO YOUR MANSE, LADY TANUMA...
ERGO, WHAT IT IS THAT I WISH...IS SIMPLY TO TURN THIS TEXTILE INTO A COMMERCIAL PRODUCT. THAT IS ALL. I DESIRE NO MONEY.
...
...

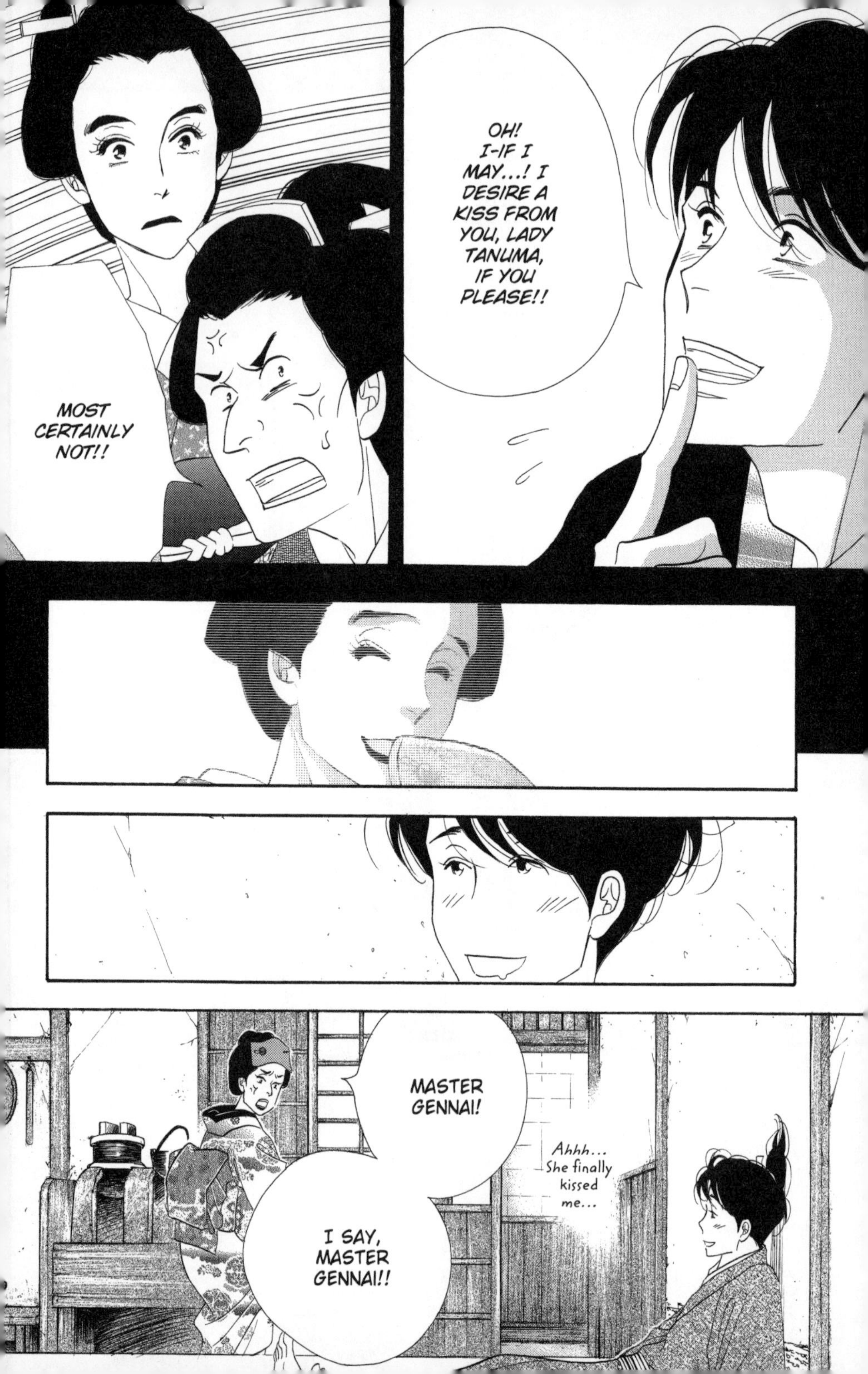
OH! I-IF I MAY...! I DESIRE A KISS FROM YOU, LADY TANUMA, IF YOU PLEASE!!
MOST CERTAINLY NOT!!
Ahhh... She finally kissed me...
MASTER GENNAI!
I SAY, MASTER GENNAI!!

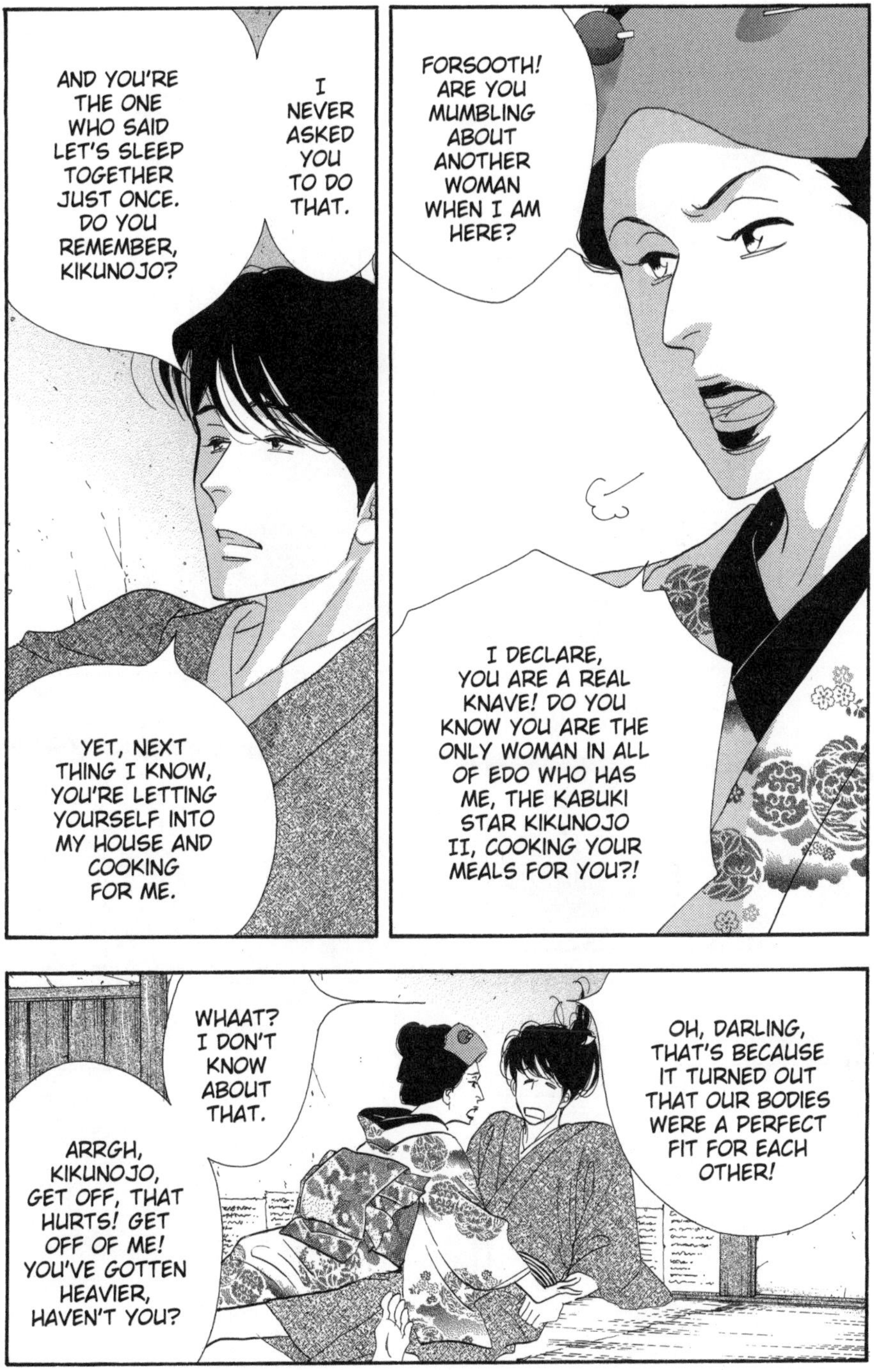
FORSOOTH! ARE YOU MUMBLING ABOUT ANOTHER WOMAN WHEN I AM HERE?
I DECLARE, YOU ARE A REAL KNAVE! DO YOU KNOW YOU ARE THE ONLY WOMAN IN ALL OF EDO WHO HAS ME, THE KABUKI STAR KIKUNOJO II, COOKING YOUR MEALS FOR YOU?!
I NEVER ASKED YOU TO DO THAT.
AND YOU'RE THE ONE WHO SAID LET'S SLEEP TOGETHER JUST ONCE. DO YOU REMEMBER, KIKUNOJO?
YET, NEXT THING I KNOW, YOU'RE LETTING YOURSELF INTO MY HOUSE AND COOKING FOR ME.
OH, DARLING, THAT'S BECAUSE IT TURNED OUT THAT OUR BODIES WERE A PERFECT FIT FOR EACH OTHER!
WHAAT? I DON'T KNOW ABOUT THAT.
ARRGH, KIKUNOJO, GET OFF, THAT HURTS! GET OFF OF ME! YOU'VE GOTTEN HEAVIER, HAVEN'T YOU?

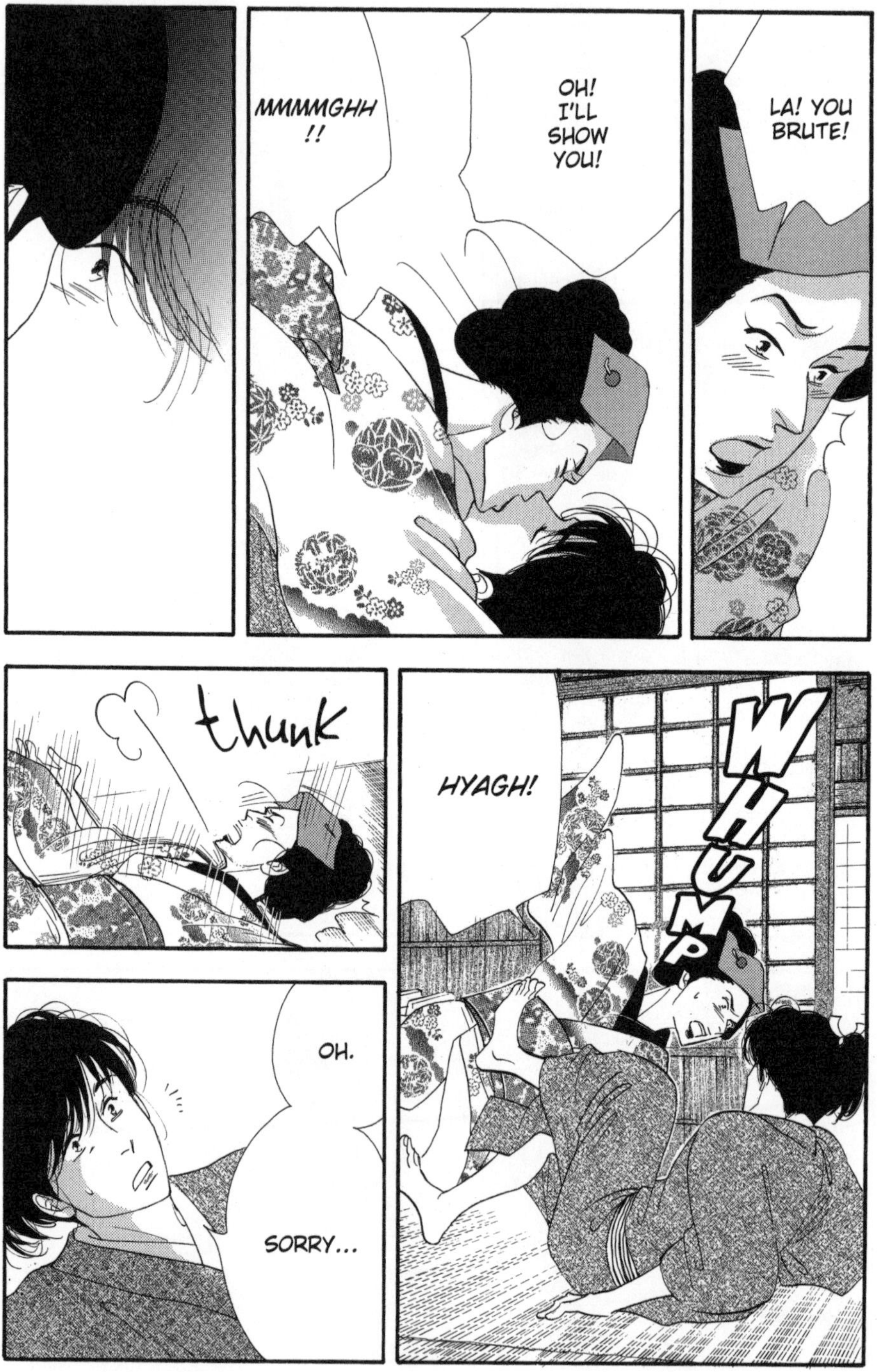
LA! YOU BRUTE!
OH! I'LL SHOW YOU!
MMMMGHH !!
WHUMP
HYAGH!
thunk
OH.
SORRY...

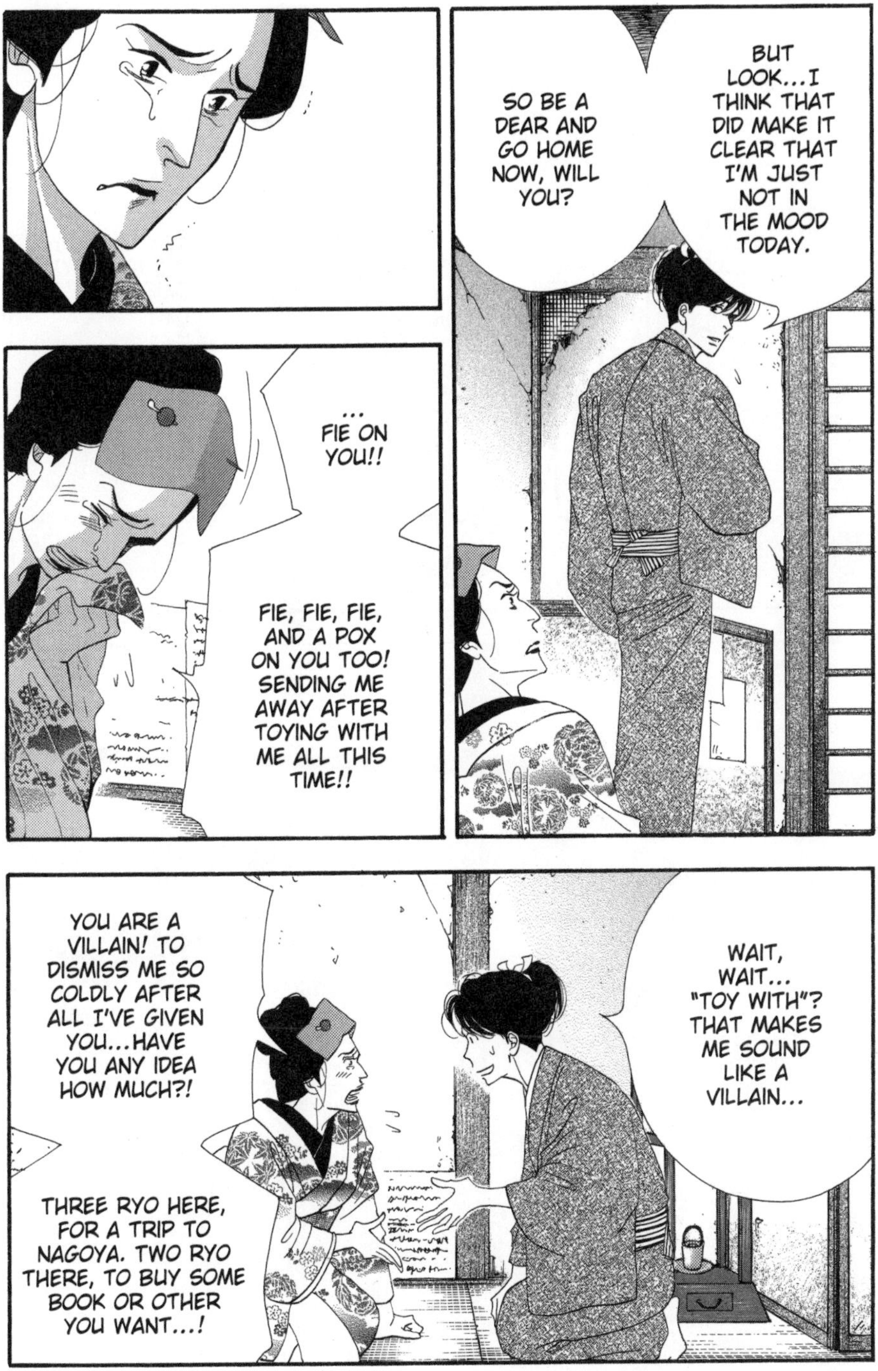
BUT LOOK...I THINK THAT DID MAKE IT CLEAR THAT I'M JUST NOT IN THE MOOD TODAY.
SO BE A DEAR AND GO HOME NOW, WILL YOU?
...FIE ON YOU!!
FIE, FIE, FIE, AND A POX ON YOU TOO! SENDING ME AWAY AFTER TOYING WITH ME ALL THIS TIME!!
WAIT, WAIT... "TOY WITH"? THAT MAKES ME SOUND LIKE A VILLAIN...
YOU ARE A VILLAIN! TO DISMISS ME SO COLDLY AFTER ALL I'VE GIVEN YOU...HAVE YOU ANY IDEA HOW MUCH?!
THREE RYO HERE, FOR A TRIP TO NAGOYA. TWO RYO THERE, TO BUY SOME BOOK OR OTHER YOU WANT...!

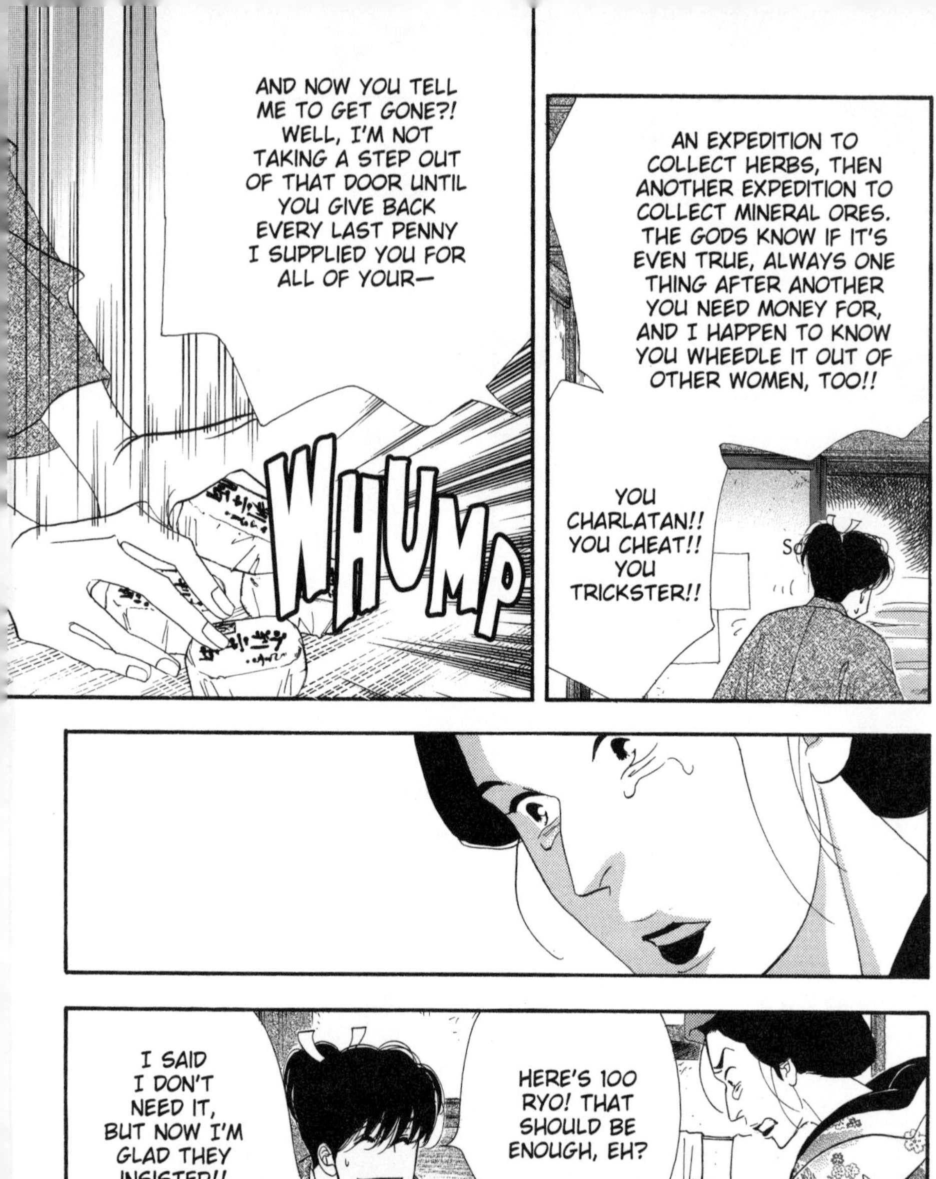
AN EXPEDITION TO COLLECT HERBS, THEN ANOTHER EXPEDITION TO COLLECT MINERAL ORES. THE GODS KNOW IF IT'S EVEN TRUE, ALWAYS ONE THING AFTER ANOTHER YOU NEED MONEY FOR, AND I HAPPEN TO KNOW YOU WHEEDLE IT OUT OF OTHER WOMEN, TOO!!
YOU CHARLATAN!! YOU CHEAT!! YOU TRICKSTER!!
AND NOW YOU TELL ME TO GET GONE?! WELL, I'M NOT TAKING A STEP OUT OF THAT DOOR UNTIL YOU GIVE BACK EVERY LAST PENNY I SUPPLIED YOU FOR ALL OF YOUR—
WHUMP
HERE'S 100 RYO! THAT SHOULD BE ENOUGH, EH?
I SAID I DON'T NEED IT, BUT NOW I'M GLAD THEY INSISTED!! TAKE IT ALL, IT'S YOURS—AND THEN YOU'LL GO, WON'T YOU?!

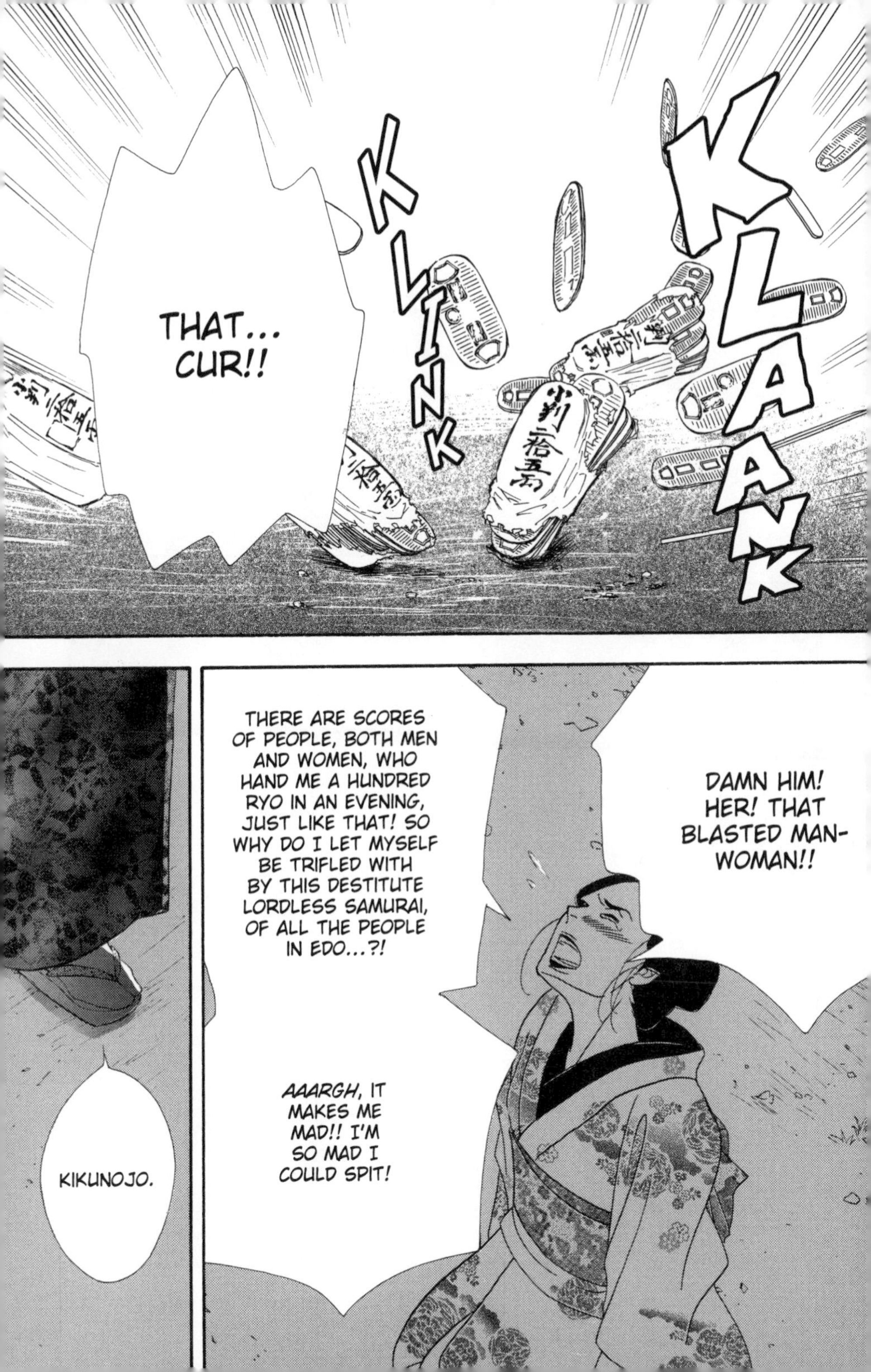
KLLANK
KLINK
THAT... CUR!!
DAMN HIM! HER! THAT BLASTED MAN-WOMAN!!
THERE ARE SCORES OF PEOPLE, BOTH MEN AND WOMEN, WHO HAND ME A HUNDRED RYO IN AN EVENING, JUST LIKE THAT! SO WHY DO I LET MYSELF BE TRIFLED WITH BY THIS DESTITUTE LORDLESS SAMURAI, OF ALL THE PEOPLE IN EDO...?!
AAARGH, IT MAKES ME MAD!! I'M SO MAD I COULD SPIT!
KIKUNOJO.

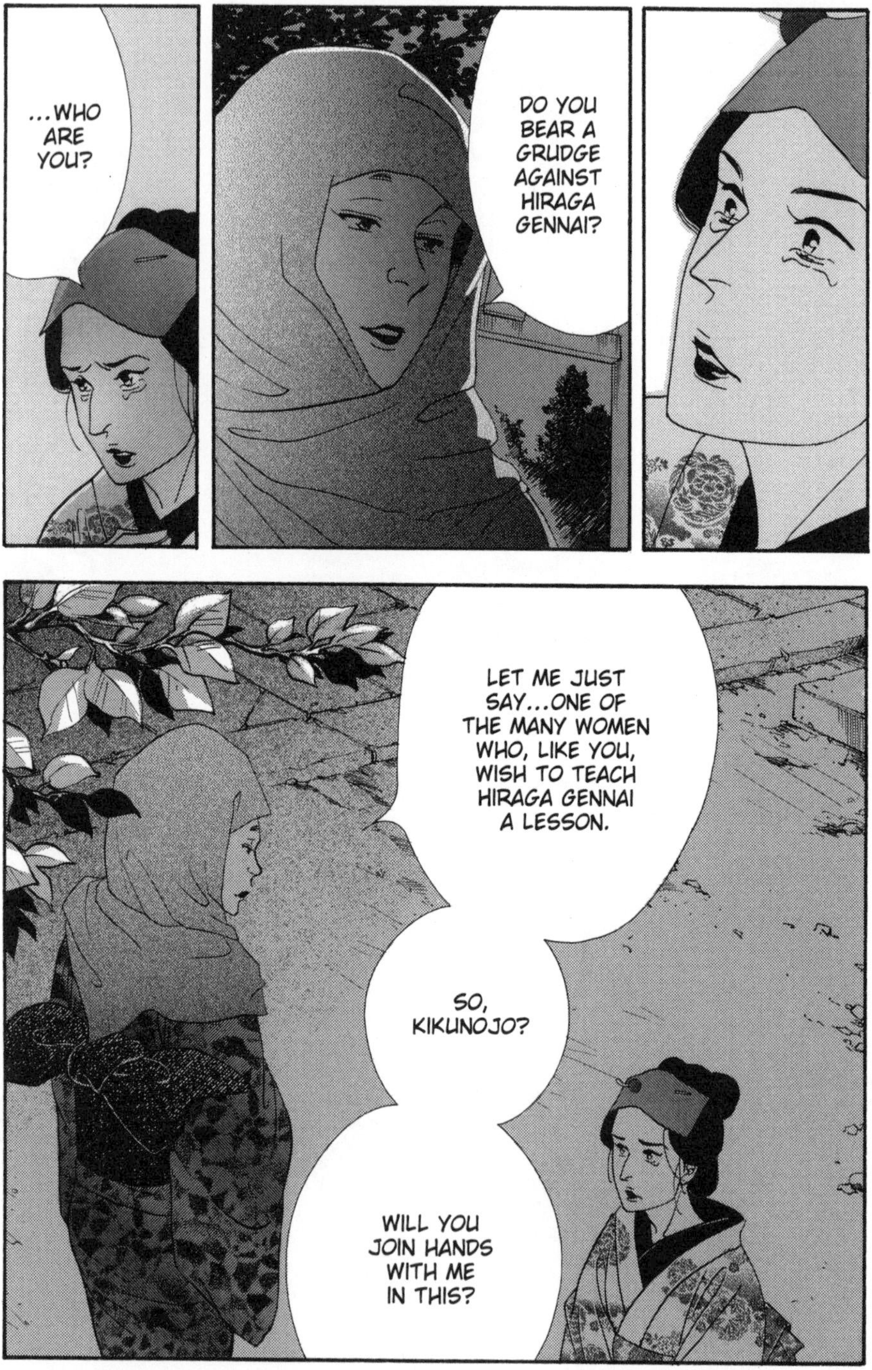
DO YOU BEAR A GRUDGE AGAINST HIRAGA GENNAI?
...WHO ARE YOU?
LET ME JUST SAY...ONE OF THE MANY WOMEN WHO, LIKE YOU, WISH TO TEACH HIRAGA GENNAI A LESSON.
SO, KIKUNOJO?
WILL YOU JOIN HANDS WITH ME IN THIS?

Ōoku
THE INNER CHAMBERS

Ōoku: The Inner Chambers

VOLUME 9 · END NOTES

by Akemi Wegmüller

Page 19, panel 2 · **KANSEI REFORMS**
The Kansei Reforms were a series of radical policy changes focused on strengthening the government, but were only partially successful.

Page 23, panel 5 · **AONUMA**
Literally means "blue pond."

Page 41, panel 4 · **GENNOSHOKO**
Geranium thunbergii, a type of geranium. It is still used as an antidiarrheic in Japan.

Page 51, panel 5 · **CINNAMON TWIG DECOCTION**
Keishitou in Japanese and *Gui Zhi Tang* in Chinese.

Panel 51, panel 5 · **MAGNOLIA BARK**
Kouboku in Japanese and *Houpu* in Chinese.

Panel 51, panel 5 · **APRICOT KERNEL**
Annin in Japanese and *Xingren* in Chinese.

Page 64, panel 3 · **TAKETOMBO**
These toys are still commonly seen in Japan today.

Page 69, panel 3 · **KAZUSA**
A province located in what is today central Chiba Prefecture.

Page 81, panel 3 · **KWART OVER ACHT'S AVONDS ETC.**
These are all times of day. "Quarter after eight in the evening. Quarter to nine in the morning. Two-thirty in the afternoon. Five to three at night."

Page 87, panel 1 · **YIN QIAO SAN, *SANG JU YIN***
Honeysuckle-forsythia powder in English, *Gingyosan* in Japanese. *Sang ju yin* is mulberry-chrysanthemum decoction in English, *Sougikuin* in Japanese.

Page 104, panel 4 · **NENASHIGUSA, HOHIRON**
Nenashigusa, when written with different kanji, means "rootless grass" and has the same meaning as "rolling stone" in English. *Hōhiron* translates as "On Farting."

Page 135. panel 1 · **EZO**
The old name for Hokkaido and its inhabitants, the Ainu.

Page 179, panel 8 · **HUO XIAN ZHENG QI SAN**
Kakkou Shouki San in Japanese, "Agastache Formula" in English.

Page 188, panel 3 · **ZHU XI**
A Song Dynasty Confucian scholar (1130–1200 CE) whose teachings formed the basis of Chinese government and bureaucracy until the dawn of the twentieth century.

Page 205, panel 3 · ENSHU
A province in what is now Shizuoka Prefecture.

Page 216, panel 4 · STONE COTTON
The literal translation of the Japanese word for asbestos (*ishiwata*).

CREATOR BIOGRAPHY

FUMI YOSHINAGA

Fumi Yoshinaga is a Tokyo-born manga creator who debuted in 1994 with *Tsuki to Sandaru* (*The Moon and the Sandals*). Yoshinaga has won numerous awards, including the 2009 Osamu Tezuka Cultural Prize for *Ōoku*, the 2002 Kodansha Manga Award for her series *Antique Bakery* and the 2006 Japan Media Arts Festival Excellence Award for *Ōoku*. She was also nominated for the 2008 Eisner Award for Best Writer/Artist.

Ōoku: The Inner Chambers
Vol. 9

VIZ Signature Edition

Story and Art by Fumi Yoshinaga

Translation & Adaptation/Akemi Wegmüller
Touch-up Art & Lettering/Monalisa De Asis
Design/Fawn Lau
Editor/Pancha Diaz

Ōoku by Fumi Yoshinaga © Fumi Yoshinaga 2012
All rights reserved. First published in Japan in 2012 by
HAKUSENSHA, Inc., Tokyo. English language translation
rights arranged with HAKUSENSHA, Inc., Tokyo.

The stories, characters and incidents mentioned in this
publication are entirely fictional.

No portion of this book may be reproduced or transmitted
in any form or by any means without written permission
from the copyright holders.

Printed in the U.S.A.

Published by VIZ Media, LLC
P.O. Box 77010
San Francisco, CA 94107

10 9 8 7 6 5 4 3 2 1
First printing, January 2014

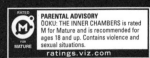

PARENTAL ADVISORY
ŌOKU: THE INNER CHAMBERS is rated
M for Mature and is recommended for
ages 18 and up. Contains violence and
sexual situations.
ratings.viz.com

THIS IS THE LAST PAGE.

Ōoku: The Inner Chambers has been printed in the original Japanese format in order to preserve the orientation of the original artwork.